The Java EE 6 Tutorial

Advanced Topics

Fourth Edition

The Java EE 6 Tutorial
Advanced Topics

Fourth Edition

Eric Jendrock
Ricardo Cervera-Navarro
Ian Evans
Devika Gollapudi
Kim Haase
William Markito
Chinmayee Srivathsa

♦♦ Addison-Wesley

Upper Saddle River, NJ • Boston • Indianapolis • San Francisco
New York • Toronto • Montreal • London • Munich • Paris • Madrid
Capetown • Sydney • Tokyo • Singapore • Mexico City

The publisher offers excellent discounts on this book when ordered in quantity for bulk purchases or special sales, which may include electronic versions and/or custom covers and content particular to your business, training goals, marketing focus, and branding interests. For more information, please contact

U.S. Corporate and Government Sales
(800) 382-3419
corpsales@pearsontechgroup.com

For sales outside the United States, please contact

International Sales international@pearsoned.com

Visit us on the Web: informit.com/aw

Library of Congress Control Number: 2012952541

ISBN-13: 978-0-13-708186-8
ISBN-10:   0-13-708186-3
Text printed in the United States on recycled paper at RR Donnelley in Crawfordsville, Indiana.
First printing, January, 2013

Contents

Preface

This tutorial is the second volume of a guide to developing enterprise applications for the Java Platform, Enterprise Edition 6 (Java EE 6) using GlassFish Server Open Source Edition.

Oracle GlassFish Server, a Java EE compatible application server, is based on GlassFish Server Open Source Edition, the leading open-source and open-community platform for building and deploying next-generation applications and services. GlassFish Server Open Source Edition, developed by the GlassFish project open-source community at `http://glassfish.java.net/`, is the first compatible implementation of the Java EE 6 platform specification. This lightweight, flexible, and open-source application server enables organizations not only to leverage the new capabilities introduced within the Java EE 6 specification, but also to add to their existing capabilities through a faster and more streamlined development and deployment cycle. Oracle GlassFish Server, the product version, and GlassFish Server Open Source Edition, the open-source version, are hereafter referred to as GlassFish Server.

Before You Read This Book

Before proceeding with this book, you should be familiar with Volume One of this tutorial, *The Java EE 6 Tutorial: Basic Concepts*. Both volumes assume that you have a good knowledge of the Java programming language. A good way to get to that point is to read the Java Tutorials, available at `http://docs.oracle.com/javase/`.

Related Documentation

The GlassFish Server documentation set describes deployment planning and system installation. To obtain documentation for GlassFish Server Open Source Edition, go to `http://glassfish.java.net/docs/`. The Uniform Resource Locator (URL) for the Oracle GlassFish Server product documentation is `http://docs.oracle.com/cd/E26576_01/index.htm`.

Javadoc tool reference documentation for packages that are provided with GlassFish Server is available as follows.

- The API specification for version 6 of Java EE is located at `http://docs.oracle.com/javaee/6/api/`.

- The API specification for GlassFish Server, including Java EE 6 platform packages and nonplatform packages that are specific to the GlassFish Server product, is located at `http://glassfish.java.net/nonav/docs/v3/api/`.

Additionally, the Java EE Specifications at `http://www.oracle.com/technetwork/java/javaee/tech/index.html` might be useful.

For information about creating enterprise applications in the NetBeans Integrated Development Environment (IDE), see `http://www.netbeans.org/kb/`.

For information about the Java DB database for use with the GlassFish Server, see `http://www.oracle.com/technetwork/java/javadb/overview/index.html`.

The GlassFish Samples project is a collection of sample applications that demonstrate a broad range of Java EE technologies. The GlassFish Samples are bundled with the Java EE Software Development Kit (SDK) and are also available from the GlassFish Samples project page at `http://glassfish-samples.java.net/`.

Typographic Conventions

Table P–1 describes the typographic changes that are used in this book.

TABLE P–1 Typographic Conventions

Typeface	Meaning	Example
AaBbCc123	The names of commands, files, and directories, and onscreen computer output	Edit your `.login` file. Use `ls -a` to list all files. `machine_name% you have mail.`
AaBbCc123	What you type, contrasted with onscreen computer output	`machine_name%` **su** `Password:`
AaBbCc123	A placeholder to be replaced with a real name or value	The command to remove a file is `rm` *filename*.
AaBbCc123	Book titles, new terms, and terms to be emphasized (note that some emphasized items appear bold online)	Read Chapter 6 in the *User's Guide*. A *cache* is a copy that is stored locally. Do *not* save the file.

Default Paths and File Names

Table P–2 describes the default paths and file names that are used in this book.

TABLE P–2 Default Paths and File Names

Placeholder	Description	Default Value
as-install	Represents the base installation directory for the GlassFish Server or the SDK of which the GlassFish Server is a part.	Installations on the Solaris operating system, Linux operating system, and Mac operating system: *user's-home-directory*/glassfish3/glassfish Windows, all installations: *SystemDrive*:\glassfish3\glassfish
as-install-parent	Represents the parent of the base installation directory for GlassFish Server.	Installations on the Solaris operating system, Linux operating system, and Mac operating system: *user's-home-directory*/glassfish3 Windows, all installations: *SystemDrive*:\glassfish3
tut-install	Represents the base installation directory for the *Java EE Tutorial* after you install the GlassFish Server or the SDK and run the Update Tool.	*as-install*/docs/javaee-tutorial
domain-root-dir	Represents the directory in which a domain is created by default.	*as-install*/domains/
domain-dir	Represents the directory in which a domain's configuration is stored.	*domain-root-dir*/*domain-name*

Third-Party Web Site References

Third-party URLs are referenced in this document and provide additional, related information.

Note – Oracle is not responsible for the availability of third-party web sites mentioned in this document. Oracle does not endorse and is not responsible or liable for any content, advertising, products, or other materials that are available on or through such sites or resources. Oracle will not be responsible or liable for any actual or alleged damage or loss caused or alleged to be caused by or in connection with use of or reliance on any such content, goods, or services that are available on or through such sites or resources.

Acknowledgments

The Java EE tutorial team would like to thank the Java EE specification leads: Roberto Chinnici, Bill Shannon, Kenneth Saks, Linda DeMichiel, Ed Burns, Roger Kitain, Ron Monzillo, Binod PG, Sivakumar Thyagarajan, Kin-Man Chung, Jitendra Kotamraju, Marc Hadley, Paul Sandoz, Gavin King, Emmanuel Bernard, Rod Johnson, Bob Lee, and Rajiv Mordani.

Thanks also to Alejandro Murillo for the original version of the connector example.

We would also like to thank the Java EE 6 SDK team, especially Carla Carlson, Snjezana Sevo-Zenzerovic, Adam Leftik, and John Clingan.

The JavaServer Faces technology chapters benefited greatly from suggestions by Manfred Riem as well as by the spec leads.

The EJB technology, Java Persistence API, and Criteria API chapters were written with extensive input from the EJB and Persistence teams, including Marina Vatkina and Mitesh Meswani.

We'd like to thank Sivakumar Thyagarajan for his reviews of the CDI chapters and Tim Quinn for assistance with the application client container. Thanks also to the NetBeans engineering and documentation teams, particularly Petr Jiricka, John Jullion-Ceccarelli, and Troy Giunipero, for their help in enabling NetBeans IDE support for the code examples.

Chang Feng, Alejandro Murillo, and Scott Fordin helped internationalize the Duke's Tutoring case study.

We would like to thank our manager, Alan Sommerer, for his support and steadying influence.

We also thank Jordan Douglas and Dawn Tyler for developing and updating the illustrations. Sheila Cepero helped smooth our path in many ways. Steve Cogorno provided invaluable help with our tools.

Finally, we would like to express our profound appreciation to Greg Doench, John Fuller, Elizabeth Ryan, Steve Freedkin, and the production team at Addison-Wesley for graciously seeing our manuscript to publication.

Introduction

Part I introduces the platform, the tutorial, and the examples. This part contains the following chapters:

- Chapter 1, "Overview"
- Chapter 2, "Using the Tutorial Examples"

1

Overview

Developers today increasingly recognize the need for distributed, transactional, and portable applications that leverage the speed, security, and reliability of server-side technology. *Enterprise applications* provide the business logic for an enterprise. They are centrally managed and often interact with other enterprise software. In the world of information technology, enterprise applications must be designed, built, and produced for less money, with greater speed, and with fewer resources.

With the Java Platform, Enterprise Edition (Java EE), development of Java enterprise applications has never been easier or faster. The aim of the Java EE platform is to provide developers with a powerful set of APIs while shortening development time, reducing application complexity, and improving application performance.

The Java EE platform is developed through the Java Community Process (JCP), which is responsible for all Java technologies. Expert groups, composed of interested parties, have created Java Specification Requests (JSRs) to define the various Java EE technologies. The work of the Java Community under the JCP program helps to ensure Java technology's standard of stability and cross-platform compatibility.

The Java EE platform uses a simplified programming model. XML deployment descriptors are optional. Instead, a developer can simply enter the information as an *annotation* directly into a Java source file, and the Java EE server will configure the component at deployment and runtime. These annotations are generally used to embed in a program data that would otherwise be furnished in a deployment descriptor. With annotations, you put the specification information in your code next to the program element affected.

In the Java EE platform, dependency injection can be applied to all resources a component needs, effectively hiding the creation and lookup of resources from application code. Dependency injection can be used in EJB containers, web containers, and application clients. Dependency injection allows the Java EE container to automatically insert references to other required components or resources, using annotations.

This tutorial uses examples to describe the features available in the Java EE platform for developing enterprise applications. Whether you are a new or experienced Enterprise developer, you should find the examples and accompanying text a valuable and accessible knowledge base for creating your own solutions.

If you are new to Java EE enterprise application development, this chapter is a good place to start. Here you will review development basics, learn about the Java EE architecture and APIs, become acquainted with important terms and concepts, and find out how to approach Java EE application programming, assembly, and deployment.

The following topics are addressed here:

Java EE 6 Platform Highlights

The most important goal of the Java EE 6 platform is to simplify development by providing a common foundation for the various kinds of components in the Java EE platform. Developers benefit from productivity improvements with more annotations and less XML configuration, more Plain Old Java Objects (POJOs), and simplified packaging. The Java EE 6 platform includes the following new features:

- Profiles: configurations of the Java EE platform targeted at specific classes of applications. Specifically, the Java EE 6 platform introduces a lightweight Web Profile targeted at next-generation web applications, as well as a Full Profile that contains all Java EE technologies and provides the full power of the Java EE 6 platform for enterprise applications.

- New technologies, including the following:

  - Java API for RESTful Web Services (JAX-RS)

  - Managed Beans

  - Contexts and Dependency Injection for the Java EE Platform (JSR 299), informally known as CDI

- Dependency Injection for Java (JSR 330)
- Bean Validation (JSR 303)
- Java Authentication Service Provider Interface for Containers (JASPIC)
- New features for Enterprise JavaBeans (EJB) components (see "Enterprise JavaBeans Technology" on page 25 for details)
- New features for servlets (see "Java Servlet Technology" on page 26 for details)
- New features for JavaServer Faces components (see "JavaServer Faces Technology" on page 26 for details)

Java EE Application Model

The Java EE application model begins with the Java programming language and the Java virtual machine. The proven portability, security, and developer productivity they provide forms the basis of the application model. Java EE is designed to support applications that implement enterprise services for customers, employees, suppliers, partners, and others who make demands on or contributions to the enterprise. Such applications are inherently complex, potentially accessing data from a variety of sources and distributing applications to a variety of clients.

To better control and manage these applications, the business functions to support these various users are conducted in the middle tier. The middle tier represents an environment that is closely controlled by an enterprise's information technology department. The middle tier is typically run on dedicated server hardware and has access to the full services of the enterprise.

The Java EE application model defines an architecture for implementing services as multitier applications that deliver the scalability, accessibility, and manageability needed by enterprise-level applications. This model partitions the work needed to implement a multitier service into the following parts:

- The business and presentation logic to be implemented by the developer
- The standard system services provided by the Java EE platform

The developer can rely on the platform to provide solutions for the hard systems-level problems of developing a multitier service.

Distributed Multitiered Applications

The Java EE platform uses a distributed multitiered application model for enterprise applications. Application logic is divided into components according to function, and the application components that make up a Java EE application are installed on various machines, depending on the tier in the multitiered Java EE environment to which the application component belongs.

Figure 1–1 shows two multitiered Java EE applications divided into the tiers described in the following list. The Java EE application parts shown in Figure 1–1 are presented in "Java EE Components" on page 8.

- Client-tier components run on the client machine.
- Web-tier components run on the Java EE server.
- Business-tier components run on the Java EE server.
- Enterprise information system (EIS)-tier software runs on the EIS server.

Although a Java EE application can consist of all tiers shown in Figure 1–1, Java EE multitiered applications are generally considered to be three-tiered applications because they are distributed over three locations: client machines, the Java EE server machine, and the database or legacy machines at the back end. Three-tiered applications that run in this way extend the standard two-tiered client-and-server model by placing a multithreaded application server between the client application and back-end storage.

FIGURE 1-1 Multitiered Applications

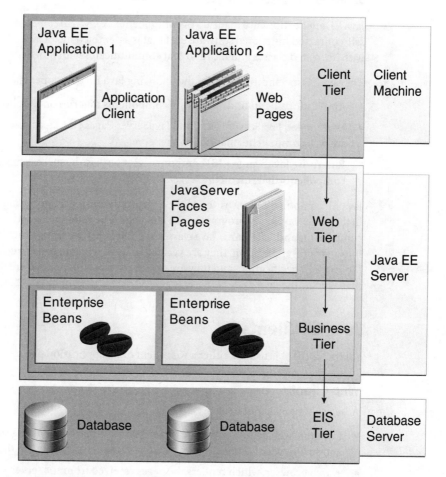

Security

Although other enterprise application models require platform-specific security measures in each application, the Java EE security environment enables security constraints to be defined at deployment time. The Java EE platform makes applications portable to a wide variety of security implementations by shielding application developers from the complexity of implementing security features.

The Java EE platform provides standard declarative access control rules that are defined by the developer and interpreted when the application is deployed on the server. Java EE also provides standard login mechanisms so application developers do not have to implement these mechanisms in their applications. The same application works in a variety of security environments without changing the source code.

Java EE Components

Java EE applications are made up of components. A *Java EE component* is a self-contained functional software unit that is assembled into a Java EE application with its related classes and files and that communicates with other components.

The Java EE specification defines the following Java EE components:

- Application clients and applets are components that run on the client.
- Java Servlet, JavaServer Faces, and JavaServer Pages (JSP) technology components are web components that run on the server.
- Enterprise JavaBeans (EJB) components (enterprise beans) are business components that run on the server.

Java EE components are written in the Java programming language and are compiled in the same way as any program in the language. The differences between Java EE components and "standard" Java classes are that Java EE components are assembled into a Java EE application, they are verified to be well formed and in compliance with the Java EE specification, and they are deployed to production, where they are run and managed by the Java EE server.

Java EE Clients

A Java EE client is usually either a web client or an application client.

Web Clients

A *web client* consists of two parts:

- Dynamic web pages containing various types of markup language (HTML, XML, and so on), which are generated by web components running in the web tier
- A web browser, which renders the pages received from the server

A web client is sometimes called a *thin client*. Thin clients usually do not query databases, execute complex business rules, or connect to legacy applications. When you use a thin client, such heavyweight operations are off-loaded to enterprise beans executing on the Java EE server, where they can leverage the security, speed, services, and reliability of Java EE server-side technologies.

Application Clients

An *application client* runs on a client machine and provides a way for users to handle tasks that require a richer user interface than can be provided by a markup language. An application client typically has a graphical user interface (GUI) created from the Swing or the Abstract Window Toolkit (AWT) API, but a command-line interface is certainly possible.

Application clients directly access enterprise beans running in the business tier. However, if application requirements warrant it, an application client can open an HTTP connection to establish communication with a servlet running in the web tier. Application clients written in languages other than Java can interact with Java EE servers, enabling the Java EE platform to interoperate with legacy systems, clients, and non-Java languages.

Applets

A web page received from the web tier can include an embedded applet. Written in the Java programming language, an *applet* is a small client application that executes in the Java virtual machine installed in the web browser. However, client systems will likely need the Java Plug-in and possibly a security policy file for the applet to successfully execute in the web browser.

Web components are the preferred API for creating a web client program, because no plug-ins or security policy files are needed on the client systems. Also, web components enable cleaner and more modular application design because they provide a way to separate applications programming from web page design. Personnel involved in web page design thus do not need to understand Java programming language syntax to do their jobs.

The JavaBeans Component Architecture

The server and client tiers might also include components based on the JavaBeans component architecture (JavaBeans components) to manage the data flow between the following:

- An application client or applet and components running on the Java EE server
- Server components and a database

JavaBeans components are not considered Java EE components by the Java EE specification.

JavaBeans components have properties and have get and set methods for accessing the properties. JavaBeans components used in this way are typically simple in design and implementation but should conform to the naming and design conventions outlined in the JavaBeans component architecture.

Java EE Server Communications

Figure 1–2 shows the various elements that can make up the client tier. The client communicates with the business tier running on the Java EE server either directly or, as in the case of a client running in a browser, by going through web pages or servlets running in the web tier.

FIGURE 1–2 Server Communication

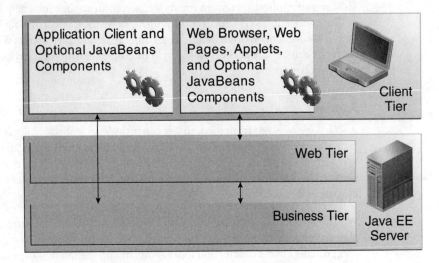

Web Components

Java EE web components are either servlets or web pages created using JavaServer Faces technology and/or JSP technology (JSP pages). *Servlets* are Java programming language classes that dynamically process requests and construct responses. *JSP pages* are text-based documents that execute as servlets but allow a more natural approach to creating static content. *JavaServer Faces technology* builds on servlets and JSP technology and provides a user interface component framework for web applications.

Static HTML pages and applets are bundled with web components during application assembly but are not considered web components by the Java EE specification. Server-side utility classes can also be bundled with web components and, like HTML pages, are not considered web components.

As shown in Figure 1–3, the web tier, like the client tier, might include a JavaBeans component to manage the user input and send that input to enterprise beans running in the business tier for processing.

FIGURE 1-3   Web Tier and Java EE Applications

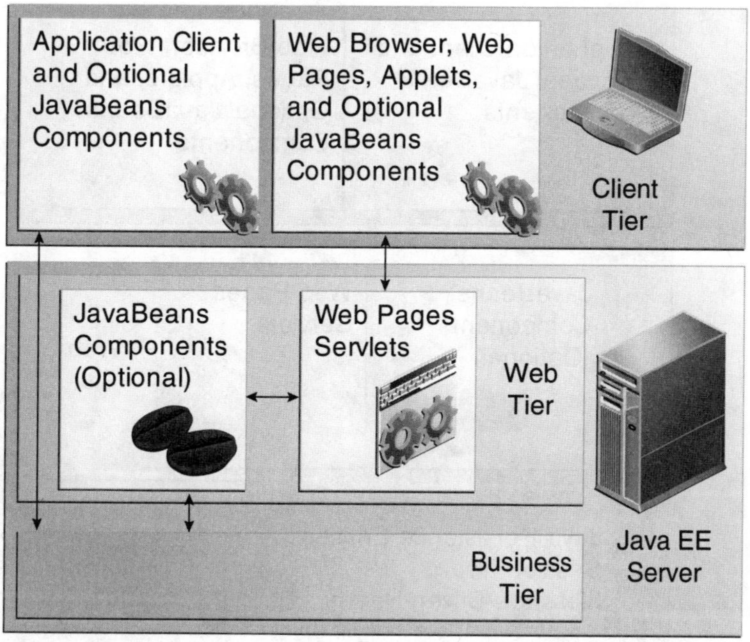

Business Components

Business code, which is logic that solves or meets the needs of a particular business domain such as banking, retail, or finance, is handled by enterprise beans running in either the business tier or the web tier. Figure 1–4 shows how an enterprise bean receives data from client programs, processes it (if necessary), and sends it to the enterprise information system tier for storage. An enterprise bean also retrieves data from storage, processes it (if necessary), and sends it back to the client program.

FIGURE 1–4 Business and EIS Tiers

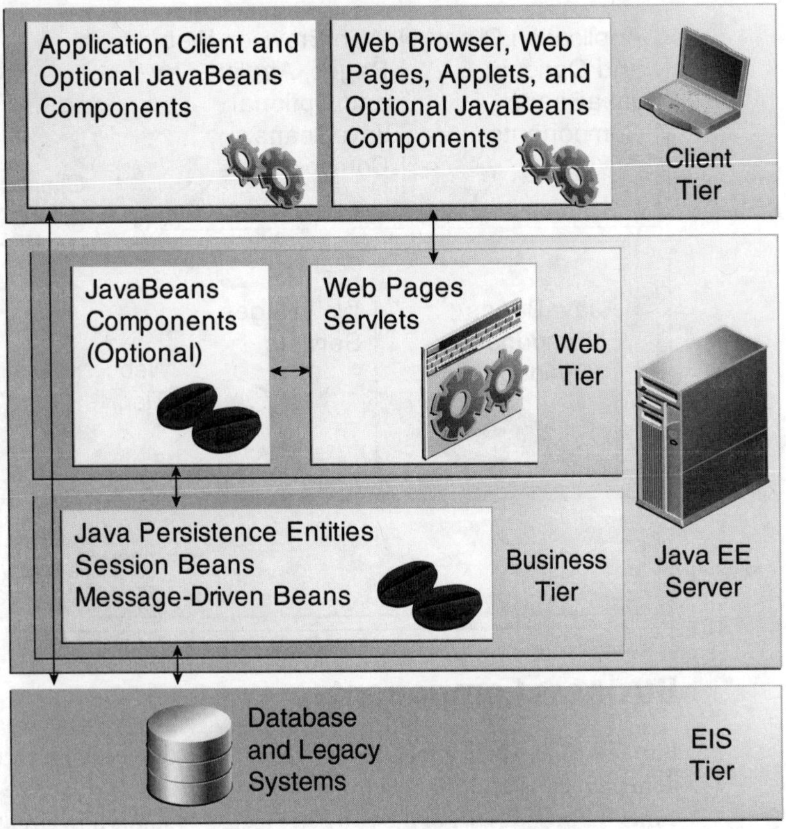

Enterprise Information System Tier

The enterprise information system tier handles EIS software and includes enterprise infrastructure systems, such as enterprise resource planning (ERP), mainframe transaction processing, database systems, and other legacy information systems. For example, Java EE application components might need access to enterprise information systems for database connectivity.

Java EE Containers

Normally, thin-client multitiered applications are hard to write because they involve many lines of intricate code to handle transaction and state management, multithreading, resource pooling, and other complex low-level details. The component-based and platform-independent Java EE architecture makes Java EE applications easy to write because business logic is organized into reusable components. In addition, the Java EE server provides underlying services in the form of a container for every component type. Because you do not have to develop these services yourself, you are free to concentrate on solving the business problem at hand.

Container Services

Containers are the interface between a component and the low-level platform-specific functionality that supports the component. Before it can be executed, a web, enterprise bean, or application client component must be assembled into a Java EE module and deployed into its container.

The assembly process involves specifying container settings for each component in the Java EE application and for the Java EE application itself. Container settings customize the underlying support provided by the Java EE server, including such services as security, transaction management, Java Naming and Directory Interface (JNDI) API lookups, and remote connectivity. Here are some of the highlights.

- The Java EE security model lets you configure a web component or enterprise bean so that system resources are accessed only by authorized users.

- The Java EE transaction model lets you specify relationships among methods that make up a single transaction so that all methods in one transaction are treated as a single unit.

- JNDI lookup services provide a unified interface to multiple naming and directory services in the enterprise so that application components can access these services.

- The Java EE remote connectivity model manages low-level communications between clients and enterprise beans. After an enterprise bean is created, a client invokes methods on it as if it were in the same virtual machine.

Because the Java EE architecture provides configurable services, application components within the same Java EE application can behave differently based on where they are deployed. For example, an enterprise bean can have security settings that allow it a certain level of access to database data in one production environment and another level of database access in another production environment.

The container also manages nonconfigurable services, such as enterprise bean and servlet lifecycles, database connection resource pooling, data persistence, and access to the Java EE platform APIs (see "Java EE 6 APIs" on page 21).

Container Types

The *deployment* process installs Java EE application components in the Java EE containers as illustrated in Figure 1–5.

FIGURE 1–5 Java EE Server and Containers

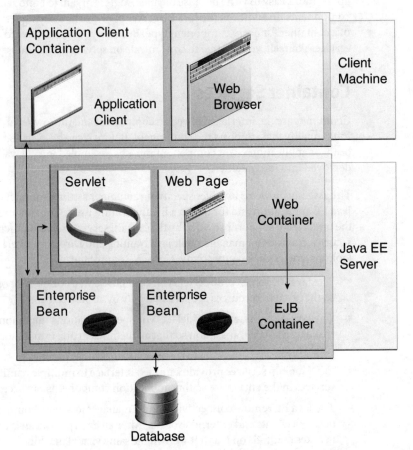

- **Java EE server:** The runtime portion of a Java EE product. A Java EE server provides EJB and web containers.

- **Enterprise JavaBeans (EJB) container:** Manages the execution of enterprise beans for Java EE applications. Enterprise beans and their container run on the Java EE server.

- **Web container:** Manages the execution of web pages, servlets, and some EJB components for Java EE applications. Web components and their container run on the Java EE server.

- **Application client container**: Manages the execution of application client components. Application clients and their container run on the client.

- **Applet container**: Manages the execution of applets. Consists of a web browser and Java Plug-in running on the client together.

Web Services Support

Web services are web-based enterprise applications that use open, XML-based standards and transport protocols to exchange data with calling clients. The Java EE platform provides the XML APIs and tools you need to quickly design, develop, test, and deploy web services and clients that fully interoperate with other web services and clients running on Java-based or non-Java-based platforms.

To write web services and clients with the Java EE XML APIs, all you do is pass parameter data to the method calls and process the data returned; for document-oriented web services, you send documents containing the service data back and forth. No low-level programming is needed, because the XML API implementations do the work of translating the application data to and from an XML-based data stream that is sent over the standardized XML-based transport protocols. These XML-based standards and protocols are introduced in the following sections.

The translation of data to a standardized XML-based data stream is what makes web services and clients written with the Java EE XML APIs fully interoperable. This does not necessarily mean that the data being transported includes XML tags, because the transported data can itself be plain text, XML data, or any kind of binary data, such as audio, video, maps, program files, computer-aided design (CAD) documents, and the like. The next section introduces XML and explains how parties doing business can use XML tags and schemas to exchange data in a meaningful way.

XML

Extensible Markup Language (XML) is a cross-platform, extensible, text-based standard for representing data. Parties that exchange XML data can create their own tags to describe the data, set up schemas to specify which tags can be used in a particular kind of XML document, and use XML style sheets to manage the display and handling of the data.

For example, a web service can use XML and a schema to produce price lists, and companies that receive the price lists and schema can have their own style sheets to handle the data in a way that best suits their needs. Here are examples.

- One company might put XML pricing information through a program to translate the XML to HTML so that it can post the price lists to its intranet.
- A partner company might put the XML pricing information through a tool to create a marketing presentation.
- Another company might read the XML pricing information into an application for processing.

SOAP Transport Protocol

Client requests and web service responses are transmitted as Simple Object Access Protocol (SOAP) messages over HTTP to enable a completely interoperable exchange between clients and web services, all running on different platforms and at various locations on the Internet. HTTP is a familiar request-and-response standard for sending messages over the Internet, and SOAP is an XML-based protocol that follows the HTTP request-and-response model.

The SOAP portion of a transported message does the following:

- Defines an XML-based envelope to describe what is in the message and explain how to process the message
- Includes XML-based encoding rules to express instances of application-defined data types within the message
- Defines an XML-based convention for representing the request to the remote service and the resulting response

WSDL Standard Format

The Web Services Description Language (WSDL) is a standardized XML format for describing network services. The description includes the name of the service, the location of the service, and ways to communicate with the service. WSDL service descriptions can be published on the Web. GlassFish Server provides a tool for generating the WSDL specification of a web service that uses remote procedure calls to communicate with clients.

Java EE Application Assembly and Deployment

A Java EE application is packaged into one or more standard units for deployment to any Java EE platform-compliant system. Each unit contains

- A functional component or components, such as an enterprise bean, web page, servlet, or applet
- An optional deployment descriptor that describes its content

Once a Java EE unit has been produced, it is ready to be deployed. Deployment typically involves using a platform's deployment tool to specify location-specific information, such as a list of local users who can access it and the name of the local database. Once deployed on a local platform, the application is ready to run.

Packaging Applications

A Java EE application is delivered in a Java Archive (JAR) file, a Web Archive (WAR) file, or an Enterprise Archive (EAR) file. A WAR or EAR file is a standard JAR (.jar) file with a .war or .ear extension. Using JAR, WAR, and EAR files and modules makes it possible to assemble a number of different Java EE applications using some of the same components. No extra coding is needed; it is only a matter of assembling (or packaging) various Java EE modules into Java EE JAR, WAR, or EAR files.

An EAR file (see Figure 1–6) contains Java EE modules and, optionally, deployment descriptors. A *deployment descriptor*, an XML document with an .xml extension, describes the deployment settings of an application, a module, or a component. Because deployment descriptor information is declarative, it can be changed without the need to modify the source code. At runtime, the Java EE server reads the deployment descriptor and acts upon the application, module, or component accordingly.

FIGURE 1-6   EAR File Structure

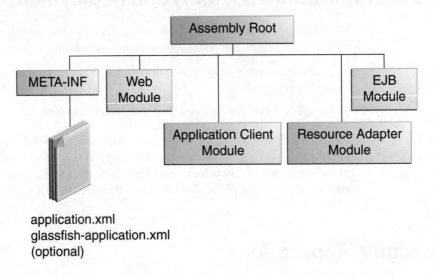

application.xml
glassfish-application.xml
(optional)

The two types of deployment descriptors are Java EE and runtime. A *Java EE deployment descriptor* is defined by a Java EE specification and can be used to configure deployment settings on any Java EE-compliant implementation. A *runtime deployment descriptor* is used to configure Java EE implementation-specific parameters. For example, the GlassFish Server runtime deployment descriptor contains such information as the context root of a web application, as well as GlassFish Server implementation-specific parameters, such as caching directives. The GlassFish Server runtime deployment descriptors are named glassfish-*moduleType*.xml and are located in the same META-INF directory as the Java EE deployment descriptor.

A *Java EE module* consists of one or more Java EE components for the same container type and, optionally, one component deployment descriptor of that type. An enterprise bean module deployment descriptor, for example, declares transaction attributes and security authorizations for an enterprise bean. A Java EE module can be deployed as a stand-alone module.

Java EE modules are of the following types:

- EJB modules, which contain class files for enterprise beans and, optionally, an EJB deployment descriptor. EJB modules are packaged as JAR files with a .jar extension.

- Web modules, which contain servlet class files, web files, supporting class files, image and HTML files, and, optionally, a web application deployment descriptor. Web modules are packaged as JAR files with a .war (web archive) extension.

- Application client modules, which contain class files and, optionally, an application client deployment descriptor. Application client modules are packaged as JAR files with a `.jar` extension.

- Resource adapter modules, which contain all Java interfaces, classes, native libraries, and, optionally, a resource adapter deployment descriptor. Together, these implement the Connector architecture (see "Java EE Connector Architecture" on page 30) for a particular EIS. Resource adapter modules are packaged as JAR files with an `.rar` (resource adapter archive) extension.

Development Roles

Reusable modules make it possible to divide the application development and deployment process into distinct roles so that different people or companies can perform different parts of the process.

The first two roles, Java EE product provider and tool provider, involve purchasing and installing the Java EE product and tools. After software is purchased and installed, Java EE components can be developed by application component providers, assembled by application assemblers, and deployed by application deployers. In a large organization, each of these roles might be executed by different individuals or teams. This division of labor works because each of the earlier roles outputs a portable file that is the input for a subsequent role. For example, in the application component development phase, an enterprise bean software developer delivers EJB JAR files. In the application assembly role, another developer may combine these EJB JAR files into a Java EE application and save it in an EAR file. In the application deployment role, a system administrator at the customer site uses the EAR file to install the Java EE application into a Java EE server.

The different roles are not always executed by different people. If you work for a small company, for example, or if you are prototyping a sample application, you might perform tasks in every phase.

Java EE Product Provider

The Java EE product provider is the company that designs and makes available for purchase the Java EE platform APIs and other features defined in the Java EE specification. Product providers are typically application server vendors that implement the Java EE platform according to the Java EE 6 Platform specification.

Tool Provider

The tool provider is the company or person who creates development, assembly, and packaging tools used by component providers, assemblers, and deployers.

Application Component Provider

The application component provider is the company or person who creates web components, enterprise beans, applets, or application clients for use in Java EE applications.

Enterprise Bean Developer

An enterprise bean developer performs the following tasks to deliver an EJB JAR file that contains one or more enterprise beans:

- Writes and compiles the source code
- Specifies the deployment descriptor (optional)
- Packages the .class files and deployment descriptor into the EJB JAR file

Web Component Developer

A web component developer performs the following tasks to deliver a WAR file containing one or more web components:

- Writes and compiles servlet source code

- Writes JavaServer Faces, JSP, and HTML files

- Specifies the deployment descriptor (optional)

- Packages the .class, .jsp, and .html files and deployment descriptor into the WAR file

Application Client Developer

An application client developer performs the following tasks to deliver a JAR file containing the application client:

- Writes and compiles the source code
- Specifies the deployment descriptor for the client (optional)
- Packages the .class files and deployment descriptor into the JAR file

Application Assembler

The application assembler is the company or person who receives application modules from component providers and may assemble them into a Java EE application EAR file. The assembler or deployer can edit the deployment descriptor directly or can use tools that correctly add XML tags according to interactive selections.

A software developer performs the following tasks to deliver an EAR file containing the Java EE application:

- Assembles EJB JAR and WAR files created in the previous phases into a Java EE application (EAR) file
- Specifies the deployment descriptor for the Java EE application (optional)
- Verifies that the contents of the EAR file are well formed and comply with the Java EE specification

Application Deployer and Administrator

The application deployer and administrator is the company or person who configures and deploys application clients, web applications, Enterprise JavaBeans components, and Java EE applications, administers the computing and networking infrastructure where Java EE components and applications run, and oversees the runtime environment. Duties include setting transaction controls and security attributes and specifying connections to databases.

During configuration, the deployer follows instructions supplied by the application component provider to resolve external dependencies, specify security settings, and assign transaction attributes. During installation, the deployer moves the application components to the server and generates the container-specific classes and interfaces.

A deployer or system administrator performs the following tasks to install and configure a Java EE application or components:

- Configures the Java EE application or components for the operational environment
- Verifies that the contents of the EAR, JAR, and/or WAR files are well formed and comply with the Java EE specification
- Deploys (installs) the Java EE application or components into the Java EE server

Java EE 6 APIs

Figure 1–7 shows the relationships among the Java EE containers.

FIGURE 1-7 Java EE Containers

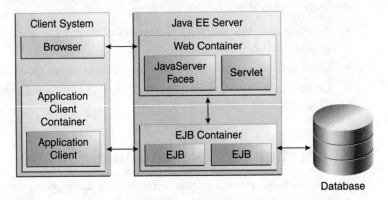

Figure 1-8 shows the availability of the Java EE 6 APIs in the web container.

FIGURE 1–8 Java EE APIs in the Web Container

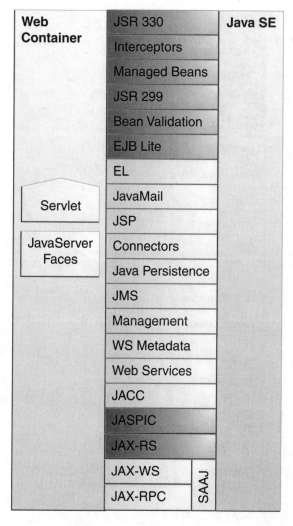

New in Java EE 6

Figure 1–9 shows the availability of the Java EE 6 APIs in the EJB container.

FIGURE 1–9   Java EE APIs in the EJB Container

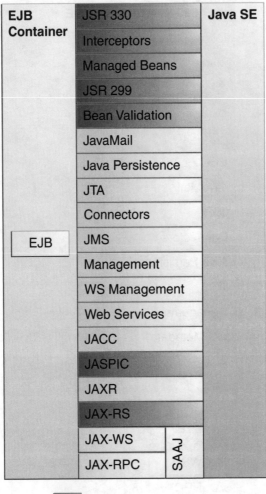

Figure 1–10 shows the availability of the Java EE 6 APIs in the application client container.

FIGURE 1–10   Java EE APIs in the Application Client Container

Application Client Container	Java Persistence	Java SE
	Management	
	WS Metadata	
Application Client	Web Services	
	JSR 299	
	JMS	
	JAXR	
	JAX-WS	SAAJ
	JAX-RPC	

■ New in Java EE 6

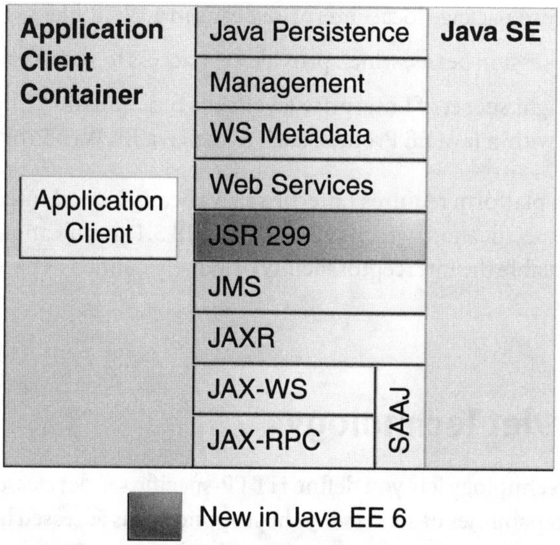

The following sections give a brief summary of the technologies required by the Java EE platform and the APIs used in Java EE applications.

Enterprise JavaBeans Technology

An *Enterprise JavaBeans (EJB) component*, or *enterprise bean*, is a body of code having fields and methods to implement modules of business logic. You can think of an enterprise bean as a building block that can be used alone or with other enterprise beans to execute business logic on the Java EE server.

Enterprise beans are either session beans or message-driven beans.

- A *session bean* represents a transient conversation with a client. When the client finishes executing, the session bean and its data are gone.

- A *message-driven bean* combines features of a session bean and a message listener, allowing a business component to receive messages asynchronously. Commonly, these are Java Message Service (JMS) messages.

In the Java EE 6 platform, new enterprise bean features include the following:

- The ability to package local enterprise beans in a WAR file
- Singleton session beans, which provide easy access to shared state
- A lightweight subset of Enterprise JavaBeans functionality (EJB Lite) that can be provided within Java EE Profiles, such as the Java EE Web Profile.

The Java EE 6 platform requires Enterprise JavaBeans 3.1 and Interceptors 1.1. The Interceptors specification, which is part of the EJB 3.1 specification, makes more generally available the interceptor facility originally defined as part of the EJB 3.0 specification.

Java Servlet Technology

Java Servlet technology lets you define HTTP-specific servlet classes. A servlet class extends the capabilities of servers that host applications accessed by way of a request-response programming model. Although servlets can respond to any type of request, they are commonly used to extend the applications hosted by web servers.

In the Java EE 6 platform, new Java Servlet technology features include the following:

- Annotation support
- Asynchronous support
- Ease of configuration
- Enhancements to existing APIs
- Pluggability

The Java EE 6 platform requires Servlet 3.0.

JavaServer Faces Technology

JavaServer Faces technology is a user interface framework for building web applications. The main components of JavaServer Faces technology are as follows:

- A GUI component framework.
- A flexible model for rendering components in different kinds of HTML or different markup languages and technologies. A Renderer object generates the markup to render the component and converts the data stored in a model object to types that can be represented in a view.
- A standard RenderKit for generating HTML/4.01 markup.

The following features support the GUI components:

- Input validation
- Event handling
- Data conversion between model objects and components
- Managed model object creation
- Page navigation configuration
- Expression Language (EL)

All this functionality is available using standard Java APIs and XML-based configuration files.

In the Java EE 6 platform, new features of JavaServer Faces include the following:

- The ability to use annotations instead of a configuration file to specify managed beans and other components
- Facelets, a display technology that replaces JavaServer Pages (JSP) technology using XHTML files
- Ajax support
- Composite components
- Implicit navigation

The Java EE 6 platform requires JavaServer Faces 2.0 and Expression Language 2.2.

JavaServer Pages Technology

JavaServer Pages (JSP) technology lets you put snippets of servlet code directly into a text-based document. A JSP page is a text-based document that contains two types of text:

- Static data, which can be expressed in any text-based format such as HTML or XML
- JSP elements, which determine how the page constructs dynamic content

For information about JSP technology, see the *The Java EE 5 Tutorial* at
`http://docs.oracle.com/javaee/5/tutorial/doc/`.

The Java EE 6 platform requires JavaServer Pages 2.2 for compatibility with earlier releases, but recommends the use of Facelets as the display technology in new applications.

JavaServer Pages Standard Tag Library

The JavaServer Pages Standard Tag Library (JSTL) encapsulates core functionality common to many JSP applications. Instead of mixing tags from numerous vendors in your JSP applications, you use a single, standard set of tags. This standardization allows you to deploy your applications on any JSP container that supports JSTL and makes it more likely that the implementation of the tags is optimized.

JSTL has iterator and conditional tags for handling flow control, tags for manipulating XML documents, internationalization tags, tags for accessing databases using SQL, and commonly used functions.

The Java EE 6 platform requires JSTL 1.2.

Java Persistence API

The Java Persistence API (JPA) is a Java standards-based solution for persistence. Persistence uses an object/relational mapping approach to bridge the gap between an object-oriented model and a relational database. The Java Persistence API can also be used in Java SE applications, outside of the Java EE environment. Java Persistence consists of the following areas:

- The Java Persistence API
- The query language
- Object/relational mapping metadata

The Java EE 6 platform requires Java Persistence API 2.0.

Java Transaction API

The Java Transaction API (JTA) provides a standard interface for demarcating transactions. The Java EE architecture provides a default auto commit to handle transaction commits and rollbacks. An auto commit means that any other applications that are viewing data will see the updated data after each database read or write operation. However, if your application performs two separate database access operations that depend on each other, you will want to use the JTA API to demarcate where the entire transaction, including both operations, begins, rolls back, and commits.

The Java EE 6 platform requires Java Transaction API 1.1.

Java API for RESTful Web Services

The Java API for RESTful Web Services (JAX-RS) defines APIs for the development of web services built according to the Representational State Transfer (REST) architectural style. A JAX-RS application is a web application that consists of classes packaged as a servlet in a WAR file along with required libraries.

The JAX-RS API is new to the Java EE 6 platform. The Java EE 6 platform requires JAX–RS 1.1.

Managed Beans

Managed Beans, lightweight container-managed objects (POJOs) with minimal requirements, support a small set of basic services, such as resource injection, lifecycle callbacks, and interceptors. Managed Beans represent a generalization of the managed beans specified by JavaServer Faces technology and can be used anywhere in a Java EE application, not just in web modules.

The Managed Beans specification is part of the Java EE 6 platform specification (JSR 316).

Managed Beans are new to the Java EE 6 platform. The Java EE 6 platform requires Managed Beans 1.0.

Contexts and Dependency Injection for the Java EE Platform (JSR 299)

Contexts and Dependency Injection (CDI) for the Java EE platform defines a set of contextual services, provided by Java EE containers, that make it easy for developers to use enterprise beans along with JavaServer Faces technology in web applications. Designed for use with stateful objects, CDI also has many broader uses, allowing developers a great deal of flexibility to integrate different kinds of components in a loosely coupled but type-safe way.

CDI is new to the Java EE 6 platform. The Java EE 6 platform requires CDI 1.0.

Dependency Injection for Java (JSR 330)

Dependency Injection for Java defines a standard set of annotations (and one interface) for use on injectable classes.

In the Java EE platform, CDI provides support for Dependency Injection. Specifically, you can use DI injection points only in a CDI-enabled application.

Dependency Injection for Java is new to the Java EE 6 platform. The Java EE 6 platform requires Dependency Injection for Java 1.0.

Bean Validation

The Bean Validation specification defines a metadata model and API for validating data in JavaBeans components. Instead of distributing validation of data over several layers, such as the browser and the server side, you can define the validation constraints in one place and share them across the different layers.

Bean Validation is new to the Java EE 6 platform. The Java EE 6 platform requires Bean Validation 1.0.

Java Message Service API

The Java Message Service (JMS) API is a messaging standard that allows Java EE application components to create, send, receive, and read messages. It enables distributed communication that is loosely coupled, reliable, and asynchronous.

The Java EE 6 platform requires JMS 1.1.

Java EE Connector Architecture

The Java EE Connector architecture is used by tools vendors and system integrators to create resource adapters that support access to enterprise information systems that can be plugged in to any Java EE product. A *resource adapter* is a software component that allows Java EE application components to access and interact with the underlying resource manager of the EIS. Because a resource adapter is specific to its resource manager, a different resource adapter typically exists for each type of database or enterprise information system.

The Java EE Connector architecture also provides a performance-oriented, secure, scalable, and message-based transactional integration of Java EE based web services with existing EISs that can be either synchronous or asynchronous. Existing applications and EISs integrated through the Java EE Connector architecture into the Java EE platform can be exposed as XML-based web services by using JAX-WS and Java EE component models. Thus JAX-WS and the Java EE Connector architecture are complementary technologies for enterprise application integration (EAI) and end-to-end business integration.

The Java EE 6 platform requires Java EE Connector architecture 1.6.

JavaMail API

Java EE applications use the JavaMail API to send email notifications. The JavaMail API has two parts:

- An application-level interface used by the application components to send mail
- A service provider interface

The Java EE platform includes the JavaMail API with a service provider that allows application components to send Internet mail.

The Java EE 6 platform requires JavaMail 1.4.

Java Authorization Contract for Containers

The Java Authorization Contract for Containers (JACC) specification defines a contract between a Java EE application server and an authorization policy provider. All Java EE containers support this contract.

The JACC specification defines `java.security.Permission` classes that satisfy the Java EE authorization model. The specification defines the binding of container-access decisions to operations on instances of these permission classes. It defines the semantics of policy providers that use the new permission classes to address the authorization requirements of the Java EE platform, including the definition and use of roles.

The Java EE 6 platform requires JACC 1.4.

Java Authentication Service Provider Interface for Containers

The Java Authentication Service Provider Interface for Containers (JASPIC) specification defines a service provider interface (SPI) by which authentication providers that implement message authentication mechanisms may be integrated in client or server message-processing containers or runtimes. Authentication providers integrated through this interface operate on network messages provided to them by their calling containers. The authentication providers transform outgoing messages so that the source of each message can be authenticated by the receiving container, and the recipient of the message can be authenticated by the message sender. Authentication providers authenticate each incoming message and return to their calling containers the identity established as a result of the message authentication.

JASPIC is new to the Java EE 6 platform. The Java EE 6 platform requires JASPIC 1.0.

Java EE 6 APIs in the Java Platform, Standard Edition 6 and 7

Several APIs that are required by the Java EE 6 platform are included in the Java Platform, Standard Edition 6 and 7 (Java SE 6 and 7) and are thus available to Java EE applications.

Java Database Connectivity API

The Java Database Connectivity (JDBC) API lets you invoke SQL commands from Java programming language methods. You use the JDBC API in an enterprise bean when you have a session bean access the database. You can also use the JDBC API from a servlet or a JSP page to access the database directly without going through an enterprise bean.

The JDBC API has two parts:

- An application-level interface used by the application components to access a database
- A service provider interface to attach a JDBC driver to the Java EE platform

The Java SE 6 platform requires JDBC 4.0.

Java Naming and Directory Interface API

The Java Naming and Directory Interface (JNDI) API provides naming and directory functionality, enabling applications to access multiple naming and directory services such as LDAP, DNS, and NIS. The JNDI API provides applications with methods for performing standard directory operations, such as associating attributes with objects and searching for objects using their attributes. Using JNDI, a Java EE application can store and retrieve any type of named Java object, allowing Java EE applications to coexist with many legacy applications and systems.

Java EE naming services provide application clients, enterprise beans, and web components with access to a JNDI naming environment. A *naming environment* allows a component to be customized without the need to access or change the component's source code. A container implements the component's environment and provides it to the component as a JNDI *naming context*.

A Java EE component can locate its environment naming context by using JNDI interfaces. A component can create a `javax.naming.InitialContext` object and look up the environment naming context in `InitialContext` under the name `java:comp/env`. A component's naming environment is stored directly in the environment naming context or in any of its direct or indirect subcontexts.

A Java EE component can access named system-provided and user-defined objects. The names of system-provided objects, such as JTA UserTransaction objects, are stored in the environment naming context java:comp/env. The Java EE platform allows a component to name user-defined objects, such as enterprise beans, environment entries, JDBC DataSource objects, and message connections. An object should be named within a subcontext of the naming environment according to the type of the object. For example, enterprise beans are named within the subcontext java:comp/env/ejb, and JDBC DataSource references are named within the subcontext java:comp/env/jdbc.

JavaBeans Activation Framework

The JavaBeans Activation Framework (JAF) is used by the JavaMail API. JAF provides standard services to determine the type of an arbitrary piece of data, encapsulate access to it, discover the operations available on it, and create the appropriate JavaBeans component to perform those operations.

Java API for XML Processing

The Java API for XML Processing (JAXP), part of the Java SE platform, supports the processing of XML documents using Document Object Model (DOM), Simple API for XML (SAX), and Extensible Stylesheet Language Transformations (XSLT). JAXP enables applications to parse and transform XML documents independently of a particular XML processing implementation.

JAXP also provides namespace support, which lets you work with schemas that might otherwise have naming conflicts. Designed to be flexible, JAXP lets you use any XML-compliant parser or XSL processor from within your application and supports the Worldwide Web Consortium (W3C) schema. You can find information on the W3C schema at this URL: http://www.w3.org/XML/Schema.

Java Architecture for XML Binding

The Java Architecture for XML Binding (JAXB) provides a convenient way to bind an XML schema to a representation in Java language programs. JAXB can be used independently or in combination with JAX-WS, where it provides a standard data binding for web service messages. All Java EE application client containers, web containers, and EJB containers support the JAXB API.

The Java EE 6 platform requires JAXB 2.2.

SOAP with Attachments API for Java

The SOAP with Attachments API for Java (SAAJ) is a low-level API on which JAX-WS depends. SAAJ enables the production and consumption of messages that conform to the SOAP 1.1 and 1.2 specifications and SOAP with Attachments note. Most developers do not use the SAAJ API, instead using the higher-level JAX-WS API.

Java API for XML Web Services

The Java API for XML Web Services (JAX-WS) specification provides support for web services that use the JAXB API for binding XML data to Java objects. The JAX-WS specification defines client APIs for accessing web services as well as techniques for implementing web service endpoints. The Implementing Enterprise Web Services specification describes the deployment of JAX-WS-based services and clients. The EJB and Java Servlet specifications also describe aspects of such deployment. JAX-WS-based applications can be deployed using any of these deployment models.

The JAX-WS specification describes the support for message handlers that can process message requests and responses. In general, these message handlers execute in the same container and with the same privileges and execution context as the JAX-WS client or endpoint component with which they are associated. These message handlers have access to the same JNDI java:comp/env namespace as their associated component. Custom serializers and deserializers, if supported, are treated in the same way as message handlers.

The Java EE 6 platform requires JAX-WS 2.2.

Java Authentication and Authorization Service

The Java Authentication and Authorization Service (JAAS) provides a way for a Java EE application to authenticate and authorize a specific user or group of users to run it.

JAAS is a Java programming language version of the standard Pluggable Authentication Module (PAM) framework, which extends the Java Platform security architecture to support user-based authorization.

GlassFish Server Tools

The GlassFish Server is a compliant implementation of the Java EE 6 platform. In addition to supporting all the APIs described in the previous sections, the GlassFish Server includes a number of Java EE tools that are not part of the Java EE 6 platform but are provided as a convenience to the developer.

This section briefly summarizes the tools that make up the GlassFish Server. Instructions for starting and stopping the GlassFish Server, starting the Administration Console, and starting and stopping the Java DB server are in Chapter 2, "Using the Tutorial Examples."

The GlassFish Server contains the tools listed in Table 1–1. Basic usage information for many of the tools appears throughout the tutorial. For detailed information, see the online help in the GUI tools.

TABLE 1–1   GlassFish Server Tools

Tool	Description
Administration Console	A web-based GUI GlassFish Server administration utility. Used to stop the GlassFish Server and to manage users, resources, and applications.
asadmin	A command-line GlassFish Server administration utility. Used to start and stop the GlassFish Server and to manage users, resources, and applications.
appclient	A command-line tool that launches the application client container and invokes the client application packaged in the application client JAR file.
capture-schema	A command-line tool to extract schema information from a database, producing a schema file that the GlassFish Server can use for container-managed persistence.
package-appclient	A command-line tool to package the application client container libraries and JAR files.
Java DB database	A copy of the Java DB server.
xjc	A command-line tool to transform, or bind, a source XML schema to a set of JAXB content classes in the Java programming language.
schemagen	A command-line tool to create a schema file for each namespace referenced in your Java classes.

TABLE 1–1 GlassFish Server Tools   *(Continued)*

Tool	Description
wsimport	A command-line tool to generate JAX-WS portable artifacts for a given WSDL file. After generation, these artifacts can be packaged in a WAR file with the WSDL and schema documents, along with the endpoint implementation, and then deployed.
wsgen	A command-line tool to read a web service endpoint class and generate all the required JAX-WS portable artifacts for web service deployment and invocation.

CHAPTER 2

Using the Tutorial Examples

This chapter tells you everything you need to know to install, build, and run the examples. The following topics are addressed here:

- "Required Software" on page 37
- "Starting and Stopping the GlassFish Server" on page 41
- "Starting the Administration Console" on page 42
- "Starting and Stopping the Java DB Server" on page 43
- "Building the Examples" on page 43
- "Tutorial Example Directory Structure" on page 44
- "Getting the Latest Updates to the Tutorial" on page 45
- "Debugging Java EE Applications" on page 45

Required Software

The following software is required to run the examples:

- "Java Platform, Standard Edition" on page 37
- "Java EE 6 Software Development Kit" on page 38
- "Java EE 6 Tutorial Component" on page 38
- "NetBeans IDE" on page 39
- "Apache Ant" on page 40

Java Platform, Standard Edition

To build, deploy, and run the examples, you need a copy of the Java Platform, Standard Edition 6.0 Development Kit (JDK 6) or the Java Platform, Standard Edition 7.0 Development Kit (JDK 7). You can download the JDK 6 or JDK 7 software from http://www.oracle.com/technetwork/java/javase/downloads/index.html.

Download the current JDK update that does not include any other software, such as NetBeans IDE or the Java EE SDK.

Java EE 6 Software Development Kit

GlassFish Server Open Source Edition 3.1.2 is targeted as the build and runtime environment for the tutorial examples. To build, deploy, and run the examples, you need a copy of the GlassFish Server and, optionally, NetBeans IDE. To obtain the GlassFish Server, you must install the Java EE 6 Software Development Kit (SDK), which you can download from `http://www.oracle.com/technetwork/java/javaee/downloads/index.html`. Make sure you download the Java EE 6 SDK, not the Java EE 6 Web Profile SDK.

SDK Installation Tips

During the installation of the SDK, do the following:

- Allow the installer to download and configure the Update Tool. If you access the Internet through a firewall, provide the proxy host and port.
- Configure the GlassFish Server administration user name as `admin`, and specify no password. This is the default setting.
- Accept the default port values for the Admin Port (4848) and the HTTP Port (8080).
- Do not select the check box to create an operating system service for the domain.

You can leave the check box to start the domain after creation selected if you wish, but this is not required.

This tutorial refers to *as-install-parent*, the directory where you install the GlassFish Server. For example, the default installation directory on Microsoft Windows is `C:\glassfish3`, so *as-install-parent* is `C:\glassfish3`. The GlassFish Server itself is installed in *as-install*, the `glassfish` directory under *as-install-parent*. So on Microsoft Windows, *as-install* is `C:\glassfish3\glassfish`.

After you install the GlassFish Server, add the following directories to your PATH to avoid having to specify the full path when you use commands:

as-install-parent/bin

as-install/bin

Java EE 6 Tutorial Component

The tutorial example source is contained in the tutorial component. To obtain the tutorial component, use the Update Tool.

▼ To Obtain the Tutorial Component Using the Update Tool

1   Start the Update Tool by doing one of the following:

   - From the command line, type the command `updatetool`.

   - On a Windows system, from the Start menu, select All Programs, then select Java EE 6 SDK, then select Start Update Tool.

2   Expand the Java EE 6 SDK node.

3   Select the Available Updates node.

4   From the list, select the Java EE 6 Tutorial check box.

5   Click Install.

6   Accept the license agreement.

   After installation, the Java EE 6 Tutorial appears in the list of installed components. The tool is installed in the *as-install*/docs/javaee-tutorial directory. This directory contains two subdirectories: docs and examples. The examples directory contains subdirectories for each of the technologies discussed in the tutorial.

Next Steps   Updates to the Java EE 6 Tutorial are published periodically. For details on obtaining these updates, see "Getting the Latest Updates to the Tutorial" on page 45.

NetBeans IDE

The NetBeans integrated development environment (IDE) is a free, open-source IDE for developing Java applications, including enterprise applications. NetBeans IDE supports the Java EE platform. You can build, package, deploy, and run the tutorial examples from within NetBeans IDE.

To run the tutorial examples, you need the latest version of NetBeans IDE. You can download NetBeans IDE from http://www.netbeans.org/downloads/index.html. Make sure that you download the Java EE bundle.

▼ To Install NetBeans IDE without GlassFish Server

When you install NetBeans IDE, do not install the version of GlassFish Server that comes with NetBeans IDE. To skip the installation of GlassFish Server, follow these steps.

1   On the first page of the NetBeans IDE Installer wizard, deselect the check box for GlassFish Server and click OK.

2   Accept both the License Agreement and the Junit License Agreement.
A few of the tutorial examples use the Junit library, so you should install it.

3   Continue with the installation of NetBeans IDE.

▼ **To Add GlassFish Server as a Server in NetBeans IDE**

To run the tutorial examples in NetBeans IDE, you must add your GlassFish Server as a server in NetBeans IDE. Follow these instructions to add the GlassFish Server to NetBeans IDE.

1   From the Tools menu, select Servers.
The Servers wizard opens.

2   Click Add Server.

3   Under Choose Server, select GlassFish Server 3+ and click Next.

4   Under Server Location, browse to the location of the Java EE 6 SDK and click Next.

5   Under Domain Location, select Register Local Domain.

6   Click Finish.

Apache Ant

Ant is a Java technology-based build tool developed by the Apache Software Foundation (http://ant.apache.org/) and is used to build, package, and deploy the tutorial examples. To run the tutorial examples, you need Ant 1.7.1 or higher. If you do not already have Ant, you can install it from the Update Tool that is part of the GlassFish Server.

▼ **To Obtain Apache Ant**

1   Start the Update Tool.

- From the command line, type the command updatetool.

- On a Windows system, from the Start menu, select All Programs, then select Java EE 6 SDK, then select Start Update Tool.

2   **Expand the Java EE 6 SDK node.**

3   **Select the Available Add-ons node.**

4   **From the list, select the Apache Ant Build Tool check box.**

5   **Click Install.**

6   **Accept the license agreement.**

After installation, Apache Ant appears in the list of installed components. The tool is installed in the *as-install-parent/*ant directory.

Next Steps   To use the ant command, add *as-install-parent/*ant/bin to your PATH environment variable.

Starting and Stopping the GlassFish Server

To start the GlassFish Server from the command line, open a terminal window or command prompt and execute the following:

```
asadmin start-domain --verbose
```

A *domain* is a set of one or more GlassFish Server instances managed by one administration server. Associated with a domain are the following:

- The GlassFish Server's port number. The default is 8080.

- The administration server's port number. The default is 4848.

- An administration user name and password. The default user name is admin, and by default no password is required.

You specify these values when you install the GlassFish Server. The examples in this tutorial assume that you chose the default ports as well as the default user name and lack of password.

With no arguments, the start-domain command initiates the default domain, which is domain1. The --verbose flag causes all logging and debugging output to appear on the terminal window or command prompt. The output also goes into the server log, which is located in *domain-dir/*logs/server.log.

Or, on Windows, from the Start menu, select All Programs, then select Java EE 6 SDK, then select Start Application Server.

To stop the GlassFish Server, open a terminal window or command prompt and execute:

```
asadmin stop-domain domain1
```

Or, on Windows, from the Start menu, select All Programs, then select Java EE 6 SDK, then select Stop Application Server.

▼ To Start the GlassFish Server Using NetBeans IDE

1 Click the Services tab.

2 Expand the Servers node.

3 Right-click the GlassFish Server instance and select Start.

Next Steps To stop the GlassFish Server using NetBeans IDE, right-click the GlassFish Server instance and select Stop.

Starting the Administration Console

To administer the GlassFish Server and manage users, resources, and Java EE applications, use the Administration Console tool. The GlassFish Server must be running before you invoke the Administration Console. To start the Administration Console, open a browser at `http://localhost:4848/`.

Or, on Windows, from the Start menu, select All Programs, then select Java EE 6 SDK, then select Administration Console.

▼ To Start the Administration Console Using NetBeans IDE

1 Click the Services tab.

2 Expand the Servers node.

3 Right-click the GlassFish Server instance and select View Domain Admin Console.

Note – NetBeans IDE uses your default web browser to open the Administration Console.

Starting and Stopping the Java DB Server

The GlassFish Server includes the Java DB database server.

To start the Java DB server from the command line, open a terminal window or command prompt and execute:

```
asadmin start-database
```

To stop the Java DB server from the command line, open a terminal window or command prompt and execute:

```
asadmin stop-database
```

For information about the Java DB included with the GlassFish Server, see
`http://www.oracle.com/technetwork/java/javadb/overview/index.html`.

▼ To Start the Database Server Using NetBeans IDE

When you start the GlassFish Server using NetBeans IDE, the database server starts automatically. If you ever need to start the database server manually, follow these steps.

1 Click the Services tab.

2 Expand the Databases node.

3 Right-click Java DB and select Start Server.

Next Steps To stop the database using NetBeans IDE, right-click Java DB and select Stop Server.

Building the Examples

The tutorial examples are distributed with a configuration file for either NetBeans IDE or Ant. Either NetBeans IDE or Ant may be used to build, package, deploy, and run the examples. Directions for building the examples are provided in each chapter.

Tutorial Example Directory Structure

To facilitate iterative development and keep application source separate from compiled files, the tutorial examples use the Java BluePrints application directory structure.

Each application module has the following structure:

- `build.xml`: Ant build file
- `src/java`: Java source files for the module
- `src/conf`: configuration files for the module, with the exception of web applications
- `web`: web pages, style sheets, tag files, and images (web applications only)
- `web/WEB-INF`: configuration files for web applications (web applications only)
- `nbproject`: NetBeans project files

When an example has multiple application modules packaged into an EAR file, its submodule directories use the following naming conventions:

- *example-name*-`app-client`: application clients
- *example-name*-`ejb`: enterprise bean JAR files
- *example-name*-`war`: web applications

The Ant build files (`build.xml`) distributed with the examples contain targets to create a `build` subdirectory and to copy and compile files into that directory; a `dist` subdirectory, which holds the packaged module file; and a `client-jar` directory, which holds the retrieved application client JAR.

The *tut-install*/`examples/bp-project/` directory contains additional Ant targets called by the `build.xml` file targets.

For some web examples, an Ant target will open the example URL in a browser if one is available. This happens automatically on Windows systems. If you are running on a UNIX system, you may want to modify a line in the *tut-install*/`examples/bp-project/build.properties` file. Remove the comment character from the line specifying the `default.browser` property and specify the path to the command that invokes a browser. If you do not make the change, you can open the URL in the browser yourself.

Getting the Latest Updates to the Tutorial

Check for any updates to the tutorial by using the Update Center included with the Java EE 6 SDK.

▼ To Update the Tutorial through the Update Center

1   Open the Services tab in NetBeans IDE and expand Servers.

2   Right-click the GlassFish Server instance and select View Update Center to display the Update Tool.

3   Select Available Updates in the tree to display a list of updated packages.

4   Look for updates to the Java EE 6 Tutorial (javaee-tutorial) package.

5   If there is an updated version of the Tutorial, select Java EE 6 Tutorial (javaee-tutorial) and click Install.

Debugging Java EE Applications

This section explains how to determine what is causing an error in your application deployment or execution.

Using the Server Log

One way to debug applications is to look at the server log in *domain-dir*/logs/server.log. The log contains output from the GlassFish Server and your applications. You can log messages from any Java class in your application with System.out.println and the Java Logging APIs (documented at http://docs.oracle.com/javase/6/docs/technotes/guides/logging/index.html) and from web components with the ServletContext.log method.

If you use NetBeans IDE, logging output appears in the Output window as well as the server log.

If you start the GlassFish Server with the --verbose flag, all logging and debugging output will appear on the terminal window or command prompt and the server log. If you start the GlassFish Server in the background, debugging information is available only in the log. You can view the server log with a text editor or with the Administration Console log viewer.

▼ To Use the Administration Console Log Viewer

1   Select the GlassFish Server node.

2   Click the View Log Files button.

The log viewer opens and displays the last 40 entries.

3   To display other entries, follow these steps.

   a.   Click the Modify Search button.

   b.   Specify any constraints on the entries you want to see.

   c.   Click the Search button at the top of the log viewer.

Using a Debugger

The GlassFish Server supports the Java Platform Debugger Architecture (JPDA). With JPDA, you can configure the GlassFish Server to communicate debugging information using a socket.

▼ To Debug an Application Using a Debugger

1   Enable debugging in the GlassFish Server using the Administration Console:

   a.   Expand the Configurations node, then expand the server-config node.

   b.   Select the JVM Settings node. The default debug options are set to:

   ```
   -Xdebug -Xrunjdwp:transport=dt_socket,server=y,suspend=n,address=9009
   ```

   As you can see, the default debugger socket port is 9009. You can change it to a port not in use by the GlassFish Server or another service.

   c.   Select the Debug Enabled check box.

   d.   Click the Save button.

2   Stop the GlassFish Server and then restart it.

The Web Tier

Part II explores advanced topics in the web tier. This part contains the following chapters:

- Chapter 3, "JavaServer Faces Technology: Advanced Concepts"
- Chapter 4, "Using Ajax with JavaServer Faces Technology"
- Chapter 5, "Composite Components: Advanced Topics and Example"
- Chapter 6, "Creating Custom UI Components and Other Custom Objects"
- Chapter 7, "Configuring JavaServer Faces Applications"
- Chapter 8, "Uploading Files with Java Servlet Technology"
- Chapter 9, "Internationalizing and Localizing Web Applications"

CHAPTER 3

JavaServer Faces Technology: Advanced Concepts

The Java EE 6 Tutorial: Basic Concepts introduces JavaServer Faces technology and Facelets, the preferred presentation layer for the Java EE platform. This chapter and the following chapters introduce advanced concepts in this area.

- This chapter describes the JavaServer Faces lifecycle in detail. Some of the complex JavaServer Faces applications use the well-defined lifecycle phases to customize application behavior.

- Chapter 4, "Using Ajax with JavaServer Faces Technology," introduces Ajax concepts and the use of Ajax in JavaServer Faces applications.

- Chapter 5, "Composite Components: Advanced Topics and Example," introduces advanced features of composite components.

- Chapter 6, "Creating Custom UI Components and Other Custom Objects," describes the process of creating new components, renderers, converters, listeners, and validators from scratch.

- Chapter 7, "Configuring JavaServer Faces Applications," introduces the process of creating and deploying JavaServer Faces applications, the use of various configuration files, and the deployment structure.

The following topics are addressed here:

The Lifecycle of a JavaServer Faces Application

The lifecycle of an application refers to the various stages of processing of that application, from its initiation to its conclusion. All applications have lifecycles. During a web application lifecycle, common tasks such as the following are performed:

- Handling incoming requests
- Decoding parameters
- Modifying and saving state
- Rendering web pages to the browser

The JavaServer Faces web application framework manages lifecycle phases automatically for simple applications or allows you to manage them manually for more complex applications as required.

JavaServer Faces applications that use advanced features may require interaction with the lifecycle at certain phases. For example, Ajax applications use partial processing features of the lifecycle. A clearer understanding of the lifecycle phases is key to creating well-designed components.

A simplified view of the JavaServer faces lifecycle, consisting of the two main phases of a JavaServer Faces web application, is introduced in "The Lifecycle of the hello Application" in *The Java EE 6 Tutorial: Basic Concepts*. This section examines the JavaServer Faces lifecycle in more detail.

Overview of the JavaServer Faces Lifecycle

The lifecycle of a JavaServer Faces application begins when the client makes an HTTP request for a page and ends when the server responds with the page, translated to HTML.

The lifecycle can be divided into two main phases, *execute* and *render*. The execute phase is further divided into subphases to support the sophisticated component tree. This structure requires that component data be converted and validated, component events be handled, and component data be propagated to beans in an orderly fashion.

A JavaServer Faces page is represented by a tree of components, called a *view*. During the lifecycle, the JavaServer Faces implementation must build the view while considering the state saved from a previous submission of the page. When the client requests a page, the JavaServer Faces implementation performs several tasks, such as validating the data input of components in the view and converting input data to types specified on the server side.

The JavaServer Faces implementation performs all these tasks as a series of steps in the JavaServer Faces request-response lifecycle. Figure 3–1 illustrates these steps.

FIGURE 3-1   JavaServer Faces Standard Request-Response Lifecycle

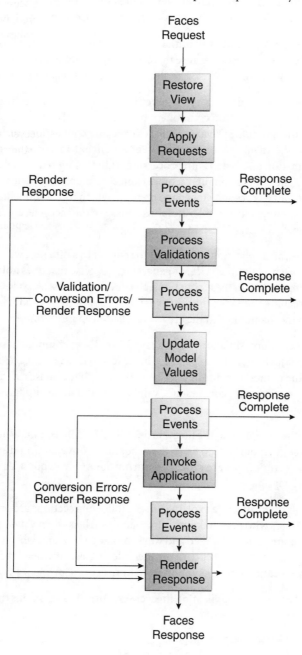

The request-response lifecycle handles two kinds of requests: initial requests and postbacks. An *initial request* occurs when a user makes a request for a page for the first time. A *postback request* occurs when a user submits the form contained on a page that was previously loaded into the browser as a result of executing an initial request.

When the lifecycle handles an initial request, it executes only the Restore View and Render Response phases, because there is no user input or action to process. Conversely, when the lifecycle handles a postback, it executes all of the phases.

Usually, the first request for a JavaServer Faces page comes in from a client, as a result of clicking a link or button component on a JavaServer Faces page. To render a response that is another JavaServer Faces page, the application creates a new view and stores it in the `javax.faces.context.FacesContext` instance, which represents all of the information associated with processing an incoming request and creating a response. The application then acquires object references needed by the view and calls the `FacesContext.renderResponse` method, which forces immediate rendering of the view by skipping to the Render Response phase of the lifecycle, as is shown by the arrows labelled Render Response in the diagram.

Sometimes, an application might need to redirect to a different web application resource, such as a web service, or generate a response that does not contain JavaServer Faces components. In these situations, the developer must skip the Render Response phase by calling the `FacesContext.responseComplete` method. This situation is also shown in the diagram, with the arrows labelled Response Complete.

The most common situation is that a JavaServer Faces component submits a request for another JavaServer Faces page. In this case, the JavaServer Faces implementation handles the request and automatically goes through the phases in the lifecycle to perform any necessary conversions, validations, and model updates, and to generate the response.

There is one exception to the lifecycle described in this section. When a component's `immediate` attribute is set to `true`, the validation, conversion, and events associated with these components are processed during the Apply Request Values phase rather than in a later phase.

The details of the lifecycle explained in the following sections are primarily intended for developers who need to know information such as when validations, conversions, and events are usually handled and ways to change how and when they are handled. For more information on each of the lifecycle phases, download the latest JavaServer Faces Specification documentation from `http://jcp.org/en/jsr/detail?id=314`.

The JavaServer Faces application lifecycle execute phase contains the following subphases:

- "Restore View Phase" on page 53
- "Apply Request Values Phase" on page 53

- "Process Validations Phase" on page 54
- "Update Model Values Phase" on page 55
- "Invoke Application Phase" on page 55
- "Render Response Phase" on page 55

Restore View Phase

When a request for a JavaServer Faces page is made, usually by an action such as when a link or a button component is clicked, the JavaServer Faces implementation begins the Restore View phase.

During this phase, the JavaServer Faces implementation builds the view of the page, wires event handlers and validators to components in the view, and saves the view in the FacesContext instance, which contains all the information needed to process a single request. All the application's components, event handlers, converters, and validators have access to the FacesContext instance.

If the request for the page is an initial request, the JavaServer Faces implementation creates an empty view during this phase and the lifecycle advances to the Render Response phase, during which the empty view is populated with the components referenced by the tags in the page.

If the request for the page is a postback, a view corresponding to this page already exists in the FacesContext instance. During this phase, the JavaServer Faces implementation restores the view by using the state information saved on the client or the server.

Apply Request Values Phase

After the component tree is restored during a postback request, each component in the tree extracts its new value from the request parameters by using its decode (processDecodes()) method. The value is then stored locally on each component.

If any decode methods or event listeners have called the renderResponse method on the current FacesContext instance, the JavaServer Faces implementation skips to the Render Response phase.

If any events have been queued during this phase, the JavaServer Faces implementation broadcasts the events to interested listeners.

If some components on the page have their immediate attributes (see "The immediate Attribute" in *The Java EE 6 Tutorial: Basic Concepts*) set to true, then the validations, conversions, and events associated with these components will be processed during this phase. If any conversion fails, an error message associated with the component is generated and queued on `FacesContext`. This message will be displayed during the Render Response phase, along with any validation errors resulting from the Process Validations phase.

At this point, if the application needs to redirect to a different web application resource or generate a response that does not contain any JavaServer Faces components, it can call the `FacesContext.responseComplete` method.

At the end of this phase, the components are set to their new values, and messages and events have been queued.

If the current request is identified as a partial request, the partial context is retrieved from the `FacesContext`, and the partial processing method is applied.

Process Validations Phase

During this phase, the JavaServer Faces implementation processes all validators registered on the components in the tree, by using its `validate (processValidators)` method. It examines the component attributes that specify the rules for the validation and compares these rules to the local value stored for the component. The JavaServer Faces implementation also completes conversions for input components that do not have the `immediate` attribute set to true.

If the local value is invalid, or if any conversion fails, the JavaServer Faces implementation adds an error message to the `FacesContext` instance, and the lifecycle advances directly to the Render Response phase so that the page is rendered again with the error messages displayed. If there were conversion errors from the Apply Request Values phase, the messages for these errors are also displayed.

If any `validate` methods or event listeners have called the `renderResponse` method on the current `FacesContext`, the JavaServer Faces implementation skips to the Render Response phase.

At this point, if the application needs to redirect to a different web application resource or generate a response that does not contain any JavaServer Faces components, it can call the `FacesContext.responseComplete` method.

If events have been queued during this phase, the JavaServer Faces implementation broadcasts them to interested listeners.

If the current request is identified as a partial request, the partial context is retrieved from the `Faces Context`, and the partial processing method is applied.

Update Model Values Phase

After the JavaServer Faces implementation determines that the data is valid, it traverses the component tree and sets the corresponding server-side object properties to the components' local values. The JavaServer Faces implementation updates only the bean properties pointed at by an input component's value attribute. If the local data cannot be converted to the types specified by the bean properties, the lifecycle advances directly to the Render Response phase so that the page is re-rendered with errors displayed. This is similar to what happens with validation errors.

If any updateModels methods or any listeners have called the renderResponse method on the current FacesContext instance, the JavaServer Faces implementation skips to the Render Response phase.

At this point, if the application needs to redirect to a different web application resource or generate a response that does not contain any JavaServer Faces components, it can call the FacesContext.responseComplete method.

If any events have been queued during this phase, the JavaServer Faces implementation broadcasts them to interested listeners.

If the current request is identified as a partial request, the partial context is retrieved from the FacesContext, and the partial processing method is applied.

Invoke Application Phase

During this phase, the JavaServer Faces implementation handles any application-level events, such as submitting a form or linking to another page.

At this point, if the application needs to redirect to a different web application resource or generate a response that does not contain any JavaServer Faces components, it can call the FacesContext.responseComplete method.

If the view being processed was reconstructed from state information from a previous request and if a component has fired an event, these events are broadcast to interested listeners.

Finally, the JavaServer Faces implementation transfers control to the Render Response phase.

Render Response Phase

During this phase, JavaServer Faces builds the view and delegates authority to the appropriate resource for rendering the pages.

If this is an initial request, the components that are represented on the page will be added to the component tree. If this is not an initial request, the components are already added to the tree, so they need not be added again.

If the request is a postback and errors were encountered during the Apply Request Values phase, Process Validations phase, or Update Model Values phase, the original page is rendered again during this phase. If the pages contain h:message or h:messages tags, any queued error messages are displayed on the page.

After the content of the view is rendered, the state of the response is saved so that subsequent requests can access it. The saved state is available to the Restore View phase.

Partial Processing and Partial Rendering

The JavaServer Faces lifecycle spans all of the execute and render processes of an application. It is also possible to process and render only parts of an application, such as a single component. For example, the JavaServer Faces Ajax framework can generate requests containing information on which particular component may be processed and which particular component may be rendered back to the client.

Once such a partial request enters the JavaServer Faces lifecycle, the information is identified and processed by a javax.faces.context.PartialViewContext object. The JavaServer Faces lifecycle is still aware of such Ajax requests and modifies the component tree accordingly.

The execute and render attributes of the f:ajax tag are used to identify which components may be executed and rendered. For more information on these attributes, see Chapter 4, "Using Ajax with JavaServer Faces Technology."

The Lifecycle of a Facelets Application

The JavaServer Faces specification defines the lifecycle of a JavaServer Faces application. For more information on this lifecycle, see "The Lifecycle of a JavaServer Faces Application" on page 50. The following steps describe that process as applied to a Facelets-based application.

1. When a client, such as a browser, makes a new request to a page that is created using Facelets, a new component tree or javax.faces.component.UIViewRoot is created and placed in the FacesContext.

2. The UIViewRoot is applied to the Facelets, and the view is populated with components for rendering.

3. The newly built view is rendered back as a response to the client.

4. On rendering, the state of this view is stored for the next request. The state of input components and form data is stored.

5. The client may interact with the view and request another view or change from the JavaServer Faces application. At this time the saved view is restored from the stored state.

6. The restored view is once again passed through the JavaServer Faces lifecycle, which eventually will either generate a new view or re-render the current view if there were no validation problems and no action was triggered.

7. If the same view is requested, the stored view is rendered once again.

8. If a new view is requested, then the process described in Step 2 is continued.

9. The new view is then rendered back as a response to the client.

User Interface Component Model

In addition to the lifecycle description, an overview of JavaServer Faces architecture provides better understanding of the technology.

JavaServer Faces components are the building blocks of a JavaServer Faces view. A component can be a user interface (UI) component or a non-UI component.

JavaServer Faces UI components are configurable, reusable elements that compose the user interfaces of JavaServer Faces applications. A component can be simple, such as a button, or can be compound, such as a table, composed of multiple components.

JavaServer Faces technology provides a rich, flexible component architecture that includes the following:

- A set of `javax.faces.component.UIComponent` classes for specifying the state and behavior of UI components
- A rendering model that defines how to render the components in various ways
- A conversion model that defines how to register data converters onto a component
- An event and listener model that defines how to handle component events
- A validation model that defines how to register validators onto a component
- A navigation model that defines page navigation and the sequence in which pages are loaded

This section briefly describes each of these pieces of the component architecture.

User Interface Component Classes

JavaServer Faces technology provides a set of UI component classes and associated behavioral interfaces that specify all the UI component functionality, such as holding component state, maintaining a reference to objects, and driving event handling and rendering for a set of standard components.

The component classes are completely extensible, allowing component writers to create their own custom components. See Chapter 6, "Creating Custom UI Components and Other Custom Objects," for more information.

The abstract base class for all components is javax.faces.component.UIComponent. JavaServer Faces UI component classes extend the UIComponentBase class (a subclass of UIComponent), which defines the default state and behavior of a component. The following set of component classes is included with JavaServer Faces technology:

- UIColumn: Represents a single column of data in a UIData component.
- UICommand: Represents a control that fires actions when activated.
- UIData: Represents a data binding to a collection of data represented by a javax.faces.model.DataModel instance.
- UIForm: Represents an input form to be presented to the user. Its child components represent (among other things) the input fields to be included when the form is submitted. This component is analogous to the form tag in HTML.
- UIGraphic: Displays an image.
- UIInput: Takes data input from a user. This class is a subclass of UIOutput.
- UIMessage: Displays a localized error message.
- UIMessages: Displays a set of localized error messages.
- UIOutcomeTarget: Displays a hyperlink in the form of a link or a button.
- UIOutput: Displays data output on a page.
- UIPanel: Manages the layout of its child components.
- UIParameter: Represents substitution parameters.
- UISelectBoolean: Allows a user to set a boolean value on a control by selecting or deselecting it. This class is a subclass of the UIInput class.
- UISelectItem: Represents a single item in a set of items.
- UISelectItems: Represents an entire set of items.
- UISelectMany: Allows a user to select multiple items from a group of items. This class is a subclass of the UIInput class.
- UISelectOne: Allows a user to select one item from a group of items. This class is a subclass of the UIInput class.

- `UIViewParameter`: Represents the query parameters in a request. This class is a subclass of the `UIInput` class.

- `UIViewRoot`: Represents the root of the component tree.

In addition to extending `UIComponentBase`, the component classes also implement one or more *behavioral interfaces*, each of which defines certain behavior for a set of components whose classes implement the interface.

These behavioral interfaces, all defined in the `javax.faces.component` package unless otherwise stated, are as follows:

- `ActionSource`: Indicates that the component can fire an action event. This interface is intended for use with components based on JavaServer Faces technology 1.1_01 and earlier versions. This interface is deprecated in JavaServer Faces 2.

- `ActionSource2`: Extends `ActionSource`, and therefore provides the same functionality. However, it allows components to use the Expression Language (EL) when they are referencing methods that handle action events.

- `EditableValueHolder`: Extends `ValueHolder` and specifies additional features for editable components, such as validation and emitting value-change events.

- `NamingContainer`: Mandates that each component rooted at this component have a unique ID.

- `StateHolder`: Denotes that a component has state that must be saved between requests.

- `ValueHolder`: Indicates that the component maintains a local value as well as the option of accessing data in the model tier.

- `javax.faces.event.SystemEventListenerHolder`: Maintains a list of `javax.faces.event.SystemEventListener` instances for each type of `javax.faces.event.SystemEvent` defined by that class.

- `javax.faces.component.behavior.ClientBehaviorHolder`: Adds the ability to attach `javax.faces.component.behavior.ClientBehavior` instances such as a reusable script.

`UICommand` implements `ActionSource2` and `StateHolder`. `UIOutput` and component classes that extend `UIOutput` implement `StateHolder` and `ValueHolder`. `UIInput` and component classes that extend `UIInput` implement `EditableValueHolder`, `StateHolder`, and `ValueHolder`. `UIComponentBase` implements `StateHolder`.

Only component writers will need to use the component classes and behavioral interfaces directly. Page authors and application developers will use a standard component by including a tag that represents it on a page. Most of the components can be rendered in different ways on a page. For example, a `UICommand` component can be rendered as a button or a hyperlink.

The next section explains how the rendering model works and how page authors can choose to render the components by selecting the appropriate tags.

Component Rendering Model

The JavaServer Faces component architecture is designed such that the functionality of the components is defined by the component classes, whereas the component rendering can be defined by a separate renderer class. This design has several benefits, including the following:

- Component writers can define the behavior of a component once but create multiple renderers, each of which defines a different way to render the component to the same client or to different clients.

- Page authors and application developers can change the appearance of a component on the page by selecting the tag that represents the appropriate combination of component and renderer.

A *render kit* defines how component classes map to component tags that are appropriate for a particular client. The JavaServer Faces implementation includes a standard HTML render kit for rendering to an HTML client.

The render kit defines a set of javax.faces.render.Renderer classes for each component that it supports. Each Renderer class defines a different way to render the particular component to the output defined by the render kit. For example, a UISelectOne component has three different renderers. One of them renders the component as a set of radio buttons. Another renders the component as a combo box. The third one renders the component as a list box. Similarly, a UICommand component can be rendered as a button or a hyperlink, using the h:commandButton or h:commandLink tag. The command part of each tag corresponds to the UICommand class, specifying the functionality, which is to fire an action. The Button or Link part of each tag corresponds to a separate Renderer class that defines how the component appears on the page.

Each custom tag defined in the standard HTML render kit is composed of the component functionality (defined in the UIComponent class) and the rendering attributes (defined by the Renderer class).

The section "Adding Components to a Page Using HTML Tags" in *The Java EE 6 Tutorial: Basic Concepts* lists all supported component tags and illustrates how to use the tags in an example.

The JavaServer Faces implementation provides a custom tag library for rendering components in HTML.

Conversion Model

A JavaServer Faces application can optionally associate a component with server-side object data. This object is a JavaBeans component, such as a managed bean. An application gets and sets the object data for a component by calling the appropriate object properties for that component.

When a component is bound to an object, the application has two views of the component's data:

- The model view, in which data is represented as data types, such as `int` or `long`.
- The presentation view, in which data is represented in a manner that can be read or modified by the user. For example, a `java.util.Date` might be represented as a text string in the format `mm/dd/yy` or as a set of three text strings.

The JavaServer Faces implementation automatically converts component data between these two views when the bean property associated with the component is of one of the types supported by the component's data. For example, if a `UISelectBoolean` component is associated with a bean property of type `java.lang.Boolean`, the JavaServer Faces implementation will automatically convert the component's data from `String` to `Boolean`. In addition, some component data must be bound to properties of a particular type. For example, a `UISelectBoolean` component must be bound to a property of type `boolean` or `java.lang.Boolean`.

Sometimes you might want to convert a component's data to a type other than a standard type, or you might want to convert the format of the data. To facilitate this, JavaServer Faces technology allows you to register a `javax.faces.convert.Converter` implementation on `UIOutput` components and components whose classes subclass `UIOutput`. If you register the `Converter` implementation on a component, the `Converter` implementation converts the component's data between the two views.

You can either use the standard converters supplied with the JavaServer Faces implementation or create your own custom converter. Custom converter creation is covered in Chapter 6, "Creating Custom UI Components and Other Custom Objects."

Event and Listener Model

The JavaServer Faces event and listener model is similar to the JavaBeans event model in that it has strongly typed event classes and listener interfaces that an application can use to handle events generated by components.

The JavaServer Faces specification defines three types of events: application events, system events, and data-model events.

Application events are tied to a particular application and are generated by a UIComponent. They represent the standard events available in previous versions of JavaServer Faces technology.

An event object identifies the component that generated the event and stores information about the event. To be notified of an event, an application must provide an implementation of the listener class and must register it on the component that generates the event. When the user activates a component, such as by clicking a button, an event is fired. This causes the JavaServer Faces implementation to invoke the listener method that processes the event.

JavaServer Faces supports two kinds of application events: action events and value-change events.

An *action event* (class javax.faces.event.ActionEvent) occurs when the user activates a component that implements javax.faces.component.ActionSource. These components include buttons and hyperlinks.

A *value-change event* (class javax.faces.event.ValueChangeEvent) occurs when the user changes the value of a component represented by UIInput or one of its subclasses. An example is selecting a check box, an action that results in the component's value changing to true. The component types that can generate these types of events are the UIInput, UISelectOne, UISelectMany, and UISelectBoolean components. Value-change events are fired only if no validation errors are detected.

Depending on the value of the immediate property (see "The immediate Attribute" in *The Java EE 6 Tutorial: Basic Concepts*) of the component emitting the event, action events can be processed during the invoke application phase or the apply request values phase, and value-change events can be processed during the process validations phase or the apply request values phase.

System events are generated by an Object rather than a UIComponent. They are generated during the execution of an application at predefined times. They are applicable to the entire application rather than to a specific component.

A *data-model event* occurs when a new row of a UIData component is selected.

There are two ways to cause your application to react to action events or value-change events that are emitted by a standard component:

- Implement an event listener class to handle the event and register the listener on the component by nesting either an f:valueChangeListener tag or an f:actionListener tag inside the component tag.

- Implement a method of a managed bean to handle the event and refer to the method with a method expression from the appropriate attribute of the component's tag.

See "Implementing an Event Listener" on page 117 for information on how to implement an event listener. See "Registering Listeners on Components" in *The Java EE 6 Tutorial: Basic Concepts* for information on how to register the listener on a component.

See "Writing a Method to Handle an Action Event" in *The Java EE 6 Tutorial: Basic Concepts* and "Writing a Method to Handle a Value-Change Event" in *The Java EE 6 Tutorial: Basic Concepts* for information on how to implement managed bean methods that handle these events.

See "Referencing a Managed Bean Method" in *The Java EE 6 Tutorial: Basic Concepts* for information on how to refer to the managed bean method from the component tag.

When emitting events from custom components, you must implement the appropriate event class and manually queue the event on the component in addition to implementing an event listener class or a managed bean method that handles the event. "Handling Events for Custom Components" on page 119 explains how to do this.

Validation Model

JavaServer Faces technology supports a mechanism for validating the local data of editable components (such as text fields). This validation occurs before the corresponding model data is updated to match the local value.

Like the conversion model, the validation model defines a set of standard classes for performing common data validation checks. The JavaServer Faces core tag library also defines a set of tags that correspond to the standard `javax.faces.validator.Validator` implementations. See "Using the Standard Validators" in *The Java EE 6 Tutorial: Basic Concepts* for a list of all the standard validation classes and corresponding tags.

Most of the tags have a set of attributes for configuring the validator's properties, such as the minimum and maximum allowable values for the component's data. The page author registers the validator on a component by nesting the validator's tag within the component's tag.

In addition to validators that are registered on the component, you can declare a default validator which is registered on all `UIInput` components in the application. For more information on default validators, see "Using Default Validators" on page 159.

The validation model also allows you to create your own custom validator and corresponding tag to perform custom validation. The validation model provides two ways to implement custom validation:

- Implement a `Validator` interface that performs the validation.
- Implement a managed bean method that performs the validation.

If you are implementing a `Validator` interface, you must also:

- Register the `Validator` implementation with the application.
- Create a custom tag or use an `f:validator` tag to register the validator on the component.

In the previously described standard validation model, the validator is defined for each input component on a page. The Bean Validation model allows the validator to be applied to all fields in a page. See "Using Bean Validation" in *The Java EE 6 Tutorial: Basic Concepts* and Chapter 22, "Bean Validation: Advanced Topics," for more information on Bean Validation.

Navigation Model

The JavaServer Faces navigation model makes it easy to define page navigation and to handle any additional processing that is needed to choose the sequence in which pages are loaded.

In JavaServer Faces technology, *navigation* is a set of rules for choosing the next page or view to be displayed after an application action, such as when a button or hyperlink is clicked.

Navigation can be implicit or user-defined. Implicit navigation comes into play when user-defined navigation rules are not available. For more information on implicit navigation, see "Implicit Navigation Rules" on page 164.

User-defined navigation rules are declared in zero or more application configuration resource files, such as `faces-config.xml`, by using a set of XML elements. The default structure of a navigation rule is as follows:

```
<navigation-rule>
    <description></description
    <from-view-id></from-view-id>
    <navigation-case>
        <from-action></from-action>
        <from-outcome></from-outcome>
        <if></if>
        <to-view-id></to-view-id>
    </navigation-case>
</navigation-rule>
```

User-defined navigation is handled as follows:

- Define the rules in the application configuration resource file.
- Refer to an outcome String from the button or hyperlink component's action attribute. This outcome String is used by the JavaServer Faces implementation to select the navigation rule.

Here is an example navigation rule:

```
<navigation-rule>
    <from-view-id>/greeting.xhtml</from-view-id>
    <navigation-case>
        <from-outcome>success</from-outcome>
        <to-view-id>/response.xhtml</to-view-id>
    </navigation-case>
</navigation-rule>
```

This rule states that when a command component (such as an h:commandButton or an h:commandLink) on greeting.xhtml is activated, the application will navigate from the greeting.xhtml page to the response.xhtml page if the outcome referenced by the button component's tag is success. Here is the h:commandButton tag from greeting.xhtml that specifies a logical outcome of success:

```
<h:commandButton id="submit" action="success"
        value="Submit" />
```

As the example demonstrates, each navigation-rule element defines how to get from one page (specified in the from-view-id element) to the other pages of the application. The navigation-rule elements can contain any number of navigation-case elements, each of which defines the page to open next (defined by to-view-id) based on a logical outcome (defined by from-outcome).

In more complicated applications, the logical outcome can also come from the return value of an *action method* in a managed bean. This method performs some processing to determine the outcome. For example, the method can check whether the password the user entered on the page matches the one on file. If it does, the method might return success; otherwise, it might return failure. An outcome of failure might result in the logon page being reloaded. An outcome of success might cause the page displaying the user's credit card activity to open. If you want the outcome to be returned by a method on a bean, you must refer to the method using a method expression, with the action attribute, as shown by this example:

```
<h:commandButton id="submit"
    action="#{userNumberBean.getOrderStatus}" value="Submit" />
```

When the user clicks the button represented by this tag, the corresponding component generates an action event. This event is handled by the default `javax.faces.event.ActionListener` instance, which calls the action method referenced by the component that triggered the event. The action method returns a logical outcome to the action listener.

The listener passes the logical outcome and a reference to the action method that produced the outcome to the default `javax.faces.application.NavigationHandler`. The `NavigationHandler` selects the page to display next by matching the outcome or the action method reference against the navigation rules in the application configuration resource file by the following process:

1. The `NavigationHandler` selects the navigation rule that matches the page currently displayed.

2. It matches the outcome or the action method reference that it received from the default `javax.faces.event.ActionListener` with those defined by the navigation cases.

3. It tries to match both the method reference and the outcome against the same navigation case.

4. If the previous step fails, the navigation handler attempts to match the outcome.

5. Finally, the navigation handler attempts to match the action method reference if the previous two attempts failed.

6. If no navigation case is matched, it displays the same view again.

When the `NavigationHandler` achieves a match, the render response phase begins. During this phase, the page selected by the `NavigationHandler` will be rendered.

The Duke's Tutoring case study example application uses navigation rules in the business methods that handle creating, editing, and deleting the users of the application. For example, the form for creating a student has the following `h:commandButton` tag:

```
<h:commandButton id="submit"
                 action="#{adminBean.createStudent(studentManager.newStudent)}"
                 value="#{bundle['action.submit']}"/>
```

The action event calls the `dukestutoring.ejb.AdminBean.createStudent` method:

```
public String createStudent(Student student) {
    em.persist(student);
    return "createdStudent";
}
```

The return value of `createdStudent` has a corresponding navigation case in the `faces-config.xml` configuration file:

```
<navigation-rule>
    <from-view-id>/admin/student/createStudent.xhtml</from-view-id>
```

```
<navigation-case>
    <from-outcome>createdStudent</from-outcome>
    <to-view-id>/admin/index.xhtml</to-view-id>
</navigation-case>
</navigation-rule>
```

After the student is created, the user is returned to the Administration index page.

For more information on how to define navigation rules, see "Configuring Navigation Rules" on page 161.

For more information on how to implement action methods to handle navigation, see "Writing a Method to Handle an Action Event" in *The Java EE 6 Tutorial: Basic Concepts*.

For more information on how to reference outcomes or action methods from component tags, see "Referencing a Method That Performs Navigation" in *The Java EE 6 Tutorial: Basic Concepts*.

Using Ajax with JavaServer Faces Technology

Early web applications were created mostly as static web pages. When a static web page is updated by a client, the entire page has to reload to reflect the update. In effect, every update needs a page reload to reflect the change. Repetitive page reloads can result in excessive network access and can impact application performance. Technologies such as Ajax were created to overcome these deficiencies.

Ajax is an acronym for Asynchronous JavaScript and XML, a group of web technologies that enable creation of dynamic and highly responsive web applications. Using Ajax, web applications can retrieve content from the server without interfering with the display on the client.

In the Java EE 6 platform, JavaServer Faces provides built-in support for Ajax. This chapter describes using Ajax functionality in JavaServer Faces web applications.

The following topics are addressed here:

- "Overview of Ajax" on page 70
- "Using Ajax Functionality with JavaServer Faces Technology" on page 70
- "Using Ajax with Facelets" on page 71
- "Sending an Ajax Request" on page 73
- "Monitoring Events on the Client" on page 75
- "Handling Errors" on page 76
- "Receiving an Ajax Response" on page 77
- "Ajax Request Lifecycle" on page 78
- "Grouping of Components" on page 78
- "Loading JavaScript as a Resource" on page 79
- "The ajaxguessnumber Example Application" on page 81
- "Further Information about Ajax in JavaServer Faces Technology" on page 85

Overview of Ajax

Ajax refers to JavaScript and XML, technologies that are widely used for creating dynamic and asynchronous web content. While Ajax is not limited to JavaScript and XML technologies, more often than not they are used together by web applications. The focus of this tutorial is on using JavaScript based Ajax functionality in JavaServer Faces web applications.

JavaScript is a dynamic scripting language for web applications. It allows users to add enhanced functionality to user interfaces and allows web pages to interact with clients asynchronously. JavaScript runs mainly on the client side (as in a browser) and thereby reduces server access by clients.

When a JavaScript function sends an asynchronous request from the client to the server, the server sends back a response that is used to update the page's Document Object Model (DOM). This response is often in the format of an XML document. The term *Ajax* refers to this interaction between the client and server.

The server response need not be in XML only; it can also be in other formats, such as JSON. This tutorial does not focus on the response formats.

Ajax enables asynchronous and partial updating of web applications. Such functionality allows for highly responsive web pages that are rendered in near real time. Ajax-based web applications can access server and process information and can also retrieve data without interfering with the display and rendering of the current web page on a client (such as a browser).

Some of the advantages of using Ajax are as follows:

- Form data validation in real time, eliminating the need to submit the form for verification
- Enhanced functionality for web pages, such as user name and password prompts
- Partial update of the web content, avoiding complete page reloads

Using Ajax Functionality with JavaServer Faces Technology

Ajax functionality can be added to a JavaServer Faces application in one of the following ways:

- Adding the required JavaScript code to an application
- Using the built-in Ajax resource library

In earlier releases of the Java EE platform, JavaServer Faces applications provided Ajax functionality by adding the necessary JavaScript to the web page. In the Java EE 6 platform, standard Ajax support is provided by a built-in JavaScript resource library.

With the support of this JavaScript resource library, JavaServer Faces standard UI components, such as buttons, labels, or text fields, can be enabled for Ajax functionality. You can also load this resource library and use its methods directly from within the managed bean code. The next sections of the tutorial describe the use of the built-in Ajax resource library.

In addition, because the JavaServer Faces technology component model can be extended, custom components can be created with Ajax functionality.

An Ajax version of the guessnumber application, ajaxguessnumber, is available in the example repository. See "The ajaxguessnumber Example Application" on page 81 for more information.

The Ajax specific f:ajax tag and its attributes are explained in the next sections.

Using Ajax with Facelets

As mentioned in the previous section, JavaServer Faces technology supports Ajax by using a built-in JavaScript resource library that is provided as part of the JavaServer Faces core libraries. This built-in Ajax resource can be used in JavaServer Faces web applications in one of the following ways:

- By using the f:ajax tag along with another standard component in a Facelets application. This method adds Ajax functionality to any UI component without additional coding and configuration.

- By using the JavaScript API method jsf.ajax.request() directly within the Facelets application. This method provides direct access to Ajax methods, and allows customized control of component behavior.

Using the f:ajax Tag

The f:ajax tag is a JavaServer Faces core tag that provides Ajax functionality to any regular UI component when used in conjunction with that component. In the following example, Ajax behavior is added to an input component by including the f:ajax core tag:

```
<h:inputText value="#{bean.message}">
    <f:ajax />
</h:inputText>
```

In this example, although Ajax is enabled, the other attributes of the f:ajax tag are not defined. If an event is not defined, the default action for the component is performed. For the inputText component, when no event attribute is specified, the default event is valueChange. Table 4–1 lists the attributes of the f:ajax tag and their default actions.

TABLE 4–1 Attributes of the f:ajax Tag

Name	Type	Description
disabled	javax.el.ValueExpression that evaluates to a Boolean	A Boolean value that identifies the tag status. A value of true indicates that the Ajax behavior should not be rendered. A value of false indicates that the Ajax behavior should be rendered. The default value is false.
event	javax.el.ValueExpression that evaluates to a String	A String that identifies the type of event to which the Ajax action will apply. If specified, it must be one of the events supported by the component. If not specified, the default event (the event that triggers the Ajax request) is determined for the component. The default event is action for javax.faces.component.ActionSource components and valueChange for javax.faces.component.EditableValueHolder components.
execute	javax.el.ValueExpression that evaluates to an Object	A Collection that identifies a list of components to be executed on the server. If a literal is specified, it must be a space-delimited String of component identifiers and/or one of the keywords. If a ValueExpression is specified, it must refer to a property that returns a Collection of String objects. If not specified, the default value is @this.
immediate	javax.el.ValueExpression that evaluates to a Boolean	A Boolean value that indicates whether inputs are to be processed early in the lifecycle. If true, behavior events generated from this behavior are broadcast during the Apply Request Values phase. Otherwise, the events will be broadcast during the Invoke Applications phase.
listener	javax.el.MethodExpression	The name of the listener method that is called when a javax.faces.event.AjaxBehaviorEvent has been broadcast for the listener.
onevent	javax.el.ValueExpression that evaluates to a String	The name of the JavaScript function that handles UI events.

TABLE 4–1 Attributes of the f:ajax Tag   *(Continued)*

Name	Type	Description
onerror	javax.el.ValueExpression that evaluates to a String	The name of the JavaScript function that handles errors.
render	javax.el.ValueExpression that evaluates to an Object	A Collection that identifies a list of components to be rendered on the client. If a literal is specified, it must be a space-delimited String of component identifiers and/or one of the keywords. If a ValueExpression is specified, it must refer to a property that returns a Collection of String objects. If not specified, the default value is @none.

The keywords listed in Table 4–2 can be used with the execute and render attributes of the f:ajax tag.

TABLE 4–2 Execute and Render Keywords

Keyword	Description
@all	All component identifiers
@form	The form that encloses the component
@none	No component identifiers
@this	The element that triggered the request

Note that when you use the f:ajax tag in a Facelets page, the JavaScript resource library is loaded implicitly. This resource library can also be loaded explicitly as described in "Loading JavaScript as a Resource" on page 79.

Sending an Ajax Request

To activate Ajax functionality, the web application must create an Ajax request and send it to the server. The server then processes the request.

The application uses the attributes of the f:ajax tag listed in Table 4–1 to create the Ajax request. The following sections explain the process of creating and sending an Ajax request using some of these attributes.

Note – Behind the scenes, the jsf.ajax.request() method of the JavaScript resource library collects the data provided by the f:ajax tag and posts the request to the JavaServer Faces lifecycle.

Using the event Attribute

The event attribute defines the event that triggers the Ajax action. Some of the possible values for this attribute are click, keyup, mouseover, focus, and blur.

If not specified, a default event based on the parent component will be applied. The default event is action for javax.faces.component.ActionSource components such as a commandButton, and valueChange for javax.faces.component.EditableValueHolder components such as inputText. In the following example, an Ajax tag is associated with the button component, and the event that triggers the Ajax action is a mouse click:

```
<h:commandButton id="submit" value="Submit">
    <f:ajax event="click" />
</h:commandButton>
<h:outputText id="result" value="#{userNumberBean.response}" />
```

Note – You may have noticed that the listed events are very similar to JavaScript events. In fact, they are based on JavaScript events, but do not have the on prefix.

For a command button, the default event is click, so that you do not actually need to specify event="click" to obtain the desired behavior.

Using the execute Attribute

The execute attribute defines the component or components to be executed on the server. The component is identified by its id attribute. You can specify more than one executable component. If more than one component is to be executed, specify a space-delimited list of components.

When a component is executed, it participates in all phases of the request processing lifecycle except the Render Response phase.

The execute attribute can also be a keyword, such as @all, @none, @this, or @form. The default value is @this, which refers to the component within which the f:ajax tag is nested.

The following code specifies that the h:inputText component with the id value of userNo should be executed when the button is clicked:

```
<h:inputText id="userNo"
             title="Type a number from 0 to 10:"
             value="#{userNumberBean.userNumber}">
    ...
</h:inputText>
<h:commandButton id="submit" value="Submit">
    <f:ajax event="click" execute="userNo" />
</h:commandButton>
```

Using the `immediate` Attribute

The immediate attribute indicates whether user inputs are to be processed early in the application lifecycle or later. If the attribute is set to true, events generated from this component are broadcast during the Apply Request Values phase. Otherwise, the events will be broadcast during the Invoke Applications phase.

If not defined, the default value of this attribute is false.

Using the `listener` Attribute

The listener attribute refers to a method expression that is executed on the server side in response to an Ajax action on the client. The listener's javax.faces.event.AjaxBehaviorListener.processAjaxBehavior method is called once during the Invoke Application phase of the lifecycle. In the following example, a listener attribute is defined by an f:ajax tag, which refers to a method from the bean.

```
<f:ajax listener="#{mybean.someaction}" render="somecomponent" />
```

The following code represents the someaction method in mybean.

```
public void someaction(AjaxBehaviorEvent event) {
    dosomething;
}
```

Monitoring Events on the Client

The ongoing Ajax requests can be monitored by using the onevent attribute of the f:ajax tag. The value of this attribute is the name of a JavaScript function. JavaServer Faces calls the onevent function at each stage of the processing of an Ajax request: begin, complete, and success.

When calling the JavaScript function assigned to the onevent property, JavaServer Faces passes a data object to it. The data object contains the properties listed in Table 4–3.

TABLE 4–3 Properties of the onEvent Data Object

Property	Description
responseXML	The response to the Ajax call in XML format
responseText	The response to the Ajax call in text format
responseCode	The response to the Ajax call in numeric code
source	The source of the current Ajax event: the DOM element
status	The status of the current Ajax call: begin, complete, or success
type	The type of the Ajax call: event

By using the status property of the data object, you can identify the current status of the Ajax request and monitor its progress. In the following example, monitormyajaxevent is a JavaScript function that monitors the Ajax request sent by the event:

```
<f:ajax event="click" render="errormessage" onevent="monitormyajaxevent"/>
```

Handling Errors

JavaServer Faces handles Ajax errors through use of the onerror attribute of the f:ajax tag. The value of this attribute is the name of a JavaScript function.

When there is an error in processing a Ajax request, JavaServer Faces calls the defined onerror JavaScript function and passes a data object to it. The data object contains all the properties available for the onevent attribute, and in addition, the following properties:

- description
- errorName
- errorMessage

The type is error. The status property of the data object contains one of the valid error values listed in Table 4–4.

TABLE 4–4   Valid Error Values for the Data Object status Property

Values	Description
emptyResponse	No Ajax response from server.
httpError	One of the valid HTTP errors: request.status==null or request.status==undefined or request.status < 200 or request.status >= 300
malformedXML	The Ajax response is not well formed.
serverError	The Ajax response contains an error element.

In the following example, any errors that occurred in processing the Ajax request are handled by the handlemyajaxerror JavaScript function:

```
<f:ajax event="click" render="test" onerror="handlemyajaxerror"/>
```

Receiving an Ajax Response

After the application sends an Ajax request, it is processed on the server side, and a response is sent back to the client. As described earlier, Ajax allows for partial updating of web pages. To enable such partial updating, JavaServer Faces technology allows for partial processing of the view. The handling of the response is defined by the render attribute of the f:ajax tag.

Similar to the execute attribute, the render attribute defines which sections of the page will be updated. The value of a render attribute can be one or more component id values, one of the keywords @this, @all, @none, and @form, or an EL expression. In the following example, the render attribute simply identifies an output component to be displayed when the Ajax action has successfully completed.

```
<h:commandButton id="submit" value="Submit">
    <f:ajax execute="userNo" render="result" />
</h:commandButton>
<h:outputText id="result" value="#{userNumberBean.response}" />
```

However, more often than not, the render attribute is likely to be associated with an event attribute. In the following example, an output component is displayed when the button component is clicked.

```
<h:commandButton id="submit" value="Submit">
    <f:ajax event="click" execute="userNo" render="result"/>
</h:commandButton>
<h:outputText id="result" value="#{userNumberBean.response}"/>
```

> **Note** – Behind the scenes, once again the `jsf.ajax.request()` method handles the
> response. It registers a response-handling callback when the original request is created.
> When the response is sent back to the client, the callback is invoked. This callback
> automatically updates the client-side DOM to reflect the rendered response.

Ajax Request Lifecycle

An Ajax request varies from other typical JavaServer Faces requests, and its processing
is also handled differently by the JavaServer Faces lifecycle.

As described in "Partial Processing and Partial Rendering" on page 56, when an Ajax
request is received, the state associated with that request is captured by the
`javax.faces.context.PartialViewContext`. This object provides access to
information such as which components are targeted for processing/rendering. The
`processPartial` method of `PartialViewContext` uses this information to perform
partial component tree processing and rendering.

The `execute` attribute of the `f:ajax` tag identifies which segments of the server side
component tree should be processed. Because components can be uniquely identified
in the JavaServer Faces component tree, it is easy to identify and process a single
component, a few components, or a whole tree. This is made possible by the
`visitTree` method of the `javax.faces.component.UIComponent` class. The identified
components then run through the JavaServer Faces request lifecycle phases.

Similar to the `execute` attribute, the `render` attribute identifies which segments of the
JavaServer Faces component tree need to be rendered during the render response
phase.

During the render response phase, the `render` attribute is examined. The identified
components are found and asked to render themselves and their children. The
components are then packaged up and sent back to the client as a response.

Grouping of Components

The previous sections describe how to associate a single UI component with Ajax
functionality. You can also associate Ajax with more than one component at a time by
grouping them together on a page. The following example shows how a number of
components can be grouped by using the `f:ajax` tag.

```
<f:ajax>
    <h:form>
        <h:inputText id="input1"/>
```

```
            <h:commandButton id="Submit"/>
        </h:form>
</f:ajax>
```

In the example, neither component is associated with any Ajax event or render attributes yet. Therefore, no action will take place in case of user input. You can associate the above components with an event and a render attribute as follows:

```
<f:ajax event="click" render="@all">
    <h:form>
        <h:inputText id="input1" value="#{user.name}"/>
        <h:commandButton id="Submit"/>
    </h:form>
</f:ajax>
```

In the updated example, when the user clicks either component, the updated results will be displayed for all components. You can further fine tune the Ajax action by adding specific events to each of the components, in which case Ajax functionality becomes cumulative. Consider the following example:

```
<f:ajax event="click" render="@all">
    ...
    <h:commandButton id="Submit">
        <f:ajax event="mouseover"/>
    </h:commandButton>
    ...
</f:ajax>
```

Now the button component will fire an Ajax action in case of a mouseover event as well as a mouse click event.

Loading JavaScript as a Resource

The JavaScript resource file bundled with JavaServer Faces technology is named jsf.js and is available in the javax.faces library. This resource library supports Ajax functionality in JavaServer Faces applications.

In order to use this resource directly with a component or a bean class, you need to explicitly load the resource library. The resource can be loaded in one of the following ways:

- By using the resource API directly in a Facelets page
- By using the javax.faces.application.ResourceDependency annotation and the resource API in a bean class

Using JavaScript API in a Facelets Application

To use the bundled JavaScript resource API directly in a web application, such as a Facelets page, you need to first identify the default JavaScript resource for the page with the help of the h:outputScript tag. For example, consider the following section of a Facelets page:

```
<h:form>
    <h:outputScript name="jsf.js" library="javax.faces" target="head"/>
</h:form>
```

Specifying the target as head causes the script resource to be rendered within the head element on the HTML page.

In the next step, identify the component to which you would like to attach the Ajax functionality. Add the Ajax functionality to the component by using the JavaScript API. For example, consider the following:

```
<h:form>
    <h:outputScript name="jsf.js" library="javax.faces" target="head">
    <h:inputText id="inputname" value="#{userBean.name}"/>
    <h:outputText id="outputname" value="#{userBean.name}"/>
    <h:commandButton id="submit" value="Submit"
                     onclick="jsf.ajax.request(this, event,
                             {execute:'inputname',render:'outputname'});
                     return false;" />
</h:form>
```

The jsf.ajax.request method takes up to three parameters that specify source, event, and options. The source parameter identifies the DOM element that triggered the Ajax request, typically this. The optional event parameter identifies the DOM event that triggered this request. The optional options parameter contains a set of name/value pairs from Table 4–5.

TABLE 4–5 Possible Values for the Options Parameter

Name	Value
execute	A space-delimited list of client identifiers or one of the keywords listed in Table 4–2. The identifiers reference the components that will be processed during the execute phase of the lifecycle.
render	A space-delimited list of client identifiers or one of the keywords listed in Table 4–2. The identifiers reference the components that will be processed during the render phase of the lifecycle.
onevent	A String that is the name of the JavaScript function to call when an event occurs.
onerror	A String that is the name of the JavaScript function to call when an error occurs.
params	An object that may include additional parameters to include in the request.

If no identifier is specified, the default assumed keyword for the execute attribute is @this, and for the render attribute it is @none.

You can also place the JavaScript method in a file and include it as a resource.

Using the @ResourceDependency Annotation in a Bean Class

Use the javax.faces.application.ResourceDependency annotation to cause the bean class to load the default jsf.js library.

To load the Ajax resource from the server side, use the jsf.ajax.request method within the bean class. This method is usually used when creating a custom component or a custom renderer for a component.

The following example shows how the resource is loaded in a bean class:

```
@ResourceDependency(name="jsf.js" library="javax.faces" target="head")
```

The ajaxguessnumber Example Application

To demonstrate the advantages of using Ajax, revisit the guessnumber example from Chapter 5, "Introduction to Facelets," in *The Java EE 6 Tutorial: Basic Concepts*. If you modify this example to use Ajax, the response need not be displayed in the response.xhtml page. Instead, an asynchronous call is made to the bean on the server side, and the response is displayed in the originating page by executing just the input component rather than by form submission.

The source code for this application is in the *tut-install*/examples/web/ajaxguessnumber/ directory.

The ajaxguessnumber Source Files

The changes to the guessnumber application occur in two source files, as well as with the addition of a JavaScript file.

The ajaxgreeting.xhtml Facelets Page

The Facelets page for ajaxguessnumber, web/ajaxgreeting.xhtml, is almost the same as the greeting.xhtml page for the guessnumber application:

```
<h:head>
    <h:outputStylesheet library="css" name="default.css"/>
    <title>Ajax Guess Number Facelets Application</title>
```

```
        </h:head>
    <h:body>
        <h:form id="AjaxGuess">
            <h:outputScript name="ui.js" target="head"/>
            <h:graphicImage library="images" name="wave.med.gif"
                            alt="Duke waving his hand"/>
            <h2>
                Hi, my name is Duke. I am thinking of a number from
                #{userNumberBean.minimum} to #{userNumberBean.maximum}.
                Can you guess it?
            </h2>
            <p>
                <h:inputText
                    id="userNo"
                    title="Type a number from 0 to 10:"
                    value="#{userNumberBean.userNumber}">
                    <f:validateLongRange
                        minimum="#{userNumberBean.minimum}"
                        maximum="#{userNumberBean.maximum}"/>
                </h:inputText>

                <h:commandButton id="submit" value="Submit" >
                    <!--<f:ajax execute="userNo" render="result errors1" />-->
                        <f:ajax execute="userNo" render="result errors1"
                                onevent="msg"/>
                </h:commandButton>
            </p>
            <p><h:outputText id="result" style="color:blue"
                            value="#{userNumberBean.response}"/>
            </p>

            <h:message id="errors1" showSummary="true" showDetail="false"
                        style="color: #d20005;
                        font-family: 'New Century Schoolbook', serif;
                        font-style: oblique;
                        text-decoration: overline"
                        for="userNo"/>
        </h:form>
    </h:body>
```

The most important change is in the h:commandButton tag. The action attribute is removed from the tag, and f:ajax tag is added.

The f:ajax tag specifies that when the button is clicked, the h:inputText component with the id value userNo is executed. The components with the id values result and errors1 are then rendered. If that was all you did (as in the commented-out version of the tag), you would see the output from both the result and errors1 components, although only one output is valid; if a validation error occurs, the managed bean is not executed, so the result output is stale.

To solve this problem, the tag also calls the JavaScript function named msg, in the file ui.js, as described in the next section. The h:outputScript tag at the top of the form calls in this script.

The ui.js JavaScript File

The ui.js file specified in the h:outputScript tag of the ajaxgreeting.xhtml file is located in the web/resources directory of the application. The file contains just one function, msg:

```javascript
var msg = function msg(data) {
    var resultArea = document.getElementById("AjaxGuess:result");
    var errorArea = document.getElementById("AjaxGuess:errors1");
    if (errorArea.innerHTML !== null && errorArea.innerHTML !== "") {
        resultArea.innerHTML="";
    }
};
```

The msg function obtains a handle to both the result and errors1 elements. If the errors1 element has any content, the function erases the content of the result element, so the stale output does not appear in the page.

The UserNumberBean Managed Bean

A small change is also made in the UserNumberBean code so that the output component does not display any message for the default (null) value of the property response. Here is the modified bean code:

```java
public String getResponse() {
    if ((userNumber != null) && (userNumber.compareTo(randomInt) == 0)) {
        return "Yay! You got it!";
    }
    if (userNumber == null) {
        return null;
    } else {
        return "Sorry, " + userNumber + " is incorrect.";
    }
}
```

Running the ajaxguessnumber Example

You can use either NetBeans IDE or Ant to build, package, deploy, and run the ajaxguessnumber example.

▼ To Build, Package, and Deploy the ajaxguessnumber Example Using NetBeans IDE

This procedure builds the application into the *tut-install*/examples/web/ajaxguessnumber/build/web/ directory. The contents of this directory are deployed to the GlassFish Server.

1   From the File menu, choose Open Project.

2   **In the Open Project dialog, navigate to:**

tut-install/examples/web/

3   **Select the ajaxguessnumber folder.**

4   **Select the Open as Main Project check box.**

5   **Click Open Project.**

6   **In the Projects tab, right-click the ajaxguessnumber project and select Deploy.**

▼ To Build, Package, and Deploy the ajaxguessnumber Example Using Ant

1   **In a terminal window, go to:**

tut-install/examples/web/ajaxguessnumber/

2   **Type the following command:**

ant

This command calls the default target, which builds and packages the application into a WAR file, ajaxguessnumber.war, located in the dist directory.

3   **Type the following command:**

ant deploy

Typing this command deploys ajaxguessnumber.war to the GlassFish Server.

▼ To Run the ajaxguessnumber Example

1   **In a web browser, type the following URL:**

http://localhost:8080/ajaxguessnumber

2   **Type a value in the input field and click Submit.**

If the value is in the range 0 to 10, a message states whether the guess is correct or incorrect. If the value is outside that range, or if the value is not a number, an error message appears in red.

To see what would happen if the JavaScript function were not included, remove the comment marks from the first f:ajax tag in ajaxgreeting.xhtml and place them around the second tag, as follows:

```
<f:ajax execute="userNo" render="result errors1" />
<!--<f:ajax execute="userNo" render="result errors1" onevent="msg"/>-->
```

If you then redeploy the application, you can see that stale output from valid guesses continues to appear if you subsequently type erroneous input.

Further Information about Ajax in JavaServer Faces Technology

For more information on Ajax in JavaServer Faces Technology, see

- JavaServer Faces project web site:

  `http://javaserverfaces.java.net/`

- JavaServer Faces JavaScript Library APIs:

  `http://javaserverfaces.java.net/`
  `nonav/docs/2.1/jsdocs/symbols/jsf.ajax.html`

CHAPTER 5

Composite Components: Advanced Topics and Example

This chapter describes the advanced features of composite components in JavaServer Faces technology.

A composite component is a special type of JavaServer Faces template that acts as a component. If you are new to composite components, see "Composite Components" in *The Java EE 6 Tutorial: Basic Concepts* before you proceed with this chapter.

The following topics are addressed here:

- "Attributes of a Composite Component" on page 87
- "Invoking a Managed Bean" on page 88
- "Validating Composite Component Values" on page 89
- "The `compositecomponentlogin` Example Application" on page 89

Attributes of a Composite Component

You define an attribute of a composite component by using the `composite:attribute` tag. Table 5–1 lists the commonly used attributes of this tag.

TABLE 5–1 Commonly Used Attributes of the `composite:attribute` Tag

Attribute	Description
name	Specifies the name of the composite component attribute to be used in the using page. Alternatively, the name attribute can specify standard event handlers such as `action`, `actionListener`, and managed bean.
default	Specifies the default value of the composite component attribute.
required	Specifies whether it is mandatory to provide a value for the attribute.

TABLE 5–1 Commonly Used Attributes of the `composite:attribute` Tag   *(Continued)*

Attribute	Description
method-signature	Specifies a subclass of `java.lang.Object` as the type of the composite component's attribute. The `method-signature` element declares that the composite component attribute is a method expression. The `type` attribute and the `method-signature` attribute are mutually exclusive. If you specify both, `method-signature` is ignored. The default type of an attribute is `java.lang.Object`. **Note** – Method expressions are similar to value expressions, but rather than supporting the dynamic retrieval and setting of properties, method expressions support the invocation of a method of an arbitrary object, passing a specified set of parameters and returning the result from the called method (if any).
type	Specifies a fully qualified class name as the type of the attribute. The `type` attribute and the `method-signature` attribute are mutually exclusive. If you specify both, `method-signature` is ignored. The default type of an attribute is `java.lang.Object`.

The following code snippet defines a composite component attribute and assigns it a default value:

```
<composite:attribute name="username" default="admin"/>
```

The following code snippet uses the `method-signature` element:

```
<composite:attribute name="myaction"
                     method-signature="java.lang.String action()"/>
```

The following code snippet uses the `type` element:

```
<composite:attribute name="dateofjoining" type="java.util.Date"/>
```

Invoking a Managed Bean

To enable a composite component to handle server-side data, you can invoke a managed bean in one of the following ways:

- Pass the reference of the managed bean to the composite component.
- Directly use the properties of the managed bean.

The example application described in "The `compositecomponentlogin` Example Application" on page 89 shows how to use a managed bean with a composite component by passing the reference of the managed bean to the component.

Validating Composite Component Values

JavaServer Faces provides the following tags for validating values of input components. These tags can be used with the `composite:valueHolder` or the `composite:editableValueHolder` tag.

Table 5–2 lists commonly used validator tags.

TABLE 5–2 Validator Tags

Tag Name	Description
f:validateBean	Delegates the validation of the local value to the Bean Validation API.
f:validateRegex	Uses the pattern attribute to validate the wrapping component. The entire pattern is matched against the String value of the component. If it matches, it is valid.
f:validateRequired	Enforces the presence of a value. Has the same effect as setting the required element of a composite component's attribute to true.

The `compositecomponentlogin` Example Application

The `compositecomponentlogin` application creates a composite component that accepts a user name and a password. The component interacts with a managed bean. The component stores the user name and password in the managed bean, retrieves the values from the bean, and displays these values on the Login page.

The `compositecomponentlogin` application has a composite component file, a using page, and a managed bean.

The source code for this application is in the *tut-install*/examples/web/compositecomponentlogin/ directory.

The Composite Component File

The composite component file is an XHTML file, /web/resources/ezcomp/LoginPanel.xhtml. It has a composite:interface section that declares the labels for the user name, password, and login button. It also declares a managed bean, which defines properties for the user name and password.

```
<composite:interface>
    <composite:attribute name="namePrompt" default="User Name: "/>
    <composite:attribute name="passwordPrompt" default="Password: "/>
```

```
        <composite:attribute name="loginButtonText" default="Log In"/>
        <composite:attribute name="loginAction"
                            method-signature="java.lang.String action()"/>
        <composite:attribute name="myLoginBean"/>
        <composite:editableValueHolder name="vals" targets="form:name"/>
        <composite:editableValueHolder name="passwordVal" targets="form:password"/>
    </composite:interface>
```

The composite component implementation accepts input values for the user name and password properties of the managed bean.

```
<composite:implementation>
    <h:form id="form">
        <table columns="2" role="presentation">
            <tr>
                <td><h:outputLabel for="name"
                                   value="#{cc.attrs.namePrompt}"/></td>
                <td><h:inputText id="name"
                                 value="#{cc.attrs.myLoginBean.name}"
                                 required="true"/></td>
            </tr>
            <tr>
                <td><h:outputLabel for="password"
                                   value="#{cc.attrs.passwordPrompt}"/></td>
                <td><h:inputSecret id="password"
                                   value="#{cc.attrs.myLoginBean.password}"
                                   required="true"/></td>
            </tr>
        </table>
        <p>
            <h:commandButton id="loginButton"
                             value="#{cc.attrs.loginButtonText}"
                             action="#{cc.attrs.loginAction}"/>
        </p>
    </h:form>
    ...
</composite:implementation>
```

The Using Page

The using page in this example application, web/index.xhtml, is an XHTML file that invokes the login composite component file along with the managed bean. It validates the user's input.

```
<div id="compositecomponent">
    <ez:LoginPanel myLoginBean="#{myLoginBean}"
                   loginAction="#{myLoginBean.login}">
        <f:validateLength maximum="10" minimum="4" for="vals" />
        <f:validateRegex pattern="((?=.*\d)(?=.*[a-z])(?=.*[A-Z]).{4,10})"
                         for="passwordVal"/>
    </ez:LoginPanel>
</div>
```

The f:validateLength tag requires the user name to have from 4 to 10 characters.

The f:validateRegex tag requires the password to have from 4 to 10 characters and to contain at least one digit, one lowercase letter, and one uppercase letter.

The Managed Bean

The managed bean, src/java/compositecomponentlogin/MyLoginBean.java, defines a method called login, which retrieves the values of the user name and password.

```
@ManagedBean
@RequestScoped
public class MyLoginBean {

    private String name;
    private String password;

    public MyLoginBean() {
    }

    public myloginBean(String name, String password) {
        this.name = name;
        this.password = password;
    }

    public String getPassword() {
        return password;
    }

    public void setPassword(String newValue) {
        password = newValue;
    }

    public String getName() {
        return name;
    }

    public void setName(String newValue) {
        name = newValue;
    }

    public String login() {
        if (getName().equals("javaee")) {
            String msg = "Success.  Your user name is " + getName()
                    + ", and your password is " + getPassword();
            FacesMessage facesMsg = new FacesMessage(msg, msg);
            FacesContext.getCurrentInstance().addMessage(null, facesMsg);
            return "index";
        } else {
            String msg = "Failure. Your user name is " + getName()
                    + ", and your password is " + getPassword();
            FacesMessage facesMsg =
                    new FacesMessage(FacesMessage.SEVERITY_ERROR, msg, msg);
            FacesContext.getCurrentInstance().addMessage(null, facesMsg);
            return "index";
        }
    }
```

```
        }
    }
```

Running the `compositecomponentlogin` Example

You can use either NetBeans IDE or Ant to build, package, deploy, and run the compositecomponentlogin example.

▼ To Build, Package, and Deploy the `compositecomponentlogin` Example Using NetBeans IDE

1 From the File menu, choose Open Project.

2 In the Open Project dialog, navigate to:
   tut-install/examples/web/

3 Select the `compositecomponentlogin` folder.

4 Select the Open as Main Project checkbox.

5 Click Open Project.

6 In the Projects tab, right-click `compositecomponentlogin` and select Deploy.

▼ To Build, Package, and Deploy the `compositecomponentlogin` Example Using Ant

1 In a terminal window, go to:
   tut-install/examples/web/compositecomponentlogin/

2 Type the following command:
   `ant`

3 Type the following command:
   `ant deploy`

▼ To Run the `compositecomponentlogin` Example

1 In a web browser, type the following URL:
   `http://localhost:8080/compositecomponentlogin/`
   The Login Component page opens.

2 Type values in the User Name and Password fields, then click the Log In button.

Because of the way the `login` method is coded, the login succeeds only if the user name is `javaee`.

Because of the `f:validateLength` tag, if the user name has fewer than 4 characters or more than 10 characters, a validation error message appears.

Because of the `f:validateRegex` tag, if the password has fewer than 4 characters or more than 10 characters or does not contain at least one digit, one lowercase letter, and one uppercase letter, a "Regex Pattern not matched" error message appears.

CHAPTER 6

Creating Custom UI Components and Other Custom Objects

JavaServer Faces technology offers a basic set of standard, reusable UI components that enable quick and easy construction of user interfaces for web applications. These components mostly map one-to-one to the elements in HTML 4. However, an application often requires a component that has additional functionality or requires a completely new component. JavaServer Faces technology allows extension of standard components to enhance their functionality or to create custom components. A rich ecosystem of third party component libraries is built on this extension capability, but it is beyond the scope of this tutorial to examine them. A web search for "JSF Component Libraries" is a good starting point to learn more about this important aspect of using JavaServer Faces technology.

In addition to extending the functionality of standard components, a component writer might want to give a page author the ability to change the appearance of the component on the page or to alter listener behavior. Alternatively, the component writer might want to render a component to a different kind of client device type, such as a smartphone or a tablet instead of a desktop computer. Enabled by the flexible JavaServer Faces architecture, a component writer can separate the definition of the component behavior from its appearance by delegating the rendering of the component to a separate renderer. In this way, a component writer can define the behavior of a custom component once but create multiple renderers, each of which defines a different way to render the component to a particular kind of client device.

A `javax.faces.component.UIComponent` is a Java class that is responsible for representing a self-contained piece of the user interface during the request processing lifecycle. It is intended to represent the meaning of the component; the visual representation of the component is the responsibility of the `javax.faces.render.Renderer`. There can be multiple instances of the same `UIComponent` class in any given JavaServer Faces view, just as there can be multiple instances of any Java class in any given Java program.

JavaServer Faces technology provides the ability to create custom components by extending the `UIComponent` class, the base class for all standard UI components. A custom component can be used anywhere an ordinary component can be used, such as within a composite component. A `UIComponent` is identified by two names: `component-family` specifies the purpose of the component (input or output, for instance), while `component-type` indicates the specific purpose of a component, such as a text input field or a command button.

A `Renderer` is a helper to the `UIComponent` that deals with how that specific `UIComponent` class should appear in a specific kind of client device. Like components, renderers are identified by two names: `render-kit-id` and `renderer-type`. A render kit is just a bucket into which a particular group of renderers is placed, and the `render-kit-id` identifies the group. Most JavaServer Faces component libraries provide their own render kits.

A `javax.faces.view.facelets.Tag` object is a helper to the `UIComponent` and `Renderer` that allows the page author to include an instance of a `UIComponent` in a JavaServer Faces view. A tag represents a specific combination of `component-type` and `renderer-type`.

See "Component, Renderer, and Tag Combinations" on page 99 for information on how components, renderers, and tags interact.

This chapter uses the image map component from the Duke's Bookstore case study example to explain how you can create simple custom components, custom renderers, and associated custom tags, and take care of all the other details associated with using the components and renderers in an application. See Chapter 25, "Duke's Bookstore Case Study Example," for more information about this example.

The chapter also describes how to create other custom objects: custom converters, custom listeners, and custom validators. It also describes how to bind component values and instances to data objects and how to bind custom objects to managed bean properties.

The following topics are addressed here:

- "Determining Whether You Need a Custom Component or Renderer" on page 97
- "Understanding the Image Map Example" on page 100
- "Steps for Creating a Custom Component" on page 105
- "Creating Custom Component Classes" on page 106
- "Delegating Rendering to a Renderer" on page 114
- "Implementing an Event Listener" on page 117
- "Handling Events for Custom Components" on page 119
- "Defining the Custom Component Tag in a Tag Library Descriptor" on page 120
- "Using a Custom Component" on page 121
- "Creating and Using a Custom Converter" on page 123
- "Creating and Using a Custom Validator" on page 128
- "Binding Component Values and Instances to Managed Bean Properties" on page 133

- "Binding Converters, Listeners, and Validators to Managed Bean Properties" on page 138

Determining Whether You Need a Custom Component or Renderer

The JavaServer Faces implementation supports a very basic set of components and associated renderers. This section helps you to decide whether you can use standard components and renderers in your application or need a custom component or custom renderer.

When to Use a Custom Component

A component class defines the state and behavior of a UI component. This behavior includes converting the value of a component to the appropriate markup, queuing events on components, performing validation, and any other behavior related to how the component interacts with the browser and the request processing lifecycle.

You need to create a custom component in the following situations:

- You need to add new behavior to a standard component, such as generating an additional type of event (for example, notifying another part of the page that something changed in this component as a result of user interaction).

- You need to take a different action in the request processing of the value of a component from what is available in any of the existing standard components.

- You want to take advantage of an HTML capability offered by your target browser, but none of the standard JavaServer Faces components take advantage of the capability in the way you want, if at all. The current release does not contain standard components for complex HTML components, such as frames; however, because of the extensibility of the component architecture, you can use JavaServer Faces technology to create components like these. The Duke's Bookstore case study creates custom components that correspond to the HTML map and area tags.

- You need to render to a non-HTML client that requires extra components not supported by HTML. Eventually, the standard HTML render kit will provide support for all standard HTML components. However, if you are rendering to a different client, such as a phone, you might need to create custom components to represent the controls uniquely supported by the client. For example, some component architectures for wireless clients include support for tickers and progress bars, which are not available on an HTML client. In this case, you might also need a custom renderer along with the component; or you might need only a custom renderer.

You do not need to create a custom component in these cases:

- You need to aggregate components to create a new component that has its own unique behavior. In this situation, you can use a composite component to combine existing standard components. For more information on composite components, see "Composite Components" in *The Java EE 6 Tutorial: Basic Concepts* and Chapter 5, "Composite Components: Advanced Topics and Example."

- You simply need to manipulate data on the component or add application-specific functionality to it. In this situation, you should create a managed bean for this purpose and bind it to the standard component rather than create a custom component. See "Managed Beans in JavaServer Faces Technology" in *The Java EE 6 Tutorial: Basic Concepts* for more information on managed beans.

- You need to convert a component's data to a type not supported by its renderer. See "Using the Standard Converters" in *The Java EE 6 Tutorial: Basic Concepts* for more information about converting a component's data.

- You need to perform validation on the component data. Standard validators and custom validators can be added to a component by using the validator tags from the page. See "Using the Standard Validators" in *The Java EE 6 Tutorial: Basic Concepts* and "Creating and Using a Custom Validator" on page 128 for more information about validating a component's data.

- You need to register event listeners on components. You can either register event listeners on components using the `f:valueChangeListener` and `f:actionListener` tags, or you can point at an event-processing method on a managed bean using the component's `actionListener` or `valueChangeListener` attributes. See "Implementing an Event Listener" on page 117 and "Writing Managed Bean Methods" in *The Java EE 6 Tutorial: Basic Concepts* for more information.

When to Use a Custom Renderer

A renderer, which generates the markup to display a component on a web page, allows you to separate the semantics of a component from its appearance. By keeping this separation, you can support different kinds of client devices with the same kind of authoring experience. You can think of a renderer as a "client adapter." It produces output suitable for consumption and display by the client, and accepts input from the client when the user interacts with that component.

If you are creating a custom component, you need to ensure, among other things, that your component class performs these operations that are central to rendering the component:

- **Decoding**: Converting the incoming request parameters to the local value of the component
- **Encoding**: Converting the current local value of the component into the corresponding markup that represents it in the response

The JavaServer Faces specification supports two programming models for handling encoding and decoding:

- **Direct implementation**: The component class itself implements the decoding and encoding.
- **Delegated implementation**: The component class delegates the implementation of encoding and decoding to a separate renderer.

By delegating the operations to the renderer, you have the option of associating your custom component with different renderers so that you can render the component on different clients. If you don't plan to render a particular component on different clients, it may be simpler to let the component class handle the rendering. However, a separate renderer enables you to preserve the separation of semantics from appearance. The Duke's Bookstore application separates the renderers from the components, although it renders only to HTML 4 web browsers.

If you aren't sure whether you will need the flexibility offered by separate renderers but you want to use the simpler direct-implementation approach, you can actually use both models. Your component class can include some default rendering code, but it can delegate rendering to a renderer if there is one.

Component, Renderer, and Tag Combinations

When you create a custom component, you can create a custom renderer to go with it. To associate the component with the renderer and to reference the component from the page, you will also need a custom tag.

Although you need to write the custom component and renderer, there is no need to write code for a custom tag (called a tag handler). If you specify the component and renderer combination, Facelets creates the tag handler automatically.

In rare situations, you might use a custom renderer with a standard component rather than a custom component. Or you might use a custom tag without a renderer or a component. This section gives examples of these situations and summarizes what's required for a custom component, renderer, and tag.

You would use a custom renderer without a custom component if you wanted to add some client-side validation on a standard component. You would implement the validation code with a client-side scripting language, such as JavaScript, and then render the JavaScript with the custom renderer. In this situation, you need a custom tag to go with the renderer so that its tag handler can register the renderer on the standard component.

Custom components as well as custom renderers need custom tags associated with them. However, you can have a custom tag without a custom renderer or custom component. For example, suppose that you need to create a custom validator that requires extra attributes on the validator tag. In this case, the custom tag corresponds to a custom validator and not to a custom component or custom renderer. In any case, you still need to associate the custom tag with a server-side object.

Table 6–1 summarizes what you must or can associate with a custom component, custom renderer, or custom tag.

TABLE 6–1 Requirements for Custom Components, Custom Renderers, and Custom Tags

Custom Item	Must Have	Can Have
Custom component	Custom tag	Custom renderer or standard renderer
Custom renderer	Custom tag	Custom component or standard component
Custom JavaServer Faces tag	Some server-side object, like a component, a custom renderer, or custom validator	Custom component or standard component associated with a custom renderer

Understanding the Image Map Example

Duke's Bookstore includes a custom image map component on the index.xhtml page. This image map displays a selection of six book titles. When the user clicks one of the book titles in the image map, the application goes to a page that displays the title of the selected book as well as information about a featured book. The page allows the user to add either book (or none) to the shopping cart.

Why Use JavaServer Faces Technology to Implement an Image Map?

JavaServer Faces technology is an ideal framework to use for implementing this kind of image map because it can perform the work that must be done on the server without requiring you to create a server-side image map.

In general, client-side image maps are preferred over server-side image maps for several reasons. One reason is that the client-side image map allows the browser to provide immediate feedback when a user positions the mouse over a hotspot. Another reason is that client-side image maps perform better because they don't require round-trips to the server. However, in some situations, your image map might need to access the server to retrieve data or to change the appearance of non-form controls, tasks that a client-side image map cannot do.

Because the image map custom component uses JavaServer Faces technology, it has the best of both styles of image maps: It can handle the parts of the application that need to be performed on the server, while allowing the other parts of the application to be performed on the client side.

Understanding the Rendered HTML

Here is an abbreviated version of the form part of the HTML page that the application needs to render:

```
<form id="j_idt13" name="j_idt13" method="post"
      action="/dukesbookstore/faces/index.xhtml" ... >
    ...
    <img id="j_idt13:mapImage"
         src="/dukesbookstore/faces/javax.faces.resource/book_all.jpg?ln=images"
         alt="Choose a Book from our Catalog"
         usemap="#bookMap" />
    ...
    <map name="bookMap">
    <area alt="Duke"
          coords="67,23,212,268"
          shape="rect"
          onmouseout=
    "document.forms[0]['j_idt13:mapImage'].src='resources/images/book_all.jpg'"
          onmouseover=
    "document.forms[0]['j_idt13:mapImage'].src='resources/images/book_201.jpg'"
          onclick=
    "document.forms[0]['bookMap_current'].value='Duke'; document.forms[0].submit()"
    />
    ...
    <input type="hidden" name="bookMap_current">
    </map>
    ...
</form>
```

The img tag associates an image (book_all.jpg) with the image map referenced in the usemap attribute value.

The map tag specifies the image map and contains a set of area tags.

Each area tag specifies a region of the image map. The onmouseover, onmouseout, and onclick attributes define which JavaScript code is executed when these events occur. When the user moves the mouse over a region, the onmouseover function associated with the region displays the map with that region highlighted. When the user moves the mouse out of a region, the onmouseout function re-displays the original image. If the user clicks on a region, the onclick function sets the value of the input tag to the ID of the selected area and submits the page.

The input tag represents a hidden control that stores the value of the currently selected area between client-server exchanges so that the server-side component classes can retrieve the value.

The server-side objects retrieve the value of bookMap_current and set the locale in the javax.faces.context.FacesContext instance according to the region that was selected.

Understanding the Facelets Page

Here is an abbreviated form of the Facelets page that the image map component uses to generate the HTML page shown in the preceding section. It uses custom bookstore:map and bookstore:area tags to represent the custom components:

```
<h:form>
    ...
    <h:graphicImage id="mapImage"
                    name="book_all.jpg"
                    library="images"
                    alt="#{bundle.ChooseBook}"
                    usemap="#bookMap" />
    <bookstore:map id="bookMap"
                    current="map1"
                    immediate="true"
                    action="bookstore">
        <f:actionListener
            type="dukesbookstore.listeners.MapBookChangeListener" />
        <bookstore:area id="map1" value="#{Book201}"
                        onmouseover="resources/images/book_201.jpg"
                        onmouseout="resources/images/book_all.jpg"
                        targetImage="mapImage" />
        <bookstore:area id="map2" value="#{Book202}"
                        onmouseover="resources/images/book_202.jpg"
                        onmouseout="resources/images/book_all.jpg"
                        targetImage="mapImage"/>
        ...
    </bookstore:map>
    ...
</h:form>
```

The alt attribute of the h:graphicImage tag maps to the localized string "Choose a Book from our Catalog".

The f:actionListener tag within the bookstore:map tag points to a listener class for an action event. The processAction method of the listener places the book ID for the selected map area into the session map. The way this event is handled is explained more in "Handling Events for Custom Components" on page 119.

The action attribute of the bookstore:map tag specifies a logical outcome String, "bookstore", which by implicit navigation rules sends the application to the page bookstore.xhtml. For more information on navigation, see the section "Configuring Navigation Rules" on page 161.

The immediate attribute of the bookstore:map tag is set to true, which indicates that the default javax.faces.event.ActionListener implementation should execute during the Apply Request Values phase of the request-processing lifecycle, instead of waiting for the Invoke Application phase. Because the request resulting from clicking the map does not require any validation, data conversion, or server-side object updates, it makes sense to skip directly to the Invoke Application phase.

The current attribute of the bookstore:map tag is set to the default area, which is map1 (the book *My Early Years: Growing Up on Star7*, by Duke).

Notice that the bookstore:area tags do not contain any of the JavaScript, coordinate, or shape data that is displayed on the HTML page. The JavaScript is generated by the dukesbookstore.renderers.AreaRenderer class. The onmouseover and onmouseout attribute values indicate the image to be loaded when these events occur. How the JavaScript is generated is explained more in "Performing Encoding" on page 109.

The coordinate, shape, and alternate text data are obtained through the value attribute, whose value refers to an attribute in application scope. The value of this attribute is a bean, which stores the coords, shape, and alt data. How these beans are stored in the application scope is explained more in the next section.

Configuring Model Data

In a JavaServer Faces application, data such as the coordinates of a hotspot of an image map is retrieved from the value attribute through a bean. However, the shape and coordinates of a hotspot should be defined together because the coordinates are interpreted differently depending on what shape the hotspot is. Because a component's value can be bound only to one property, the value attribute cannot refer to both the shape and the coordinates.

To solve this problem, the application encapsulates all of this information in a set of ImageArea objects. These objects are initialized into application scope by the managed bean creation facility (see "Managed Beans in JavaServer Faces Technology" in *The Java EE 6 Tutorial: Basic Concepts*). Here is part of the managed bean declaration for the ImageArea bean corresponding to the South America hotspot:

```
<managed-bean eager="true">
   ...
   <managed-bean-name> Book201 </managed-bean-name>
   <managed-bean-class> dukesbookstore.model.ImageArea /managed-bean-class>
   <managed-bean-scope> application </managed-bean-scope>
```

```
    <managed-property>
        ...
        <property-name>shape</property-name>
        <value>rect</value>
    </managed-property>
    <managed-property>
        ...
        <property-name>alt</property-name>
        <value>Duke</value>
    </managed-property>
    <managed-property>
        ...
        <property-name>coords</property-name>
        <value>67,23,212,268</value>
    </managed-property>
</managed-bean>
```

For more information on initializing managed beans with the managed bean creation facility, see the section "Application Configuration Resource File" on page 144.

The `value` attributes of the `bookstore:area` tags refer to the beans in the application scope, as shown in this `bookstore:area` tag from `index.xhtml`:

```
<bookstore:area id="map1" value="#{Book201}"
                onmouseover="resources/images/book_201.jpg"
                onmouseout="resources/images/book_all.jpg"
                targetImage="mapImage" />
```

To reference the `ImageArea` model object bean values from the component class, you implement a `getValue` method in the component class. This method calls `super.getValue`. The superclass of *tut-install*/examples/case-studies/dukes-bookstore/ src/java/dukesbookstore/components/AreaComponent.java, `UIOutput`, has a `getValue` method that does the work of finding the `ImageArea` object associated with `AreaComponent`. The `AreaRenderer` class, which needs to render the `alt`, `shape`, and `coords` values from the `ImageArea` object, calls the `getValue` method of `AreaComponent` to retrieve the `ImageArea` object.

```
ImageArea iarea = (ImageArea) area.getValue();
```

`ImageArea` is a simple bean, so you can access the shape, coordinates, and alternative text values by calling the appropriate accessor methods of `ImageArea`. "Creating the Renderer Class" on page 115 explains how to do this in the `AreaRenderer` class.

Summary of the Image Map Application Classes

Table 6–2 summarizes all the classes needed to implement the image map component.

TABLE 6–2 Image Map Classes

Class	Function
AreaSelectedEvent	The `javax.faces.event.ActionEvent` indicating that an `AreaComponent` from the `MapComponent` has been selected.
AreaComponent	The class that defines `AreaComponent`, which corresponds to the `bookstore:area` custom tag.
MapComponent	The class that defines `MapComponent`, which corresponds to the `bookstore:map` custom tag.
AreaRenderer	This `javax.faces.render.Renderer` performs the delegated rendering for `AreaComponent`.
ImageArea	The bean that stores the shape and coordinates of the hotspots.
MapBookChangeListener	The action listener for the `MapComponent`.

The Duke's Bookstore source directory, called *bookstore-dir*, is *tut-install*/examples/case-studies/dukes-bookstore/src/java/dukesbookstore/. The event and listener classes are located in *bookstore-dir*/listeners/. The component classes are located in *bookstore-dir*/components/. The renderer classes are located in *bookstore-dir*/renderers/. `ImageArea` is located in *bookstore-dir*/model/.

Steps for Creating a Custom Component

You can apply the following steps while developing your own custom component.

1. Create a custom component class that does the following:
   a. Overrides the `getFamily` method to return the component family, which is used to look up renderers that can render the component.
   b. Includes the rendering code or delegates it to a renderer (explained in step 2).
   c. Enables component attributes to accept expressions.
   d. Queues an event on the component if the component generates events.
   e. Saves and restores the component state.

2. Delegate rendering to a renderer if your component does not handle the rendering. To do this:
   a. Create a custom renderer class by extending `javax.faces.render.Renderer`.
   b. Register the renderer to a render kit.

3. Register the component.

4. Create an event handler if your component generates events.

5. Create a tag library descriptor (TLD) that defines the custom tag.

See "Registering a Custom Component" on page 167 and "Registering a Custom Renderer with a Render Kit" on page 165 for information on registering the custom component and the renderer. The section "Using a Custom Component" on page 121 discusses how to use the custom component in a JavaServer Faces page.

Creating Custom Component Classes

As explained in "When to Use a Custom Component" on page 97, a component class defines the state and behavior of a UI component. The state information includes the component's type, identifier, and local value. The behavior defined by the component class includes the following:

- Decoding (converting the request parameter to the component's local value)
- Encoding (converting the local value into the corresponding markup)
- Saving the state of the component
- Updating the bean value with the local value
- Processing validation on the local value
- Queueing events

The javax.faces.component.UIComponentBase class defines the default behavior of a component class. All the classes representing the standard components extend from UIComponentBase. These classes add their own behavior definitions, as your custom component class will do.

Your custom component class must either extend UIComponentBase directly or extend a class representing one of the standard components. These classes are located in the javax.faces.component package and their names begin with UI.

If your custom component serves the same purpose as a standard component, you should extend that standard component rather than directly extend UIComponentBase. For example, suppose you want to create an editable menu component. It makes sense to have this component extend UISelectOne rather than UIComponentBase because you can reuse the behavior already defined in UISelectOne. The only new functionality you need to define is to make the menu editable.

Whether you decide to have your component extend UIComponentBase or a standard component, you might also want your component to implement one or more of these behavioral interfaces defined in the javax.faces.component package:

- ActionSource: Indicates that the component can fire a javax.faces.event.ActionEvent.

- ActionSource2: Extends ActionSource and allows component properties referencing methods that handle action events to use method expressions as defined by the unified EL.

- EditableValueHolder: Extends ValueHolder and specifies additional features for editable components, such as validation and emitting value-change events.

- NamingContainer: Mandates that each component rooted at this component have a unique ID.

- StateHolder: Denotes that a component has state that must be saved between requests.

- ValueHolder: Indicates that the component maintains a local value as well as the option of accessing data in the model tier.

If your component extends UIComponentBase, it automatically implements only StateHolder. Because all components directly or indirectly extend UIComponentBase, they all implement StateHolder. Any component that implements StateHolder also implements the StateHelper interface, which extends StateHolder and defines a Map-like contract that makes it easy for components to save and restore a partial view state.

If your component extends one of the other standard components, it might also implement other behavioral interfaces in addition to StateHolder. If your component extends UICommand, it automatically implements ActionSource2. If your component extends UIOutput or one of the component classes that extend UIOutput, it automatically implements ValueHolder. If your component extends UIInput, it automatically implements EditableValueHolder and ValueHolder. See the JavaServer Faces API documentation to find out what the other component classes implement.

You can also make your component explicitly implement a behavioral interface that it doesn't already by virtue of extending a particular standard component. For example, if you have a component that extends UIInput and you want it to fire action events, you must make it explicitly implement ActionSource2 because a UIInput component doesn't automatically implement this interface.

The Duke's Bookstore image map example has two component classes: AreaComponent and MapComponent. The MapComponent class extends UICommand and therefore implements ActionSource2, which means it can fire action events when a user clicks on the map. The AreaComponent class extends the standard component UIOutput. The @FacesComponent annotation registers the components with the JavaServer Faces implementation:

```
@FacesComponent("DemoMap")
public class MapComponent extends UICommand {...}

@FacesComponent("DemoArea")
public class AreaComponent extends UIOutput {...}
```

The MapComponent class represents the component corresponding to the bookstore:map tag:

```
<bookstore:map id="bookMap"
               current="map1"
               immediate="true"
               action="bookstore">
   ...
</bookstore:map>
```

The AreaComponent class represents the component corresponding to the bookstore:area tag:

```
<bookstore:area id="map1" value="#{Book201}"
                onmouseover="resources/images/book_201.jpg"
                onmouseout="resources/images/book_all.jpg"
                targetImage="mapImage"/>
```

MapComponent has one or more AreaComponent instances as children. Its behavior consists of the following actions:

- Retrieving the value of the currently selected area
- Defining the properties corresponding to the component's values
- Generating an event when the user clicks on the image map
- Queuing the event
- Saving its state
- Rendering the HTML map tag and the HTML input tag

MapComponent delegates the rendering of the HTML map and input tags to the MapRenderer class.

AreaComponent is bound to a bean that stores the shape and coordinates of the region of the image map. You will see how all this data is accessed through the value expression in "Creating the Renderer Class" on page 115. The behavior of AreaComponent consists of the following:

- Retrieving the shape and coordinate data from the bean
- Setting the value of the hidden tag to the id of this component
- Rendering the area tag, including the JavaScript for the onmouseover, onmouseout, and onclick functions

Although these tasks are actually performed by AreaRenderer, AreaComponent must delegate the tasks to AreaRenderer. See "Delegating Rendering to a Renderer" on page 114 for more information.

The rest of this section describes the tasks that MapComponent performs as well as the encoding and decoding that it delegates to MapRenderer. "Handling Events for Custom Components" on page 119 details how MapComponent handles events.

Specifying the Component Family

If your custom component class delegates rendering, it needs to override the getFamily method of UIComponent to return the identifier of a *component family*, which is used to refer to a component or set of components that can be rendered by a renderer or set of renderers.

The component family is used along with the renderer type to look up renderers that can render the component:

```
public String getFamily() {
    return ("Map");
}
```

The component family identifier, Map, must match that defined by the component-family elements included in the component and renderer configurations in the application configuration resource file. "Registering a Custom Renderer with a Render Kit" on page 165 explains how to define the component family in the renderer configuration. "Registering a Custom Component" on page 167 explains how to define the component family in the component configuration.

Performing Encoding

During the Render Response phase, the JavaServer Faces implementation processes the encoding methods of all components and their associated renderers in the view. The encoding methods convert the current local value of the component into the corresponding markup that represents it in the response.

The UIComponentBase class defines a set of methods for rendering markup: encodeBegin, encodeChildren, and encodeEnd. If the component has child components, you might need to use more than one of these methods to render the component; otherwise, all rendering should be done in encodeEnd. Alternatively, you can use the encodeALL method, which encompasses all the methods.

Because MapComponent is a parent component of AreaComponent, the area tags must be rendered after the beginning map tag and before the ending map tag. To accomplish this, the MapRenderer class renders the beginning map tag in encodeBegin and the rest of the map tag in encodeEnd.

The JavaServer Faces implementation automatically invokes the encodeEnd method of AreaComponent's renderer after it invokes MapRenderer's encodeBegin method and before it invokes MapRenderer's encodeEnd method. If a component needs to perform the rendering for its children, it does this in the encodeChildren method.

Here are the encodeBegin and encodeEnd methods of MapRenderer:

```
@Override
public void encodeBegin(FacesContext context, UIComponent component)
        throws IOException {
    if ((context == null)|| (component == null)){
        throw new NullPointerException();
    }
    MapComponent map = (MapComponent) component;
    ResponseWriter writer = context.getResponseWriter();
    writer.startElement("map", map);
    writer.writeAttribute("name", map.getId(), "id");
}

@Override
public void encodeEnd(FacesContext context, UIComponent component)
        throws IOException {
    if ((context == null) || (component == null)){
        throw new NullPointerException();
    }
    MapComponent map = (MapComponent) component;
    ResponseWriter writer = context.getResponseWriter();
    writer.startElement("input", map);
    writer.writeAttribute("type", "hidden", null);
    writer.writeAttribute("name", getName(context,map), "clientId");(
    writer.endElement("input");
    writer.endElement("map");
}
```

Notice that encodeBegin renders only the beginning map tag. The encodeEnd method renders the input tag and the ending map tag.

The encoding methods accept a UIComponent argument and a javax.faces.context.FacesContext argument. The FacesContext instance contains all the information associated with the current request. The UIComponent argument is the component that needs to be rendered.

The rest of the method renders the markup to the javax.faces.context.ResponseWriter instance, which writes out the markup to the current response. This basically involves passing the HTML tag names and attribute names to the ResponseWriter instance as strings, retrieving the values of the component attributes, and passing these values to the ResponseWriter instance.

The startElement method takes a String (the name of the tag) and the component to which the tag corresponds (in this case, map). (Passing this information to the ResponseWriter instance helps design-time tools know which portions of the generated markup are related to which components.)

After calling startElement, you can call writeAttribute to render the tag's attributes. The writeAttribute method takes the name of the attribute, its value, and the name of a property or attribute of the containing component corresponding to the attribute. The last parameter can be null, and it won't be rendered.

The name attribute value of the map tag is retrieved using the getId method of UIComponent, which returns the component's unique identifier. The name attribute value of the input tag is retrieved using the getName(FacesContext, UIComponent) method of MapRenderer.

If you want your component to perform its own rendering but delegate to a renderer if there is one, include the following lines in the encoding method to check whether there is a renderer associated with this component:

```
if (getRendererType() != null) {
    super.encodeEnd(context);
    return;
}
```

If there is a renderer available, this method invokes the superclass's encodeEnd method, which does the work of finding the renderer. The MapComponent class delegates all rendering to MapRenderer, so it does not need to check for available renderers.

In some custom component classes that extend standard components, you might need to implement other methods in addition to encodeEnd. For example, if you need to retrieve the component's value from the request parameters, you must also implement the decode method.

Performing Decoding

During the Apply Request Values phase, the JavaServer Faces implementation processes the decode methods of all components in the tree. The decode method extracts a component's local value from incoming request parameters and uses a javax.faces.convert.Converter implementation to convert the value to a type that is acceptable to the component class.

A custom component class or its renderer must implement the decode method only if it must retrieve the local value or if it needs to queue events. The component queues the event by calling queueEvent.

Here is the decode method of MapRenderer:

```
@Override
public void decode(FacesContext context, UIComponent component) {
    if ((context == null) || (component == null)) {
        throw new NullPointerException();
    }
    MapComponent map = (MapComponent) component;
    String key = getName(context, map);
    String value = (String) context.getExternalContext().
            getRequestParameterMap().get(key);
    if (value != null)
```

```
        map.setCurrent(value);
    }
}
```

The decode method first gets the name of the hidden input field by calling getName(FacesContext, UIComponent). It then uses that name as the key to the request parameter map to retrieve the current value of the input field. This value represents the currently selected area. Finally, it sets the value of the MapComponent class's current attribute to the value of the input field.

Enabling Component Properties to Accept Expressions

Nearly all the attributes of the standard JavaServer Faces tags can accept expressions, whether they are value expressions or method expressions. It is recommended that you also enable your component attributes to accept expressions because it gives you much more flexibility when you write Facelets pages.

To enable the attributes to accept expressions, the component class must implement getter and setter methods for the component properties. These methods can use the facilities offered by the StateHelper interface to store and retrieve not only the values for these properties, but also the state of the components across multiple requests.

Because MapComponent extends UICommand, the UICommand class already does the work of getting the ValueExpression and MethodExpression instances associated with each of the attributes that it supports. Similarly, the UIOutput class that AreaComponent extends already obtains the ValueExpression instances for its supported attributes. For both components, the simple getter and setter methods store and retrieve the key values and state for the attributes, as shown in this code fragment from AreaComponent:

```
enum PropertyKeys {
    alt, coords, shape, targetImage;
}

public String getAlt() {
    return (String) getStateHelper().eval(PropertyKeys.alt, null);
}

public void setAlt(String alt) {
    getStateHelper().put(PropertyKeys.alt, alt);
}
...
```

However, if you have a custom component class that extends UIComponentBase, you will need to implement the methods that get the ValueExpression and MethodExpression instances associated with those attributes that are enabled to accept expressions. For example, you could include a method that gets the ValueExpression instance for the immediate attribute:

```
public boolean isImmediate() {
    if (this.immediateSet) {
        return (this.immediate);
    }
    ValueExpression ve = getValueExpression("immediate");
    if (ve != null) {
        Boolean value = (Boolean) ve.getValue(
            getFacesContext().getELContext());
        return (value.booleanValue());
    } else {
        return (this.immediate);
    }
}
```

The properties corresponding to the component attributes that accept method expressions must accept and return a `MethodExpression` object. For example, if `MapComponent` extended `UIComponentBase` instead of `UICommand`, it would need to provide an `action` property that returns and accepts a `MethodExpression` object:

```
public MethodExpression getAction() {
    return (this.action);
}
public void setAction(MethodExpression action) {
    this.action = action;
}
```

Saving and Restoring State

As described in "Enabling Component Properties to Accept Expressions" on page 112, use of the `StateHelper` interface facilities allows you to save the component's state at the same time you set and retrieve property values. The `StateHelper` implementation allows partial state saving: it saves only the changes in the state since the initial request, not the entire state, because the full state can be restored during the Restore View phase.

Component classes that implement `StateHolder` may prefer to implement the `saveState(FacesContext)` and `restoreState(FacesContext, Object)` methods to help the JavaServer Faces implementation save and restore the full state of components across multiple requests.

To save a set of values, you can implement the `saveState(FacesContext)` method. This method is called during the Render Response phase, during which the state of the response is saved for processing on subsequent requests. Here is a hypothetical method from `MapComponent`, which has only one attribute, `current`:

```
@Override
public Object saveState(FacesContext context) {
    Object values[] = new Object[2];
    values[0] = super.saveState(context);
    values[1] = current;
```

```
        return (values);
    }
```

This method initializes an array, which will hold the saved state. It next saves all of the state associated with the component.

A component that implements StateHolder may also provide an implementation for restoreState(FacesContext, Object), which restores the state of the component to that saved with the saveState(FacesContext) method. The restoreState(FacesContext, Object) method is called during the Restore View phase, during which the JavaServer Faces implementation checks whether there is any state that was saved during the last Render Response phase and needs to be restored in preparation for the next postback.

Here is a hypothetical restoreState(FacesContext, Object) method from MapComponent:

```
public void restoreState(FacesContext context, Object state) {
    Object values[] = (Object[]) state;
    super.restoreState(context, values[0]);
    current = (String) values[1];
}
```

This method takes a FacesContext and an Object instance, representing the array that is holding the state for the component. This method sets the component's properties to the values saved in the Object array.

Whether or not you implement these methods in a component class, you can use the javax.faces.STATE_SAVING_METHOD context parameter to specify in the deployment descriptor where you want the state to be saved: either client or server. If state is saved on the client, the state of the entire view is rendered to a hidden field on the page. By default, the state is saved on the server.

The web applications in the Duke's Forest case study save their view state on the client.

Saving state on the client uses more bandwidth as well as more client resources, while saving it on the server uses more server resources. You may also want to save state on the client if you expect your users to disable cookies.

Delegating Rendering to a Renderer

Both MapComponent and AreaComponent delegate all of their rendering to a separate renderer. The section "Performing Encoding" on page 109 explains how MapRenderer performs the encoding for MapComponent. This section explains in detail the process of delegating rendering to a renderer using AreaRenderer, which performs the rendering for AreaComponent.

To delegate rendering, you perform these tasks:

- Create the Renderer class.

- Register the renderer with a render kit by using the @FacesRenderer annotation (or by using the application configuration resource file, as explained in "Registering a Custom Renderer with a Render Kit" on page 165).

- Identify the renderer type in the @FacesRenderer annotation.

Creating the Renderer Class

When delegating rendering to a renderer, you can delegate all encoding and decoding to the renderer, or you can choose to do part of it in the component class. The AreaComponent class delegates encoding to the AreaRenderer class.

The renderer class begins with a @FacesRenderer annotation:

```
@FacesRenderer(componentFamily = "Area",
rendererType = "dukesbookstore.renderers.AreaRenderer")
public class AreaRenderer extends Renderer {
```

The @FacesRenderer annotation registers the renderer class with the JavaServer Faces implementation as a renderer class. The annotation identifies the component family as well as the renderer type.

To perform the rendering for AreaComponent, AreaRenderer must implement an encodeEnd method. The encodeEnd method of AreaRenderer retrieves the shape, coordinates, and alternative text values stored in the ImageArea bean that is bound to AreaComponent. Suppose that the area tag currently being rendered has a value attribute value of "book203". The following line from encodeEnd gets the value of the attribute "book203" from the FacesContext instance.

```
ImageArea ia = (ImageArea)area.getValue();
```

The attribute value is the ImageArea bean instance, which contains the shape, coords, and alt values associated with the book203 AreaComponent instance. "Configuring Model Data" on page 103 describes how the application stores these values.

After retrieving the ImageArea object, the method renders the values for shape, coords, and alt by simply calling the associated accessor methods and passing the returned values to the javax.faces.context.ResponseWriter instance, as shown by these lines of code, which write out the shape and coordinates:

```
writer.startElement("area", area);
writer.writeAttribute("alt", iarea.getAlt(), "alt");
writer.writeAttribute("coords", iarea.getCoords(), "coords");
writer.writeAttribute("shape", iarea.getShape(), "shape");
```

The encodeEnd method also renders the JavaScript for the onmouseout, onmouseover, and onclick attributes. The Facelets page need only provide the path to the images that are to be loaded during an onmouseover or onmouseout action:

```
<bookstore:area id="map3" value="#{Book203}"
                onmouseover="resources/images/book_203.jpg"
                onmouseout="resources/images/book_all.jpg"
                targetImage="mapImage"/>
```

The AreaRenderer class takes care of generating the JavaScript for these actions, as shown in the following code from encodeEnd. The JavaScript that AreaRenderer generates for the onclick action sets the value of the hidden field to the value of the current area's component ID and submits the page.

```
sb = new StringBuffer("document.forms[0]['").append(targetImageId).
        append("'].src='");
sb.append(
        getURI(context,
        (String) area.getAttributes().get("onmouseout")));
sb.append("'");
writer.writeAttribute("onmouseout", sb.toString(), "onmouseout");
sb = new StringBuffer("document.forms[0]['").append(targetImageId).
        append("'].src='");
sb.append(
        getURI(context,
        (String) area.getAttributes().get("onmouseover")));
sb.append("'");
writer.writeAttribute("onmouseover", sb.toString(), "onmouseover");
sb = new StringBuffer("document.forms[0]['");
sb.append(getName(context, area));
sb.append("'].value='");
sb.append(iarea.getAlt());
sb.append("'; document.forms[0].submit()");
writer.writeAttribute("onclick", sb.toString(), "value");
writer.endElement("area");
```

By submitting the page, this code causes the JavaServer Faces lifecycle to return back to the Restore View phase. This phase saves any state information, including the value of the hidden field, so that a new request component tree is constructed. This value is retrieved by the decode method of the MapComponent class. This decode method is called by the JavaServer Faces implementation during the Apply Request Values phase, which follows the Restore View phase.

In addition to the encodeEnd method, AreaRenderer contains an empty constructor. This is used to create an instance of AreaRenderer so that it can be added to the render kit.

The @FacesRenderer annotation registers the renderer class with the JavaServer Faces implementation as a renderer class. The annotation identifies the component family as well as the renderer type.

Identifying the Renderer Type

During the Render Response phase, the JavaServer Faces implementation calls the `getRendererType` method of the component's tag handler to determine which renderer to invoke, if there is one.

You identify the type associated with the renderer in the `rendererType` element of the `@FacesRenderer` annotation for `AreaRenderer` as well as in the `renderer-type` element of the tag library descriptor file.

Implementing an Event Listener

The JavaServer Faces technology supports action events and value-change events for components.

Action events occur when the user activates a component that implements `javax.faces.component.ActionSource`. These events are represented by the class `javax.faces.event.ActionEvent`.

Value-change events occur when the user changes the value of a component that implements `javax.faces.component.EditableValueHolder`. These events are represented by the class `javax.faces.event.ValueChangeEvent`.

One way to handle events is to implement the appropriate listener classes. Listener classes that handle the action events in an application must implement the interface `javax.faces.event.ActionListener`. Similarly, listeners that handle the value-change events must implement the interface `javax.faces.event.ValueChangeListener`.

This section explains how to implement the two listener classes.

To handle events generated by custom components, you must implement an event listener and an event handler and manually queue the event on the component. See "Handling Events for Custom Components" on page 119 for more information.

Note – You do not need to create an `ActionListener` implementation to handle an event that results solely in navigating to a page and does not perform any other application-specific processing. See "Writing a Method to Handle Navigation" in *The Java EE 6 Tutorial: Basic Concepts* for information on how to manage page navigation.

Implementing Value-Change Listeners

A `javax.faces.event.ValueChangeListener` implementation must include a `processValueChange(ValueChangeEvent)` method. This method processes the specified value-change event and is invoked by the JavaServer Faces implementation when the value-change event occurs. The ValueChangeEvent instance stores the old and the new values of the component that fired the event.

In the Duke's Bookstore case study, the NameChanged listener implementation is registered on the name UIInput component on the bookcashier.xhtml page. This listener stores into session scope the name the user entered in the text field corresponding to the name component.

The bookreceipt.xhtml subsequently retrieves the name from the session scope:

```
<h:outputFormat title="thanks"
                value="#{bundle.ThankYouParam}">
    <f:param value="#{sessionScope.name}"/>
</h:outputFormat>
```

When the bookreceipt.xhtml page is loaded, it displays the name inside the message:

```
"Thank you, {0}, for purchasing your books from us."
```

Here is part of the NameChanged listener implementation:

```
public class NameChanged extends Object implements ValueChangeListener {

    @Override
    public void processValueChange(ValueChangeEvent event)
        throws AbortProcessingException {

        if (null != event.getNewValue()) {
            FacesContext.getCurrentInstance().getExternalContext().
                getSessionMap().put("name", event.getNewValue());
        }
    }
}
```

When the user enters the name in the text field, a value-change event is generated, and the processValueChange(ValueChangeEvent) method of the NameChanged listener implementation is invoked. This method first gets the ID of the component that fired the event from the ValueChangeEvent object, and it puts the value, along with an attribute name, into the session map of the FacesContext instance.

"Registering a Value-Change Listener on a Component" in *The Java EE 6 Tutorial: Basic Concepts* explains how to register this listener onto a component.

Implementing Action Listeners

A javax.faces.event.ActionListener implementation must include a processAction(ActionEvent) method. The processAction(ActionEvent) method processes the specified action event. The JavaServer Faces implementation invokes the processAction(ActionEvent) method when the ActionEvent occurs.

The Duke's Bookstore case study uses two ActionListener implementations, LinkBookChangeListener and MapBookChangeListener. See "Handling Events for Custom Components" on page 119 for details on MapBookChangeListener.

"Registering an Action Listener on a Component" in *The Java EE 6 Tutorial: Basic Concepts* explains how to register this listener onto a component.

Handling Events for Custom Components

As explained in "Implementing an Event Listener" on page 117, events are automatically queued on standard components that fire events. A custom component, on the other hand, must manually queue events from its decode method if it fires events.

"Performing Decoding" on page 111 explains how to queue an event on MapComponent using its decode method. This section explains how to write the class that represents the event of clicking on the map and how to write the method that processes this event.

As explained in "Understanding the Facelets Page" on page 102, the actionListener attribute of the bookstore:map tag points to the MapBookChangeListener class. The listener class's processAction method processes the event of clicking the image map. Here is the processAction method:

```
@Override
public void processAction(ActionEvent actionEvent)
        throws AbortProcessingException {

    AreaSelectedEvent event = (AreaSelectedEvent) actionEvent;
    String current = event.getMapComponent().getCurrent();
    FacesContext context = FacesContext.getCurrentInstance();
    String bookId = books.get(current);
    context.getExternalContext().getSessionMap().put("bookId", bookId);
}
```

When the JavaServer Faces implementation calls this method, it passes in an ActionEvent object that represents the event generated by clicking on the image map. Next, it casts it to an AreaSelectedEvent object (see *tut-install*/examples/case-studies/dukes-bookstore/src/java/dukesbookstore/listeners/AreaSelectedEvent.java). Then this method gets the MapComponent associated with the event. It then gets the value of the MapComponent object's current attribute, which indicates the currently selected area. The method then uses the value of the current attribute to get the book's ID value from a HashMap object, which is constructed elsewhere in the MapBookChangeListener class. Finally the method places the ID obtained from the HashMap object into the session map for the application.

In addition to the method that processes the event, you need the event class itself. This class is very simple to write: You have it extend `ActionEvent` and provide a constructor that takes the component on which the event is queued and a method that returns the component.

Here is the `AreaSelectedEvent` class used with the image map:

```
public class AreaSelectedEvent extends ActionEvent {
    public AreaSelectedEvent(MapComponent map) {
        super(map);
    }
    public MapComponent getMapComponent() {
        return ((MapComponent) getComponent());
    }
}
```

As explained in the section "Creating Custom Component Classes" on page 106, in order for `MapComponent` to fire events in the first place, it must implement `ActionSource`. Because `MapComponent` extends `UICommand`, it also implements `ActionSource`.

Defining the Custom Component Tag in a Tag Library Descriptor

To use a custom tag, you declare it in a Tag Library Descriptor (TLD). The TLD file defines how the custom tag is used in a JavaServer Faces page. The web container uses the TLD to validate the tag. The set of tags that are part of the HTML render kit are defined in the HTML_BASIC TLD, available at `http://docs.oracle.com/javaee/6/javaserverfaces/2.1/docs/renderkitdocs/`.

The TLD file name must end with `taglib.xml`. In the Duke's Bookstore case study, the custom tags `area` and `map` are defined in the file `web/WEB-INF/bookstore.taglib.xml`.

All tag definitions must be nested inside the `facelet-taglib` element in the TLD. Each tag is defined by a `tag` element that specifies a particular combination of a component type and a renderer type. Here are the tag definitions for the `area` and `map` components:

```
<facelet-taglib xmlns="http://java.sun.com/xml/ns/javaee"
... >
    <namespace>http://dukesbookstore</namespace>
    <tag>
        <tag-name>area</tag-name>
        <component>
            <component-type>DemoArea</component-type>
            <renderer-type>DemoArea</renderer-type>
```

```
        </component>
    </tag>
    <tag>
        <tag-name>map</tag-name>
        <component>
            <component-type>DemoMap</component-type>
            <renderer-type>DemoMap</renderer-type>
        </component>
    </tag>
</facelet-taglib>
```

The component-type element specifies the name defined in the @FacesComponent annotation, while the renderer-type element specifies the rendererType defined in the @FacesRenderer annotation.

The facelet-taglib element must also include a namespace element, which defines the namespace to be specified in pages that use the custom component. See "Using a Custom Component" on page 121 for information on specifying the namespace in pages.

The TLD file is located in the WEB-INF directory. In addition, an entry is included in the web deployment descriptor (web.xml) to identify the custom tag library descriptor file, as follows:

```
<context-param>
    <param-name>javax.faces.FACELETS_LIBRARIES</param-name>
    <param-value>/WEB-INF/bookstore.taglib.xml</param-value>
</context-param>
```

Using a Custom Component

To use a custom component in a page, you add the custom tag associated with the component to the page.

As explained in "Defining the Custom Component Tag in a Tag Library Descriptor" on page 120, you must ensure that the TLD that defines any custom tags is packaged in the application if you intend to use the tags in your pages. TLD files are stored in the WEB-INF/ directory or subdirectory of the WAR file or in the META-INF/ directory or subdirectory of a tag library packaged in a JAR file.

You also need to include a namespace declaration in the page so that the page has access to the tags. The custom tags for the Duke's Bookstore case study are defined in bookstore.taglib.xml. The ui:composition tag on the index.xhtml page declares the namespace defined in the tag library:

```
<ui:composition xmlns="http://www.w3.org/1999/xhtml"
                xmlns:ui="http://java.sun.com/jsf/facelets"
                xmlns:h="http://java.sun.com/jsf/html"
```

```
                      xmlns:f="http://java.sun.com/jsf/core"
                      xmlns:bookstore="http://dukesbookstore"
                      template="./bookstoreTemplate.xhtml">
```

Finally, to use a custom component in a page, you add the component's tag to the page.

The Duke's Bookstore case study includes a custom image map component on the index.xhtml page. This component allows you to select a book by clicking on a region of the image map:

```
...
<h:graphicImage id="mapImage"
                name="book_all.jpg"
                library="images
                alt="#{bundle.chooseLocale}"
                usemap="#bookMap" />
<bookstore:map id="bookMap"
               current="map1"
               immediate="true"
               action="bookstore">
    <f:actionListener
        type="dukesbookstore.listeners.MapBookChangeListener" />
    <bookstore:area id="map1" value="#{Book201}"
                    onmouseover="resources/images/book_201.jpg"
                    onmouseout="resources/images/book_all.jpg"
                    targetImage="mapImage" />
    ...
    <bookstore:area id="map6" value="#{Book207}"
                    onmouseover="resources/images/book_207.jpg"
                    onmouseout="resources/images//book_all.jpg"
                    targetImage="mapImage" />
</bookstore:map>
```

The standard h:graphicImage tag associates an image (book_all.jpg) with an image map that is referenced in the usemap attribute value.

The custom bookstore:map tag that represents the custom component, MapComponent, specifies the image map, and contains a set of area tags. Each custom bookstore:area tag represents a custom AreaComponent and specifies a region of the image map.

On the page, the onmouseover and onmouseout attributes specify the image that is displayed when the user performs the actions described by the attributes. The custom renderer also renders an onclick attribute.

In the rendered HTML page, the onmouseover, onmouseout, and onclick attributes define which JavaScript code is executed when these events occur. When the user moves the mouse over a region, the onmouseover function associated with the region displays the map with that region highlighted. When the user moves the mouse out of a region, the onmouseout function redisplays the original image. When the user clicks a region, the onclick function sets the value of a hidden input tag to the ID of the selected area and submits the page.

When the custom renderer renders these attributes in HTML, it also renders the JavaScript code. The custom renderer also renders the entire onclick attribute rather than let the page author set it.

The custom renderer that renders the HTML map tag also renders a hidden input component that holds the current area. The server-side objects retrieve the value of the hidden input field and set the locale in the FacesContext instance according to which region was selected.

Creating and Using a Custom Converter

A JavaServer Faces converter class converts strings to objects and objects to strings as required. Several standard converters are provided by JavaServer Faces for this purpose. See "Using the Standard Converters" in *The Java EE 6 Tutorial: Basic Concepts* for more information on these included converters.

As explained in "Conversion Model" on page 61, if the standard converters included with JavaServer Faces cannot perform the data conversion that you need, you can create a custom converter to perform this specialized conversion. This implementation, at a minimum, must define how to convert data both ways between the two views of the data described in "Conversion Model" on page 61.

All custom converters must implement the javax.faces.convert.Converter interface. This section explains how to implement this interface to perform a custom data conversion.

The Duke's Bookstore case study uses a custom Converter implementation, located in *tut-install*/examples/case-studies/dukes-bookstore/src/java/dukesbookstore/converters/CreditCardConverter.java, to convert the data entered in the Credit Card Number field on the bookcashier.xhtml page. It strips blanks and hyphens from the text string and formats it so that a blank space separates every four characters.

Another common use case for a custom converter is in a drop-down menu for a nonstandard object type. In the Duke's Tutoring case study, the Student and Guardian entities require a custom converter so they can be converted to and from a UISelectItems input component.

Creating a Custom Converter

The CreditCardConverter custom converter class is created as follows:

```
@FacesConverter("ccno")
public class CreditCardConverter implements Converter {
    ...
}
```

The @FacesConverter annotation registers the custom converter class as a converter with the name of ccno with the JavaServer Faces implementation. Alternatively, you can register the converter with entries in the application configuration resource file, as shown in "Registering a Custom Converter" on page 160.

To define how the data is converted from the presentation view to the model view, the Converter implementation must implement the getAsObject(FacesContext, UIComponent, String) method from the Converter interface. Here is the implementation of this method from CreditCardConverter:

```
@Override
public Object getAsObject(FacesContext context,
        UIComponent component, String newValue)
        throws ConverterException {

    String convertedValue = null;
    if ( newValue == null ) {
        return newValue;
    }
    // Since this is only a String to String conversion,
    // this conversion does not throw ConverterException.

    convertedValue = newValue.trim();
    if ( (convertedValue.contains("-")) ||
        (convertedValue.contains(" "))) {
        char[] input = convertedValue.toCharArray();
        StringBuilder builder = new StringBuilder(input.length);
        for ( int i = 0; i < input.length; ++i ) {
            if ( input[i] == '-' || input[i] == ' ' ) {
                continue;
            } else {
                builder.append(input[i]);
            }
        }
        convertedValue = builder.toString();
    }
    return convertedValue;
}
```

During the Apply Request Values phase, when the components' decode methods are processed, the JavaServer Faces implementation looks up the component's local value in the request and calls the getAsObject method. When calling this method, the JavaServer Faces implementation passes in the current FacesContext instance, the component whose data needs conversion, and the local value as a String. The method then writes the local value to a character array, trims the hyphens and blanks, adds the rest of the characters to a String, and returns the String.

To define how the data is converted from the model view to the presentation view, the Converter implementation must implement the getAsString(FacesContext, UIComponent, Object) method from the Converter interface. Here is an implementation of this method:

```
@Override
public String getAsString(FacesContext context,
        UIComponent component, Object value)
        throws ConverterException {

    String inputVal = null;
    if ( value == null ) {
        return null;
    }
    // value must be of a type that can be cast to a String.
    try {
        inputVal = (String)value;
    } catch (ClassCastException ce) {
        FacesMessage errMsg = new FacesMessage(CONVERSION_ERROR_MESSAGE_ID);
        FacesContext.getCurrentInstance().addMessage(null, errMsg);
        throw new ConverterException(errMsg.getSummary());
    }
    // insert spaces after every four characters for better
    // readability if they are not already present.
    char[] input = inputVal.toCharArray();
    StringBuilder builder = new StringBuilder(input.length + 3);
    for ( int i = 0; i < input.length; ++i ) {
        if ( (i % 4) == 0 && i != 0) {
            if (input[i] != ' ' || input[i] != '-'){
                builder.append(" ");
                // if there are any "-"'s convert them to blanks.
            } else if (input[i] == '-') {
                builder.append(" ");
            }
        }
        builder.append(input[i]);
    }
    String convertedValue = builder.toString();
    return convertedValue;
}
```

During the Render Response phase, in which the components' encode methods are called, the JavaServer Faces implementation calls the getAsString method in order to generate the appropriate output. When the JavaServer Faces implementation calls this method, it passes in the current FacesContext, the UIComponent whose value needs to be converted, and the bean value to be converted. Because this converter does a String-to-String conversion, this method can cast the bean value to a String.

If the value cannot be converted to a String, the method throws an exception, passing an error message from the resource bundle that is registered with the application. "Registering Application Messages" on page 155 explains how to register custom error messages with the application.

If the value can be converted to a String, the method reads the String to a character array and loops through the array, adding a space after every four characters.

You can also create a custom converter with a @FacesConverter annotation that specifies the forClass attribute, as shown in the following example from the Duke's Tutoring case study:

```
@FacesConverter(forClass=Guardian.class)
public class GuardianConverter implements Converter { ...
```

The forClass attribute registers the converter as the default converter for the Guardian class. Therefore, whenever that class is specified by a value attribute of an input component, the converter is invoked automatically.

A converter class can be a separate Java POJO class, as in the Duke's Bookstore and Duke's Tutoring case studies. If it needs to access objects defined in a managed bean class, however, it can be a subclass of a JavaServer Faces managed bean, as in the Duke's Forest case study, where the converters use an enterprise bean that is injected into the managed bean class.

Using a Custom Converter

To apply the data conversion performed by a custom converter to a particular component's value, you must do one of the following:

- Reference the converter from the component tag's converter attribute.
- Nest an f:converter tag inside the component's tag and reference the custom converter from one of the f:converter tag's attributes.

If you are using the component tag's converter attribute, this attribute must reference the Converter implementation's identifier or the fully-qualified class name of the converter. "Creating and Using a Custom Converter" on page 123 explains how to implement a custom converter.

The identifier for the credit card converter class is ccno, the value specified in the @FacesConverter annotation:

```
@FacesConverter("ccno")
public class CreditCardConverter implements Converter {
    ...
```

Therefore, the CreditCardConverter instance can be registered on the ccno component as shown in the following example:

```
<h:inputText id="ccno"
    size="19"
    converter="ccno"
    value="#{cashier.creditCardNumber}"
    required="true"
    requiredMessage="#{bundle.ReqCreditCard}">
    ...
</h:inputText>
```

By setting the converter attribute of a component's tag to the converter's identifier or its class name, you cause that component's local value to be automatically converted according to the rules specified in the Converter implementation.

Instead of referencing the converter from the component tag's `converter` attribute, you can reference the converter from an `f:converter` tag nested inside the component's tag. To reference the custom converter using the `f:converter` tag, you do one of the following:

- Set the `f:converter` tag's `converterId` attribute to the `Converter` implementation's identifier defined in the `@FacesConverter` annotation or in the application configuration resource file. This method is shown in `bookcashier.xhtml`:

```
<h:inputText id="ccno"
             size="19"
             value="#{cashier.creditCardNumber}"
             required="true"
             requiredMessage="#{bundle.ReqCreditCard}" >
    <f:converter converterId="ccno"/>
    <f:validateRegex
        pattern="\d{16}|\d{4} \d{4} \d{4} \d{4}|\d{4}-\d{4}-\d{4}-\d{4}" />
</h:inputText>
```

- Bind the `Converter` implementation to a managed bean property using the `f:converter` tag's `binding` attribute, as described in "Binding Converters, Listeners, and Validators to Managed Bean Properties" on page 138.

The JavaServer Faces implementation calls the converter's `getAsObject` method to strip spaces and hyphens from the input value. The `getAsString` method is called when the `bookcashier.xhtml` page is redisplayed; this happens if the user orders more than $100 worth of books.

In the Duke's Tutoring case study, each converter is registered as the converter for a particular class. The converter is automatically invoked whenever that class is specified by a `value` attribute of an input component. In the following example, the `itemValue` attribute (highlighted in bold) calls the converter for the `Guardian` class:

```
<h:selectManyListbox id="selectGuardiansMenu"
                     value="#{guardianManager.selectedGuardians}"
                     size="5">
    <f:selectItems value="#{guardianManager.allGuardians}"
                   var="selectedGuardian"
                   itemLabel="#{selectedGuardian.name}"
                   itemValue="#{selectedGuardian}" />
</h:selectManyListbox>
```

Creating and Using a Custom Validator

If the standard validators or Bean Validation don't perform the validation checking you need, you can create a custom validator to validate user input. As explained in "Validation Model" on page 63, there are two ways to implement validation code:

- Implement a managed bean method that performs the validation.
- Provide an implementation of the `javax.faces.validator.Validator` interface to perform the validation.

"Writing a Method to Perform Validation" in *The Java EE 6 Tutorial: Basic Concepts* explains how to implement a managed bean method to perform validation. The rest of this section explains how to implement the `Validator` interface.

If you choose to implement the `Validator` interface and you want to allow the page author to configure the validator's attributes from the page, you also must specify a custom tag for registering the validator on a component.

If you prefer to configure the attributes in the `Validator` implementation, you can forgo specifying a custom tag and instead let the page author register the validator on a component using the `f:validator` tag, as described in "Using a Custom Validator" on page 132.

You can also create a managed bean property that accepts and returns the `Validator` implementation you create, as described in "Writing Properties Bound to Converters, Listeners, or Validators" in *The Java EE 6 Tutorial: Basic Concepts*. You can use the `f:validator` tag's binding attribute to bind the `Validator` implementation to the managed bean property.

Usually, you will want to display an error message when data fails validation. You need to store these error messages in a resource bundle.

After creating the resource bundle, you have two ways to make the messages available to the application. You can queue the error messages onto the `FacesContext` programmatically, or you can register the error messages in the application configuration resource file, as explained in "Registering Application Messages" on page 155.

For example, an e-commerce application might use a general-purpose custom validator called `FormatValidator.java` to validate input data against a format pattern that is specified in the custom validator tag. This validator would be used with a Credit Card Number field on a Facelets page. Here is the custom validator tag:

```
<mystore:formatValidator
    formatPatterns="9999999999999999|9999 9999 9999 9999|9999-9999-9999-9999"/>
```

According to this validator, the data entered in the field must be one of the following:

- A 16–digit number with no spaces
- A 16–digit number with a space between every four digits
- A 16–digit number with hyphens between every four digits

The f:validateRegex tag makes a custom validator unnecessary in this situation. However, the rest of this section describes how this validator would be implemented and how to specify a custom tag so that the page author could register the validator on a component.

Implementing the Validator Interface

A Validator implementation must contain a constructor, a set of accessor methods for any attributes on the tag, and a validate method, which overrides the validate method of the Validator interface.

The hypothetical FormatValidator class also defines accessor methods for setting the formatPatterns attribute, which specifies the acceptable format patterns for input into the fields. The setter method calls the parseFormatPatterns method, which separates the components of the pattern string into a string array, formatPatternsList.

```
public String getFormatPatterns() {
    return (this.formatPatterns);
}
public void setFormatPatterns(String formatPatterns) {
    this.formatPatterns = formatPatterns;
    parseFormatPatterns();
}
```

In addition to defining accessor methods for the attributes, the class overrides the validate method of the Validator interface. This method validates the input and also accesses the custom error messages to be displayed when the String is invalid.

The validate method performs the actual validation of the data. It takes the FacesContext instance, the component whose data needs to be validated, and the value that needs to be validated. A validator can validate only data of a component that implements javax.faces.component.EditableValueHolder.

Here is an implementation of the validate method:

```
@FacesValidator
public class FormatValidator implements Validator, StateHolder {
    ...
    public void validate(FacesContext context, UIComponent component,
                         Object toValidate) {
```

```
                    boolean valid = false;
                    String value = null;
                    if ((context == null) || (component == null)) {
                        throw new NullPointerException();
                    }
                    if (!(component instanceof UIInput)) {
                        return;
                    }
                    if ( null == formatPatternsList || null == toValidate) {
                        return;
                    }
                    value = toValidate.toString();
                    // validate the value against the list of valid patterns.
                    Iterator patternIt = formatPatternsList.iterator();
                    while (patternIt.hasNext()) {
                        valid = isFormatValid(
                            ((String)patternIt.next()), value);
                        if (valid) {
                            break;
                        }
                    }
                    if ( !valid ) {
                        FacesMessage errMsg =
                            new FacesMessage(FORMAT_INVALID_MESSAGE_ID);
                        FacesContext.getCurrentInstance().addMessage(null, errMsg);
                        throw new ValidatorException(errMsg);
                    }
                }
            }
        }
```

The @FacesValidator annotation registers the FormatValidator class as a validator with the JavaServer Faces implementation. The validate method gets the local value of the component and converts it to a String. It then iterates over the formatPatternsList list, which is the list of acceptable patterns that was parsed from the formatPatterns attribute of the custom validator tag.

While iterating over the list, this method checks the pattern of the component's local value against the patterns in the list. If the pattern of the local value does not match any pattern in the list, this method generates an error message. It then creates a javax.faces.application.FacesMessage and queues it on the FacesContext for display during the Render Response phase, using a String that represents the key in the Properties file:

```
public static final String FORMAT_INVALID_MESSAGE_ID =
    "FormatInvalid";
}
```

Finally, the method passes the message to the constructor of javax.faces.validator.ValidatorException.

When the error message is displayed, the format pattern will be substituted for the {0} in the error message, which, in English, is as follows:

```
Input must match one of the following patterns: {0}
```

You may wish to save and restore state for your validator, although state saving is not usually necessary. To do so, you will need to implement the `StateHolder` interface in addition to the `Validator` interface. To implement `StateHolder`, you would need to implement its four methods: `saveState(FacesContext)`, `restoreState(FacesContext, Object)`, `isTransient`, and `setTransient(boolean)`. See "Saving and Restoring State" on page 113 for more information.

Specifying a Custom Tag

If you implemented a `Validator` interface rather than implementing a managed bean method that performs the validation, you need to do one of the following:

- Allow the page author to specify the `Validator` implementation to use with the `f:validator` tag. In this case, the `Validator` implementation must define its own properties. "Using a Custom Validator" on page 132 explains how to use the `f:validator` tag.

- Specify a custom tag that provides attributes for configuring the properties of the validator from the page.

To specify a custom tag, you need to add the tag to the tag library descriptor for the application, `bookstore.taglib.xml`.

```
<tag>
    <tag-name>formatValidator</tag-name>
    <validator>
        <validator-id>formatValidator</validator-id>
        <validator-class>dukesbookstore.validators.FormatValidator</validator-class>
    </validator>
</tag>
```

The `tag-name` element defines the name of the tag as it must be used in a Facelets page. The `validator-id` element identifies the custom validator. The `validator-class` element wires the custom tag to its implementation class.

"Using a Custom Validator" on page 132 explains how to use the custom validator tag on the page.

Using a Custom Validator

To register a custom validator on a component, you must do one of the following:

- Nest the validator's custom tag inside the tag of the component whose value you want to be validated.

- Nest the standard f:validator tag within the tag of the component and reference the custom Validator implementation from the f:validator tag.

Here is a hypothetical custom formatValidator tag for the Credit Card Number field, nested within the h:inputText tag:

```
<h:inputText id="ccno" size="19"
    ...
    required="true">
    <mystore:formatValidator
        formatPatterns="9999999999999999|9999 9999 9999 9999|9999-9999-9999-9999" />
</h:inputText>
<h:message styleClass="validationMessage" for="ccno"/>
```

This tag validates the input of the ccno field against the patterns defined by the page author in the formatPatterns attribute.

You can use the same custom validator for any similar component by simply nesting the custom validator tag within the component tag.

If the application developer who created the custom validator prefers to configure the attributes in the Validator implementation rather than allow the page author to configure the attributes from the page, the developer will not create a custom tag for use with the validator.

In this case, the page author must nest the f:validator tag inside the tag of the component whose data needs to be validated. Then the page author needs to do one of the following:

- Set the f:validator tag's validatorId attribute to the ID of the validator that is defined in the application configuration resource file.

- Bind the custom Validator implementation to a managed bean property using the f:validator tag's binding attribute, as described in "Binding Converters, Listeners, and Validators to Managed Bean Properties" on page 138.

The following tag registers a hypothetical validator on a component using a `validator` tag and references the ID of the validator:

```
<h:inputText id="name" value="#{CustomerBean.name}"
             size="10" ... >
    <f:validator validatorId="customValidator" />
    ...
</h:inputText>
```

Binding Component Values and Instances to Managed Bean Properties

A component tag can wire its data to a managed bean by one of the following methods:

- Binding its component's value to a bean property
- Binding its component's instance to a bean property

To bind a component's value to a managed bean property, a component tag's `value` attribute uses a EL value expression. To bind a component instance to a bean property, a component tag's `binding` attribute uses a value expression.

When a component instance is bound to a managed bean property, the property holds the component's local value. Conversely, when a component's value is bound to a managed bean property, the property holds the value stored in the managed bean. This value is updated with the local value during the Update Model Values phase of the lifecycle. There are advantages to both of these methods.

Binding a component instance to a bean property has these advantages:

- The managed bean can programmatically modify component attributes.

- The managed bean can instantiate components rather than let the page author do so.

Binding a component's value to a bean property has these advantages:

- The page author has more control over the component attributes.

- The managed bean has no dependencies on the JavaServer Faces API (such as the component classes), allowing for greater separation of the presentation layer from the model layer.

- The JavaServer Faces implementation can perform conversions on the data based on the type of the bean property without the developer needing to apply a converter.

In most situations, you will bind a component's value rather than its instance to a bean property. You'll need to use a component binding only when you need to change one of the component's attributes dynamically. For example, if an application renders a component only under certain conditions, it can set the component's rendered property accordingly by accessing the property to which the component is bound.

When referencing the property using the component tag's value attribute, you need to use the proper syntax. For example, suppose a managed bean called MyBean has this int property:

```
protected int currentOption = null;
public int getCurrentOption(){...}
public void setCurrentOption(int option){...}
```

The value attribute that references this property must have this value-binding expression:

```
#{myBean.currentOption}
```

In addition to binding a component's value to a bean property, the value attribute can specify a literal value or can map the component's data to any primitive (such as int), structure (such as an array), or collection (such as a list), independent of a JavaBeans component. Table 6–3 lists some example value-binding expressions that you can use with the value attribute.

TABLE 6–3 Examples of Value-Binding Expressions

Value	Expression
A Boolean	cart.numberOfItems > 0
A property initialized from a context initialization parameter	initParam.quantity
A bean property	cashierBean.name
Value in an array	books[3]
Value in a collection	books["fiction"]
Property of an object in an array of objects	books[3].price

The next two sections explain how to use the value attribute to bind a component's value to a bean property or other data objects, and how to use the binding attribute to bind a component instance to a bean property.

Binding a Component Value to a Property

To bind a component's value to a managed bean property, you specify the name of the bean and the property using the value attribute.

This means that the first part of the EL value expression must match the name of the managed bean up to the first period (.) and the part of the value expression after the period must match the property of the managed bean.

For example, in the Duke's Bookstore case study, the h:dataTable tag in bookcatalog.xhtml sets the value of the component to the value of the books property of the stateless session bean BookRequestBean:

```
<h:dataTable id="books"
             value="#{bookRequestBean.books}"
             var="book"
             headerClass="list-header"
             styleClass="list-background"
             rowClasses="list-row-even, list-row-odd"
             border="1"
             summary="#{bundle.BookCatalog}" >
```

The value is obtained by calling the bean's getBooks method.

If you use the application configuration resource file to configure managed beans instead of defining them in managed bean classes, the name of the bean in the value expression must match the managed-bean-name element of the managed bean declaration up to the first period (.) in the expression. Similarly, the part of the value expression after the period must match the name specified in the corresponding property-name element in the application configuration resource file.

For example, consider this managed bean configuration, which configures the ImageArea bean corresponding to the top left book in the image map on the index.html page of the Duke's Bookstore case study:

```
<managed-bean eager="true">
    ...
    <managed-bean-name> Book201 </managed-bean-name>
    <managed-bean-class> dukesbookstore.model.ImageArea </managed-bean-class>
    <managed-bean-scope> application </managed-bean-scope>
    <managed-property>
        ...
        <property-name>shape</property-name>
        <value>rect</value>
    </managed-property>
    <managed-property>
        ...
        <property-name>alt</property-name>
        <value>Duke</value>
    </managed-property>
    ...
```

This example configures a bean called Book201, which has several properties, one of which is called shape.

Although the `bookstore:area` tags on the `index.xhtml` page do not bind to an `ImageArea` property (they bind to the bean itself), you could refer to the property using a value expression from the `value` attribute of the component's tag:

```
<h:outputText value="#{Book201.shape}" />
```

See "Configuring Managed Beans" on page 146 for information on how to configure beans in the application configuration resource file.

Binding a Component Value to an Implicit Object

One external data source that a `value` attribute can refer to is an implicit object.

The `bookreceipt.xhtml` page of the Duke's Bookstore case study has a reference to an implicit object:

```
<h:outputFormat title="thanks"
                value="#{bundle.ThankYouParam}">
    <f:param value="#{sessionScope.name}"/>
</h:outputFormat>
```

This tag gets the name of the customer from the session scope and inserts it into the parameterized message at the key `ThankYouParam` from the resource bundle. For example, if the name of the customer is Gwen Canigetit, this tag will render:

```
Thank you, Gwen Canigetit, for purchasing your books from us.
```

Retrieving values from other implicit objects is done in a similar way to the example shown in this section. Table 6–4 lists the implicit objects to which a value attribute can refer. All of the implicit objects, except for the scope objects, are read-only and therefore should not be used as a value for a `UIInput` component.

TABLE 6–4 Implicit Objects

Implicit Object	What It Is
`applicationScope`	A Map of the application scope attribute values, keyed by attribute name
`cookie`	A Map of the cookie values for the current request, keyed by cookie name
`facesContext`	The `FacesContext` instance for the current request
`header`	A Map of HTTP header values for the current request, keyed by header name
`headerValues`	A Map of `String` arrays containing all the header values for HTTP headers in the current request, keyed by header name
`initParam`	A Map of the context initialization parameters for this web application
`param`	A Map of the request parameters for this request, keyed by parameter name

TABLE 6–4 Implicit Objects *(Continued)*

Implicit Object	What It Is
paramValues	A Map of String arrays containing all the parameter values for request parameters in the current request, keyed by parameter name
requestScope	A Map of the request attributes for this request, keyed by attribute name
sessionScope	A Map of the session attributes for this request, keyed by attribute name
view	The root UIComponent in the current component tree stored in the FacesRequest for this request

Binding a Component Instance to a Bean Property

A component instance can be bound to a bean property using a value expression with the binding attribute of the component's tag. You usually bind a component instance rather than its value to a bean property if the bean must dynamically change the component's attributes.

Here are two tags from the bookcashier.xhtml page that bind components to bean properties:

```
<h:selectBooleanCheckbox id="fanClub"
                         rendered="false"
                         binding="#{cashier.specialOffer}" />
<h:outputLabel for="fanClub"
               rendered="false"
               binding="#{cashier.specialOfferText}"
               value="#{bundle.DukeFanClub}"/>
```

The h:selectBooleanCheckbox tag renders a check box and binds the fanClub UISelectBoolean component to the specialOffer property of the cashier bean. The h:outputLabel tag binds the component representing the check box's label to the specialOfferText property of the cashier bean. If the application's locale is English, the h:outputLabel tag renders:

```
I'd like to join the Duke Fan Club, free with my purchase of over $100
```

The rendered attributes of both tags are set to false, to prevent the check box and its label from being rendered. If the customer makes a large order and clicks the Submit button, the submit method of CashierBean sets both components' rendered properties to true, causing the check box and its label to be rendered.

These tags use component bindings rather than value bindings, because the managed bean must dynamically set the values of the components' rendered properties.

If the tags were to use value bindings instead of component bindings, the managed bean would not have direct access to the components, and would therefore require additional code to access the components from the FacesContext instance to change the components' rendered properties.

"Writing Properties Bound to Component Instances" in *The Java EE 6 Tutorial: Basic Concepts* explains how to write the bean properties bound to the example components.

Binding Converters, Listeners, and Validators to Managed Bean Properties

As described in "Adding Components to a Page Using HTML Tags" in *The Java EE 6 Tutorial: Basic Concepts*, a page author can bind converter, listener, and validator implementations to managed bean properties using the binding attributes of the tags that are used to register the implementations on components.

This technique has similar advantages to binding component instances to managed bean properties, as described in "Binding Component Values and Instances to Managed Bean Properties" on page 133. In particular, binding a converter, listener, or validator implementation to a managed bean property yields the following benefits:

- The managed bean can instantiate the implementation instead of allowing the page author to do so.

- The managed bean can programmatically modify the attributes of the implementation. In the case of a custom implementation, the only other way to modify the attributes outside of the implementation class would be to create a custom tag for it and require the page author to set the attribute values from the page.

Whether you are binding a converter, listener, or validator to a managed bean property, the process is the same for any of the implementations:

- Nest the converter, listener, or validator tag within an appropriate component tag.

- Make sure that the managed bean has a property that accepts and returns the converter, listener, or validator implementation class that you want to bind to the property.

- Reference the managed bean property using a value expression from the binding attribute of the converter, listener, or validator tag.

For example, say that you want to bind the standard DateTime converter to a managed bean property because you want to set the formatting pattern of the user's input in the managed bean rather than on the Facelets page. First, the page registers the converter onto the component by nesting the f:convertDateTime tag within the component tag.

Then, the page references the property with the `binding` attribute of the `f:convertDateTime` tag:

```
<h:inputText value="#{loginBean.birthDate}">
    <f:convertDateTime binding="#{loginBean.convertDate}" />
</h:inputText>
```

The `convertDate` property would look something like this:

```
private DateTimeConverter convertDate;
public DateTimeConverter getConvertDate() {
    ...
    return convertDate;
}
public void setConvertDate(DateTimeConverter convertDate) {
    convertDate.setPattern("EEEEEEEE, MMM dd, yyyy");
    this.convertDate = convertDate;
}
```

See "Writing Properties Bound to Converters, Listeners, or Validators" in *The Java EE 6 Tutorial: Basic Concepts* for more information on writing managed bean properties for converter, listener, and validator implementations.

Configuring JavaServer Faces Applications

The process of building and deploying simple JavaServer Faces applications is described in *The Java EE 6 Tutorial: Basic Concepts*. When you create large and complex applications, however, various additional configuration tasks are required. These tasks include the following:

- Registering managed beans with the application so that all parts of the application have access to them

- Configuring managed beans and model beans so that they are instantiated with the proper values when a page makes reference to them

- Defining navigation rules for each of the pages in the application so that the application has a smooth page flow, if non-default navigation is needed

- Packaging the application to include all the pages, resources, and other files so that the application can be deployed on any compliant container

The following topics are addressed here:

Using Annotations to Configure Managed Beans

JavaServer Faces support for bean annotations is introduced in Chapter 4, "JavaServer Faces Technology," in *The Java EE 6 Tutorial: Basic Concepts*. Bean annotations can be used for configuring JavaServer Faces applications.

The @ManagedBean (javax.faces.bean.ManagedBean) annotation in a class automatically registers that class as a resource with the JavaServer Faces implementation. Such a registered managed bean does not need managed-bean configuration entries in the application configuration resource file.

An example of using the @ManagedBean annotation in a class is as follows:

```
@ManagedBean
@SessionScoped
public class DukesBday{
...
}
```

The above code snippet shows a bean that is managed by the JavaServer Faces implementation and is available for the length of the session. You do not need to configure the managed bean instance in the faces-config.xml file. In effect, this is an alternative to the application configuration resource file approach and reduces the task of configuring managed beans.

You can also define the scope of the managed bean within the class file, as shown in the above example. You can annotate beans with request, session, application, or view scope.

All classes will be scanned for annotations at startup unless the faces-config element in the faces-config.xml file has the metadata-complete attribute set to true.

Annotations are also available for other artifacts, such as components, converters, validators, and renderers, to be used in place of application configuration resource file entries. These are discussed, along with registration of custom listeners, custom validators, and custom converters, in Chapter 6, "Creating Custom UI Components and Other Custom Objects."

Using Managed Bean Scopes

You can use annotations to define the scope in which the bean will be stored. You can specify one of the following scopes for a bean class:

- Application (@ApplicationScoped): Application scope persists across all users' interactions with a web application.

- Session (@SessionScoped): Session scope persists across multiple HTTP requests in a web application.

- View (@ViewScoped): View scope persists during a user's interaction with a single page (view) of a web application.

- Request (@RequestScoped): Request scope persists during a single HTTP request in a web application.

- None (@NoneScoped): Indicates a scope is not defined for the application.

- Custom (@CustomScoped): A user-defined, nonstandard scope. Its value must be configured as a java.util.Map. Custom scopes are used infrequently.

You may want to use @NoneScoped when a managed bean references another managed bean. The second bean should not be in a scope (@NoneScoped) if it is supposed to be created only when it is referenced. If you define a bean as @NoneScoped, the bean is instantiated anew each time it is referenced, so it does not get saved in any scope.

If your managed bean is referenced by the binding attribute of a component tag, you should define the bean with a request scope. If you placed the bean in session or application scope instead, the bean would need to take precautions to ensure thread safety, because javax.faces.component.UIComponent instances each depend on running inside of a single thread.

If you are configuring a bean that allows attributes to be associated with the view, you can use the view scope. The attributes persist until the user has navigated to the next view.

Eager Application-Scoped Beans

Managed beans are lazily instantiated. That is, that they are instantiated when a request is made from the application.

To force an application-scoped bean to be instantiated and placed in the application scope as soon as the application is started and before any request is made, the eager attribute of the managed bean should be set to true as shown in the following example:

```
@ManagedBean(eager=true)
@ApplicationScoped
```

Application Configuration Resource File

JavaServer Faces technology provides a portable configuration format (as an XML document) for configuring application resources. One or more XML documents, called *application configuration resource files*, may use this format to register and configure objects and resources, and to define navigation rules for applications. An application configuration resource file is usually named `faces-config.xml`.

You need an application configuration resource file in the following cases:

- To specify configuration elements for your application that are not available through managed bean annotations, such as localized messages and navigation rules

- To override managed bean annotations when the application is deployed

The application configuration resource file must be valid against the XML schema located at `http://java.sun.com/xml/ns/javaee/web-facesconfig_2_0.xsd`.

In addition, each file must include the following information, in the following order:

- The XML version number, usually with an `encoding` attribute:

  ```
  <?xml version="1.0" encoding='UTF-8'?>
  ```

- A `faces-config` tag enclosing all the other declarations:

  ```
  <faces-config version="2.0" xmlns="http://java.sun.com/xml/ns/javaee"
      xmlns:xsi="http://www.w3.org/2001/XMLSchema-instance"
      xsi:schemaLocation="http://java.sun.com/xml/ns/javaee
      http://java.sun.com/xml/ns/javaee/web-facesconfig_2_0.xsd">
      ...
  </faces-config>
  ```

You can have more than one application configuration resource file for an application. The JavaServer Faces implementation finds the configuration file or files by looking for the following:

- A resource named `/META-INF/faces-config.xml` in any of the JAR files in the web application's `/WEB-INF/lib/` directory and in parent class loaders. If a resource with this name exists, it is loaded as a configuration resource. This method is practical for a packaged library containing some components and renderers. In addition, any file with a name that ends in `faces-config.xml` is also considered a configuration resource and is loaded as such.

- A context initialization parameter, `javax.faces.application.CONFIG_FILES`, in your web deployment descriptor file that specifies one or more (comma-delimited) paths to multiple configuration files for your web application. This method is most often used for enterprise-scale applications that delegate to separate groups the responsibility for maintaining the file for each portion of a big application.

- A resource named `faces-config.xml` in the `/WEB-INF/` directory of your application. Simple web applications make their configuration files available in this way.

To access the resources registered with the application, an application developer can use an instance of the `javax.faces.application.Application` class, which is automatically created for each application. The `Application` instance acts as a centralized factory for resources that are defined in the XML file.

When an application starts up, the JavaServer Faces implementation creates a single instance of the `Application` class and configures it with the information you provided in the application configuration resource file.

Ordering of Application Configuration Resource Files

Because JavaServer Faces technology allows the use of multiple application configuration resource files stored in different locations, the order in which they are loaded by the implementation becomes important in certain situations (for example, when using application-level objects). This order can be defined through an `ordering` element and its subelements in the application configuration resource file itself. The ordering of application configuration resource files can be absolute or relative.

Absolute ordering is defined by an `absolute-ordering` element in the file. With absolute ordering, the user specifies the order in which application configuration resource files will be loaded. The following example shows an entry for absolute ordering:

File `my-faces-config.xml`:

```
<faces-config>
    <name>myJSF</name>
    <absolute-ordering>
        <name>A</name>
        <name>B</name>
        <name>C</name>
    </absolute-ordering>
</faces-config>
```

In this example, A, B, and C are different application configuration resource files and are to be loaded in the listed order.

If there is an `absolute-ordering` element in the file, only the files listed by the subelement name are processed. To process any other application configuration resource files, an `others` subelement is required. In the absence of the `others` subelement, all other unlisted files will be ignored at load time.

Relative ordering is defined by an ordering element and its subelements before and after. With relative ordering, the order in which application configuration resource files will be loaded is calculated by considering ordering entries from the different files. The following example shows some of these considerations. In the following example, config-A, config-B, and config-C are different application configuration resource files.

File config-A contains the following elements:

```
<faces-config>
    <name>config-A</name>
    <ordering>
        <before>
            <name>config-B</name>
        </before>
    </ordering>
</faces-config>
```

File config-B (not shown here) does not contain any ordering elements.

File config-C contains the following elements:

```
<faces-config>
    <name>config-C</name>
    <ordering>
        <after>
            <name>config-B</name>
        </after>
    </ordering>
</faces-config>
```

Based on the before subelement entry, file config-A will be loaded before the config-B file. Based on the after subelement entry, file config-C will be loaded after the config-B file.

In addition, a subelement others can also be nested within the before and after subelements. If the others element is present, the specified file may receive highest or lowest preference among both listed and unlisted configuration files.

If an ordering element is not present in an application configuration file, then that file will be loaded after all the files that contain ordering elements.

Configuring Managed Beans

When a page references a managed bean for the first time, the JavaServer Faces implementation initializes it based on a @ManagedBean annotation in the bean class (or a @Named annotation for CDI managed beans) or according to its configuration in the application configuration resource file. For information on using annotations to initialize beans, see "Using Annotations to Configure Managed Beans" on page 142.

You can use either annotations or the application configuration resource file to instantiate managed beans that are used in a JavaServer Faces application and to store them in scope. The managed bean creation facility is configured in the application configuration resource file using managed-bean XML elements to define each bean. This file is processed at application startup time. For information on using this facility, see "Using the managed-bean Element" on page 147.

With the managed bean creation facility, you can:

- Create beans in one centralized file that is available to the entire application, rather than conditionally instantiate beans throughout the application

- Customize a bean's properties without any additional code

- Customize a bean's property values directly from within the configuration file so that it is initialized with these values when it is created

- Using value elements, set a property of one managed bean to be the result of evaluating another value expression

This section shows you how to initialize beans using the managed bean creation facility. See "Writing Bean Properties" in *The Java EE 6 Tutorial: Basic Concepts* and "Writing Managed Bean Methods" in *The Java EE 6 Tutorial: Basic Concepts* for information on programming managed beans.

Using the managed-bean Element

A managed bean is initiated in the application configuration resource file using a managed-bean element, which represents an instance of a bean class that must exist in the application. At runtime, the JavaServer Faces implementation processes the managed-bean element. If a page references the bean, and if no bean instance exists, the JavaServer Faces implementation instantiates the bean as specified by the element configuration.

Here is an example managed bean configuration from the Duke's Bookstore case study:

```
<managed-bean eager="true">
    <managed-bean-name> Book201 </managed-bean-name>
    <managed-bean-class> dukesbookstore.model.ImageArea </managed-bean-class>
    <managed-bean-scope> application </managed-bean-scope>
    <managed-property>
        <property-name>shape</property-name>
        <value>rect</value>
    </managed-property>
    <managed-property>
        <property-name>alt</property-name>
        <value>Duke</value>
    </managed-property>
    <managed-property>
```

```
            <property-name>coords</property-name>
            <value>67,23,212,268</value>
        </managed-property>
</managed-bean>
```

Using NetBeans IDE, you can add a managed bean declaration by doing the following:

1. After opening your project in NetBeans IDE, expand the project node in the Projects pane.

2. Expand the Web Pages and WEB-INF nodes of the project node.

3. If there is no `faces-config.xml` in the project, create one as follows:

    a. From the File menu, choose New File.

    b. In the New File wizard, select the JavaServer Faces category, then select JSF Faces Configuration and click Next.

    c. On the Name and Location page, change the name and location of the file if necessary. The default file name is `faces-config.xml`.

    d. Click Finish.

4. Double-click `faces-config.xml` if the file is not already open.

5. After `faces-config.xml` opens in the editor pane, select XML from the sub-tab panel options.

6. Right-click in the editor pane.

7. From the Insert menu, choose Managed Bean.

8. In the Add Managed Bean dialog box:

    a. Type the display name of the bean in the Bean Name field.
    b. Click Browse to locate the bean's class.

9. In the Browse Class dialog box:

    a. Start typing the name of the class you are looking for in the Class Name field. While you are typing, the dialog will show the matching classes.

    b. Select the class from the Matching Classes box.

    c. Click OK.

10. In the Add Managed Bean dialog box:

    a. Select the bean's scope from the Scope menu.
    b. Click Add.

The preceding steps will add the `managed-bean` element and three elements inside of that element: a `managed-bean-name` element, a `managed-bean-class` element, and a `managed-bean-scope` element. You will need to edit the XML of the configuration file directly to further configure this managed bean.

The managed-bean-name element defines the key under which the bean will be stored in a scope. For a component's value to map to this bean, the component tag's value attribute must match the managed-bean-name up to the first period.

The managed-bean-class element defines the fully qualified name of the JavaBeans component class used to instantiate the bean.

The managed-bean element can contain zero or more managed-property elements, each corresponding to a property defined in the bean class. These elements are used to initialize the values of the bean properties. If you don't want a particular property initialized with a value when the bean is instantiated, do not include a managed-property definition for it in your application configuration resource file.

If a managed-bean element does not contain other managed-bean elements, it can contain one map-entries element or list-entries element. The map-entries element configures a set of beans that are instances of Map. The list-entries element configures a set of beans that are instances of List.

In the following example, the newsletters managed bean, representing a UISelectItems component, is configured as an ArrayList that represents a set of SelectItem objects. Each SelectItem object is in turn configured as a managed bean with properties:

```
<managed-bean>
    <managed-bean-name>newsletters</managed-bean-name>
    <managed-bean-class>java.util.ArrayList</managed-bean-class>
    <managed-bean-scope>application</managed-bean-scope>
    <list-entries>
        <value-class>javax.faces.model.SelectItem</value-class>
        <value>#{newsletter0}</value>
        <value>#{newsletter1}</value>
        <value>#{newsletter2}</value>
        <value>#{newsletter3}</value>
    </list-entries>
</managed-bean>
<managed-bean>
    <managed-bean-name>newsletter0</managed-bean-name>
    <managed-bean-class>javax.faces.model.SelectItem</managed-bean-class>
    <managed-bean-scope>none</managed-bean-scope>
    <managed-property>
        <property-name>label</property-name>
        <value>Duke's Quarterly</value>
    </managed-property>
    <managed-property>
        <property-name>value</property-name>
        <value>200</value>
    </managed-property>
</managed-bean>
...
```

This approach may be useful for quick-and-dirty creation of selection item lists, before a development team has had time to create such lists from the database. Note that each of the individual newsletter beans has a managed-bean-scope setting of none, so that they will not themselves be placed into any scope.

See "Initializing Array and List Properties" on page 153 for more information on configuring collections as beans.

To map to a property defined by a managed-property element, you must ensure that the part of a component tag's value expression after the period matches the managed-property element's property-name element. In the earlier example, the maximum property is initialized with the value 10. The following section, "Initializing Properties Using the managed-property Element" on page 150, explains in more detail how to use the managed-property element. See "Initializing Managed Bean Properties" on page 153 for an example of initializing a managed bean property.

Initializing Properties Using the managed-property Element

A managed-property element must contain a property-name element, which must match the name of the corresponding property in the bean. A managed-property element must also contain one of a set of elements that defines the value of the property. This value must be of the same type as that defined for the property in the corresponding bean. Which element you use to define the value depends on the type of the property defined in the bean. Table 7–1 lists all the elements that are used to initialize a value.

TABLE 7–1   Subelements of managed-property Elements That Define Property Values

Element	Value It Defines
list-entries	Defines the values in a list
map-entries	Defines the values of a map
null-value	Explicitly sets the property to null
value	Defines a single value, such as a String, int, or JavaServer Faces EL expression

"Using the managed-bean Element" on page 147 includes an example of initializing an int property (a primitive type) using the value subelement. You also use the value subelement to initialize String and other reference types. The rest of this section describes how to use the value subelement and other subelements to initialize properties of Java Enum types, Map, array, and Collection, as well as initialization parameters.

Referencing a Java Enum Type

A managed bean property can also be a Java Enum type (see http://docs.oracle.com/javase/6/docs/api/java/lang/Enum.html). In this case, the value element of the managed-property element must be a String that matches one of the String constants of the Enum. In other words, the String must be one of the valid values that can be returned if you were to call valueOf(Class, String) on enum, where Class is the Enum class and String is the contents of the value subelement. For example, suppose the managed bean property is the following:

```
public enum Suit { Hearts, Spades, Diamonds, Clubs}
  ...
public Suit getSuit() { ... return Suit.Hearts; }
```

Assuming you want to configure this property in the application configuration resource file, the corresponding managed-property element looks like this:

```
<managed-property>
    <property-name>Suit</property-name>
    <value>Hearts</value>
</managed-property>
```

When the system encounters this property, it iterates over each of the members of the enum and calls toString() on each member until it finds one that is exactly equal to the value from the value element.

Referencing a Context Initialization Parameter

Another powerful feature of the managed bean creation facility is the ability to reference implicit objects from a managed bean property.

Suppose you have a page that accepts data from a customer, including the customer's address. Suppose also that most of your customers live in a particular area code. You can make the area code component render this area code by saving it in an implicit object and referencing it when the page is rendered.

You can save the area code as an initial default value in the context initParam implicit object by adding a context parameter to your web application and setting its value in the deployment descriptor. For example, to set a context parameter called defaultAreaCode to 650, add a context-param element to the deployment descriptor, and give the parameter the name defaultAreaCode and the value 650.

Next, you write a managed-bean declaration that configures a property that references the parameter:

```
<managed-bean>
    <managed-bean-name>customer</managed-bean-name>
        <managed-bean-class>CustomerBean</managed-bean-class>
        <managed-bean-scope>request</managed-bean-scope>
```

```
<managed-property>
    <property-name>areaCode</property-name>
        <value>#{initParam.defaultAreaCode}</value>
    </managed-property>
    ...
</managed-bean>
```

To access the area code at the time the page is rendered, refer to the property from the area component tag's `value` attribute:

```
<h:inputText id=area value="#{customer.areaCode}"
```

Values are retrieved from other implicit objects in a similar way.

Initializing Map Properties

The `map-entries` element is used to initialize the values of a bean property with a type of `java.util.Map` if the `map-entries` element is used within a `managed-property` element. A `map-entries` element contains an optional `key-class` element, an optional `value-class` element, and zero or more `map-entry` elements.

Each of the `map-entry` elements must contain a key element and either a `null-value` or value element. Here is an example that uses the `map-entries` element:

```
<managed-bean>
    ...
    <managed-property>
        <property-name>prices</property-name>
        <map-entries>
            <map-entry>
                <key>My Early Years: Growing Up on *7</key>
                <value>30.75</value>
            </map-entry>
            <map-entry>
                <key>Web Servers for Fun and Profit</key>
                <value>40.75</value>
            </map-entry>
        </map-entries>
    </managed-property>
</managed-bean>
```

The map created from this `map-entries` tag contains two entries. By default, all the keys and values are converted to `String`. If you want to specify a different type for the keys in the map, embed the `key-class` element just inside the `map-entries` element:

```
<map-entries>
    <key-class>java.math.BigDecimal</key-class>
    ...
</map-entries>
```

This declaration will convert all the keys into `java.math.BigDecimal`. Of course, you must make sure the keys can be converted to the type you specify. The key from the example in this section cannot be converted to a `BigDecimal`, because it is a `String`.

If you want to specify a different type for all the values in the map, include the value-class element after the key-class element:

```
<map-entries>
    <key-class>int</key-class>
    <value-class>java.math.BigDecimal</value-class>
    ...
</map-entries>
```

Note that this tag sets only the type of all the value subelements.

Each map-entry in the preceding example includes a value subelement. The value subelement defines a single value, which will be converted to the type specified in the bean.

Instead of using a map-entries element, it is also possible to assign the entire map using a value element that specifies a map-typed expression.

Initializing Array and List Properties

The list-entries element is used to initialize the values of an array or List property. Each individual value of the array or List is initialized using a value or null-value element. Here is an example:

```
<managed-bean>
    ...
    <managed-property>
        <property-name>books</property-name>
        <list-entries>
            <value-class>java.lang.String</value-class>
            <value>Web Servers for Fun and Profit</value>
            <value>#{myBooks.bookId[3]}</value>
            <null-value/>
        </list-entries>
    </managed-property>
</managed-bean>
```

This example initializes an array or a List. The type of the corresponding property in the bean determines which data structure is created. The list-entries element defines the list of values in the array or List. The value element specifies a single value in the array or List and can reference a property in another bean. The null-value element will cause the setBooks method to be called with an argument of null. A null property cannot be specified for a property whose data type is a Java primitive, such as int or boolean.

Initializing Managed Bean Properties

Sometimes you might want to create a bean that also references other managed beans so you can construct a graph or a tree of beans. For example, suppose you want to create a bean representing a customer's information, including the mailing address and street address, each of which is also a bean. The following managed-bean declarations create a CustomerBean instance that has two AddressBean properties: one representing the mailing address, and the other representing the street address. This declaration results in a tree of beans with CustomerBean as its root and the two AddressBean objects as children.

```
<managed-bean>
    <managed-bean-name>customer</managed-bean-name>
    <managed-bean-class>
        com.example.mybeans.CustomerBean
    </managed-bean-class>
    <managed-bean-scope> request </managed-bean-scope>
    <managed-property>
        <property-name>mailingAddress</property-name>
        <value>#{addressBean}</value>
    </managed-property>
    <managed-property>
        <property-name>streetAddress</property-name>
        <value>#{addressBean}</value>
    </managed-property>
    <managed-property>
        <property-name>customerType</property-name>
        <value>New</value>
    </managed-property>
</managed-bean>
<managed-bean>
    <managed-bean-name>addressBean</managed-bean-name>
    <managed-bean-class>
        com.example.mybeans.AddressBean
    </managed-bean-class>
    <managed-bean-scope> none </managed-bean-scope>
    <managed-property>
        <property-name>street</property-name>
        <null-value/>
    <managed-property>
        ...
</managed-bean>
```

The first CustomerBean declaration (with the managed-bean-name of customer) creates a CustomerBean in request scope. This bean has two properties, mailingAddress and streetAddress. These properties use the value element to reference a bean named addressBean.

The second managed bean declaration defines an AddressBean, but does not create it, because its managed-bean-scope element defines a scope of none. Recall that a scope of none means that the bean is created only when something else references it. Because both the mailingAddress and the streetAddress properties reference addressBean using the value element, two instances of AddressBean are created when CustomerBean is created.

When you create an object that points to other objects, do not try to point to an object with a shorter life span, because it might be impossible to recover that scope's resources when it goes away. A session-scoped object, for example, cannot point to a request-scoped object. And objects with none scope have no effective life span managed by the framework, so they can point only to other none-scoped objects. Table 7–2 outlines all of the allowed connections.

TABLE 7–2   Allowable Connections Between Scoped Objects

An Object of This Scope	May Point to an Object of This Scope
none	none
application	none, application
session	none, application, session
request	none, application, session, request, view
view	none, application, session, view

Be sure not to allow cyclical references between objects. For example, neither of the AddressBean objects in the preceding example should point back to the CustomerBean object, because CustomerBean already points to the AddressBean objects.

Initializing Maps and Lists

In addition to configuring Map and List properties, you can also configure a Map and a List directly so that you can reference them from a tag rather than referencing a property that wraps a Map or a List.

Registering Application Messages

Application messages can include any strings displayed to the user, as well as custom error messages (which are displayed by the message and messages tags) for your custom converters or validators. To make messages available at application startup time, do one of the following:

- Queue an individual message onto the javax.faces.context.FacesContext instance programmatically, as described in "Using FacesMessage to Create a Message" on page 157

- Register all the messages with your application using the application configuration resource file

Here is the section of the `faces-config.xml` file that registers the messages for the Duke's Bookstore case study application:

```
<application>
    <resource-bundle>
        <base-name>dukesbookstore.web.messages.Messages</base-name>
        <var>bundle</var>
    </resource-bundle>
    <locale-config>
        <default-locale>en</default-locale>
        <supported-locale>es</supported-locale>
        <supported-locale>de</supported-locale>
        <supported-locale>fr</supported-locale>
    </locale-config>
</application>
```

This set of elements causes the application to be populated with the messages that are contained in the specified resource bundle.

The `resource-bundle` element represents a set of localized messages. It must contain the fully qualified path to the resource bundle containing the localized messages (in this case, `dukestutoring.web.messages.Messages`). The `var` element defines the EL name by which page authors refer to the resource bundle.

The `locale-config` element lists the default locale and the other supported locales. The `locale-config` element enables the system to find the correct locale based on the browser's language settings.

The `supported-locale` and `default-locale` tags accept the lowercase, two-character codes defined by ISO 639 (see `http://ftp.ics.uci.edu/pub/ietf/http/related/iso639.txt`). Make sure your resource bundle actually contains the messages for the locales you specify with these tags.

To access the localized message, the application developer merely references the key of the message from the resource bundle.

You can pull localized text into an `alt` tag for a graphic image, as in the following example:

```
<h:graphicImage id="mapImage"
                name="book_all.jpg"
                library="images"
                alt="#{bundle.ChooseBook}"
                usemap="#bookMap" />
```

The `alt` attribute can accept value expressions. In this case, the `alt` attribute refers to localized text that will be included in the alternative text of the image rendered by this tag.

Using FacesMessage to Create a Message

Instead of registering messages in the application configuration resource file, you can access the java.util.ResourceBundle directly from managed bean code. The code snippet below locates an email error message:

```
String message = "";
...
message = ExampleBean.loadErrorMessage(context,
    ExampleBean.EX_RESOURCE_BUNDLE_NAME,
        "EMailError");
context.addMessage(toValidate.getClientId(context),
    new FacesMessage(message));
```

These lines call the bean's loadErrorMessage method to get the message from the ResourceBundle. Here is the loadErrorMessage method:

```
public static String loadErrorMessage(FacesContext context,
    String basename, String key) {
    if ( bundle == null ) {
        try {
            bundle = ResourceBundle.getBundle(basename,
                context.getViewRoot().getLocale());
        } catch (Exception e) {
            return null;
        }
    }
    return bundle.getString(key);
}
```

Referencing Error Messages

A JavaServer Faces page uses the message or messages tags to access error messages, as explained in "Displaying Error Messages with the h:message and h:messages Tags" in *The Java EE 6 Tutorial: Basic Concepts*.

The error messages these tags access include:

- The standard error messages that accompany the standard converters and validators that ship with the API. See Section 2.5.2.4 of the JavaServer Faces specification for a complete list of standard error messages.

- Custom error messages contained in resource bundles registered with the application by the application architect using the resource-bundle element in the configuration file.

When a converter or validator is registered on an input component, the appropriate error message is automatically queued on the component.

A page author can override the error messages queued on a component by using the following attributes of the component's tag:

- `converterMessage`: References the error message to display when the data on the enclosing component can not be converted by the converter registered on this component.

- `requiredMessage`: References the error message to display when no value has been entered into the enclosing component.

- `validatorMessage`: References the error message to display when the data on the enclosing component cannot be validated by the validator registered on this component.

All three attributes are enabled to take literal values and value expressions. If an attribute uses a value expression, this expression references the error message in a resource bundle. This resource bundle must be made available to the application in one of the following ways:

- By the application architect using the `resource-bundle` element in the configuration file

- By the page author using the `f:loadBundle` tag

Conversely, the `resource-bundle` element must be used to make available to the application those resource bundles containing custom error messages that are queued on the component as a result of a custom converter or validator being registered on the component.

The following tags show how to specify the `requiredMessage` attribute using a value expression to reference an error message:

```
<h:inputText id="ccno" size="19"
    required="true"
    requiredMessage="#{customMessages.ReqMessage}" >
    ...
</h:inputText>
<h:message styleClass="error-message" for="ccno"/>
```

The value expression used by `requiredMessage` in this example references the error message with the ReqMessage key in the resource bundle, `customMessages`.

This message replaces the corresponding message queued on the component and will display wherever the `message` or `messages` tag is placed on the page.

Using Default Validators

In addition to the validators you declare on the components, you can also specify zero or more default validators in the application configuration resource file. The default validator applies to all javax.faces.component.UIInput instances in a view or component tree and is appended after the local defined validators. Here is an example of a default validator registered in the application configuration resource file:

```
<faces-config>
    <application>
        <default-validators>
            <validator-id>javax.faces.Bean</validator-id>
        </default-validators>
    <application/>
</faces-config>
```

Registering a Custom Validator

If the application developer provides an implementation of the javax.faces.validator.Validator interface to perform validation, you must register this custom validator either by using the @FacesValidator annotation, as described in "Implementing the Validator Interface" on page 129, or by using the validator XML element in the application configuration resource file:

```
<validator>
    ...
    <validator-id>FormatValidator</validator-id>
    <validator-class>
        myapplication.validators.FormatValidator
    </validator-class>
    <attribute>
        ...
        <attribute-name>formatPatterns</attribute-name>
        <attribute-class>java.lang.String</attribute-class>
    </attribute>
</validator>
```

Attributes specified in a validator tag override any settings in the @FacesValidator annotation.

The validator-id and validator-class elements are required subelements. The validator-id element represents the identifier under which the Validator class should be registered. This ID is used by the tag class corresponding to the custom validator tag.

The validator-class element represents the fully qualified class name of the Validator class.

The attribute element identifies an attribute associated with the Validator implementation. It has required attribute-name and attribute-class subelements.

The attribute-name element refers to the name of the attribute as it appears in the validator tag. The attribute-class element identifies the Java type of the value associated with the attribute.

"Creating and Using a Custom Validator" on page 128 explains how to implement the Validator interface.

"Using a Custom Validator" on page 132 explains how to reference the validator from the page.

Registering a Custom Converter

As is the case with a custom validator, if the application developer creates a custom converter, you must register it with the application either by using the @FacesConverter annotation, as described in "Creating a Custom Converter" on page 123, or by using the converter XML element in the application configuration resource file. Here is a hypothetical converter configuration for CreditCardConverter from the Duke's Bookstore case study:

```
<converter>
    <description>
        Converter for credit card numbers that normalizes
        the input to a standard format
    </description>
    <converter-id>CreditCardConverter</converter-id>
    <converter-class>
        dukesbookstore.converters.CreditCardConverter
    </converter-class>
</converter>
```

Attributes specified in a converter tag override any settings in the @FacesConverter annotation.

The converter element represents a javax.faces.convert.Converter implementation and contains required converter-id and converter-class elements.

The converter-id element identifies an ID that is used by the converter attribute of a UI component tag to apply the converter to the component's data. "Using a Custom Converter" on page 126 includes an example of referencing the custom converter from a component tag.

The converter-class element identifies the Converter implementation.

"Creating and Using a Custom Converter" on page 123 explains how to create a custom converter.

Configuring Navigation Rules

Navigation between different pages of a JavaServer Faces application, such as choosing the next page to be displayed after a button or hyperlink component is clicked, is defined by a set of rules. Navigation rules can be implicit, or they can be explicitly defined in the application configuration resource file. For more information on implicit navigation rules, see "Implicit Navigation Rules" on page 164.

Each navigation rule specifies how to navigate from one page to another page or set of pages. The JavaServer Faces implementation chooses the proper navigation rule according to which page is currently displayed.

After the proper navigation rule is selected, the choice of which page to access next from the current page depends on two factors:

- The action method invoked when the component was clicked
- The logical outcome referenced by the component's tag or returned from the action method

The outcome can be anything the developer chooses, but Table 7–3 lists some outcomes commonly used in web applications.

TABLE 7–3 Common Outcome Strings

Outcome	What It Means
success	Everything worked. Go on to the next page.
failure	Something is wrong. Go on to an error page.
login	The user needs to log in first. Go on to the login page.
no results	The search did not find anything. Go to the search page again.

Usually, the action method performs some processing on the form data of the current page. For example, the method might check whether the user name and password entered in the form match the user name and password on file. If they match, the method returns the outcome success. Otherwise, it returns the outcome failure. As this example demonstrates, both the method used to process the action and the outcome returned are necessary to determine the correct page to access.

Here is a navigation rule that could be used with the example just described:

```
<navigation-rule>
    <from-view-id>/login.xhtml</from-view-id>
    <navigation-case>
        <from-action>#{LoginForm.login}</from-action>
        <from-outcome>success</from-outcome>
```

```
            <to-view-id>/storefront.xhtml</to-view-id>
        </navigation-case>
        <navigation-case>
            <from-action>#{LoginForm.logon}</from-action>
            <from-outcome>failure</from-outcome>
            <to-view-id>/logon.xhtml</to-view-id>
        </navigation-case>
    </navigation-rule>
```

This navigation rule defines the possible ways to navigate from login.xhtml. Each navigation-case element defines one possible navigation path from login.xhtml. The first navigation-case says that if LoginForm.login returns an outcome of success, then storefront.xhtml will be accessed. The second navigation-case says that login.xhtml will be re-rendered if LoginForm.login returns failure.

The configuration of an application's page flow consists of a set of navigation rules. Each rule is defined by the navigation-rule element in the faces-config.xml file.

Each navigation-rule element corresponds to one component tree identifier defined by the optional from-view-id element. This means that each rule defines all the possible ways to navigate from one particular page in the application. If there is no from-view-id element, the navigation rules defined in the navigation-rule element apply to all the pages in the application. The from-view-id element also allows wildcard matching patterns. For example, this from-view-id element says that the navigation rule applies to all the pages in the books directory:

```
<from-view-id>/books/*</from-view-id>
```

A navigation-rule element can contain zero or more navigation-case elements. The navigation-case element defines a set of matching criteria. When these criteria are satisfied, the application will navigate to the page defined by the to-view-id element contained in the same navigation-case element.

The navigation criteria are defined by optional from-outcome and from-action elements. The from-outcome element defines a logical outcome, such as success. The from-action element uses a method expression to refer to an action method that returns a String, which is the logical outcome. The method performs some logic to determine the outcome and returns the outcome.

The navigation-case elements are checked against the outcome and the method expression in this order:

1. Cases specifying both a from-outcome value and a from-action value. Both of these elements can be used if the action method returns different outcomes depending on the result of the processing it performs.

2. Cases specifying only a from-outcome value. The from-outcome element must match either the outcome defined by the action attribute of the javax.faces.component.UICommand component or the outcome returned by the method referred to by the UICommand component.

3. Cases specifying only a from-action value. This value must match the action expression specified by the component tag.

When any of these cases is matched, the component tree defined by the to-view-id element will be selected for rendering.

▼ To Configure a Navigation Rule

Using NetBeans IDE, you can configure a navigation rule by doing the following.

1 After opening your project in NetBeans IDE, expand the project node in the Projects pane.

2 Expand the Web Pages and WEB-INF nodes of the project node.

3 Double-click faces-config.xml.

4 After faces-config.xml opens in the editor pane, right-click in the editor pane.

5 From the Insert menu, choose Navigation Rule.

6 In the Add Navigation Rule dialog:

   a. Enter or browse for the page that represents the starting view for this navigation rule.

   b. Click Add.

7 Right-click again in the editor pane.

8 From the Insert menu, choose Navigation Case.

9　In the Add Navigation Case dialog box:

a.　From the From View menu, choose the page that represents the starting view for the navigation rule (from Step 6 a).

b.　(optional) In the From Action field, type the action method invoked when the component that triggered navigation is activated.

c.　(optional) In the From Outcome field, enter the logical outcome string that the activated component references from its `action` attribute.

d.　From the To View menu, choose or browse for the page that will be opened if this navigation case is selected by the navigation system.

e.　Click Add.

See Also　"Referencing a Method That Performs Navigation" in *The Java EE 6 Tutorial: Basic Concepts* explains how to use a component tag's `action` attribute to point to an action method. "Writing a Method to Handle Navigation" in *The Java EE 6 Tutorial: Basic Concepts* explains how to write an action method.

Implicit Navigation Rules

JavaServer Faces technology supports implicit navigation rules for Facelets applications. Implicit navigation applies when `navigation-rules` are not configured in the application configuration resource files.

When you add a component such as a `commandButton` in a page, and assign another page as the value for its `action` property, the default navigation handler will try to match a suitable page within the application implicitly.

```
<h:commandButton value="submit" action="response">
```

In the above example, the default navigation handler will try to locate a page named `response.xhtml` within the application and navigate to it.

Registering a Custom Renderer with a Render Kit

When the application developer creates a custom renderer, as described in "Delegating Rendering to a Renderer" on page 114, you must register it using the appropriate render kit. Because the image map application implements an HTML image map, the AreaRenderer and MapRenderer classes in the Duke's Bookstore case study should be registered using the HTML render kit.

You register the renderer either by using the @FacesRenderer annotation, as described in "Creating the Renderer Class" on page 115, or by using the render-kit element of the application configuration resource file. Here is a hypothetical configuration of AreaRenderer:

```
<render-kit>
    <renderer>
        <component-family>Area</component-family>
        <renderer-type>DemoArea</renderer-type>
        <renderer-class>
            dukesbookstore.renderers.AreaRenderer
        </renderer-class>
        <attribute>
            <attribute-name>onmouseout</attribute-name>
            <attribute-class>java.lang.String</attribute-class>
        </attribute>
        <attribute>
            <attribute-name>onmouseover</attribute-name>
            <attribute-class>java.lang.String</attribute-class>
        </attribute>
        <attribute>
            <attribute-name>styleClass</attribute-name>
            <attribute-class>java.lang.String</attribute-class>
        </attribute>
    </renderer>
    ...
```

Attributes specified in a renderer tag override any settings in the @FacesRenderer annotation.

The render-kit element represents a javax.faces.render.RenderKit implementation. If no render-kit-id is specified, the default HTML render kit is assumed. The renderer element represents a javax.faces.render.Renderer implementation. By nesting the renderer element inside the render-kit element, you are registering the renderer with the RenderKit implementation associated with the render-kit element.

The renderer-class is the fully qualified class name of the Renderer.

The component-family and renderer-type elements are used by a component to find renderers that can render it. The component-family identifier must match that returned by the component class's getFamily method. The component family represents a component or set of components that a particular renderer can render. The renderer-type must match that returned by the getRendererType method of the tag handler class.

By using the component family and renderer type to look up renderers for components, the JavaServer Faces implementation allows a component to be rendered by multiple renderers and allows a renderer to render multiple components.

Each of the attribute tags specifies a render-dependent attribute and its type. The attribute element doesn't affect the runtime execution of your application. Rather, it provides information to tools about the attributes the Renderer supports.

The object responsible for rendering a component (be it the component itself or a renderer to which the component delegates the rendering) can use facets to aid in the rendering process. These facets allow the custom component developer to control some aspects of rendering the component. Consider this custom component tag example:

```
<d:dataScroller>
    <f:facet name="header">
        <h:panelGroup>
            <h:outputText value="Account Id"/>
            <h:outputText value="Customer Name"/>
            <h:outputText value="Total Sales"/>
        </h:panelGroup>
    </f:facet>
    <f:facet name="next">
        <h:panelGroup>
            <h:outputText value="Next"/>
            <h:graphicImage url="/images/arrow-right.gif" />
        </h:panelGroup>
    </f:facet>
    ...
</d:dataScroller>
```

The dataScroller component tag includes a component that will render the header and a component that will render the Next button. If the renderer associated with this component renders the facets, you can include the following facet elements in the renderer element:

```
<facet>
    <description>This facet renders as the header of the table. It should be
        a panelGroup with the same number of columns as the data
    </description>
    <display-name>header</display-name>
    <facet-name>header</facet-name>
</facet>
<facet>
    <description>This facet renders as the content of the "next" button in
        the scroller. It should be a panelGroup that includes an outputText
        tag that has the text "Next" and a right arrow icon.
    </description>
```

```
    <display-name>Next</display-name>
    <facet-name>next</facet-name>
</facet>
```

If a component that supports facets provides its own rendering and you want to include facet elements in the application configuration resource file, you need to put them in the component's configuration rather than the renderer's configuration.

Registering a Custom Component

In addition to registering custom renderers (as explained in the preceding section), you also must register the custom components that are usually associated with the custom renderers. You use either a @FacesComponent annotation, as described in "Creating Custom Component Classes" on page 106, or the component element of the application configuration resource file.

Here is a hypothetical component element from the application configuration resource file that registers AreaComponent:

```
<component>
    <component-type>DemoArea</component-type>
    <component-class>
        dukesbookstore.components.AreaComponent
    </component-class>
    <property>
        <property-name>alt</property-name>
        <property-class>java.lang.String</property-class>
    </property>
    <property>
        <property-name>coords</property-name>
        <property-class>java.lang.String</property-class>
    </property>
    <property>
        <property-name>shape</property-name>
        <property-class>java.lang.String</property-class>
    </property>
</component>
```

Attributes specified in a component tag override any settings in the @FacesComponent annotation.

The component-type element indicates the name under which the component should be registered. Other objects referring to this component use this name. For example, the component-type element in the configuration for AreaComponent defines a value of DemoArea, which matches the value returned by the AreaTag class's getComponentType method.

The component-class element indicates the fully qualified class name of the component. The property elements specify the component properties and their types.

If the custom component can include facets, you can configure the facets in the component configuration using facet elements, which are allowed after the component-class elements. See "Registering a Custom Renderer with a Render Kit" on page 165 for further details on configuring facets.

Basic Requirements of a JavaServer Faces Application

In addition to configuring your application, you must satisfy other requirements of JavaServer Faces applications, including properly packaging all the necessary files and providing a deployment descriptor. This section describes how to perform these administrative tasks.

JavaServer Faces applications can be packaged in a WAR file, which must conform to specific requirements to execute across different containers. At a minimum, a WAR file for a JavaServer Faces application must contain the following:

- A web application deployment descriptor, called web.xml, to configure resources required by a web application
- A specific set of JAR files containing essential classes
- A set of application classes, JavaServer Faces pages, and other required resources, such as image files

A WAR file may also contain:

- An application configuration resource file, which configures application resources
- A set of tag library descriptor files

For example, a Java Server Faces web application WAR file using Facelets typically has the following directory structure:

```
$PROJECT_DIR
[Web Pages]
+- /[xhtml documents]
+- /resources
+- /WEB-INF
   +- /classes
   +- /lib
   +- /web.xml
   +- /faces-config.xml (optional)
   +- /*.taglib.xml (optional)
   +- /glassfish-web.xml
```

The web.xml file (or web deployment descriptor), the set of JAR files, and the set of application files must be contained in the WEB-INF directory of the WAR file.

Configuring an Application with a Web Deployment Descriptor

Web applications are commonly configured using elements contained in the web application deployment descriptor, web.xml. The deployment descriptor for a JavaServer Faces application must specify certain configurations, including the following:

- The servlet used to process JavaServer Faces requests
- The servlet mapping for the processing servlet
- The path to the configuration resource file, if it exists and is not located in a default location

The deployment descriptor can also include other, optional configurations, such as:

- Specifying where component state is saved
- Encrypting state saved on the client
- Compressing state saved on the client
- Restricting access to pages containing JavaServer Faces tags
- Turning on XML validation
- Specifying the Project Stage
- Verifying custom objects

This section gives more details on these configurations. Where appropriate, it also describes how you can make these configurations using NetBeans IDE.

Identifying the Servlet for Lifecycle Processing

A requirement of a JavaServer Faces application is that all requests to the application that reference previously saved JavaServer Faces components must go through javax.faces.webapp.FacesServlet. A FacesServlet instance manages the request processing lifecycle for web applications and initializes the resources required by JavaServer Faces technology.

Before a JavaServer Faces application can launch its first web page, the web container must invoke the FacesServlet instance in order for the application lifecycle process to start. See "The Lifecycle of a JavaServer Faces Application" on page 50 for more information.

The following example shows the default configuration of the FacesServlet:

```
<servlet>
    <servlet-name>FacesServlet</servlet-name>
    <servlet-class>javax.faces.webapp.FacesServlet</servlet-class>
    </servlet>
```

You provide a mapping configuration entry to make sure the FacesServlet instance is invoked. The mapping to FacesServlet can be a prefix mapping, such as /faces/*, or an extension mapping, such as *.xhtml. The mapping is used to identify a page as having JavaServer Faces content. Because of this, the URL to the first page of the application must include the URL pattern mapping.

The following elements, commonly used in the tutorial examples, specify a prefix mapping:

```
<servlet-mapping>
    <servlet-name>FacesServlet</servlet-name>
    <url-pattern>/faces/* </url-pattern>
</servlet-mapping>
...
<welcome-file-list>
    <welcome-file>faces/greeting.xhtml</welcome-file>
</welcome-file-list>
```

The following elements, also commonly used in the tutorial examples, specify an extension mapping:

```
<servlet-mapping>
    <servlet-name>Faces Servlet</servlet-name>
    <url-pattern>*.xhtml</url-pattern>
</servlet-mapping>
...
<welcome-file-list>
    <welcome-file>index.xhtml</welcome-file>
</welcome-file-list>
```

When you use this mechanism, users access the application as shown in the following example:

```
http://localhost:8080/guessNumber
```

In the case of extension mapping, if a request comes to the server for a page with an .xhtml extension, the container will send the request to the FacesServlet instance, which will expect a corresponding page of the same name containing the content to exist.

If you are using NetBeans IDE to create your application, a web deployment descriptor is automatically created for you with default configurations. If you created your application without an IDE, you can create a web deployment descriptor.

▼ To Specify a Path to an Application Configuration Resource File

As explained in "Application Configuration Resource File" on page 144, an application can have multiple application configuration resource files. If these files are not located in the directories that the implementation searches by default or the files are not named faces-config.xml, you need to specify paths to these files.

To specify these paths using NetBeans IDE, do the following.

1   Expand the node of your project in the Projects pane.

2   Expand the Web Pages and WEB-INF nodes that are under the project node.

3   Double-click web.xml.

4   After the web.xml file appears in the editor pane, click General at the top of the editor pane.

5   Expand the Context Parameters node.

6   Click Add.

7   In the Add Context Parameter dialog:

    a. Type javax.faces.CONFIG_FILES in the Param Name field.

    b. Type the path to your configuration file in the Param Value field.

    c. Click OK.

8   Repeat steps 1 through 7 for each configuration file.

▼ To Specify Where State Is Saved

For all the components in a web application, you can specify in your deployment descriptor where you want the state to be saved, on either client or server. You do this by setting a context parameter in your deployment descriptor. By default, state is saved on the server, so you need to specify this context parameter only if you want to save state on the client. See "Saving and Restoring State" on page 113 for information on the advantages and disadvantages of each location.

To specify where state is saved using NetBeans IDE, do the following.

1   Expand the node of your project in the Projects pane.

2   Expand the Web Pages and WEB-INF nodes under the project node.

3   Double-click web.xml.

4   After the web.xml file appears in the editor pane, click General at the top of the editor pane.

5   Expand the Context Parameters node.

6   In the Add Context Parameter dialog:

   a. Type `javax.faces.STATE_SAVING_METHOD` in the Param Name field.

   b. Type `client` or `server` in the Param Value field.

   c. Click OK.

More Information   Implementation of State Saving

If state is saved on the client, the state of the entire view is rendered to a hidden field on the page. The JavaServer Faces implementation saves the state on the server by default. Duke's Forest saves its state on the client.

Configuring Project Stage

Project Stage is a context parameter identifying the status of a JavaServer Faces application in the software lifecycle. The stage of an application can affect the behavior of the application. For example, error messages can be displayed during the Development stage but suppressed during the Production stage.

The possible Project Stage values are as follows:

- `Development`
- `UnitTest`
- `SystemTest`
- `Production`

Project Stage is configured through a context parameter in the web deployment descriptor file. Here is an example:

```
<context-param>
    <param-name>javax.faces.PROJECT_STAGE</param-name>
    <param-value>Development</param-value>
</context-param>
```

If no Project Stage is defined, the default stage is `Development`. You can also add custom stages according to your requirements.

Including the Classes, Pages, and Other Resources

When packaging web applications using the included build scripts, you'll notice that the scripts package resources in the following ways:

- All web pages are placed at the top level of the WAR file.
- The faces-config.xml file and the web.xml file are packaged in the WEB-INF directory.
- All packages are stored in the WEB-INF/classes/ directory.
- All application JAR files are packaged in the WEB-INF/lib/ directory.
- All resource files are either under the root of the web application /resources directory, or in the web application's classpath, META-INF/resources/*resourceIdentifier* directory. For more information on resources, see Chapter 5, "Introduction to Facelets," in *The Java EE 6 Tutorial: Basic Concepts*.

When packaging your own applications, you can use NetBeans IDE or you can use the build scripts such as those created for Ant. You can modify the build scripts to fit your situation. However, you can continue to package your WAR files by using the directory structure described in this section, because this technique complies with the commonly accepted practice for packaging web applications.

Uploading Files with Java Servlet Technology

Supporting file uploads is a very basic and common requirement for many web applications. Prior to Servlet 3.0, implementing file upload required the use of external libraries or complex input processing. Version 3.0 of the Java Servlet specification helps to provide a viable solution to the problem in a generic and portable way. The Servlet 3.0 specification supports file upload out of the box, so any web container that implements the specification can parse multipart requests and make mime attachments available through the `HttpServletRequest` object.

A new annotation, `javax.servlet.annotation.MultipartConfig`, is used to indicate that the servlet on which it is declared expects requests to made using the `multipart/form-data` MIME type. Servlets that are annotated with `@MultipartConfig` can retrieve the `Part` components of a given `multipart/form-data` request by calling the `request.getPart(String name)` or `request.getParts()` method.

The following topics are addressed here:

- "The `@MultipartConfig` Annotation" on page 175
- "The `getParts` and `getPart` Methods" on page 176
- "The `fileupload` Example Application" on page 177

The `@MultipartConfig` Annotation

The `@MultipartConfig` annotation supports the following optional attributes:

- `location`: An absolute path to a directory on the file system. The `location` attribute does *not* support a path relative to the application context. This location is used to store files temporarily while the parts are processed or when the size of the file exceeds the specified `fileSizeThreshold` setting. The default location is "".
- `fileSizeThreshold`: The file size in bytes after which the file will be temporarily stored on disk. The default size is 0 bytes.

- MaxFileSize: The maximum size allowed for uploaded files, in bytes. If the size of any uploaded file is greater than this size, the web container will throw an exception (IllegalStateException). The default size is unlimited.

- maxRequestSize: The maximum size allowed for a multipart/form-data request, in bytes. The web container will throw an exception if the overall size of all uploaded files exceeds this threshold. The default size is unlimited.

For, example, the @MultipartConfig annotation could be constructed as follows:

```
@MultipartConfig(location="/tmp", fileSizeThreshold=1024*1024,
    maxFileSize=1024*1024*5, maxRequestSize=1024*1024*5*5)
```

Instead of using the @MultipartConfig annotation to hard-code these attributes in your file upload servlet, you could add the following as a child element of the servlet configuration element in the web.xml file.

```
<multipart-config>
    <location>/tmp</location>
    <max-file-size>20848820</max-file-size>
    <max-request-size>418018841</max-request-size>
    <file-size-threshold>1048576</file-size-threshold>
</multipart-config>
```

The getParts and getPart Methods

Servlet 3.0 supports two additional HttpServletRequest methods:

- Collection<Part> getParts()
- Part getPart(String name)

The request.getParts() method returns collections of all Part objects. If you have more than one input of type file, multiple Part objects are returned. Since Part objects are named, the getPart(String name) method can be used to access a particular Part. Alternatively, the getParts() method, which returns an Iterable<Part>, can be used to get an Iterator over all the Part objects.

The javax.servlet.http.Part interface is a simple one, providing methods that allow introspection of each Part. The methods do the following:

- Retrieve the name, size, and content-type of the Part
- Query the headers submitted with a Part
- Delete a Part
- Write a Part out to disk

For example, the Part interface provides the write(String filename) method to write the file with the specified name. The file can then be saved in the directory specified with the location attribute of the @MultipartConfig annotation or, in the case of the fileupload example, in the location specified by the Destination field in the form.

The fileupload Example Application

The fileupload example illustrates how to implement and use the file upload feature.

The Duke's Forest case study provides a more complex example that uploads an image file and stores its content in a database.

Architecture of the fileupload Example Application

The fileupload example application consists of a single servlet and an HTML form that makes a file upload request to the servlet.

This example includes a very simple HTML form with two fields, File and Destination. The input type, file, enables a user to browse the local file system to select the file. When the file is selected, it is sent to the server as a part of a POST request. During this process two mandatory restrictions are applied to the form with input type file:

- The enctype attribute must be set to a value of multipart/form-data.
- Its method must be POST.

When the form is specified in this manner, the entire request is sent to the server in encoded form. The servlet then handles the request to process the incoming file data and to extract a file from the stream. The destination is the path to the location where the file will be saved on your computer. Pressing the Upload button at the bottom of the form posts the data to the servlet, which saves the file in the specified destination.

The HTML form in *tut-install*/examples/web/fileupload/web/index.html is as follows:

```
<!DOCTYPE html>
<html lang="en">
    <head>
        <title>File Upload</title>
        <meta http-equiv="Content-Type" content="text/html; charset=UTF-8">
    </head>
    <body>
        <form method="POST" action="upload" enctype="multipart/form-data" >
            File:
            <input type="file" name="file" id="file" /> <br/>
            Destination:
            <input type="text" value="/tmp" name="destination"/>
            </br>
            <input type="submit" value="Upload" name="upload" id="upload" />
```

```
        </form>
      </body>
</html>
```

A POST request method is used when the client needs to send data to the server as part of the request, such as when uploading a file or submitting a completed form. In contrast, a GET request method sends a URL and headers only to the server, whereas POST requests also include a message body. This allows arbitrary-length data of any type to be sent to the server. A header field in the POST request usually indicates the message body's Internet media type.

When submitting a form, the browser streams the content in, combining all parts, with each part representing a field of a form. Parts are named after the input elements and are separated from each other with string delimiters named boundary.

This is what submitted data from the fileupload form looks like, after selecting sample.txt as the file that will be uploaded to the tmp directory on the local file system:

```
POST /fileupload/upload HTTP/1.1
Host: localhost:8080
Content-Type: multipart/form-data;
boundary=-------------------------263081694432439
Content-Length: 441
---------------------------263081694432439
Content-Disposition: form-data; name="file"; filename="sample.txt"
Content-Type: text/plain

Data from sample file
---------------------------263081694432439
Content-Disposition: form-data; name="destination"

/tmp
---------------------------263081694432439
Content-Disposition: form-data; name="upload"

Upload
---------------------------263081694432439--
```

The servlet FileUploadServlet.java can be found in the *tut-install*/examples/web/fileupload/src/java/fileupload/ directory. The servlet begins as follows:

```
@WebServlet(name = "FileUploadServlet", urlPatterns = {"/upload"})
@MultipartConfig
public class FileUploadServlet extends HttpServlet {

    private final static Logger LOGGER =
            Logger.getLogger(FileUploadServlet.class.getCanonicalName());
```

The @WebServlet annotation uses the urlPatterns property to define servlet mappings.

The @MultipartConfig annotation indicates that the servlet expects requests to made using the multipart/form-data MIME type.

The processRequest method retrieves the destination and file part from the request, then calls the getFileName method to retrieve the file name from the file part. The method then creates a FileOutputStream and copies the file to the specified destination. The error-handling section of the method catches and handles some of the most common reasons why a file would not be found. The processRequest and getFileName methods look like this:

```
protected void processRequest(HttpServletRequest request,
        HttpServletResponse response)
        throws ServletException, IOException {
    response.setContentType("text/html;charset=UTF-8");

    // Create path components to save the file
    final String path = request.getParameter("destination");
    final Part filePart = request.getPart("file");
    final String fileName = getFileName(filePart);

    OutputStream out = null;
    InputStream filecontent = null;
    final PrintWriter writer = response.getWriter();

    try {
        out = new FileOutputStream(new File(path + File.separator
                + fileName));
        filecontent = filePart.getInputStream();

        int read = 0;
        final byte[] bytes = new byte[1024];

        while ((read = filecontent.read(bytes)) != -1) {
            out.write(bytes, 0, read);
        }
        writer.println("New file " + fileName + " created at " + path);
        LOGGER.log(Level.INFO, "File{0}being uploaded to {1}",
                new Object[]{fileName, path});
    } catch (FileNotFoundException fne) {
        writer.println("You either did not specify a file to upload or are "
                + "trying to upload a file to a protected or nonexistent "
                + "location.");
        writer.println("<br/> ERROR: " + fne.getMessage());

        LOGGER.log(Level.SEVERE, "Problems during file upload. Error: {0}",
                new Object[]{fne.getMessage()});
    } finally {
        if (out != null) {
            out.close();
        }
        if (filecontent != null) {
            filecontent.close();
        }
        if (writer != null) {
            writer.close();
        }
```

```
        }
    }

    private String getFileName(final Part part) {
        final String partHeader = part.getHeader("content-disposition");
        LOGGER.log(Level.INFO, "Part Header = {0}", partHeader);
        for (String content : part.getHeader("content-disposition").split(";")) {
            if (content.trim().startsWith("filename")) {
                return content.substring(
                        content.indexOf('=') + 1).trim().replace("\"", "");
            }
        }
        return null;
    }
```

Running the fileupload Example

You can use either NetBeans IDE or Ant to build, package, deploy, and run the fileupload example.

▼ To Build, Package, and Deploy the fileupload Example Using NetBeans IDE

1 From the File menu, choose Open Project.

2 In the Open Project dialog, navigate to:

   tut-install/examples/web/

3 Select the fileupload folder.

4 Select the Open as Main Project checkbox.

5 Click Open Project.

6 In the Projects tab, right-click fileupload and select Deploy.

▼ To Build, Package, and Deploy the fileupload Example Using Ant

1 In a terminal window, go to:

   tut-install/examples/web/fileupload/

2 Type the following command:

   ant

3 Type the following command:

   ant deploy

▼ To Run the `fileupload` Example

1   **In a web browser, type the following URL:**

`http://localhost:8080/fileupload/`

The File Upload page opens.

2   **Click Browse to display a file browser window.**

3   **Select a file to upload and click Open.**

The name of the file you selected is displayed in the File field. If you do not select a file, an exception will be thrown.

4   **In the Destination field, type a directory name.**

The directory must have already been created and must also be writable. If you do not enter a directory name, or if you enter the name of a nonexistent or protected directory, an exception will be thrown.

5   **Click Upload to upload the file you selected to the directory you specified in the Destination field.**

A message reports that the file was created in the directory you specified.

6   **Go to the directory you specified in the Destination field and verify that the uploaded file is present.**

CHAPTER 9

Internationalizing and Localizing Web Applications

The process of preparing an application to support more than one language and data format is called *internationalization*. *Localization* is the process of adapting an internationalized application to support a specific region or locale. Examples of locale-dependent information include messages and user interface labels, character sets and encoding, and date and currency formats. Although all client user interfaces should be internationalized and localized, these processes are particularly important for web applications because of the global nature of the web.

The following topics are addressed here:

- "Java Platform Localization Classes" on page 183
- "Providing Localized Messages and Labels" on page 184
- "Date and Number Formatting" on page 187
- "Character Sets and Encodings" on page 188

Java Platform Localization Classes

In the Java platform, `java.util.Locale` (`http://docs.oracle.com/javase/6/docs/api/java/util/Locale.html`) represents a specific geographical, political, or cultural region. The string representation of a locale consists of the international standard two-character abbreviation for language and country and an optional variant, separated by underscore (_) characters. Examples of locale strings include `fr` (French), `de_CH` (Swiss German), and `en_US_POSIX` (English on a POSIX-compliant platform).

Locale-sensitive data is stored in a `java.util.ResourceBundle` (`http://docs.oracle.com/javase/6/docs/api/java/util/ResourceBundle.html`). A resource bundle contains key-value pairs, where the key uniquely identifies a locale-specific object in the bundle. A resource bundle can be backed by a text file (properties resource bundle) or a class (list resource bundle) containing the pairs. You construct a resource bundle instance by appending a locale string representation to a base name.

The Duke's Tutoring application contains resource bundles with the base name `messages.properties` for the locales pt (Portuguese), de (German), es (Spanish), and zh (Chinese). The default locale, en (English), which is specified in the `faces-config.xml` file, uses the resource bundle with the base name, `messages.properties`.

For more details on internationalization and localization in the Java platform, see (`http://docs.oracle.com/javase/tutorial/i18n/index.html`).

Providing Localized Messages and Labels

Messages and labels should be tailored according to the conventions of a user's language and region. There are two approaches to providing localized messages and labels in a web application:

- Provide a version of the web page in each of the target locales and have a controller servlet dispatch the request to the appropriate page depending on the requested locale. This approach is useful if large amounts of data on a page or an entire web application need to be internationalized.

- Isolate any locale-sensitive data on a page into resource bundles, and access the data so that the corresponding translated message is fetched automatically and inserted into the page. Thus, instead of creating strings directly in your code, you create a resource bundle that contains translations and read the translations from that bundle using the corresponding key.

The Duke's Tutoring application follows the second approach. Here are a few lines from the default resource bundle `messages.properties`:

```
nav.main=Main page
nav.status=View status
nav.current_session=View current tutoring session
nav.park=View students at the park
nav.admin=Administration

admin.nav.main=Administration main page
admin.nav.create_student=Create new student
admin.nav.edit_student=Edit student
admin.nav.create_guardian=Create new guardian
admin.nav.edit_guardian=Edit guardian
admin.nav.create_address=Create new address
admin.nav.edit_address=Edit address
admin.nav.activate_student=Activate student
```

Establishing the Locale

To get the correct strings for a given user, a web application either retrieves the locale (set by a browser language preference) from the request using the getLocale method, or allows the user to explicitly select the locale.

A component can explicitly set the locale by using the fmt:setLocale tag.

The locale-config element in the configuration file registers the default locale and other supported locales. This element in Duke's Tutoring registers English as the default locale and indicates that German, Spanish, Portuguese, and Chinese are supported locales.

```
<locale-config>
    <default-locale>en</default-locale>
    <supported-locale>de</supported-locale>
    <supported-locale>es</supported-locale>
    <supported-locale>pt</supported-locale>
    <supported-locale>zh</supported-locale>
</locale-config>
```

The Status Manager in the Duke's Tutoring application uses the getLocale method to retrieve the locale and a toString method to return a localized translation of a student's status based on the locale.

```
public class StatusManager {

    private FacesContext ctx = FacesContext.getCurrentInstance();
    private Locale locale;

    /** Creates a new instance of StatusManager */
    public StatusManager() {
        locale = ctx.getViewRoot().getLocale();
    }

    public String getLocalizedStatus(StatusType status) {
        return status.toString(locale);
    }

}
```

Setting the Resource Bundle

The resource bundle is set with the resource-bundle element in the configuration file. The setting for Duke's Tutoring looks like this:

```
<resource-bundle>
    <base-name>dukestutoring.web.messages.Messages</base-name>
    <var>bundle</var>
</resource-bundle>
```

After the locale is set, the controller of a web application could retrieve the resource bundle for that locale and save it as a session attribute (see "Associating Objects with a Session" in *The Java EE 6 Tutorial: Basic Concepts*) for use by other components or simply to return a text string appropriate for the selected locale:

```
public String toString(Locale locale) {
    ResourceBundle res = ResourceBundle.getBundle(
            "dukestutoring.web.messages.Messages", locale);
    return res.getString(name() + ".string");
}
```

Alternatively, an application could use the f:loadBundle tag to set the resource bundle. This tag loads the correct resource bundle according to the locale stored in FacesContext.

```
<f:loadBundle basename="dukestutoring.web.messages.Messages"
              var="bundle"/>
```

Resource bundles containing messages that are explicitly referenced from a JavaServer Faces tag attribute using a value expression must be registered using the resource-bundle element of the configuration file.

For more information on using this element, see "Registering Application Messages" on page 155.

Retrieving Localized Messages

A web component written in the Java programming language retrieves the resource bundle from the session:

```
ResourceBundle messages = (ResourceBundle)session.getAttribute("messages");
```

Then it looks up the string associated with the key person.lastName as follows:

```
messages.getString("person.lastName");
```

You can only use a message or messages tag to display messages that are queued onto a component as a result of a converter or validator being registered on the component. The following example shows a message tag that displays the error message queued on the userNo input component if the validator registered on the component fails to validate the value the user enters into the component.

```
<h:inputText id="userNo" value="#{UserNumberBean.userNumber}">
    <f:validateLongRange minimum="0" maximum="10" />
    ...
<h:message
    style="color: red;
    text-decoration: overline" id="errors1" for="userNo"/>
```

For more information on using the message or messages tags, see "Displaying Error Messages with the h:message and h:messages Tags" in *The Java EE 6 Tutorial: Basic Concepts*.

Messages that are not queued on a component and are therefore not loaded automatically are referenced using a value expression. You can reference a localized message from almost any JavaServer Faces tag attribute.

The value expression that references a message has the same notation whether you loaded the resource bundle with the f:loadBundle tag or registered it with the resource-bundle element in the configuration file.

The value expression notation is var.message, in which var matches the var attribute of the f:loadBundle tag or the var element defined in the resource-bundle element of the configuration file, and message matches the key of the message contained in the resource bundle, referred to by the var attribute.

Here is an example from editAddress.xhtml in Duke's Tutoring:

```
<h:outputLabel for="country" value="#{bundle['address.country']}:" />
```

Notice that bundle matches the var element from the configuration file and that country matches the key in the resource bundle.

Date and Number Formatting

Java programs use the DateFormat.getDateInstance(int, locale) to parse and format dates in a locale-sensitive manner. Java programs use the NumberFormat.get*XXX*Instance(locale) method, where *XXX* can be Currency, Number, or Percent, to parse and format numerical values in a locale-sensitive manner.

An application can use date/time and number converters to format dates and numbers in a locale-sensitive manner. For example, a shipping date could be converted as follows:

```
<h:outputText value="#{cashier.shipDate}">
    <f:convertDateTime dateStyle="full"/>
</h:outputText>
```

For information on JavaServer Faces converters, see "Using the Standard Converters" in *The Java EE 6 Tutorial: Basic Concepts*.

Character Sets and Encodings

The following sections describe character sets and character encodings.

Character Sets

A *character set* is a set of textual and graphic symbols, each of which is mapped to a set of nonnegative integers.

The first character set used in computing was US-ASCII. It is limited in that it can represent only American English. US-ASCII contains uppercase and lowercase Latin letters, numerals, punctuation, control codes, and a few miscellaneous symbols.

Unicode defines a standardized, universal character set that can be extended to accommodate additions. When the Java program source file encoding doesn't support Unicode, you can represent Unicode characters as escape sequences by using the notation \u*XXXX*, where *XXXX* is the character's 16-bit representation in hexadecimal. For example, the Spanish version of the Duke's Tutoring message file uses Unicode for non-ASCII characters:

```
nav.main=P\u00e1gina Principal
nav.status=Mirar el estado
nav.current_session=Ver sesi\u00f3n actual del tutorial
nav.park=Ver estudiantes en el Parque
nav.admin=Administraci\u00f3n

admin.nav.main=P\u00e1gina principal de administraci\u00f3n
admin.nav.create_student=Crear un nuevo estudiante
admin.nav.edit_student=Editar informaci\u00f3n del estudiante
admin.nav.create_guardian=Crear un nuevo guardia
admin.nav.edit_guardian=Editar guardia
admin.nav.create_address=Crear una nueva direcci\u00f3n
admin.nav.edit_address=Editar direcci\u00f3n
admin.nav.activate_student=Activar estudiante
```

Character Encoding

A *character encoding* maps a character set to units of a specific width and defines byte serialization and ordering rules. Many character sets have more than one encoding. For example, Java programs can represent Japanese character sets using the EUC-JP or Shift-JIS encodings, among others. Each encoding has rules for representing and serializing a character set.

The ISO 8859 series defines 13 character encodings that can represent texts in dozens of languages. Each ISO 8859 character encoding can have up to 256 characters. ISO-8859-1 (Latin-1) comprises the ASCII character set, characters with diacritics (accents, diaereses, cedillas, circumflexes, and so on), and additional symbols.

UTF-8 (Unicode Transformation Format, 8-bit form) is a variable-width character encoding that encodes 16-bit Unicode characters as one to four bytes. A byte in UTF-8 is equivalent to 7-bit ASCII if its high-order bit is zero; otherwise, the character comprises a variable number of bytes.

UTF-8 is compatible with the majority of existing web content and provides access to the Unicode character set. Current versions of browsers and email clients support UTF-8. In addition, many new web standards specify UTF-8 as their character encoding. For example, UTF-8 is one of the two required encodings for XML documents (the other is UTF-16).

Web components usually use `PrintWriter` to produce responses; `PrintWriter` automatically encodes using ISO-8859-1. Servlets can also output binary data using `OutputStream` classes, which perform no encoding. An application that uses a character set that cannot use the default encoding must explicitly set a different encoding.

Web Services

Part III explores advanced web services topics. This part contains the following chapter:

- Chapter 10, "JAX-RS: Advanced Topics and Example"

JAX-RS: Advanced Topics and Example

The Java API for RESTful Web Services (JAX-RS, defined in JSR 311) is designed to make it easy to develop applications that use the REST architecture. This chapter describes advanced features of JAX-RS. If you are new to JAX-RS, see Chapter 13, "Building RESTful Web Services with JAX-RS," in *The Java EE 6 Tutorial: Basic Concepts* before you proceed with this chapter.

JAX-RS is part of the Java EE 6 full profile. JAX-RS is integrated with Contexts and Dependency Injection for the Java EE Platform (CDI), Enterprise JavaBeans (EJB) technology, and Java Servlet technology.

The following topics are addressed here:

Annotations for Field and Bean Properties of Resource Classes

JAX-RS annotations for resource classes let you extract specific parts or values from a Uniform Resource Identifier (URI) or request header.

JAX-RS provides the annotations listed in Table 10–1.

TABLE 10–1   Advanced JAX-RS Annotations

Annotation	Description
@Context	Injects information into a class field, bean property, or method parameter
@CookieParam	Extracts information from cookies declared in the cookie request header
@FormParam	Extracts information from a request representation whose content type is application/x-www-form-urlencoded
@HeaderParam	Extracts the value of a header
@MatrixParam	Extracts the value of a URI matrix parameter
@PathParam	Extracts the value of a URI template parameter
@QueryParam	Extracts the value of a URI query parameter

Extracting Path Parameters

URI path templates are URIs with variables embedded within the URI syntax. The @PathParam annotation lets you use variable URI path fragments when you call a method.

The following code snippet shows how to extract the last name of an employee when the employee's email address is provided:

```
@Path(/employees/"{firstname}.{lastname}@{domain}.com")
public class EmpResource {

    @GET
    @Produces("text/xml")
    public String getEmployeelastname(@PathParam("lastname") String lastName) {
    ...
    }
}
```

In this example, the @Path annotation defines the URI variables (or path parameters) {firstname}, {lastname}, and {domain}. The @PathParam in the method parameter of the request method extracts the last name from the email address.

If your HTTP request is GET /employees/john.doe@example.com, the value "doe" is injected into {lastname}.

You can specify several path parameters in one URI.

You can declare a regular expression with a URI variable. For example, if it is required that the last name must consist only of lower and upper case characters, you can declare the following regular expression:

```
@Path(/employees/{"firstname}.{lastname[a-zA-Z]*}@{domain}.com")
```

If the last name does not match the regular expression, a 404 response is returned.

Extracting Query Parameters

Use the @QueryParam annotation to extract query parameters from the query component of the request URI.

For instance, to query all employees who have joined within a specific range of years, use a method signature like the following:

```
@Path(/employees/")
@GET
public Response getEmployees(
        @DefaultValue("2002") @QueryParam("minyear") int minyear,
        @DefaultValue("2010") @QueryParam("maxyear") int maxyear)
    {...}
```

This code snippet defines two query parameters, minyear and maxyear. The following HTTP request would query for all employees who have joined between 1999 and 2009:

```
GET /employees?maxyear=2009&minyear=1999
```

The @DefaultValue annotation defines a default value, which is to be used if no values are provided for the query parameters. By default, JAX-RS assigns a null value for Object values and zero for primitive data types. You can use the @DefaultValue annotation to eliminate null or zero values and define your own default values for a parameter.

Extracting Form Data

Use the @FormParam annotation to extract form parameters from HTML forms. For example, the following form accepts the name, address, and manager's name of an employee:

```
<FORM action="http://example.com/employees/" method="post">
<p>
<fieldset>
Employee name: <INPUT type="text" name="empname" tabindex="1">
Employee address: <INPUT type="text" name="empaddress" tabindex="2">
Manager name: <INPUT type="text" name="managername" tabindex="3">
</fieldset>
</p>
</FORM>
```

Use the following code snippet to extract the manager name from this HTML form:

```
@POST
@Consumes("application/x-www-form-urlencoded")
public void post(@FormParam("managername") String managername) {
    // Store the value
    ...
}
```

To obtain a map of form parameter names to values, use a code snippet like the following:

```
@POST
@Consumes("application/x-www-form-urlencoded")
public void post(MultivaluedMap<String. String> formParams) {
    // Store the message
}
```

Extracting the Java Type of a Request or Response

The javax.ws.rs.core.Context annotation retrieves the Java types related to a request or response.

The javax.ws.rs.core.UriInfo interface provides information about the components of a request URI. The following code snippet shows how to obtain a map of query and path parameter names to values:

```
@GET
public String getParams(@Context UriInfo ui) {
    MultivaluedMap<String, String> queryParams = ui.getQueryParameters();
    MultivaluedMap<String, String> pathParams = ui.getPathParameters();
}
```

The javax.ws.rs.core.HttpHeaders interface provides information about request headers and cookies. The following code snippet shows how to obtain a map of header and cookie parameter names to values:

```
@GET
public String getHeaders(@Context HttpHeaders hh) {
    MultivaluedMap<String, String> headerParams = hh.getRequestHeaders();
    MultivaluedMap<String, Cookie> pathParams = hh.getCookies();
}
```

Subresources and Runtime Resource Resolution

You can use a resource class to process only a part of the URI request. A root resource can then implement subresources that can process the remainder of the URI path.

A resource class method that is annotated with @Path is either a subresource method or a subresource locator:

- A subresource method is used to handle requests on a subresource of the corresponding resource.

- A subresource locator is used to locate subresources of the corresponding resource.

Subresource Methods

A *subresource method* handles an HTTP request directly. The method must be annotated with a request method designator such as @GET or @POST, in addition to @Path. The method is invoked for request URIs that match a URI template created by concatenating the URI template of the resource class with the URI template of the method.

The following code snippet shows how a subresource method can be used to extract the last name of an employee when the employee's email address is provided:

```
@Path("/employeeinfo")
Public class EmployeeInfo {

    public employeeinfo() {}

    @GET
    @Path("/employees/{firstname}.{lastname}@{domain}.com")
    @Produces("text/xml")
    public String getEmployeeLastName(@PathParam("lastname") String lastName) {
        ...
    }

}
```

The getEmployeeLastName method returns doe for the following GET request:

```
GET /employeeinfo/employees/john.doe@example.com
```

Subresource Locators

A *subresource locator* returns an object that will handle an HTTP request. The method must not be annotated with a request method designator. You must declare a subresource locator within a subresource class, and only subresource locators are used for runtime resource resolution.

The following code snippet shows a subresource locator:

```
// Root resource class
@Path("/employeeinfo")
public class EmployeeInfo {

    // Subresource locator: obtains the subresource Employee
    // from the path /employeeinfo/employees/{empid}
    @Path("/employees/{empid}")
    public Employee getEmployee(@PathParam("empid") String id) {
        // Find the Employee based on the id path parameter
        Employee emp = ...;
        ...
        return emp;
    }
}

// Subresource class
public class Employee {

    // Subresource method: returns the employee's last name
    @GET
    @Path("/lastname")
    public String getEmployeeLastName() {
        ...
        return lastName
    }
}
```

In this code snippet, the getEmployee method is the subresource locator that provides the Employee object, which services requests for lastname.

If your HTTP request is GET /employeeinfo/employees/as209/, the getEmployee method returns an Employee object whose id is as209. At runtime, JAX-RS sends a GET /employeeinfo/employees/as209/lastname request to the getEmployeeLastName method . The getEmployeeLastName method retrieves and returns the last name of the employee whose id is as209.

Integrating JAX-RS with EJB Technology and CDI

JAX-RS works with Enterprise JavaBeans technology (enterprise beans) and Contexts and Dependency Injection for the Java EE Platform (CDI).

In general, for JAX-RS to work with enterprise beans, you need to annotate the class of a bean with @Path to convert it to a root resource class. You can use the @Path annotation with stateless session beans and singleton POJO beans.

The following code snippet shows a stateless session bean and a singleton bean that have been converted to JAX-RS root resource classes.

```
@Stateless
@Path("stateless-bean")
public class StatelessResource {...}

@Singleton
@Path("singleton-bean")
public class SingletonResource {...}
```

Session beans can also be used for subresources.

JAX-RS and CDI have slightly different component models. By default, JAX-RS root resource classes are managed in the request scope, and no annotations are required for specifying the scope. CDI managed beans annotated with @RequestScoped or @ApplicationScoped can be converted to JAX-RS resource classes.

The following code snippet shows a JAX-RS resource class.

```
@Path("/employee/{id}")
public class Employee {
    public Employee(@PathParam("id") String id) {...}
}

@Path("{lastname}")
public final class EmpDetails {...}
```

The following code snippet shows this JAX-RS resource class converted to a CDI bean. The beans must be proxyable, so the Employee class requires a non-private constructor with no parameters, and the EmpDetails class must not be final.

```
@Path("/employee/{id}")
@RequestScoped
public class Employee {
    public Employee() {...}

    @Inject
    public Employee(@PathParam("id") String id) {...}
}

@Path("{lastname}")
@RequestScoped
public class EmpDetails {...}
```

Conditional HTTP Requests

JAX-RS provides support for conditional GET and PUT HTTP requests. Conditional GET requests help save bandwidth by improving the efficiency of client processing.

A GET request can return a Not Modified (304) response if the representation has not changed since the previous request. For example, a web site can return 304 responses for all its static images that have not changed since the previous request.

A PUT request can return a Precondition Failed (412) response if the representation has been modified since the last request. The conditional PUT can help avoid the lost update problem.

Conditional HTTP requests can be used with the Last-Modified and ETag headers. The Last-Modified header can represent dates with granularity of one second.

```
@Path("/employee/{joiningdate}")
public class Employee {

    Date joiningdate;

    @GET
    @Produces("application/xml")
    public Employee(@PathParam("joiningdate") Date joiningdate,
            @Context Request req,
            @Context UriInfo ui) {

        this.joiningdate = joiningdate;
        ...
        this.tag = computeEntityTag(ui.getRequestUri());
        if (req.getMethod().equals("GET")) {
            Response.ResponseBuilder rb = req.evaluatePreconditions(tag);
            if (rb != null) {
                throw new WebApplicationException(rb.build());
            }
        }
    }
}
```

In this code snippet, the constructor of the Employee class computes the entity tag from the request URI and calls the request.evaluatePreconditions method with that tag. If a client request returns an If-none-match header with a value that has the same entity tag that was computed, evaluate.Preconditions returns a pre-filled-out response with a 304 status code and an entity tag set that may be built and returned.

Runtime Content Negotiation

The @Produces and @Consumes annotations handle static content negotiation in JAX-RS. These annotations specify the content preferences of the server. HTTP headers such as Accept, Content-Type, and Accept-Language define the content negotiation preferences of the client.

For more details on the HTTP headers for content negotiation, see HTTP /1.1 - Content Negotiation (http://www.w3.org/Protocols/rfc2616/rfc2616-sec12.html).

The following code snippet shows the server content preferences:

```
@Produces("text/plain")
@Path("/employee")
```

```
public class Employee {

    @GET
    public String getEmployeeAddressText(String address) { ... }

    @Produces("text/xml")
    @GET
    public String getEmployeeAddressXml(Address address) { ... }
}
```

The getEmployeeAddressText method is called for an HTTP request that looks as follows:

```
GET /employee
Accept: text/plain
```

This will produce the following response:

```
500 Oracle Parkway, Redwood Shores, CA
```

The getEmployeeAddressXml method is called for an HTTP request that looks as follows:

```
GET /employee
Accept: text/xml
```

This will produce the following response:

```
<address street="500 Oracle Parkway, Redwood Shores, CA" country="USA"/>
```

With static content negotiation, you can also define multiple content and media types for the client and server.

```
@Produces("text/plain", "text/xml")
```

In addition to supporting static content negotiation, JAX-RS also supports runtime content negotiation using the javax.ws.rs.core.Variant class and Request objects. The Variant class specifies the resource representation of content negotiation. Each instance of the Variant class may contain a media type, a language, and an encoding. The Variant object defines the resource representation that is supported by the server. The Variant.VariantListBuilder class is used to build a list of representation variants.

The following code snippet shows how to create a list of resource representation variants:

```
List<Variant> vs =
    Variant.mediatypes("application/xml", "application/json")
            .languages("en", "fr").build();
```

This code snippet calls the build method of the VariantListBuilder class. The VariantListBuilder class is invoked when you call the mediatypes, languages, or encodings methods. The build method builds a series of resource representations. The Variant list created by the build method has all possible combinations of items specified in the mediatypes, languages, and encodings methods.

In this example, the size of the vs object as defined in this code snippet is 4, and the contents are as follows:

```
[["application/xml","en"], ["application/json","en"],
    ["application/xml","fr"],["application/json","fr"]]
```

The javax.ws.rs.core.Request.selectVariant method accepts a list of Variant objects and chooses the Variant object that matches the HTTP request. This method compares its list of Variant objects with the Accept, Accept-Encoding, Accept-Language, and Accept-Charset headers of the HTTP request.

The following code snippet shows how to use the selectVariant method to select the most acceptable Variant from the values in the client request.

```
@GET
public Response get(@Context Request r) {
    List<Variant> vs = ...;
    Variant v = r.selectVariant(vs);
    if (v == null) {
        return Response.notAcceptable(vs).build();
    } else {
        Object rep = selectRepresentation(v);
        return Response.ok(rep, v);
    }
}
```

The selectVariant method returns the Variant object that matches the request, or null if no matches are found. In this code snippet, if the method returns null, a Response object for a non-acceptable response is built. Otherwise, a Response object with an OK status and containing a representation in the form of an Object entity and a Variant is returned.

Using JAX-RS With JAXB

Java Architecture for XML Binding (JAXB) is an XML-to-Java binding technology that simplifies the development of web services by enabling transformations between schema and Java objects and between XML instance documents and Java object instances. An XML schema defines the data elements and structure of an XML document. You can use JAXB APIs and tools to establish mappings between Java classes and XML schema. JAXB technology provides the tools that enable you to convert your XML documents to and from Java objects.

By using JAXB, you can manipulate data objects in the following ways:

- You can start with an XML schema definition (XSD) and use xjc, the JAXB schema compiler tool, to create a set of JAXB-annotated Java classes that map to the elements and types defined in the XSD schema.

- You can start with a set of Java classes and use schemagen, the JAXB schema generator tool, to generate an XML schema.

- Once a mapping between the XML schema and the Java classes exists, you can use the JAXB binding runtime to marshal and unmarshal your XML documents to and from Java objects and use the resulting Java classes to assemble a web services application.

XML is a common media format that RESTful services consume and produce. To deserialize and serialize XML, you can represent requests and responses by JAXB annotated objects. Your JAX-RS application can use the JAXB objects to manipulate XML data. JAXB objects can be used as request entity parameters and response entities. The JAX-RS runtime environment includes standard MessageBodyReader and MessageBodyWriter provider interfaces for reading and writing JAXB objects as entities.

With JAX-RS, you enable access to your services by publishing resources. Resources are just simple Java classes with some additional JAX-RS annotations. These annotations express the following:

- The path of the resource (the URL you use to access it)

- The HTTP method you use to call a certain method (for example, the GET or POST method)

- The MIME type with which a method accepts or responds

As you define the resources for your application, consider the type of data you want to expose. You may already have a relational database that contains information you want to expose to users, or you may have static content that does not reside in a database but does need to be distributed as resources. Using JAX-RS, you can distribute content from multiple sources. RESTful web services can use various types of input/output formats for request and response. The customer example, described in "The customer Example Application" on page 209, uses XML.

Resources have representations. A resource representation is the content in the HTTP message that is sent to, or returned from, the resource using the URI. Each representation a resource supports has a corresponding media type. For example, if a resource is going to return content formatted as XML, you can use application/xml as the associated media type in the HTTP message. Depending on the requirements of your application, resources can return representations in a preferred single format or in multiple formats. JAX-RS provides @Consumes and @Produces annotations to declare the media types that are acceptable for a resource method to read and write.

JAX-RS also maps Java types to and from resource representations using entity providers. A MessageBodyReader entity provider reads a request entity and deserializes the request entity into a Java type. A MessageBodyWriter entity provider serializes from a Java type into a response entity. For example, if a String value is used as the request entity parameter, the MessageBodyReader entity provider deserializes the request body into a new String. If a JAXB type is used as the return type on a resource method, the MessageBodyWriter serializes the JAXB object into a response body.

By default, the JAX-RS runtime environment attempts to create and use a default JAXBContext class for JAXB classes. However, if the default JAXBContext class is not suitable, then you can supply a JAXBContext class for the application using a JAX-RS ContextResolver provider interface.

The following sections explain how to use JAXB with JAX-RS resource methods.

Using Java Objects to Model Your Data

If you do not have an XML schema definition for the data you want to expose, you can model your data as Java classes, add JAXB annotations to these classes, and use JAXB to generate an XML schema for your data. For example, if the data you want to expose is a collection of products and each product has an ID, a name, a description, and a price, you can model it as a Java class as follows:

```
@XmlRootElement(name="product")
@XmlAccessorType(XmlAccessType.FIELD)
public class Product {

    @XmlElement(required=true)
    protected int id;
    @XmlElement(required=true)
    protected String name;
    @XmlElement(required=true)
    protected String description;
    @XmlElement(required=true)
    protected int price;

    public Product() {}

    // Getter and setter methods
    // ...
}
```

Run the JAXB schema generator on the command line to generate the corresponding XML schema definition:

```
schemagen Product.java
```

This command produces the XML schema as an .xsd file:

```
<?xml version="1.0" encoding="UTF-8" standalone="yes"?>
<xs:schema version="1.0" xmlns:xs="http://www.w3.org/2001/XMLSchema">

  <xs:element name="product" type="product"/>

  <xs:complexType name="product">
    <xs:sequence>
      <xs:element name="id" type="xs:int"/>
      <xs:element name="name" type="xs:string"/>
      <xs:element name="description" type="xs:string"/>
      <xs:element name="price" type="xs:int"/>
    </xs:sequence>
  <xs:complexType>
</xs:schema>
```

Once you have this mapping, you can create Product objects in your application, return them, and use them as parameters in JAX-RS resource methods. The JAX-RS runtime uses JAXB to convert the XML data from the request into a Product object and to convert a Product object into XML data for the response. The following resource class provides a simple example:

```
@Path("/product")
public class ProductService {
    @GET
    @Path("/get")
    @Produces("application/xml")
    public Product getProduct() {
        Product prod = new Product();
        prod.setId(1);
        prod.setName("Mattress");
        prod.setDescription("Queen size mattress");
        prod.setPrice(500);
        return prod;
    }

    @POST
    @Path("/create")
    @Consumes("application/xml")
    public Response createProduct(Product prod) {
        // Process or store the product and return a response
        // ...
    }
}
```

Some IDEs, such as NetBeans IDE, will run the schema generator tool automatically during the build process if you add Java classes that have JAXB annotations to your project. For a detailed example, see "The customer Example Application" on page 209. The customer example contains a more complex relationship between the Java classes that model the data, which results in a more hierarchical XML representation.

Starting from an Existing XML Schema Definition

If you already have an XML schema definition in an .xsd file for the data you want to
expose, use the JAXB schema compiler tool. Consider this simple example of an .xsd
file:

```
<?xml version="1.0"?>
<xs:schema targetNamespace="http://xml.product"
           xmlns:xs="http://www.w3.org/2001/XMLSchema"
           elementFormDefault="qualified"
           xmlns:myco="http://xml.product">

  <xs:element name="product" type="myco:Product"/>

  <xs:complexType name="Product">
    <xs:sequence>
      <xs:element name="id" type="xs:int"/>
      <xs:element name="name" type="xs:string"/>
      <xs:element name="description" type="xs:string"/>
      <xs:element name="price" type="xs:int"/>
    </xs:sequence>
  </xs:complexType>
</xs:schema>
```

Run the schema compiler tool on the command line as follows:

xjc Product.xsd

This command generates the source code for Java classes that correspond to the types
defined in the .xsd file. The schema compiler tool generates a Java class for each
complexType defined in the .xsd file. The fields of each generated Java class are the
same as the elements inside the corresponding complexType, and the class contains
getter and setter methods for these fields.

In this case the schema compiler tool generates the classes product.xml.Product and
product.xml.ObjectFactory. The Product class contains JAXB annotations, and its
fields correspond to those in the .xsd definition:

```
@XmlAccessorType(XmlAccessType.FIELD)
@XmlType(name = "Product", propOrder = {
    "id",
    "name",
    "description",
    "price"
})
public class Product {
    protected int id;
    @XmlElement(required = true)
    protected String name;
    @XmlElement(required = true)
    protected String description;
    protected int price;
```

```
    // Setter and getter methods
    // ...
}
```

You can create instances of the Product class from your application (for example, from a database). The generated class product.xml.ObjectFactory contains a method that allows you to convert these objects to JAXB elements that can be returned as XML inside JAX-RS resource methods:

```
@XmlElementDecl(namespace = "http://xml.product", name = "product")
public JAXBElement<Product> createProduct(Product value) {
  return new JAXBElement<Product>(_Product_QNAME, Product.class, null, value);
}
```

The following code shows how to use the generated classes to return a JAXB element as XML in a JAX-RS resource method:

```
@Path("/product")
public class ProductService {
    @GET
    @Path("/get")
    @Produces("application/xml")
    public JAXBElement<Product> getProduct() {
        Product prod = new Product();
        prod.setId(1);
        prod.setName("Mattress");
        prod.setDescription("Queen size mattress");
        prod.setPrice(500);
        return new ObjectFactory().createProduct(prod);
    }
}
```

For @POST and @PUT resource methods, you can use a Product object directly as a parameter. JAX-RS maps the XML data from the request into a Product object.

```
@Path("/product")
public class ProductService {
    @GET
    // ...

    @POST
    @Path("/create")
    @Consumes("application/xml")
    public Response createProduct(Product prod) {
        // Process or store the product and return a response
        // ...
    }
}
```

Some IDEs, such as NetBeans IDE, will run the schema compiler tool automatically during the build process if you add an .xsd file to your project sources. For a detailed example, see "Modifying the Example to Generate Entity Classes from an Existing Schema" on page 216. The modified customer example contains a more hierarchical XML schema definition, which results in a more complex relationship between the Java classes that model the data.

Using JSON with JAX-RS and JAXB

JAX-RS can automatically read and write XML using JAXB, but it can also work with JSON data. JSON is a simple text-based format for data exchange derived from JavaScript. For the examples above, the XML representation of a product is:

```
<?xml version="1.0" encoding="UTF-8"?>
<product>
  <id>1</id>
  <name>Mattress</name>
  <description>Queen size mattress</description>
  <price>500</price>
</product>
```

The equivalent JSON representation is:

```
{
    "id":"1",
    "name":"Mattress",
    "description":"Queen size mattress",
    "price":500
}
```

You can add the format `application/json` to the `@Produces` annotation in resource methods to produce responses with JSON data:

```
@GET
@Path("/get")
@Produces({"application/xml","application/json"})
public Product getProduct() { ... }
```

In this example the default response is XML, but the response is a JSON object if the client makes a GET request that includes this header:

```
Accept: application/json
```

The resource methods can also accept JSON data for JAXB annotated classes:

```
@POST
@Path("/create")
@Consumes({"application/xml","application/json"})
public Response createProduct(Product prod) { ... }
```

The client should include the following header when submitting JSON data with a POST request:

```
Content-Type: application/json
```

The customer **Example Application**

This section describes how to build and run the customer sample application. This example application is a RESTful web service that uses JAXB to perform the Create, Read, Update, Delete (CRUD) operations for a specific entity.

The customer sample application is in the *tut-install*/examples/jaxrs/customer/ directory. See Chapter 2, "Using the Tutorial Examples," for basic information on building and running sample applications.

Overview of the customer **Example Application**

The source files of this application are at *tut-install*/examples/jaxrs/customer/src/java/. The application has three parts:

- The Customer and Address entity classes. These classes model the data of the application and contain JAXB annotations. See "The Customer and Address Entity Classes" on page 209 for details.

- The CustomerService resource class. This class contains JAX-RS resource methods that perform operations on Customer instances represented as XML or JSON data using JAXB. See "The CustomerService Class" on page 212 for details.

- The CustomerClientXML and CustomerClientJSON client classes. These classes test the resource methods of the web service using XML and JSON representations of Customer instances. See "The CustomerClientXML and CustomerClientJSON Classes" on page 214 for details.

The customer sample application shows you how to model your data entities as Java classes with JAXB annotations. The JAXB schema generator produces an equivalent XML schema definition file (.xsd) for your entity classes. The resulting schema is used to automatically marshal and unmarshal entity instances to and from XML or JSON in the JAX-RS resource methods.

In some cases you may already have an XML schema definition for your entities. See "Modifying the Example to Generate Entity Classes from an Existing Schema" on page 216 for instructions on how to modify the customer example to model your data starting from an .xsd file and using JAXB to generate the equivalent Java classes.

The Customer **and** Address **Entity Classes**

The following class represents a customer's address:

```
@XmlRootElement(name="address")
@XmlAccessorType(XmlAccessType.FIELD)
public class Address {
```

```
        @XmlElement(required=true)
        protected int number;

        @XmlElement(required=true)
        protected String street;

        @XmlElement(required=true)
        protected String city;

        @XmlElement(required=true)
        protected String state;

        @XmlElement(required=true)
        protected String zip;

        @XmlElement(required=true)
        protected String country;

        public Address() { }

        // Getter and setter methods
        // ...
}
```

The @XmlRootElement(name="address") annotation maps this class to the address XML element. The @XmlAccessorType(XmlAccessType.FIELD) annotation specifies that all the fields of this class are bound to XML by default. The @XmlElement(required=true) annotation specifies that an element must be present in the XML representation.

The following class represents a customer:

```
@XmlRootElement(name="customer")
@XmlAccessorType(XmlAccessType.FIELD)
public class Customer {

        @XmlAttribute(required=true)
        protected int id;

        @XmlElement(required=true)
        protected String firstname;

        @XmlElement(required=true)
        protected String lastname;

        @XmlElement(required=true)
        protected Address address;

        @XmlElement(required=true)
        protected String email;

        @XmlElement (required=true)
        protected String phone;
```

```
        public Customer() { }

        // Getter and setter methods
        // ...
}
```

The Customer class contains the same JAXB annotations as the previous class, except for the @XmlAttribute(required=true) annotation, which maps a property to an attribute of the XML element representing the class.

The Customer class contains a property whose type is another entity, the Address class. This mechanism allows you to define in Java code the hierarchical relationships between entities without having to write an .xsd file yourself.

JAXB generates the following XML schema definition for the two classes above:

```
<?xml version="1.0" encoding="UTF-8" standalone="yes"?>
<xs:schema version="1.0" xmlns:xs="http://www.w3.org/2001/XMLSchema">

  <xs:element name="address" type="address"/>
  <xs:element name="customer" type="customer"/>

  <xs:complexType name="address">
    <xs:sequence>
      <xs:element name="number" type="xs:int"/>
      <xs:element name="street" type="xs:string"/>
      <xs:element name="city" type="xs:string"/>
      <xs:element name="state" type="xs:string"/>
      <xs:element name="zip" type="xs:string"/>
      <xs:element name="country" type="xs:string"/>
    </xs:sequence>
  </xs:complexType>

  <xs:complexType name="customer">
    <xs:sequence>
      <xs:element name="firstname" type="xs:string"/>
      <xs:element name="lastname" type="xs:string"/>
      <xs:element ref="address"/>
      <xs:element name="email" type="xs:string"/>
      <xs:element name="phone" type="xs:string"/>
    </xs:sequence>
    <xs:attribute name="id" type="xs:int" use="required"/>
  </xs:complexType>
</xs:schema>
```

The file sample-input.xml in the top-level directory of the project contains an example of an XML representation of a customer:

```
<?xml version="1.0" encoding="UTF-8"?>
<customer id="1">
  <firstname>Duke</firstname>
  <lastname>OfJava</lastname>
  <address>
    <number>1</number>
    <street>Duke's Way</street>
```

```
        <city>JavaTown</city>
        <state>JA</state>
        <zip>12345</zip>
        <country>USA</country>
    </address>
    <email>duke@example.com</email>
    <phone>123-456-7890</phone>
</customer>
```

The file `sample-input.json` contains an example of a JSON representation of a customer:

```
{
    "@id": "1",
    "firstname": "Duke",
    "lastname": "OfJava",
    "address": {
        "number": 1,
        "street": "Duke's Way",
        "city": "JavaTown",
        "state": "JA",
        "zip": "12345",
        "country": "USA"
    },
    "email": "duke@example.com",
    "phone": "123-456-7890"
}
```

The `CustomerService` Class

The `CustomerService` class has a `createCustomer` method that creates a customer resource based on the `Customer` class and returns a URI for the new resource. The persist method emulates the behavior of the JPA entity manager. This example uses a `java.util.Properties` file to store data. If you are using the default configuration of GlassFish Server, the properties file is at *domain-dir*/`CustomerDATA.txt`.

```
@Path("/Customer")
public class CustomerService {
    public static final String DATA_STORE = "CustomerDATA.txt";
    public static final Logger logger =
            Logger.getLogger(CustomerService.class.getCanonicalName());
    ...

    @POST
    @Consumes({"application/xml", "application/json"})
    public Response createCustomer(Customer customer) {
        try {
            long customerId = persist(customer);
            return Response.created(URI.create("/" + customerId)).build();
        } catch (Exception e) {
            throw new WebApplicationException(e,
                    Response.Status.INTERNAL_SERVER_ERROR);
        }
    }
```

```
...
    private long persist(Customer customer) throws IOException {

        File dataFile = new File(DATA_STORE);

        if (!dataFile.exists()) {
            dataFile.createNewFile();
        }

        long customerId = customer.getId();
        Address address = customer.getAddress();

        Properties properties = new Properties();
        properties.load(new FileInputStream(dataFile));

        properties.setProperty(String.valueOf(customerId),
                customer.getFirstname() + ","
                + customer.getLastname() + ","
                + address.getNumber() + ","
                + address.getStreet() + ","
                + address.getCity() + ","
                + address.getState() + ","
                + address.getZip() + ","
                + address.getCountry() + ","
                + customer.getEmail() + ","
                + customer.getPhone());

        properties.store(new FileOutputStream(DATA_STORE),null);

        return customerId;
    }
    ...
}
```

The response returned to the client has a URI to the newly created resource. The return type is an entity body mapped from the property of the response with the status code specified by the status property of the response. The WebApplicationException is a RuntimeException that is used to wrap the appropriate HTTP error status code, such as 404, 406, 415, or 500.

The @Consumes({"application/xml","application/json"}) and @Produces({"application/xml","application/json"}) annotations set the request and response media types to use the appropriate MIME client. These annotations can be applied to a resource method, a resource class, or even an entity provider. If you do not use these annotations, JAX-RS allows the use of any media type ("*/*").

The following code snippet shows the implementation of the getCustomer and findbyId methods. The getCustomer method uses the @Produces annotation and returns a Customer object, which is converted to an XML or JSON representation depending on the Accept: header specified by the client.

```
@GET
@Path("{id}")
@Produces({"application/xml", "application/json"})
```

```
public Customer getCustomer(@PathParam("id") String customerId) {
    Customer customer = null;

    try {
        customer = findById(customerId);
    } catch (Exception ex) {
        logger.log(Level.SEVERE,
                "Error calling searchCustomer() for customerId {0}. {1}",
                new Object[]{customerId, ex.getMessage()});
    }
    return customer;
}

private Customer findById(String customerId) throws IOException {
    properties properties = new Properties();
    properties.load(new FileInputStream(DATA_STORE));
    String rawData = properties.getProperty(customerId);

    if (rawData != null) {
        final String[] field = rawData.split(",");

        Address address = new Address();
        Customer customer = new Customer();
        customer.setId(Integer.parseInt(customerId));
        customer.setAddress(address);

        customer.setFirstname(field[0]);
        customer.setLastname(field[1]);
        address.setNumber(Integer.parseInt(field[2]));
        address.setStreet(field[3]);
        address.setCity(field[4]);
        address.setState(field[5]);
        address.setZip(field[6]);
        address.setCountry(field[7]);
        customer.setEmail(field[8]);
        customer.setPhone(field[9]);

        return customer;
    }
    return null;
}
```

The CustomerClientXML and CustomerClientJSON Classes

Jersey is the reference implementation of JAX-RS (JSR 311). You can use the Jersey client API to write a test client for the customer example application. You can find the Jersey APIs at http://jersey.java.net/nonav/apidocs/latest/jersey/.

The CustomerClientXML class calls Jersey APIs to test the CustomerService web service:

```
package customer.rest.client;

import com.sun.jersey.api.client.Client;
```

```java
import com.sun.jersey.api.client.ClientResponse;
import com.sun.jersey.api.client.WebResource;
import customer.data.Address;
import customer.data.Customer;
import java.util.logging.Level;
import java.util.logging.Logger;
import javax.ws.rs.core.MediaType;

public class CustomerClientXML {
    public static final Logger logger =
            Logger.getLogger(CustomerClientXML.class.getCanonicalName());

    public static void main(String[] args) {

        Client client = Client.create();
        // Define the URL for testing the example application
        WebResource webResource =
                client.resource("http://localhost:8080/customer/rest/Customer");

        // Test the POST method
        Customer customer = new Customer();
        Address address = new Address();
        customer.setAddress(address);

        customer.setId(1);
        customer.setFirstname("Duke");
        customer.setLastname("OfJava");
        address.setNumber(1);
        address.setStreet("Duke's Drive");
        address.setCity("JavaTown");
        address.setZip("1234");
        address.setState("JA");
        address.setCountry("USA");
        customer.setEmail("duke@java.net");
        customer.setPhone("12341234");

        ClientResponse response =
                webResource.type("application/xml").post(ClientResponse.class,
                customer);

        logger.info("POST status: {0}" + response.getStatus());
        if (response.getStatus() == 201) {
            logger.info("POST succeeded");
        } else {
            logger.info("POST failed");
        }

        // Test the GET method using content negotiation
        response = webResource.path("1").accept(MediaType.APPLICATION_XML)
                .get(ClientResponse.class);
        Customer entity = response.getEntity(Customer.class);

        logger.log(Level.INFO, "GET status: {0}", response.getStatus());
        if (response.getStatus() == 200) {
            logger.log(Level.INFO, "GET succeeded, city is {0}",
                    entity.getAddress().getCity());
        } else {
            logger.info("GET failed");
        }
```

```
// Test the DELETE method
response = webResource.path("1").delete(ClientResponse.class);

logger.log(Level.INFO, "DELETE status: {0}", response.getStatus());
if (response.getStatus() == 204) {
    logger.info("DELETE succeeded (no content)");
} else {
    logger.info("DELETE failed");
}

response = webResource.path("1").accept(MediaType.APPLICATION_XML)
        .get(ClientResponse.class);
logger.log(Level.INFO, "GET status: {0}", response.getStatus());
if (response.getStatus() == 204) {
    logger.info("After DELETE, the GET request returned no content.");
} else {
    logger.info("Failed, after DELETE, GET returned a response.");
}
    }
}
```

This Jersey client tests the POST, GET, and DELETE methods using XML representations.

All of these HTTP status codes indicate success: 201 for POST, 200 for GET, and 204 for DELETE. For details about the meanings of HTTP status codes, see `http://www.w3.org/Protocols/rfc2616/rfc2616-sec10.html`.

The `CustomerClientJSON` class is similar to `CustomerClientXML` but it uses JSON representations to test the web service. In the `CustomerClientJSON` class `"application/xml"` is replaced by `"application/json"`, and `MediaType.APPLICATION_XML` is replaced by `MediaType.APPLICATION_JSON`.

Modifying the Example to Generate Entity Classes from an Existing Schema

This section describes how you can modify the customer example if you provide an XML schema definition file for your entities instead of providing Java classes. In this case JAXB generates the equivalent Java entity classes from the schema definition.

For the customer example you provide the following .xsd file:

```xml
<?xml version="1.0"?>
<xs:schema targetNamespace="http://xml.customer"
    xmlns:xs="http://www.w3.org/2001/XMLSchema" elementFormDefault="qualified"
    xmlns:ora="http://xml.customer">

  <xs:element name="customer" type="ora:Customer"/>

  <xs:complexType name="Address">
```

```
<xs:sequence>
  <xs:element name="number" type="xs:int"/>
  <xs:element name="street" type="xs:string"/>
  <xs:element name="city" type="xs:string"/>
  <xs:element name="state" type="xs:string"/>
  <xs:element name="zip" type="xs:string"/>
  <xs:element name="country" type="xs:string"/>
</xs:sequence>
</xs:complexType>

<xs:complexType name="Customer">
  <xs:sequence>
    <xs:element name="firstname" type="xs:string"/>
    <xs:element name="lastname" type="xs:string"/>
    <xs:element name="address" type="ora:Address"/>
    <xs:element name="email" type="xs:string"/>
    <xs:element name="phone" type="xs:string"/>
  </xs:sequence>
  <xs:attribute name="id" type="xs:int" use="required"/>
</xs:complexType>
</xs:schema>
```

You can modify the customer example as follows:

▼ To Modify the customer Example to Generate Java Entity Classes from an Existing XML Schema Definition

1 Create a JAXB binding to generate the entity Java classes from the schema definition. For example, in NetBeans IDE, follow these steps:

   a. Right click on the customer project and select New > Other...

   b. Under the XML folder, select JAXB Binding and click Next.

   c. In the Binding Name field, type `CustomerBinding`.

   d. Click Browse and choose the .xsd file from your file system.

   e. In the Package Name field, type `customer.xml`.

   f. Click Finish.

This procedure creates the Customer class, the Address class, and some JAXB auxiliary classes in the package customer.xml.

2 Modify the CustomerService class as follows:

a. Replace the customer.data.* imports with customer.xml.* imports and import the JAXBElement and ObjectFactory classes:

```
import customer.xml.Customer;
import customer.xml.Address;
import customer.xml.ObjectFactory;
import javax.xml.bind.JAXBElement;
```

b. Replace the return type of the getCustomer method:

```
public JAXBElement<Customer> getCustomer(
        @PathParam("id") String customerId) {
    ...
    return new ObjectFactory().createCustomer(customer);
}
```

3 Modify the CustomerClientXML and CustomerClientJSON classes as follows:

a. Replace the customer.data.* imports with customer.xml.* imports and import the JAXBElement and ObjectFactory classes:

```
import customer.xml.Address;
import customer.xml.Customer;
import customer.xml.ObjectFactory;
import javax.xml.bind.JAXBElement;
```

b. Create an ObjectFactory instance and a JAXBElement<Customer> instance at the beginning of the main method:

```
public static void main(String[] args) {
    Client client = Client.create();
    ObjectFactory factory = new ObjectFactory();
    WebResource webResource = ...;
    ...
    customer.setPhone("12341234");
    JAXBElement<Customer> customerJAXB = factory.createCustomer(customer);
    ClientResponse response = webResource.type("application/xml")
            .post(ClientResponse.class, customerJAXB);
    ...
}
```

c. Modify the GET request after testing the DELETE method:

```
response = webResource.path("1").accept(MediaType.APPLICATION_XML)
        .get(ClientResponse.class);
entity = response.getEntity(Customer.class);
logger.log(Level.INFO, "GET status: {0}", response.getStatus());
try {
    logger.info(entity.getAddress().getCity());
} catch (NullPointerException ne) {
    // null after deleting the only customer
    logger.log(Level.INFO, "After DELETE, city is: {0}", ne.getCause());
}
```

The instructions for building, deploying, and running the example are the same for the original customer example and for the modified version using this procedure.

Running the customer Example

You can use either NetBeans IDE or Ant to build, package, deploy, and run the customer application.

▼ To Build, Package, and Deploy the customer Example Using NetBeans IDE

This procedure builds the application into the
tut-install/examples/jax-rs/customer/build/web/ directory. The contents of this directory are deployed to the GlassFish Server.

1   From the File menu, choose Open Project.

2   In the Open Project dialog, navigate to:

   tut-install/examples/jaxrs/

3   Select the customer folder.

4   Select the Open as Main Project check box.

5   Click Open Project.

   It may appear that there are errors in the source files, because the files refer to JAXB classes that will be generated when you build the application. You can ignore these errors.

6   In the Projects tab, right-click the customer project and select Deploy.

▼ To Build, Package, and Deploy the customer Example Using Ant

1   In a terminal window, go to:

   tut-install/examples/jaxrs/customer/

2   Type the following command:

   `ant`

   This command calls the default target, which builds and packages the application into a WAR file, customer.war, located in the dist directory.

3   Type the following command:

   `ant deploy`

   Typing this command deploys customer.war to the GlassFish Server.

▼ To Run the customer Example Using the Jersey Client

1 In NetBeans IDE, expand the Source Packages node.

2 Expand the customer.rest.client node.

3 Right-click the CustomerClientXML.java file and select Run File.

The output of the client looks like this:

```
run:
Jun 12, 2012 2:40:20 PM customer.rest.client.CustomerClientXML main
INFO: POST status: 201
Jun 12, 2012 2:40:20 PM customer.rest.client.CustomerClientXML main
INFO: POST succeeded
Jun 12, 2012 2:40:20 PM customer.rest.client.CustomerClientXML main
INFO: GET status: 200
Jun 12, 2012 2:40:20 PM customer.rest.client.CustomerClientXML main
INFO: GET succeeded, city is JavaTown
Jun 12, 2012 2:40:20 PM customer.rest.client.CustomerClientXML main
INFO: DELETE status: 204
Jun 12, 2012 2:40:20 PM customer.rest.client.CustomerClientXML main
INFO: DELETE succeeded (no content)
Jun 12, 2012 2:40:20 PM customer.rest.client.CustomerClientXML main
INFO: GET status: 204
Jun 12, 2012 2:40:20 PM customer.rest.client.CustomerClientXML main
INFO: After DELETE, the GET request returned no content.
BUILD SUCCESSFUL (total time: 5 seconds)
```

The output is slightly different for the modified customer example:

```
run:
Jun 12, 2012 2:40:20 PM customer.rest.client.CustomerClientXML main
INFO: POST status: 201
[...]
Jun 12, 2012 2:40:20 PM customer.rest.client.CustomerClientXML main
INFO: DELETE succeeded (no content)
Jun 12, 2012 2:40:20 PM customer.rest.client.CustomerClientXML main
INFO: GET status: 200
Jun 12, 2012 2:40:20 PM customer.rest.client.CustomerClientXML main
INFO: After DELETE, city is: null
BUILD SUCCESSFUL (total time: 5 seconds)
```

▼ To Run the customer Example Using the Web Services Tester

1 In NetBeans IDE, right-click the customer node and select Test RESTful Web Services.

Note – The Web Services Tester works only with the modified version of the customer example.

2 In the Configure REST Test Client dialog, select Web Test Client in Project and click Browse.

3 In the Select Project dialog, choose the customer project and click OK.

4 In the Configure REST Test Client dialog, click OK.

5 When the test client appears in the browser, select the Customer resource node in the left pane.

6 Paste the following XML code into the Content text area, replacing "Insert content here":

```
<?xml version="1.0" encoding="UTF-8"?>
<customer id="1">
  <firstname>Duke</firstname>
  <lastname>OfJava</lastname>
  <address>
    <number>1</number>
    <street>Duke's Way</street>
    <city>JavaTown</city>
    <state>JA</state>
    <zip>12345</zip>
    <country>USA</country>
  </address>
  <email>duke@example.com</email>
  <phone>123-456-7890</phone>
</customer>
```

You can find the code in the file customer/sample-input.xml.

7 Click Test.

The following message appears in the window below:

```
Status: 201 (Created)
```

8 Expand the Customer node and click {id}.

9 Type 1 in the id field and click Test to test the GET method.

The following status message appears:

```
Status: 200 (OK)
```

The XML output for the resource appears in the Response window:

```
<?xml version="1.0" encoding="UTF-8"?>
<customer xmlns="http://xml.customer" id="1">
  <firstname>Duke</firstname>
  <lastname>OfJava</lastname>
  <address>
    <number>1</number>
    <street>Duke's Way</street>
    <city>JavaTown</city>
    <state>JA</state>
    <zip>12345</zip>
    <country>USA</country>
  </address>
```

```
  <email>duke@example.com</email>
  <phone>123-456-7890</phone>
</customer>
```

A GET for a nonexistent ID also returns a 200 (OK) status, but the output in the Response window shows no content:

```
<?xml version="1.0" encoding="UTF-8"?>
  <customer xmlns="http://xml.customer"
    xmlns:xsi="http://www.w3.org/2001/XMLSchema-instance" xsi:nil="true"/>
```

You can test other methods as follows:

- Select PUT, type the input for an existing customer, modify any content except the id value, and click Test to update the customer fields. A successful update returns the following status message:

  ```
  Status: 303 (See Other)
  ```

- Select DELETE, type the ID for an existing customer, and click Test to remove the customer. A successful delete returns the following status message:

  ```
  Status: 204 (See Other)
  ```

Using Curl to Run the customer Example Application

Curl is a command-line tool you can use to run the customer application on UNIX platforms. You can download Curl from http://curl.haxx.se or add it to a Cygwin installation.

Run the following commands in the directory *tut-install*/examples/jaxrs/customer/ after deploying the application.

To add a new customer and test the POST method using XML data, use the following command:

```
curl -i --data @sample-input.xml \
--header Content-type:application/xml \
http://localhost:8080/customer/rest/Customer
```

To add a new customer using JSON data instead, use the following command:

```
curl -i --data @sample-input.json \
--header Content-type:application/json \
http://localhost:8080/customer/rest/Customer
```

A successful POST returns HTTP Status: 201 (Created).

To retrieve the details of the customer whose ID is 1, use the following command:

```
curl -i -X GET http://localhost:8080/customer/rest/Customer/1
```

To retrieve the details of the same customer represented as JSON data, use the following command:

```
curl -i --header Accept:application/json
    -X GET http://localhost:8080/customer/rest/Customer/1
```

A successful GET returns HTTP Status: 200 (OK).

To delete a customer record, use the following command:

```
curl -i -X DELETE http://localhost:8080/customer/rest/Customer/1
```

A successful DELETE returns HTTP Status: 204.

The customer example and the modified version respond differently to a GET request for a customer ID that does not exist. The original customer example returns HTTP Status: 204 (No content), whereas the modified version returns HTTP Status: 200 (OK) with a response that contains the XML header but no customer data.

Enterprise Beans

Part IV explores advanced topics related to Enterprise JavaBeans components. This part contains the following chapters:

- Chapter 11, "A Message-Driven Bean Example"
- Chapter 12, "Using the Embedded Enterprise Bean Container"
- Chapter 13, "Using Asynchronous Method Invocation in Session Beans"

11

A Message-Driven Bean Example

Message-driven beans can implement any messaging type. Most commonly, they implement the Java Message Service (JMS) technology. The example in this chapter uses JMS technology, so you should be familiar with basic JMS concepts such as queues and messages. To learn about these concepts, see Chapter 20, "Java Message Service Concepts."

This chapter describes the source code of a simple message-driven bean example. Before proceeding, you should read the basic conceptual information in the section "What Is a Message-Driven Bean?" in *The Java EE 6 Tutorial: Basic Concepts* as well as "Using Message-Driven Beans to Receive Messages Asynchronously" on page 370.

The following topics are addressed here:

- "Overview of the `simplemessage` Example" on page 227
- "The `simplemessage` Application Client" on page 228
- "The Message-Driven Bean Class" on page 229
- "Running the `simplemessage` Example" on page 231

Overview of the `simplemessage` Example

The `simplemessage` application has the following components:

- `SimpleMessageClient`: An application client that sends several messages to a queue
- `SimpleMessageBean`: A message-driven bean that asynchronously receives and processes the messages that are sent to the queue

Figure 11–1 illustrates the structure of this application. The application client sends messages to the queue, which was created administratively using the Administration Console. The JMS provider (in this case, the GlassFish Server) delivers the messages to the instances of the message-driven bean, which then processes the messages.

FIGURE 11–1   The simplemessage Application

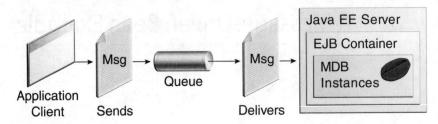

The source code for this application is in the
tut-install/examples/ejb/simplemessage/ directory.

The simplemessage Application Client

The SimpleMessageClient sends messages to the queue that the SimpleMessageBean listens to. The client starts by injecting the connection factory and queue resources:

```
@Resource(mappedName="jms/ConnectionFactory")
private static ConnectionFactory connectionFactory;

@Resource(mappedName="jms/Queue")
private static Queue queue;
```

Next, the client creates the connection, session, and message producer:

```
connection = connectionFactory.createConnection();
session = connection.createSession(false, Session.AUTO_ACKNOWLEDGE);
messageProducer = session.createProducer(queue);
```

Finally, the client sends several messages to the queue:

```
message = session.createTextMessage();

for (int i = 0; i < NUM_MSGS; i++) {
    message.setText("This is message " + (i + 1));
    System.out.println("Sending message: " + message.getText());
    messageProducer.send(message);
}
```

The Message-Driven Bean Class

The code for the `SimpleMessageBean` class illustrates the requirements of a message-driven bean class:

- It must be annotated with the `@MessageDriven` annotation if it does not use a deployment descriptor.

- The class must be defined as `public`.

- The class cannot be defined as `abstract` or `final`.

- It must contain a public constructor with no arguments.

- It must not define the `finalize` method.

It is recommended, but not required, that a message-driven bean class implement the message listener interface for the message type it supports. A bean that supports the JMS API implements the `javax.jms.MessageListener` interface.

Unlike session beans and entities, message-driven beans do not have the remote or local interfaces that define client access. Client components do not locate message-driven beans and invoke methods on them. Although message-driven beans do not have business methods, they may contain helper methods that are invoked internally by the `onMessage` method.

For the GlassFish Server, the `@MessageDriven` annotation typically contains a `mappedName` element that specifies the JNDI name of the destination from which the bean will consume messages. For complex message-driven beans, there can also be an `activationconfig` element containing `@ActivationConfigProperty` annotations used by the bean.

A message-driven bean can also inject a `MessageDrivenContext` resource. Commonly you use this resource to call the `setRollbackOnly` method to handle exceptions for a bean that uses container-managed transactions.

Therefore, the first few lines of the `SimpleMessageBean` class look like this:

```
@MessageDriven(mappedName="jms/Queue", activationConfig =  {
    @ActivationConfigProperty(propertyName = "acknowledgeMode",
                              propertyValue = "Auto-acknowledge"),
    @ActivationConfigProperty(propertyName = "destinationType",
                              propertyValue = "javax.jms.Queue")
})
public class SimpleMessageBean implements MessageListener {
    @Resource
    private MessageDrivenContext mdc;
    ...
```

NetBeans IDE typically creates a message-driven bean with a default set of `@ActivationConfigProperty` settings. You can delete those you do not need, or add others. Table 11–1 lists commonly used properties.

TABLE 11-1 `@ActivationConfigProperty` Settings for Message-Driven Beans

Property Name	Description
`acknowledgeMode`	Acknowledgment mode; see "Controlling Message Acknowledgment" on page 360 for information
`destinationType`	Either `javax.jms.Queue` or `javax.jms.Topic`
`subscriptionDurability`	For durable subscribers, set to `Durable`; see "Creating Durable Subscriptions" on page 364 for information
`clientId`	For durable subscribers, the client ID for the connection
`subscriptionName`	For durable subscribers, the name of the subscription
`messageSelector`	A string that filters messages; see "JMS Message Selectors" on page 355 for information, and see "An Application That Uses the JMS API with a Session Bean" on page 416 for an example
`addressList`	Remote system or systems with which to communicate; see "An Application Example That Consumes Messages from a Remote Server" on page 429 for an example

The onMessage Method

When the queue receives a message, the EJB container invokes the message listener method or methods. For a bean that uses JMS, this is the `onMessage` method of the `MessageListener` interface.

A message listener method must follow these rules:

- The method must be declared as `public`.
- The method must not be declared as `final` or `static`.

The `onMessage` method is called by the bean's container when a message has arrived for the bean to service. This method contains the business logic that handles the processing of the message. It is the message-driven bean's responsibility to parse the message and perform the necessary business logic.

The `onMessage` method has a single argument: the incoming message.

The signature of the `onMessage` method must follow these rules:

- The return type must be `void`.
- The method must have a single argument of type `javax.jms.Message`.

In the SimpleMessageBean class, the onMessage method casts the incoming message to a TextMessage and displays the text:

```
public void onMessage(Message inMessage) {
    TextMessage msg = null;

    try {
        if (inMessage instanceof TextMessage) {
            msg = (TextMessage) inMessage;
            logger.info("MESSAGE BEAN: Message received: " +
                msg.getText());
        } else {
            logger.warning("Message of wrong type: " +
                inMessage.getClass().getName());
        }
    } catch (JMSException e) {
        e.printStackTrace();
        mdc.setRollbackOnly();
    } catch (Throwable te) {
        te.printStackTrace();
    }
}
```

Running the simplemessage Example

You can use either NetBeans IDE or Ant to build, package, deploy, and run the simplemessage example.

Administered Objects for the simplemessage Example

This example requires the following:

- A JMS connection factory resource
- A JMS destination resource

If you have run the simple JMS examples in Chapter 20, "Java Message Service Concepts," and have not deleted the resources, you already have these resources. Otherwise, the resources will be created automatically when you deploy the application.

For more information on creating JMS resources, see "JMS Administered Objects for the Synchronous Receive Example" on page 381.

▼ To Run the simplemessage Application Using NetBeans IDE

1 From the File menu, choose Open Project.

2 In the Open Project dialog, navigate to:

tut-install/examples/ejb/

3 Select the simplemessage folder.

4 Select the Open as Main Project check box and the Open Required Projects check box.

5 Click Open Project.

6 In the Projects tab, right-click the simplemessage project and choose Build.

This task packages the application client and the message-driven bean, then creates a file named simplemessage.ear in the dist directory.

7 Right-click the project and choose Run.

This command creates any needed resources, deploys the project, returns a JAR file named simplemessageClient.jar, and then executes it.

The output of the application client in the Output pane looks like this (preceded by application client container output):

```
Sending message: This is message 1
Sending message: This is message 2
Sending message: This is message 3
To see if the bean received the messages,
 check <install_dir>/domains/domain1/logs/server.log.
```

The output from the message-driven bean appears in the server log (*domain-dir*/logs/server.log), wrapped in logging information.

```
MESSAGE BEAN: Message received: This is message 1
MESSAGE BEAN: Message received: This is message 2
MESSAGE BEAN: Message received: This is message 3
```

The received messages may appear in a different order from the order in which they were sent.

▼ To Run the simplemessage Application Using Ant

1 In a terminal window, go to:

tut-install/examples/ejb/simplemessage/

2   To compile the source files and package the application, use the following command:

`ant`

This target packages the application client and the message-driven bean, then creates a file named `simplemessage.ear` in the `dist` directory.

By using resource injection and annotations, you avoid having to create deployment descriptor files for the message-driven bean and application client. You need to use deployment descriptors only if you want to override the values specified in the annotated source files.

3   To create any needed resources, deploy the application, and run the client using Ant, use the following command:

`ant run`

Ignore the message that states that the application is deployed at a URL.

The output in the terminal window looks like this (preceded by application client container output):

```
Sending message: This is message 1
Sending message: This is message 2
Sending message: This is message 3
To see if the bean received the messages,
 check <install_dir>/domains/domain1/logs/server.log.
```

In the server log file, the following lines appear, wrapped in logging information:

```
MESSAGE BEAN: Message received: This is message 1
MESSAGE BEAN: Message received: This is message 2
MESSAGE BEAN: Message received: This is message 3
```

The received messages may appear in a different order from the order in which they were sent.

Removing the Administered Objects for the simplemessage Example

After you run the example, you can use NetBeans IDE to remove the connection factory and queue, as described in "To Delete JMS Resources Using NetBeans IDE" on page 382. If you are not using NetBeans IDE, you can use the `asadmin list-jms-resources` command to list the resources, and the `asadmin delete-jms-resource` command to remove each one.

CHAPTER 12

Using the Embedded Enterprise Bean Container

This chapter demonstrates how to use the embedded enterprise bean container to run enterprise bean applications in the Java SE environment, outside of a Java EE server.

The following topics are addressed here:

- "Overview of the Embedded Enterprise Bean Container" on page 235
- "Developing Embeddable Enterprise Bean Applications" on page 236
- "The `standalone` Example Application" on page 239

Overview of the Embedded Enterprise Bean Container

The embedded enterprise bean container is used to access enterprise bean components from client code executed in a Java SE environment. The container and the client code are executed within the same virtual machine. The embedded enterprise bean container is typically used for testing enterprise beans without having to deploy them to a server.

Most of the services present in the enterprise bean container in a Java EE server are available in the embedded enterprise bean container, including injection, container-managed transactions, and security. Enterprise bean components execute similarly in both embedded and Java EE environments, and therefore the same enterprise bean can be easily reused in both standalone and networked applications.

Developing Embeddable Enterprise Bean Applications

All embeddable enterprise bean containers support the features listed in Table 12–1.

TABLE 12–1   Required Enterprise Bean Features in the Embeddable Container

Enterprise Bean Feature	Description
Local session beans	Local and no-interface view stateless, stateful, and singleton session beans. All method access is synchronous. Session beans must not be web service endpoints.
Transactions	Container-managed and bean-managed transactions.
Security	Declarative and programmatic security.
Interceptors	Class-level and method-level interceptors for session beans.
Deployment descriptor	The optional ejb-jar.xml deployment descriptor, with the same overriding rules for the enterprise bean container in Java EE servers.

Container providers are allowed to support the full set of features in enterprise beans, but applications that use the embedded container will not be portable if they use enterprise bean features not listed in Table 12–1, such as the timer service, session beans as web service endpoints, or remote business interfaces.

Running Embedded Applications

The embedded container, the enterprise bean components, and the client all are executed in the same virtual machine using the same classpath. As a result, developers can run an application that uses the embedded container just like a typical Java SE application as follows:

```
java -classpath mySessionBean.jar:containerProviderRuntime.jar:myClient.jar
com.example.ejb.client.Main
```

In the above example, mySessionBean.jar is an EJB JAR containing a local stateless session bean, containerProviderRuntime.jar is a JAR file supplied by the enterprise bean provider that contains the needed runtime classes for the embedded container, and myClient.jar is a JAR file containing a Java SE application that calls the business methods in the session bean through the embedded container.

Creating the Enterprise Bean Container

The `javax.ejb.embedded.EJBContainer` abstract class represents an instance of the enterprise bean container and includes factory methods for creating a container instance. The `EJBContainer.createEJBContainer` method is used to create and initialize an embedded container instance.

The following code snippet shows how to create an embedded container that is initialized with the container provider's default settings:

```
EJBContainer ec = EJBContainer.createEJBContainer();
```

By default, the embedded container will search the virtual machine classpath for enterprise bean modules: directories containing a `META-INF/ejb-jar.xml` deployment descriptor, directories containing a class file with one of the enterprise bean component annotations (such as `@Stateless`), or JAR files containing an `ejb-jar.xml` deployment descriptor or class file with an enterprise bean annotation. Any matching entries are considered enterprise bean modules within the same application. Once all the valid enterprise bean modules have been found in the classpath, the container will begin initializing the modules. When the `createEJBContainer` method successfully returns, the client application can obtain references to the client view of any enterprise bean module found by the embedded container.

An alternate version of the `EJBContainer.createEJBContainer` method takes a `Map` of properties and settings for customizing the embeddable container instance:

```
Properties props = new Properties();
props.setProperty(...);
...
EJBContainer ec = EJBContainer.createEJBContainer(props);
```

Explicitly Specifying Enterprise Bean Modules to be Initialized

Developers can specify exactly which enterprise bean modules the embedded container will initialize. To explicitly specify the enterprise bean modules initialized by the embedded container, set the `EJBContainer.MODULES` property.

The modules may be located either in the virtual machine classpath in which the embedded container and client code run, or alternately outside the virtual machine classpath.

To specify modules in the virtual machine classpath, set `EJBContainer.MODULES` to a `String` to specify a single module name, or a `String` array containing the module names. The embedded container searches the virtual machine classpath for enterprise bean modules matching the specified names.

```
Properties props = new Properties();
props.setProperty(EJBContainer.MODULES, "mySessionBean");
EJBContainer ec = EJBContainer.createEJBContainer(props);
```

To specify enterprise bean modules outside the virtual machine classpath, set
EJBContainer.MODULES to a java.io.File object or an array of File objects. Each
File object refers to an EJB JAR file, or a directory containing an expanded EJB JAR.

```
Properties props = new Properties();
File ejbJarFile = new File(...);
props.setProperty(EJBContainer.MODULES, ejbJarFile);
EJBContainer ec = EJBContainer.createEJBContainer(props);
```

Looking Up Session Bean References

To look up session bean references in an application using the embedded container,
use an instance of EJBContainer to retrieve a javax.naming.Context object. Call the
EJBContainer.getContext method to retrieve the Context object.

```
EJBContainer ec = EJBContainer.createEJBContainer();
Context ctx = ec.getContext();
```

References to session beans can then be obtained using the portable JNDI syntax
detailed in "Portable JNDI Syntax" in *The Java EE 6 Tutorial: Basic Concepts*. For
example, to obtain a reference to MySessionBean, a local session bean with a
no-interface view, use the following code:

```
MySessionBean msb = (MySessionBean)
            ctx.lookup("java:global/mySessionBean/MySessionBean");
```

Shutting Down the Enterprise Bean Container

From the client, call the close method of the instance of EJBContainer to shut down
the embedded container:

```
EJBContainer ec = EJBContainer.createEJBContainer();
...
ec.close();
```

While clients are not required to shut down EJBContainer instances, doing so frees
resources consumed by the embedded container. This is particularly important when
the virtual machine under which the client application is running has a longer lifetime
than the client application.

The standalone **Example Application**

The standalone example application demonstrates how to create an instance of the embedded enterprise bean container in a JUnit test class and call a session bean business method. Testing the business methods of an enterprise bean in a unit test allows developers to exercise the business logic of an application separately from the other application layers, such as the presentation layer, and without having to deploy the application to a Java EE server.

The standalone example has two main components: StandaloneBean, a stateless session bean, and StandaloneBeanTest, a JUnit test class that acts as a client to StandaloneBean using the embedded container.

StandaloneBean is a simple session bean exposing a local, no-interface view with a single business method, returnMessage, which returns "Greetings!" as a String.

```
@Stateless
public class StandaloneBean {

    private static final String message = "Greetings!";

    public String returnMessage() {
        return message;
    }

}
```

StandaloneBeanTest calls StandaloneBean.returnMessage and tests that the returned message is correct. First, an embedded container instance and initial context are created within the setUp method, which is annotated with org.junit.Before to indicate that the method should be executed before the test methods.

```
@Before
public void setUp() {
    ec = EJBContainer.createEJBContainer();
    ctx = ec.getContext();
}
```

The testReturnMessage method, annotated with org.junit.Test to indicate that the method includes a unit test, obtains a reference to StandaloneBean through the Context instance, and calls StandaloneBean.returnMessage. The result is compared with the expected result using a JUnit assertion, assertEquals. If the string returned from StandaloneBean.returnMessage is equal to "Greetings!" the test passes.

```
@Test
public void testReturnMessage() throws Exception {
    logger.info("Testing standalone.ejb.StandalonBean.returnMessage()");
    StandaloneBean instance = (StandaloneBean)
            ctx.lookup("java:global/classes/StandaloneBean");
    String expResult = "Greetings!";
```

```
        String result = instance.returnMessage();
        assertEquals(expResult, result);
}
```

Finally, the tearDown method, annotated with org.junit.After to indicate that the method should be executed after all the unit tests have run, closes the embedded container instance.

```
@After
public void tearDown() {
    if (ec != null) {
        ec.close();
    }
}
```

▼ To Run the standalone Example Application

Before You Begin You must run the standalone example application within NetBeans IDE.

1   **From the File menu, choose Open Project.**

2   **In the Open Project dialog, navigate to:**

    tut-install/examples/ejb/

3   **Select the standalone folder and click Open Project.**

4   **In the Projects tab, right-click standalone and select Test.**

    This will execute the JUnit test class StandaloneBeanTest. The Output tab shows the progress of the test and the output log.

Using Asynchronous Method Invocation in Session Beans

This chapter discusses how to implement asynchronous business methods in session beans and call them from enterprise bean clients.

The following topics are addressed here:

- "Asynchronous Method Invocation" on page 241
- "The async Example Application" on page 244

Asynchronous Method Invocation

Session beans can implement *asynchronous methods*, business methods where control is returned to the client by the enterprise bean container before the method is invoked on the session bean instance. Clients may then use the Java SE concurrency API to retrieve the result, cancel the invocation, and check for exceptions. Asynchronous methods are typically used for long-running operations, for processor-intensive tasks, for background tasks, to increase application throughput, or to improve application response time if the method invocation result isn't required immediately.

When a session bean client invokes a typical non-asynchronous business method, control is not returned to the client until the method has completed. Clients calling asynchronous methods, however, immediately have control returned to them by the enterprise bean container. This allows the client to perform other tasks while the method invocation completes. If the method returns a result, the result is an implementation of the `java.util.concurrent.Future<V>` interface, where "V" is the result value type. The `Future<V>` interface defines methods the client may use to check whether the computation is completed, wait for the invocation to complete, retrieve the final result, and cancel the invocation.

Creating an Asynchronous Business Method

Annotate a business method with `javax.ejb.Asynchronous` to mark that method as an asynchronous method, or apply `@Asynchronous` at the class level to mark all the business methods of the session bean as asynchronous methods. Session bean methods that expose web services can't be asynchronous.

Asynchronous methods must return either `void` or an implementation of the `Future<V>` interface. Asynchronous methods that return `void` can't declare application exceptions, but if they return `Future<V>`, they may declare application exceptions. For example:

```
@Asynchronous
public Future<String> processPayment(Order order) throws PaymentException {
    ...
}
```

This method will attempt to process the payment of an order, and return the status as a `String`. Even if the payment processor takes a long time, the client can continue working, and display the result when the processing finally completes.

The `javax.ejb.AsyncResult<V>` class is a concrete implementation of the `Future<V>` interface provided as a helper class for returning asynchronous results. `AsyncResult` has a constructor with the result as a parameter, making it easy to create `Future<V>` implementations. For example, the `processPayment` method would use `AsyncResult` to return the status as a `String`:

```
@Asynchronous
public Future<String> processPayment(Order order) throws PaymentException {
    ...
    String status = ...;
    return new AsyncResult<String>(status);
}
```

The result is returned to the enterprise bean container, not directly to the client, and the enterprise bean container makes the result available to the client. The session bean can check whether the client requested that the invocation be cancelled by calling the `javax.ejb.SessionContext.wasCancelled` method. For example:

```
@Asynchronous
public Future<String> processPayment(Order order) throws PaymentException {
    ...
    if (SessionContext.wasCancelled()) {
        // clean up
    } else {
        // process the payment
    }
    ...
}
```

Calling Asynchronous Methods from Enterprise Bean Clients

Session bean clients call asynchronous methods just like non-asynchronous business methods. If the asynchronous method returns a result, the client receives a Future<V> instance as soon as the method is invoked. This instance can be used to retrieve the final result, cancel the invocation, check whether the invocation has completed, check whether any exceptions were thrown during processing, and check whether the invocation was cancelled.

Retrieving the Final Result from an Asynchronous Method Invocation

The client may retrieve the result using one of the Future<V>.get methods. If processing hasn't been completed by the session bean handling the invocation, calling one of the get methods will result in the client halting execution until the invocation completes. Use the Future<V>.isDone method to determine whether processing has completed before calling one of the get methods.

The get() method returns the result as the type specified in the type value of the Future<V> instance. For example, calling Future<String>.get() will return a String object. If the method invocation was cancelled, calls to get() result in a java.util.concurrent.CancellationException being thrown. If the invocation resulted in an exception during processing by the session bean, calls to get() result in a java.util.concurrent.ExecutionException being thrown. The cause of the ExecutionException may be retrieved by calling the ExecutionException.getCause method.

The get(long timeout, java.util.concurrent.TimeUnit unit) method is similar to the get() method, but allows the client to set a timeout value. If the timeout value is exceeded, a java.util.concurrent.TimeoutException is thrown. See the Javadoc for the TimeUnit class for the available units of time to specify the timeout value.

Cancelling an Asynchronous Method Invocation

Call the cancel(boolean mayInterruptIfRunning) method on the Future<V> instance to attempt to cancel the method invocation. The cancel method returns true if the cancellation was successful, and false if the method invocation cannot be cancelled.

When the invocation cannot be cancelled, the mayInterruptIfRunning parameter is used to alert the session bean instance on which the method invocation is running that the client attempted to cancel the invocation. If mayInterruptIfRunning is set to true, calls to SessionContext.wasCancelled by the session bean instance will return true. If mayInterruptIfRunning is to set false, calls to SessionContext.wasCancelled by the session bean instance will return false.

The `Future<V>.isCancelled` method is used to check whether the method invocation was cancelled before the asynchronous method invocation completed by calling `Future<V>.cancel`. The `isCancelled` method returns `true` if the invocation was cancelled.

Checking the Status of an Asynchronous Method Invocation

The `Future<V>.isDone` method returns `true` if the session bean instance completed processing the method invocation. The `isDone` method returns `true` if the asynchronous method invocation completed normally, was cancelled, or resulted in an exception. That is, `isDone` indicates only whether the session bean has completed processing the invocation.

The async **Example Application**

The `async` example demonstrates how to define an asynchronous business method on a session bean and call it from a web client. The `MailerBean` stateless session bean defines an asynchronous method, `sendMessage`, which uses the JavaMail API to send an email to a specified email address.

Note – This example needs to be configured for your environment before it runs correctly, and requires access to an SMTPS server.

Architecture of the async **Example Application**

The `async` application consists of a single stateless session bean, `MailerBean`, and a JavaServer Faces web application front end that uses Facelets tags in XHTML files to display a form for users to enter the email address for the recipient of an email. The status of the email is updated when the email is finally sent.

The `MailerBean` session bean injects a JavaMail resource used to send an email message to an address specified by the user. The message is created, modified, and sent using the JavaMail API. The injected JavaMail resource is configured through the GlassFish Server Administration Console, or through a resource configuration file packaged with the application. The resource configuration can be modified at runtime by the GlassFish Server administrator to use a different mail server or transport protocol.

```
@Asynchronous
public Future<String> sendMessage(String email) {
    String status;
    try {
        Message message = new MimeMessage(session);
```

```
        message.setFrom();
        message.setRecipients(Message.RecipientType.TO,
                InternetAddress.parse(email, false));
        message.setSubject("Test message from async example");
        message.setHeader("X-Mailer", "JavaMail");
        DateFormat dateFormatter = DateFormat
                .getDateTimeInstance(DateFormat.LONG, DateFormat.SHORT);
        Date timeStamp = new Date();
        String messageBody = "This is a test message from the async example "
                + "of the Java EE Tutorial. It was sent on "
                + dateFormatter.format(timeStamp)
                + ".";
        message.setText(messageBody);
        message.setSentDate(timeStamp);
        Transport.send(message);
        status = "Sent";
        logger.log(Level.INFO, "Mail sent to {0}", email);
    } catch (MessagingException ex) {
        logger.severe("Error in sending message.");
        status = "Encountered an error";
        logger.severe(ex.getMessage() + ex.getNextException().getMessage());
        logger.severe(ex.getCause().getMessage());
    }
    return new AsyncResult<String>(status);
}
```

The web client consists of a Facelets template, `template.xhtml`, two Facelets clients, `index.xhtml` and `response.xhtml`, and a JavaServer Faces managed bean, `MailerManagedBean`. The `index.xhtml` file contains a form for the target email address. When the user submits the form, the `MailerManagedBean.send` method is called. This method uses an injected instance of the `MailerBean` session bean to call `MailerBean.sendMessage`. The result is sent to the `response.xhtml` Facelets view.

Running the async Example

You can use either NetBeans IDE or Ant to build, package, deploy, and run the `async` example. First, however, you must configure the keystore and truststore.

▼ To Configure the Keystore and Truststore in GlassFish Server

The GlassFish Server domain needs to be configured with the server's master password to access the keystore and truststore used to initiate secure communications using the SMTPS transport protocol.

1   Open the GlassFish Server Administration Console in a web browser at
    `http://localhost:4848`.

2   Expand Configurations, then expand server-config, then click JVM Settings.

3   Click JVM Options, then click Add JVM Option and enter
    `-Djavax.net.ssl.keyStorePassword=`*master-password*, replacing *master-password*
    with the keystore master password. The default master password is `changeit`.

4   Click Add JVM Option and enter
    `-Djavax.net.ssl.trustStorePassword=`*master-password*, replacing
    master-password with the truststore master password. The default master password is
    `changeit`.

5   Click Save, then restart GlassFish Server.

▼ To Run the `async` Example Using NetBeans IDE

Before You Begin   Before running this example, you must configure your GlassFish Server instance to
access the keystore and truststore used by GlassFish Server to create a secure
connection to the target SMTPS server.

1   From the File menu, choose Open Project.

2   In the Open Project dialog, navigate to:
    tut-install/examples/ejb/

3   Select the `async` folder and click Open Project.

4   Under `async` in the project pane, expand the Server Resources node and double-click
    `glassfish-resources.xml`.

5   Enter the configuration settings for your SMTPS server in `glassfish-resources.xml`.

    The SMTPS server host name is set in the `host` attribute; the email address from which
    you want the message sent is set in the `from` attribute; and the SMTPS user name is set
    in the `user` attribute. Set the `mail-smtps-password` property value to the password for
    the SMTPS server user. The following code snippet shows an example resource
    configuration. Lines in bold need to be modified.

```
<resources>
    <mail-resource debug="false"
            enabled="true"
            from="user@example.com"
            host="smtp.example.com"
            jndi-name="mail/myExampleSession"
            object-type="user" store-protocol="imap"
            store-protocol-class="com.sun.mail.imap.IMAPStore"
            transport-protocol="smtps"
            transport-protocol-class="com.sun.mail.smtp.SMTPSSLTransport"
            user="user@example.com">
        <description/>
        <property name="mail-smtps-auth" value="true"/>
        <property name="mail-smtps-password" value="mypassword"/>
```

```
    </mail-resource>
</resources>
```

6 **Right-click async in the project pane and select Run.**

This will compile, assemble, and deploy the application, and start a web browser at the following URL: http://localhost:8080/async.

7 **In the web browser window, enter the email to which you want the test message sent and click Send email.**

If your configuration settings are correct, a test email will be sent, and the status message will read Sent in the web client. The test message should appear momentarily in the inbox of the recipient.

If an error occurs, the status will read Encountered an error. Check the server.log file for your domain to find the cause of the error.

▼ To Run the async Example Using Ant

1 **In a terminal window, navigate to** *tut-install*/**examples/ejb/async/.**

2 **In a text editor, open setup/glassfish-resources.xml and enter the configuration settings for your SMTPS server.**

The SMTPS server host name is set in the host attribute, email address from which you want the message sent is the from attribute, the SMTPS user name is the user attribute. Set the mail-smtps-password property value to the password for the SMTPS server user. The following code snippet shows an example resource configuration. Lines in bold need to be modified.

```
<resources>
    <mail-resource debug="false"
            enabled="true"
            from="user@example.com"
            host="smtp.example.com"
            jndi-name="mail/myExampleSession"
            object-type="user" store-protocol="imap"
            store-protocol-class="com.sun.mail.imap.IMAPStore"
            transport-protocol="smtps"
            transport-protocol-class="com.sun.mail.smtp.SMTPSSLTransport"
            user="user@example.com">
        <description/>
        <property name="mail-smtps-auth" value="true"/>
        <property name="mail-smtps-password" value="mypassword"/>
    </mail-resource>
</resources>
```

3 **Enter the following command:**

`ant all`

This will compile, assemble, and deploy the application, and start a web browser at the following URL: http://localhost:8080/async.

Note – If your build system isn't configured to automatically open a web browser, open the above URL in a browser window.

---

4   In the web browser window, enter the email to which you want the test message sent and click Send email.

If your configuration settings are correct, a test email will be sent, and the status message will read Sent in the web client. The test message should appear momentarily in the inbox of the recipient.

If an error occurs, the status will read Encountered an error. Check the server.log file for your domain to find the cause of the error.

Contexts and Dependency Injection for the Java EE Platform

Part V explores advanced topics related to Contexts and Dependency Injection for the Java EE Platform. This part contains the following chapters:

- Chapter 14, "Contexts and Dependency Injection for the Java EE Platform: Advanced Topics"
- Chapter 15, "Running the Advanced Contexts and Dependency Injection Examples"

Contexts and Dependency Injection for the Java EE Platform: Advanced Topics

This chapter describes more advanced features of Contexts and Dependency Injection for the Java EE Platform. Specifically, it covers additional features CDI provides to enable loose coupling of components with strong typing, in addition to those described in "Overview of CDI" in *The Java EE 6 Tutorial: Basic Concepts*.

The following topics are addressed here:

- "Using Alternatives in CDI Applications" on page 251
- "Using Producer Methods, Producer Fields, and Disposer Methods in CDI Applications" on page 254
- "Using Predefined Beans in CDI Applications" on page 256
- "Using Events in CDI Applications" on page 257
- "Using Interceptors in CDI Applications" on page 260
- "Using Decorators in CDI Applications" on page 262
- "Using Stereotypes in CDI Applications" on page 263

Using Alternatives in CDI Applications

When you have more than one version of a bean you use for different purposes, you can choose between them during the development phase by injecting one qualifier or another, as shown in "The simplegreeting CDI Example" in *The Java EE 6 Tutorial: Basic Concepts*.

Instead of having to change the source code of your application, however, you can make the choice at deployment time by using *alternatives*.

Alternatives are commonly used for purposes like the following:

- To handle client-specific business logic that is determined at runtime
- To specify beans that are valid for a particular deployment scenario (for example, when country-specific sales tax laws require country-specific sales tax business logic)
- To create dummy (mock) versions of beans to be used for testing

To make a bean available for lookup, injection, or EL resolution using this mechanism, give it a javax.enterprise.inject.Alternative annotation and then use the alternative element to specify it in the beans.xml file.

For example, you might want to create a full version of a bean and also a simpler version that you use only for certain kinds of testing. The example described in "The encoder Example: Using Alternatives" on page 265 contains two such beans, CoderImpl and TestCoderImpl. The test bean is annotated as follows:

```
@Alternative
public class TestCoderImpl implements Coder { ... }
```

The full version is not annotated:

```
public class CoderImpl implements Coder { ... }
```

The managed bean injects an instance of the Coder interface:

```
@Inject
Coder coder;
```

The alternative version of the bean is used by the application only if that version is declared as follows in the beans.xml file:

```
<beans ... >
    <alternatives>
        <class>encoder.TestCoderImpl</class>
    </alternatives>
</beans>
```

If the alternatives element is commented out in the beans.xml file, the CoderImpl class is used.

You can also have several beans that implement the same interface, all annotated @Alternative. In this case, you must specify in the beans.xml file which of these alternative beans you want to use. If CoderImpl were also annotated @Alternative, one of the two beans would always have to be specified in the beans.xml file.

Using Specialization

Specialization has a function similar to that of alternatives, in that it allows you to substitute one bean for another. However, you might want to make one bean override the other in all cases. Suppose you defined the following two beans:

```
@Default @Asynchronous
public class AsynchronousService implements Service { ... }

@Alternative
public class MockAsynchronousService extends AsynchronousService { ... }
```

If you then declared `MockAsynchronousService` as an alternative in your `beans.xml` file, the following injection point would resolve to `MockAsynchronousService`:

```
@Inject Service service;
```

The following, however, would resolve to `AsynchronousService` rather than `MockAsynchronousService`, because `MockAsynchronousService` does not have the `@Asynchronous` qualifier:

```
@Inject @Asynchronous Service service;
```

To make sure `MockAsynchronousService` was always injected, you would have to implement all bean types and bean qualifiers of `AsynchronousService`. However, if `AsynchronousService` declared a producer method or observer method, even this cumbersome mechanism would not ensure that the other bean was never invoked. Specialization provides a simpler mechanism.

Specialization happens at development time as well as at runtime. If you declare that one bean specializes another, it extends the other bean class, and at runtime the specialized bean completely replaces the other bean. If the first bean is produced by means of a producer method, you must also override the producer method.

You specialize a bean by giving it the `javax.enterprise.inject.Specializes` annotation. For example, you might declare a bean as follows:

```
@Specializes
public class MockAsynchronousService extends AsynchronousService { ... }
```

In this case, the `MockAsynchronousService` class will always be invoked instead of the `AsynchronousService` class.

Usually, a bean marked with the `@Specializes` annotation is also an alternative and is declared as an alternative in the `beans.xml` file. Such a bean is meant to stand in as a replacement for the default implementation, and the alternative implementation automatically inherits all qualifiers of the default implementation as well as its EL name, if it has one.

Using Producer Methods, Producer Fields, and Disposer Methods in CDI Applications

A *producer method* generates an object that can then be injected. Typically, you use producer methods in the following situations:

- When you want to inject an object that is not itself a bean
- When the concrete type of the object to be injected may vary at runtime
- When the object requires some custom initialization that the bean constructor does not perform

For more information on producer methods, see "Injecting Objects by Using Producer Methods" in *The Java EE 6 Tutorial: Basic Concepts*.

A *producer field* is a simpler alternative to a producer method; it is a field of a bean that generates an object. It can be used instead of a simple getter method. Producer fields are particularly useful for declaring Java EE resources such as data sources, JMS resources, and web service references.

A producer method or field is annotated with the `javax.enterprise.inject.Produces` annotation.

Using Producer Methods

A producer method can allow you to select a bean implementation at runtime, instead of at development time or deployment time. For example, in the example described in "The producermethods Example: Using a Producer Method To Choose a Bean Implementation" on page 271, the managed bean defines the following producer method:

```
@Produces
@Chosen
@RequestScoped
public Coder getCoder(@New TestCoderImpl tci,
        @New CoderImpl ci) {

    switch (coderType) {
        case TEST:
            return tci;
        case SHIFT:
            return ci;
        default:
            return null;
    }
}
```

The javax.enterprise.inject.New qualifier instructs the CDI runtime to instantiate both of the coder implementations and provide them as arguments to the producer method. Here, getCoder becomes in effect a getter method, and when the coder property is injected with the same qualifier and other annotations as the method, the selected version of the interface is used.

```
@Inject
@Chosen
@RequestScoped
Coder coder;
```

Specifying the qualifier is essential: It tells CDI which Coder to inject. Without it, the CDI implementation would not be able to choose between CoderImpl, TestCoderImpl, and the one returned by getCoder, and would cancel deployment, informing the user of the ambiguous dependency.

Using Producer Fields to Generate Resources

A common use of a producer field is to generate an object such as a JDBC DataSource or a Java Persistence API EntityManager. The object can then be managed by the container. For example, you could create a @UserDatabase qualifier and then declare a producer field for an entity manager as follows:

```
@Produces
@UserDatabase
@PersistenceContext
private EntityManager em;
```

The @UserDatabase qualifier can be used when you inject the object into another bean, RequestBean, elsewhere in the application:

```
@Inject
@UserDatabase
EntityManager em;
...
```

"The producerfields Example: Using Producer Fields to Generate Resources" on page 273 shows how to use producer fields to generate an entity manager. You can use a similar mechanism to inject @Resource, @EJB, or @WebServiceRef objects.

To minimize the reliance on resource injection, specify the producer field for the resource in one place in the application, then inject the object wherever in the application you need it.

Using a Disposer Method

You can use a producer method to generate an object that needs to be removed when its work is completed. If you do, you need a corresponding *disposer method*, annotated with a @Disposes annotation. For example, if you used a producer method instead of a producer field to create the entity manager, you would create and close it as follows:

```
@PersistenceContext
private EntityManager em;

@Produces
@UserDatabase
public EntityManager create() {
    return em;
}

public void close(@Disposes @UserDatabase EntityManager em) {
    em.close();
}
```

The disposer method is called automatically when the context ends (in this case, at the end of the conversation, because RequestBean has conversation scope), and the parameter in the close method receives the object produced by the producer method, create.

Using Predefined Beans in CDI Applications

CDI provides predefined beans that implement the following interfaces:

javax.transaction.UserTransaction
A Java Transaction API (JTA) user transaction.

java.security.Principal
The abstract notion of a principal, which represents any entity, such as an individual, a corporation, or a login ID. Whenever the injected principal is accessed, it always represents the identity of the current caller. For example, a principal is injected into a field at initialization. Later, a method that uses the injected principal is called on the object into which the principal was injected. In this situation, the injected principal represents the identity of the current caller when the method is run.

javax.validation.Validator
A validator for bean instances. The bean that implements this interface enables a Validator object for the default bean validation ValidatorFactory object to be injected.

`javax.validation.ValidatorFactory`
> A factory class for returning initialized `Validator` instances. The bean that implements this interface enables the default bean validation object `ValidatorFactory` to be injected.

To inject a predefined bean, create an injection point by using the `javax.annotation.Resource` annotation to obtain an instance of the bean. For the bean type, specify the class name of the interface the bean implements.

Predefined beans are injected with dependent scope and the predefined default qualifier `@Default`.

For more information about injecting resources, see "Resource Injection" in *The Java EE 6 Tutorial: Basic Concepts*.

The following code snippet shows how to use the `@Resource` annotation to inject a predefined bean. This code snippet injects a user transaction into the servlet class `TransactionServlet`. The user transaction is an instance of the predefined bean that implements the `javax.transaction.UserTransaction` interface.

```java
import javax.annotation.Resource;
import javax.servlet.http.HttpServlet;
import javax.transaction.UserTransaction;
...
public class TransactionServlet extends HttpServlet {
    @Resource UserTransaction transaction;
    ...
}
```

Using Events in CDI Applications

Events allow beans to communicate without any compile-time dependency. One bean can define an event, another bean can fire the event, and yet another bean can handle the event. The beans can be in separate packages and even in separate tiers of the application.

Defining Events

An event consists of the following:

- The event object, a Java object
- Zero or more qualifier types, the event qualifiers

For example, in the `billpayment` example described in "The `billpayment` Example: Using Events and Interceptors" on page 280, a `PaymentEvent` bean defines an event using three properties, which have setter and getter methods:

```
public String paymentType;
public BigDecimal value;
public Date datetime;

public PaymentEvent() {
}
```

The example also defines qualifiers that distinguish between two kinds of `PaymentEvent`. Every event also has the default qualifier `@Any`.

Using Observer Methods to Handle Events

An event handler uses an *observer method* to consume events.

Each observer method takes as a parameter an event of a specific event type that is annotated with the `@Observes` annotation and with any qualifiers for that event type. The observer method is notified of an event if the event object matches the event type and if all the qualifiers of the event match the observer method event qualifiers.

The observer method can take other parameters in addition to the event parameter. The additional parameters are injection points and can declare qualifiers.

The event handler for the `billpayment` example, `PaymentHandler`, defines two observer methods, one for each type of `PaymentEvent`:

```
public void creditPayment(@Observes @Credit PaymentEvent event) {
    ...
}

public void debitPayment(@Observes @Debit PaymentEvent event) {
    ...
}
```

Observer methods can also be conditional or transactional:

- A conditional observer method is notified of an event only if an instance of the bean that defines the observer method already exists in the current context. To declare a conditional observer method, specify `notifyObserver=IF_EXISTS` as an argument to `@Observes`:

  ```
  @Observes(notifyObserver=IF_EXISTS)
  ```

  To obtain the default unconditional behavior, you can specify `@Observes(notifyObserver=ALWAYS)`.

- A transactional observer method is notified of an event during the before-completion or after-completion phase of the transaction in which the event was fired. You can also specify that the notification is to occur only after the transaction has completed successfully or unsuccessfully. To specify a transactional observer method, use any of the following arguments to @Observes:

```
@Observes(during=BEFORE_COMPLETION)
```

```
@Observes(during=AFTER_COMPLETION)
```

```
@Observes(during=AFTER_SUCCESS)
```

```
@Observes(during=AFTER_FAILURE)
```

To obtain the default non-transactional behavior, specify @Observes(during=IN_PROGRESS).

An observer method that is called before completion of a transaction may call the setRollbackOnly method on the transaction instance to force a transaction rollback.

Observer methods may throw exceptions. If a transactional observer method throws an exception, the exception is caught by the container. If the observer method is non-transactional, the exception terminates processing of the event, and no other observer methods for the event are called.

Firing Events

To activate an event, call the javax.enterprise.event.Event.fire method. This method fires an event and notifies any observer methods.

In the billpayment example, a managed bean called PaymentBean fires the appropriate event by using information it receives from the user interface. There are actually four event beans, two for the event object and two for the payload. The managed bean injects the two event beans. The pay method uses a switch statement to choose which event to fire, using new to create the payload.

```
@Inject
@Credit
Event<PaymentEvent> creditEvent;

@Inject
@Debit
Event<PaymentEvent> debitEvent;

private static final int DEBIT = 1;
private static final int CREDIT = 2;
private int paymentOption = DEBIT;
...
```

```
@Logged
public String pay() {
    ...
    switch (paymentOption) {
        case DEBIT:
            PaymentEvent debitPayload = new PaymentEvent();
            // populate payload ...
            debitEvent.fire(debitPayload);
            break;
        case CREDIT:
            PaymentEvent creditPayload = new PaymentEvent();
            // populate payload ...
            creditEvent.fire(creditPayload);
            break;
        default:
            logger.severe("Invalid payment option!");
    }
    ...
}
```

The argument to the `fire` method is a `PaymentEvent` that contains the payload. The fired event is then consumed by the observer methods.

Using Interceptors in CDI Applications

An *interceptor* is a class used to interpose in method invocations or lifecycle events that occur in an associated target class. The interceptor performs tasks, such as logging or auditing, that are separate from the business logic of the application and are repeated often within an application. Such tasks are often called *cross-cutting* tasks. Interceptors allow you to specify the code for these tasks in one place for easy maintenance. When interceptors were first introduced to the Java EE platform, they were specific to enterprise beans. On the Java EE 6 platform you can use them with Java EE managed objects of all kinds, including managed beans.

For information on Java EE interceptors, see Chapter 23, "Using Java EE Interceptors."

An interceptor class often contains a method annotated @AroundInvoke, which specifies the tasks the interceptor will perform when intercepted methods are invoked. It can also contain a method annotated @PostConstruct, @PreDestroy, @PrePassivate, or @PostActivate, to specify lifecycle callback interceptors, and a method annotated @AroundTimeout, to specify EJB timeout interceptors. An interceptor class can contain more than one interceptor method, but it must have no more than one method of each type.

Along with an interceptor, an application defines one or more *interceptor binding types*, which are annotations that associate an interceptor with target beans or methods. For example, the `billpayment` example contains an interceptor binding type named @Logged and an interceptor named LoggedInterceptor.

The interceptor binding type declaration looks something like a qualifier declaration, but it is annotated with `javax.interceptor.InterceptorBinding`:

```
@Inherited
@InterceptorBinding
@Retention(RUNTIME)
@Target({METHOD, TYPE})
public @interface Logged {
}
```

An interceptor binding also has the `java.lang.annotation.Inherited` annotation, to specify that the annotation can be inherited from superclasses. The @Inherited annotation also applies to custom scopes (not discussed in this tutorial), but does not apply to qualifiers.

An interceptor binding type may declare other interceptor bindings.

The interceptor class is annotated with the interceptor binding as well as with the @Interceptor annotation. For an example, see "The LoggedInterceptor Interceptor Class" on page 284.

Every @AroundInvoke method takes a `javax.interceptor.InvocationContext` argument, returns a `java.lang.Object`, and throws an `Exception`. It can call `InvocationContext` methods. The @AroundInvoke method must call the proceed method, which causes the target class method to be invoked.

Once an interceptor and binding type are defined, you can annotate beans and individual methods with the binding type to specify that the interceptor is to be invoked either on all methods of the bean or on specific methods. For example, in the billpayment example, the PaymentHandler bean is annotated @Logged, which means that any invocation of its business methods will cause the interceptor's @AroundInvoke method to be invoked:

```
@Logged
@SessionScoped
public class PaymentHandler implements Serializable {...}
```

However, in the PaymentBean bean, only the pay and reset methods have the @Logged annotation, so the interceptor is invoked only when these methods are invoked:

```
@Logged
public String pay() {...}
```

```
@Logged
public void reset() {...}
```

In order for an interceptor to be invoked in a CDI application, it must, like an alternative, be specified in the beans.xml file. For example, the LoggedInterceptor class is specified as follows:

```
<interceptors>
    <class>billpayment.interceptors.LoggedInterceptor</class>
</interceptors>
```

If an application uses more than one interceptor, the interceptors are invoked in the order specified in the beans.xml file.

Using Decorators in CDI Applications

A *decorator* is a Java class that is annotated javax.decorator.Decorator and that has a corresponding decorators element in the beans.xml file.

A decorator bean class must also have a delegate injection point, which is annotated javax.decorator.Delegate. This injection point can be a field, a constructor parameter, or an initializer method parameter of the decorator class.

Decorators are outwardly similar to interceptors. However, they actually perform tasks complementary to those performed by interceptors. Interceptors perform cross-cutting tasks associated with method invocation and with the lifecycles of beans, but cannot perform any business logic. Decorators, on the other hand, do perform business logic by intercepting business methods of beans. This means that instead of being reusable for different kinds of applications as are interceptors, their logic is specific to a particular application.

For example, instead of using an alternative TestCoderImpl class for the encoder example, you could create a decorator as follows:

```
@Decorator
public abstract class CoderDecorator implements Coder {

    @Inject
    @Delegate
    @Any
    Coder coder;

    public String codeString(String s, int tval) {
        int len = s.length();

        return "\"" + s + "\" becomes " + "\"" + coder.codeString(s, tval)
                + "\", " + len + " characters in length";
    }
}
```

See "The decorators Example: Decorating a Bean" on page 286 for an example that uses this decorator.

This simple decorator returns more detailed output than the encoded string returned by the CoderImpl.codeString method. A more complex decorator could store information in a database or perform some other business logic.

A decorator can be declared as an abstract class, so that it does not have to implement all the business methods of the interface.

In order for a decorator to be invoked in a CDI application, it must, like an interceptor or an alternative, be specified in the beans.xml file. For example, the CoderDecorator class is specified as follows:

```
<decorators>
    <class>decorators.CoderDecorator</class>
</decorators>
```

If an application uses more than one decorator, the decorators are invoked in the order in which they are specified in the beans.xml file.

If an application has both interceptors and decorators, the interceptors are invoked first. This means, in effect, that you cannot intercept a decorator.

Using Stereotypes in CDI Applications

A *stereotype* is a kind of annotation, applied to a bean, that incorporates other annotations. Stereotypes can be particularly useful in large applications where you have a number of beans that perform similar functions. A stereotype is a kind of annotation that specifies the following:

- A default scope
- Zero or more interceptor bindings
- Optionally, a @Named annotation, guaranteeing default EL naming
- Optionally, an @Alternative annotation, specifying that all beans with this stereotype are alternatives

A bean annotated with a particular stereotype will always use the specified annotations, so you do not have to apply the same annotations to many beans.

For example, you might create a stereotype named Action, using the javax.enterprise.inject.Stereotype annotation:

```
@RequestScoped
@Secure
@Transactional
@Named
@Stereotype
@Target(TYPE)
@Retention(RUNTIME)
public @interface Action {}
```

All beans annotated @Action will have request scope, use default EL naming, and have the interceptor bindings @Transactional and @Secure.

You could also create a stereotype named Mock:

```
@Alternative
@Stereotype
@Target(TYPE)
@Retention(RUNTIME)
public @interface Mock {}
```

All beans with this annotation are alternatives.

It is possible to apply multiple stereotypes to the same bean, so you can annotate a bean as follows:

```
@Action
@Mock
public class MockLoginAction extends LoginAction { ... }
```

It is also possible to override the scope specified by a stereotype, simply by specifying a different scope for the bean. The following declaration gives the MockLoginAction bean session scope instead of request scope:

```
@SessionScoped
@Action
@Mock
public class MockLoginAction extends LoginAction { ... }
```

CDI makes available a built-in stereotype called Model, which is intended for use with beans that define the model layer of a model-view-controller application architecture. This stereotype specifies that a bean is both @Named and @RequestScoped:

```
@Named
@RequestScoped
@Stereotype
@Target({TYPE, METHOD, FIELD})
@Retention(RUNTIME)
public @interface Model {}
```

15

Running the Advanced Contexts and Dependency Injection Examples

This chapter describes in detail how to build and run several advanced examples that use CDI. The examples are in the *tut-install*/examples/cdi/ directory.

To build and run the examples, you will do the following:

1. Use NetBeans IDE or the Ant tool to compile, package, and deploy the example.
2. Run the example in a web browser.

Each example has a build.xml file that refers to files in the *tut-install*/examples/bp-project/ directory.

See Chapter 2, "Using the Tutorial Examples," for basic information on installing, building, and running the examples.

The following topics are addressed here:

The encoder Example: Using Alternatives

The encoder example shows how to use alternatives to choose between two beans at deployment time, as described in "Using Alternatives in CDI Applications" on page 251. The example includes an interface and two implementations of it, a managed bean, a Facelets page, and configuration files.

The `Coder` Interface and Implementations

The `Coder` interface contains just one method, `codeString`, that takes two arguments: a string, and an integer value that specifies how the letters in the string should be transposed.

```
public interface Coder {

    public String codeString(String s, int tval);
}
```

The interface has two implementation classes, `CoderImpl` and `TestCoderImpl`. The implementation of `codeString` in `CoderImpl` shifts the string argument forward in the alphabet by the number of letters specified in the second argument; any characters that are not letters are left unchanged. (This simple shift code is known as a Caesar cipher, for Julius Caesar, who reportedly used it to communicate with his generals.) The implementation in `TestCoderImpl` merely displays the values of the arguments. The `TestCoderImpl` implementation is annotated @`Alternative`:

```
import javax.enterprise.inject.Alternative;

@Alternative
public class TestCoderImpl implements Coder {

    public String codeString(String s, int tval) {
        return ("input string is " + s + ", shift value is " + tval);
    }
}
```

The beans.xml file for the encoder example contains an `alternatives` element for the `TestCoderImpl` class, but by default the element is commented out:

```
<beans ... >
    <!--<alternatives>
        <class>encoder.TestCoderImpl</class>
    </alternatives>-->
</beans>
```

This means that by default, the `TestCoderImpl` class, annotated @`Alternative`, will not be used. Instead, the `CoderImpl` class will be used.

The `encoder` Facelets Page and Managed Bean

The simple Facelets page for the encoder example, index.xhtml, asks the user to type the string and integer values and passes them to the managed bean, `CoderBean`, as `coderBean.inputString` and `coderBean.transVal`:

```
<html lang="en"
      xmlns="http://www.w3.org/1999/xhtml"
      xmlns:h="http://java.sun.com/jsf/html">
```

```
<h:head>
    <h:outputStylesheet library="css" name="default.css"/>
    <title>String Encoder</title>
</h:head>
<h:body>
    <h2>String Encoder</h2>
    <p>Type a string and an integer, then click Encode.</p>
    <p>Depending on which alternative is enabled, the coder bean
        will either display the argument values or return a string that
        shifts the letters in the original string by the value you specify.
        The value must be between 0 and 26.</p>
    <h:form id="encodeit">
        <p><h:outputLabel value="Type a string: " for="inputString"/>
            <h:inputText id="inputString"
                        value="#{coderBean.inputString}"/>
            <h:outputLabel value="Type the number of letters to shift by: "
                            for="transVal"/>
            <h:inputText id="transVal" value="#{coderBean.transVal}"/></p>
        <p><h:commandButton value="Encode"
                            action="#{coderBean.encodeString()}"/></p>
        <p><h:outputLabel value="Result: " for="outputString"/>
            <h:outputText id="outputString" value="#{coderBean.codedString}"
                            style="color:blue"/> </p>
        <p><h:commandButton value="Reset" action="#{coderBean.reset}"/></p>
    </h:form>
    ...
</h:body>
</html>
```

When the user clicks the Encode button, the page invokes the managed bean's
encodeString method and displays the result, coderBean.codedString, in blue. The
page also has a Reset button that clears the fields.

The managed bean, CoderBean, is a @RequestScoped bean that declares its input and
output properties. The transVal property has three Bean Validation constraints that
enforce limits on the integer value, so that if the user types an invalid value, a default
error message appears on the Facelets page. The bean also injects an instance of the
Coder interface:

```
@Named
@RequestScoped
public class CoderBean {

    private String inputString;
    private String codedString;
    @Max(26)
    @Min(0)
    @NotNull
    private int transVal;

    @Inject
    Coder coder;
    ...
```

In addition to simple getter and setter methods for the three properties, the bean defines the encodeString action method called by the Facelets page. This method sets the codedString property to the value returned by a call to the codeString method of the Coder implementation:

```
public void encodeString() {
    setCodedString(coder.codeString(inputString, transVal));
}
```

Finally, the bean defines the reset method to empty the fields of the Facelets page:

```
public void reset() {
    setInputString("");
    setTransVal(0);
}
```

Running the encoder Example

You can use either NetBeans IDE or Ant to build, package, deploy, and run the encoder application.

▼ To Build, Package, and Deploy the encoder Example Using NetBeans IDE

1 From the File menu, choose Open Project.

2 In the Open Project dialog, navigate to:

   tut-install/examples/cdi/

3 Select the encoder folder.

4 Select the Open as Main Project check box.

5 Click Open Project.

6 In the Projects tab, right-click the encoder project and select Deploy.

▼ To Run the encoder Example Using NetBeans IDE

1 In a web browser, type the following URL:

   http://localhost:8080/encoder

   The String Encoder page opens.

2　Type a string and the number of letters to shift by, then click Encode.

The encoded string appears in blue on the Result line. For example, if you type Java and 4, the result is Neze.

3　Now, edit the beans.xml file to enable the alternative implementation of Coder.

   a.　In the Projects tab, under the encoder project, expand the Web Pages node, then the WEB-INF node.

   b.　Double-click the beans.xml file to open it.

   c.　Remove the comment characters that surround the alternatives element, so that it looks like this:

```
<alternatives>
    <class>encoder.TestCoderImpl</class>
</alternatives>
```

   d.　Save the file.

4　Right-click the encoder project and select Deploy.

5　In the web browser, retype the URL to show the String Encoder page for the redeployed project:

```
http://localhost:8080/encoder/
```

6　Type a string and the number of letters to shift by, then click Encode.

This time, the Result line displays your arguments. For example, if you type Java and 4, the result is:

```
Result: input string is Java, shift value is 4
```

▼ To Build, Package, and Deploy the encoder Example Using Ant

1　In a terminal window, go to:

tut-install/examples/cdi/encoder/

2　Type the following command:

ant

This command calls the default target, which builds and packages the application into a WAR file, encoder.war, located in the dist directory.

3　Type the following command:

ant deploy

▼ **To Run the encoder Example Using Ant**

1   **In a web browser, type the following URL:**

```
http://localhost:8080/encoder/
```

The String Encoder page opens.

2   **Type a string and the number of letters to shift by, then click Encode.**

The encoded string appears in blue on the Result line. For example, if you type Java and 4, the result is Neze.

3   **Now, edit the beans.xml file to enable the alternative implementation of Coder.**

a.   **In a text editor, open the following file:**

tut-install/examples/cdi/encoder/web/WEB-INF/beans.xml

b.   **Remove the comment characters that surround the alternatives element, so that it looks like this:**

```
<alternatives>
    <class>encoder.TestCoderImpl</class>
</alternatives>
```

c.   **Save and close the file.**

4   **Type the following commands:**

```
ant undeploy
ant
ant deploy
```

5   **In the web browser, retype the URL to show the String Encoder page for the redeployed project:**

```
http://localhost:8080/encoder
```

6   **Type a string and the number of letters to shift by, then click Encode.**

This time, the Result line displays your arguments. For example, if you type Java and 4, the result is:

```
Result: input string is Java, shift value is 4
```

The producermethods Example: Using a Producer Method To Choose a Bean Implementation

The producermethods example shows how to use a producer method to choose between two beans at runtime, as described in "Using Producer Methods, Producer Fields, and Disposer Methods in CDI Applications" on page 254. It is very similar to the encoder example described in "The encoder Example: Using Alternatives" on page 265. The example includes the same interface and two implementations of it, a managed bean, a Facelets page, and configuration files. It also contains a qualifier type. When you run it, you do not need to edit the beans.xml file and redeploy the application to change its behavior.

Components of the producermethods Example

The components of producermethods are very much like those for encoder, with some significant differences.

Neither implementation of the Coder bean is annotated @Alternative, and the beans.xml file does not contain an alternatives element.

The Facelets page and the managed bean, CoderBean, have an additional property, coderType, that allows the user to specify at runtime which implementation to use. In addition, the managed bean has a producer method that selects the implementation using a qualifier type, @Chosen.

The bean declares two constants that specify whether the coder type is the test implementation or the implementation that actually shifts letters:

```
private final static int TEST = 1;
private final static int SHIFT = 2;
private int coderType = SHIFT; // default value
```

The producer method, annotated with @Produces and @Chosen as well as @RequestScoped (so that it lasts only for the duration of a single request and response), takes both implementations as arguments, then returns one or the other, based on the coderType supplied by the user.

```
@Produces
@Chosen
@RequestScoped
public Coder getCoder(@New TestCoderImpl tci,
        @New CoderImpl ci) {

    switch (coderType) {
        case TEST:
            return tci;
```

```
        case SHIFT:
            return ci;
        default:
            return null;
    }
}
```

Finally, the managed bean injects the chosen implementation, specifying the same qualifier as that returned by the producer method to resolve ambiguities:

```
@Inject
@Chosen
@RequestScoped
Coder coder;
```

The Facelets page contains modified instructions and a pair of radio buttons whose selected value is assigned to the property coderBean.coderType:

```
<h2>String Encoder</h2>
    <p>Select Test or Shift, type a string and an integer, then click
        Encode.</p>
    <p>If you select Test, the TestCoderImpl bean will display the
        argument values.</p>
    <p>If you select Shift, the CoderImpl bean will return a string that
        shifts the letters in the original string by the value you specify.
        The value must be between 0 and 26.</p>
    <h:form id="encodeit">
        <h:selectOneRadio id="coderType"
                          required="true"
                          value="#{coderBean.coderType}">
            <f:selectItem
                itemValue="1"
                itemLabel="Test"/>
            <f:selectItem
                itemValue="2"
                itemLabel="Shift Letters"/>
        </h:selectOneRadio>
        ...
```

Running the producermethods Example

You can use either NetBeans IDE or Ant to build, package, deploy, and run the producermethods application.

▼ To Build, Package, and Deploy the producermethods Example Using NetBeans IDE

1 **From the File menu, choose Open Project.**

2 **In the Open Project dialog, navigate to:**

tut-install/examples/cdi/

3   Select the producermethods folder.

4   Select the Open as Main Project check box.

5   Click Open Project.

6   In the Projects tab, right-click the producermethods project and select Deploy.

▼ **To Build, Package, and Deploy the producermethods Example Using Ant**

1   In a terminal window, go to:

tut-install/examples/cdi/producermethods/

2   Type the following command:

ant

This command calls the default target, which builds and packages the application into a WAR file, producermethods.war, located in the dist directory.

3   Type the following command:

ant deploy

▼ **To Run the producermethods Example**

1   In a web browser, type the following URL:

http://localhost:8080/producermethods

The String Encoder page opens.

2   Select either the Test or Shift Letters radio button, type a string and the number of letters to shift by, then click Encode.

Depending on your selection, the Result line displays either the encoded string or the input values you specified.

The producerfields Example: Using Producer Fields to Generate Resources

The producerfields example, which allows you to create a to-do list, shows how to use a producer field to generate objects that can then be managed by the container. This example generates an EntityManager object, but resources such as JDBC connections and datasources can also be generated this way.

The producerfields example is the simplest possible entity example. It also contains a qualifier and a class that generates the entity manager. It also contains a single entity, a stateful session bean, a Facelets page, and a managed bean.

The Producer Field for the producerfields Example

The most important component of the producerfields example is the smallest, the db.UserDatabaseEntityManager class, which isolates the generation of the EntityManager object so it can easily be used by other components in the application. The class uses a producer field to inject an EntityManager annotated with the @UserDatabase qualifier, also defined in the db package:

```
@Singleton
public class UserDatabaseEntityManager {

    @Produces
    @PersistenceContext
    @UserDatabase
    private EntityManager em;
    ...
}
```

The class does not explicitly produce a persistence unit field, but the application has a persistence.xml file that specifies a persistence unit. The class is annotated javax.inject.Singleton to specify that the injector should instantiate it only once.

The db.UserDatabaseEntityManager class also contains commented-out code that uses create and close methods to generate and remove the producer field:

```
/* @PersistenceContext
   private EntityManager em;

   @Produces
   @UserDatabase
   public EntityManager create() {
       return em;
   } */

   public void close(@Disposes @UserDatabase EntityManager em) {
       em.close();
   }
```

You can remove the comment indicators from this code and place them around the field declaration to test how the methods work. The behavior of the application is the same with either mechanism.

The advantage of producing the EntityManager in a separate class rather than simply injecting it into an enterprise bean is that the object can easily be reused in a typesafe way. Also, a more complex application can create multiple entity managers using multiple persistence units, and this mechanism isolates this code for easy maintenance, as in the following example:

```
@Singleton
public class JPAResourceProducer {
    @Produces
    @PersistenceUnit(unitName="pu3")
    @TestDatabase
    EntityManagerFactory customerDatabasePersistenceUnit;

    @Produces
    @PersistenceContext(unitName="pu3")
    @TestDatabase
    EntityManager customerDatabasePersistenceContext;

    @Produces
    @PersistenceUnit(unitName="pu4")
    @Documents
    EntityManagerFactory customerDatabasePersistenceUnit;

    @Produces
    @PersistenceContext(unitName="pu4")
    @Documents
    EntityManager docDatabaseEntityManager;"
}
```

The EntityManagerFactory declarations also allow applications to use an application-managed entity manager.

The producerfields Entity and Session Bean

The producerfields example contains a simple entity class, entity.ToDo, and a stateful session bean, ejb.RequestBean, that uses it.

The entity class contains three fields: an autogenerated id field, a string specifying the task, and a timestamp. The timestamp field, timeCreated, is annotated with @Temporal, which is required for persistent Date fields.

```
@Entity
public class ToDo implements Serializable {

    ...
    @Id
    @GeneratedValue(strategy = GenerationType.AUTO)
    private Long id;
    protected String taskText;
    @Temporal(TIMESTAMP)
    protected Date timeCreated;

    public ToDo() {
    }

    public ToDo(Long id, String taskText, Date timeCreated) {
        this.id = id;
        this.taskText = taskText;
        this.timeCreated = timeCreated;
    }
    ...
```

The remainder of the ToDo class contains the usual getters, setters, and other entity methods.

The RequestBean class injects the EntityManager generated by the producer method, annotated with the @UserDatabase qualifier:

```
@ConversationScoped
@Stateful
public class RequestBean {

    @Inject
    @UserDatabase
    EntityManager em;
```

It then defines two methods, one that creates and persists a single ToDo list item, and another that retrieves all the ToDo items created so far by creating a query:

```
public ToDo createToDo(String inputString) {
    ToDo toDo;
    Date currentTime = Calendar.getInstance().getTime();

    try {
        toDo = new ToDo();
        toDo.setTaskText(inputString);
        toDo.setTimeCreated(currentTime);
        em.persist(toDo);
        return toDo;
    } catch (Exception e) {
        throw new EJBException(e.getMessage());
    }
}

public List<ToDo> getToDos() {
    try {
        List<ToDo> toDos =
                (List<ToDo>) em.createQuery(
                "SELECT t FROM ToDo t ORDER BY t.timeCreated")
                .getResultList();
        return toDos;
    } catch (Exception e) {
        throw new EJBException(e.getMessage());
    }
}
}
```

The producerfields Facelets Pages and Managed Bean

The producerfields example has two Facelets pages, index.xhtml and todolist.xhtml. The simple form on the index.xhtml page asks the user only for the task. When the user clicks the Submit button, the listBean.createTask method is called. When the user clicks the Show Items button, the action specifies that the todolist.xhtml file should be displayed:

```
<h:body>
    <h2>To Do List</h2>
    <p>Type a task to be completed.</p>
    <h:form id="todolist">
        <p><h:outputLabel value="Type a string: " for="inputString"/>
            <h:inputText id="inputString"
                         value="#{listBean.inputString}"/></p>
        <p><h:commandButton value="Submit"
                            action="#{listBean.createTask()}"/></p>
        <p><h:commandButton value="Show Items"
                            action="todolist"/></p>
    </h:form>
    ...
</h:body>
```

The managed bean, `web.ListBean`, injects the `ejb.RequestBean` session bean. It declares the `entity.ToDo` entity and a list of the entity, along with the input string that it passes to the session bean. The `inputString` is annotated with the `@NotNull` Bean Validation constraint, so an attempt to submit an empty string results in an error.

```
@Named
@ConversationScoped
public class ListBean implements Serializable {

    ...
    @EJB
    private RequestBean request;
    @NotNull
    private String inputString;
    private ToDo toDo;
    private List<ToDo> toDos;
```

The `createTask` method called by the Submit button calls the `createToDo` method of `RequestBean`:

```
public void createTask() {
    this.toDo = request.createToDo(inputString);
}
```

The `getToDos` method, which is called by the `todolist.xhtml` page, calls the `getToDos` method of `RequestBean`:

```
public List<ToDo> getToDos() {
    return request.getToDos();
}
```

To force the Facelets page to recognize an empty string as a null value and return an error, the `web.xml` file sets the context parameter `javax.faces.INTERPRET_EMPTY_STRING_SUBMITTED_VALUES_AS_NULL` to true:

```
<context-param>
  <param-name>
      javax.faces.INTERPRET_EMPTY_STRING_SUBMITTED_VALUES_AS_NULL
  </param-name>
```

```
        <param-value>true</param-value>
    </context-param>
```

The `todolist.xhtml` page is a little more complicated than the `index.html` page. It contains a `dataTable` element that displays the contents of the ToDo list. The body of the page looks like this:

```
<body>
    <h2>To Do List</h2>
    <h:form id="showlist">
        <h:dataTable var="toDo"
                    value="#{listBean.toDos}"
                    rules="all"
                    border="1"
                    cellpadding="5">
            <h:column>
                <f:facet name="header">
                    <h:outputText value="Time Stamp" />
                </f:facet>
                <h:outputText value="#{toDo.timeCreated}" />
            </h:column>
            <h:column>
                <f:facet name="header">
                    <h:outputText value="Task" />
                </f:facet>
                <h:outputText value="#{toDo.taskText}" />
            </h:column>
        </h:dataTable>
        <p><h:commandButton id="back" value="Back" action="index" /></p>
    </h:form>
</body>
```

The value of the `dataTable` is `listBean.toDos`, the list returned by the managed bean's `getToDos` method, which in turn calls the session bean's `getToDos` method. Each row of the table displays the `timeCreated` and `taskText` fields of the individual task. Finally, a Back button returns the user to the `index.xhtml` page.

Running the `producerfields` Example

You can use either NetBeans IDE or Ant to build, package, deploy, and run the `producerfields` application.

▼ To Build, Package, and Deploy the `producerfields` Example Using NetBeans IDE

1   If the database server is not already running, start it by following the instructions in "Starting and Stopping the Java DB Server" on page 43.

2   From the File menu, choose Open Project.

3   In the Open Project dialog, navigate to:

    tut-install/examples/cdi/

4   Select the `producerfields` folder.

5   Select the Open as Main Project check box.

6   Click Open Project.

7   In the Projects tab, right-click the `producerfields` project and select Deploy.

▼ To Build, Package, and Deploy the `producerfields` Example Using Ant

1   If the database server is not already running, start it by following the instructions in "Starting and Stopping the Java DB Server" on page 43.

2   In a terminal window, go to:

    tut-install/examples/cdi/producerfields/

3   Type the following command:

    ```
    ant
    ```

    This command calls the `default` target, which builds and packages the application into a WAR file, `producerfields.war`, located in the `dist` directory.

4   Type the following command:

    ```
    ant deploy
    ```

▼ To Run the `producerfields` Example

1   In a web browser, type the following URL:

    ```
    http://localhost:8080/producerfields
    ```

    The Create To Do List page opens.

2   Type a string in the text field and click Submit.

    You can type additional strings and click Submit to create a task list with multiple items.

3   Click the Show Items button.

    The To Do List page opens, showing the timestamp and text for each item you created.

4 **Click the Back button to return to the Create To Do List page.**

On this page, you can enter more items in the list.

The `billpayment` Example: Using Events and Interceptors

The `billpayment` example shows how to use both events and interceptors.

The example simulates paying an amount using a debit card or credit card. When the user chooses a payment method, the managed bean creates an appropriate event, supplies its payload, and fires it. A simple event listener handles the event using observer methods.

The example also defines an interceptor that is set on a class and on two methods of another class.

The `PaymentEvent` Event Class

The event class, `event.PaymentEvent`, is a simple bean class that contains a no-argument constructor. It also has a `toString` method and getter and setter methods for the payload components: a `String` for the payment type, a `BigDecimal` for the payment amount, and a `Date` for the timestamp.

```
public class PaymentEvent implements Serializable {

    ...
    public String paymentType;
    public BigDecimal value;
    public Date datetime;

    public PaymentEvent() {
    }
    @Override
    public String toString() {
        return this.paymentType
                + " = $" + this.value.toString()
                + " at " + this.datetime.toString();
    }
    ...
```

The event class is a simple bean that is instantiated by the managed bean using new and then populated. For this reason, the CDI container cannot intercept the creation of the bean, and hence it cannot allow interception of its getter and setter methods.

The PaymentHandler Event Listener

The event listener, listener.PaymentHandler, contains two observer methods, one for each of the two event types:

```
@Logged
@SessionScoped
public class PaymentHandler implements Serializable {

    ...
    public void creditPayment(@Observes @Credit PaymentEvent event) {
        logger.log(Level.INFO, "PaymentHandler - Credit Handler: {0}",
                event.toString());

        // call a specific Credit handler class...
    }

    public void debitPayment(@Observes @Debit PaymentEvent event) {
        logger.log(Level.INFO, "PaymentHandler - Debit Handler: {0}",
                event.toString());

        // call a specific Debit handler class...
    }
}
```

Each observer method takes as an argument the event, annotated with @Observes and with the qualifier for the type of payment. In a real application, the observer methods would pass the event information on to another component that would perform business logic on the payment.

The qualifiers are defined in the payment package, described in "The billpayment Facelets Pages and Managed Bean" on page 281.

Like PaymentEvent, the PaymentHandler bean is annotated @Logged, so that all its methods can be intercepted.

The billpayment Facelets Pages and Managed Bean

The billpayment example contains two Facelets pages, index.xhtml and the very simple response.xhtml. The body of index.xhtml looks like this:

```
<h:body>
    <h3>Bill Payment Options</h3>
    <p>Type an amount, select Debit Card or Credit Card,
       then click Pay.</p>
    <h:form>
        <p>
        <h:outputLabel value="Amount: $" for="amt"/>
        <h:inputText id="amt" value="#{paymentBean.value}"
                    required="true"
                    requiredMessage="An amount is required."
```

```
                        maxlength="15" />
        </p>
        <h:outputLabel value="Options:" for="opt"/>
        <h:selectOneRadio id="opt" value="#{paymentBean.paymentOption}">
            <f:selectItem id="debit" itemLabel="Debit Card"
                        itemValue="1"/>
            <f:selectItem id="credit" itemLabel="Credit Card"
                        itemValue="2" />
        </h:selectOneRadio>
        <p><h:commandButton id="submit" value="Pay"
                        action="#{paymentBean.pay}" /></p>
        <p><h:commandButton value="Reset"
                        action="#{paymentBean.reset}" /></p>
    </h:form>
    ...
</h:body>
```

The input text field takes a payment amount, passed to paymentBean.value. Two radio buttons ask the user to select a Debit Card or Credit Card payment, passing the integer value to paymentBean.paymentOption. Finally, the Pay command button's action is set to the method paymentBean.pay, while the Reset button's action is set to the paymentBean.reset method.

The payment.PaymentBean managed bean uses qualifiers to differentiate between the two kinds of payment event:

```
@Named
@SessionScoped
public class PaymentBean implements Serializable {

    ...
    @Inject
    @Credit
    Event<PaymentEvent> creditEvent;

    @Inject
    @Debit
    Event<PaymentEvent> debitEvent;
```

The qualifiers, @Credit and @Debit, are defined in the payment package along with PaymentBean.

Next, the PaymentBean defines the properties it obtains from the Facelets page and will pass on to the event:

```
public static final int DEBIT = 1;
public static final int CREDIT = 2;
private int paymentOption = DEBIT;

@Digits(integer = 10, fraction = 2, message = "Invalid value")
private BigDecimal value;

private Date datetime;
```

The `paymentOption` value is an integer passed in from the radio button component; the default value is `DEBIT`. The `value` is a `BigDecimal` with a Bean Validation constraint that enforces a currency value with a maximum number of digits. The timestamp for the event, `datetime`, is a `Date` object initialized when the pay method is called.

The pay method of the bean first sets the timestamp for this payment event. It then creates and populates the event payload, using the constructor for the `PaymentEvent` and calling the event's setter methods using the bean properties as arguments. It then fires the event.

```
@Logged
public String pay() {
    this.setDatetime(Calendar.getInstance().getTime());
    switch (paymentOption) {
        case DEBIT:
            PaymentEvent debitPayload = new PaymentEvent();
            debitPayload.setPaymentType("Debit");
            debitPayload.setValue(value);
            debitPayload.setDatetime(datetime);
            debitEvent.fire(debitPayload);
            break;
        case CREDIT:
            PaymentEvent creditPayload = new PaymentEvent();
            creditPayload.setPaymentType("Credit");
            creditPayload.setValue(value);
            creditPayload.setDatetime(datetime);
            creditEvent.fire(creditPayload);
            break;
        default:
            logger.severe("Invalid payment option!");
    }
    return "/response.xhtml";
}
```

The pay method returns the page to which the action is redirected, `response.xhtml`.

The `PaymentBean` class also contains a reset method that empties the value field on the `index.xhtml` page and sets the payment option to the default:

```
@Logged
public void reset() {
    setPaymentOption(DEBIT);
    setValue(BigDecimal.ZERO);
}
```

In this bean, only the pay and reset methods are intercepted.

The `response.xhtml` page displays the amount paid. It uses a `rendered` expression to display the payment method:

```
<h:body>
    <h:form>
        <h2>Bill Payment: Result</h2>
```

```
                    <h3>Amount Paid with
                        <h:outputText id="debit" value="Debit Card: "
                                        rendered="#{paymentBean.paymentOption eq 1}" />
                        <h:outputText id="credit" value="Credit Card: "
                                        rendered="#{paymentBean.paymentOption eq 2}" />
                        <h:outputText id="result" value="#{paymentBean.value}" >
                            <f:convertNumber type="currency"/>
                        </h:outputText>
                    </h3>
                    <p><h:commandButton id="back" value="Back" action="index" /></p>
            </h:form>
        </h:body>
```

The LoggedInterceptor Interceptor Class

The interceptor class, LoggedInterceptor, and its interceptor binding, Logged, are both defined in the interceptor package. The Logged interceptor binding is defined as follows:

```
@Inherited
—@InterceptorBinding
@Retention(RUNTIME)
@Target({METHOD, TYPE})
public @interface Logged {
}
```

The LoggedInterceptor class looks like this:

```
@Logged
@Interceptor
public class LoggedInterceptor implements Serializable {

    ...

    public LoggedInterceptor() {
    }

    @AroundInvoke
    public Object logMethodEntry(InvocationContext invocationContext)
            throws Exception {
        System.out.println("Entering method: "
                + invocationContext.getMethod().getName() + " in class "
                + invocationContext.getMethod().getDeclaringClass().getName());

        return invocationContext.proceed();
    }
}
```

The class is annotated with both the @Logged and the @Interceptor annotations. The @AroundInvoke method, logMethodEntry, takes the required InvocationContext argument, and calls the required proceed method. When a method is intercepted, logMethodEntry displays the name of the method being invoked as well as its class.

To enable the interceptor, the beans.xml file defines it as follows:

```
<interceptors>
    <class>billpayment.interceptor.LoggedInterceptor</class>
</interceptors>
```

In this application, the PaymentEvent and PaymentHandler classes are annotated @Logged, so all their methods are intercepted. In PaymentBean, only the pay and reset methods are annotated @Logged, so only those methods are intercepted.

Running the billpayment Example

You can use either NetBeans IDE or Ant to build, package, deploy, and run the billpayment application.

▼ To Build, Package, and Deploy the billpayment Example Using NetBeans IDE

1 From the File menu, choose Open Project.

2 In the Open Project dialog, navigate to:

tut-install/examples/cdi/

3 Select the billpayment folder.

4 Select the Open as Main Project check box.

5 Click Open Project.

6 In the Projects tab, right-click the billpayment project and select Deploy.

▼ To Build, Package, and Deploy the billpayment Example Using Ant

1 In a terminal window, go to:

tut-install/examples/cdi/billpayment/

2 Type the following command:

ant

This command calls the default target, which builds and packages the application into a WAR file, billpayment.war, located in the dist directory.

3 Type the following command:

ant deploy

▼ **To Run the billpayment Example**

1 **In a web browser, type the following URL:**

   `http://localhost:8080/billpayment`

   The Bill Payment Options page opens.

2 **Type a value in the Amount field.**

   The amount can contain up to 10 digits and include up to 2 decimal places. For example:

   9876.54

3 **Select Debit Card or Credit Card and click Pay.**

   The Bill Payment: Result page opens, displaying the amount paid and the method of payment:

   `Amount Paid with Credit Card: $9,876.34`

4 **(Optional) Click Back to return to the Bill Payment Options page.**

   You can also click Reset to return to the initial page values.

5 **Examine the server log output.**

   In NetBeans IDE, the output is visible in the GlassFish Server 3+ output window. Otherwise, view *domain-dir*/`logs/server.log`.

   The output from each interceptor appears in the log, followed by the additional logger output defined by the constructor and methods.

The decorators Example: Decorating a Bean

The decorators example, which is yet another variation on the encoder example, shows how to use a decorator to implement additional business logic for a bean. Instead of having the user choose between two alternative implementations of an interface at deployment time or runtime, a decorator adds some additional logic to a single implementation of the interface.

The example includes an interface, an implementation of it, a decorator, an interceptor, a managed bean, a Facelets page, and configuration files.

Components of the decorators Example

The decorators example is very similar to the encoder example described in "The encoder Example: Using Alternatives" on page 265. Instead of providing two implementations of the Coder interface, however, this example provides only the CoderImpl class. The decorator class, CoderDecorator, rather than simply return the coded string, displays the input and output strings' values and length.

The CoderDecorator class, like CoderImpl, implements the business method of the Coder interface, codeString:

```
@Decorator
public abstract class CoderDecorator implements Coder {

    @Inject
    @Delegate
    @Any
    Coder coder;

    @Override
    public String codeString(String s, int tval) {
        int len = s.length();

        return "\"" + s + "\" becomes " + "\"" + coder.codeString(s, tval)
                + "\", " + len + " characters in length";
    }
}
```

The decorator's codeString method calls the delegate object's codeString method to perform the actual encoding.

The decorators example includes the Logged interceptor binding and LoggedInterceptor class from the billpayment example. For this example, the interceptor is set on the CoderBean.encodeString method and the CoderImpl.codeString method. The interceptor code is unchanged; interceptors are usually reusable for different applications.

Except for the interceptor annotations, the CoderBean and CoderImpl classes are identical to the versions in the encoder example.

The beans.xml file specifies both the decorator and the interceptor:

```
<decorators>
    <class>decorators.CoderDecorator</class>
</decorators>
<interceptors>
    <class>decorators.LoggedInterceptor</class>
</interceptors>
```

Running the decorators Example

You can use either NetBeans IDE or Ant to build, package, deploy, and run the decorators application.

▼ To Build, Package, and Deploy the decorators Example Using NetBeans IDE

1   From the File menu, choose Open Project.

2   In the Open Project dialog, navigate to:

    tut-install/examples/cdi/

3   Select the decorators folder.

4   Select the Open as Main Project check box.

5   Click Open Project.

6   In the Projects tab, right-click the decorators project and select Deploy.

▼ To Build, Package, and Deploy the decorators Example Using Ant

1   In a terminal window, go to:

    tut-install/examples/cdi/decorators/

2   Type the following command:

    ```
    ant
    ```

    This command calls the default target, which builds and packages the application into a WAR file, decorators.war, located in the dist directory.

3   Type the following command:

    ```
    ant deploy
    ```

▼ To Run the decorators Example

1   In a web browser, type the following URL:

    ```
    http://localhost:8080/decorators
    ```

    The Decorated String Encoder page opens.

2   Type a string and the number of letters to shift by, then click Encode.

    The output from the decorator method appears in blue on the Result line. For example, if you typed Java and 4, you would see the following:

    ```
    "Java" becomes "Neze", 4 characters in length
    ```

3   Examine the server log output.

In NetBeans IDE, the output is visible in the GlassFish Server 3+ output window. Otherwise, view *domain-dir*/logs/server.log.

The output from the interceptors appears:

```
INFO: Entering method: encodeString in class decorators.CoderBean
INFO: Entering method: codeString in class decorators.CoderImpl
```

Persistence

Part VI explores advanced topics related to the Java Persistence API. This part consists of the following chapters:

- Chapter 16, "Creating and Using String-Based Criteria Queries"
- Chapter 17, "Controlling Concurrent Access to Entity Data with Locking"
- Chapter 18, "Using a Second-Level Cache with Java Persistence API Applications"

◆ ◆ ◆   C H A P T E R   1 6

16

Creating and Using String-Based Criteria Queries

This chapter describes how to create weakly-typed string-based Criteria API queries.

The following topics are addressed here:

- "Overview of String-Based Criteria API Queries" on page 293
- "Creating String-Based Queries" on page 294
- "Executing String-Based Queries" on page 295

Overview of String-Based Criteria API Queries

String-based Criteria API queries ("string-based queries") are Java programming language queries that use strings rather than strongly-typed metamodel objects to specify entity attributes when traversing a data hierarchy. String-based queries are constructed similarly to metamodel queries, can be static or dynamic, and can express the same kind of queries and operations as strongly-typed metamodel queries.

Strongly-typed metamodel queries are the preferred method of constructing Criteria API queries. The main advantage of string-based queries over metamodel queries is the ability to construct Criteria queries at development time without the need to generate static metamodel classes or otherwise access dynamically generated metamodel classes. The main disadvantage to string-based queries is their lack of type safety, which may lead to runtime errors due to type mismatches that would be caught at development time when using strongly-typed metamodel queries.

For information on constructing criteria queries, see Chapter 22, "Using the Criteria API to Create Queries," in *The Java EE 6 Tutorial: Basic Concepts*.

Creating String-Based Queries

To create a string-based query, specify the attribute names of entity classes directly as strings, rather than the attributes of the metamodel class. For example, this query finds all Pet entities where the value of the name attribute is Fido:

```
CriteriaQuery<Pet> cq = cb.createQuery(Pet.class);
Root<Pet> pet = cq.from(Pet.class);
cq.where(cb.equal(pet.get("name"), "Fido"));
...
```

The name of the attribute is specified as a string. This query is the equivalent of the following metamodel query:

```
CriteriaQuery<Pet> cq = cb.createQuery(Pet.class);
Metamodel m = em.getMetamodel();
EntityType<Pet> Pet_ = m.entity(Pet.class);
Root<Pet> pet = cq.from(Pet.class);
cq.where(cb.equal(pet.get(Pet_.name), "Fido"));
```

Note – Type mismatch errors in string-based queries won't appear until the code is executed at runtime, unlike in the above metamodel query, where type mismatches will be caught at compile time.

Joins are specified in the same way:

```
CriteriaQuery<Pet> cq = cb.createQuery(Pet.class);
Root<Pet> pet = cq.from(Pet.class);
Join<Owner, Address> address = pet.join("owners").join("addresses");
...
```

All the conditional expressions, method expressions, path navigation methods, and result restriction methods used in metamodel queries can be used in string-based queries. In each case, the attributes are specified using strings. For example, here is a string-based query that uses the in expression:

```
CriteriaQuery<Pet> cq = cb.createQuery(Pet.class);
Root<Pet> pet = cq.from(Pet.class);
cq.where(pet.get("color").in("brown", "black"));
```

Here is a string-based query that orders the results in descending order by date:

```
CriteriaQuery<Pet> cq = cb.createQuery(Pet.class);
Root<Pet> pet = cq.from(Pet.class);
cq.select(pet);
cq.orderBy(cb.desc(pet.get("birthday")));
```

Executing String-Based Queries

String-based queries are executed similarly to strongly-typed Criteria queries. First create a javax.persistence.TypedQuery object by passing the criteria query object to the EntityManager.createQuery method and then call either getSingleResult or getResultList on the query object to execute the query.

```
CriteriaQuery<Pet> cq = cb.createQuery(Pet.class);
Root<Pet> pet = cq.from(Pet.class);
cq.where(cb.equal(pet.get("name"), "Fido"));
TypedQuery<Pet> q = em.createQuery(cq);
List<Pet> results = q.getResultList();
```

Controlling Concurrent Access to Entity Data with Locking

This chapter details how to handle concurrent access to entity data, and the locking strategies available to Java Persistence API application developers.

The following topics are addressed here:

Overview of Entity Locking and Concurrency

Entity data is *concurrently accessed* if the data in a data source is accessed at the same time by multiple applications. Special care must be taken to ensure that the underlying data's integrity is preserved when accessed concurrently.

When data is updated in the database tables in a transaction, the persistence provider assumes the database management system will hold short-term read locks and long-term write locks to maintain data integrity. Most persistence providers will delay database writes until the end of the transaction, except when the application explicitly calls for a flush (that is, the application calls the `EntityManager.flush` method or executes queries with the flush mode set to `AUTO`).

By default, persistence providers use *optimistic locking*, where, before committing changes to the data, the persistence provider checks that no other transaction has modified or deleted the data since the data was read. This is accomplished by a version column in the database table, with a corresponding version attribute in the entity class. When a row is modified, the version value is incremented. The original transaction checks the version attribute, and if the data has been modified by another transaction, a `javax.persistence.OptimisticLockException` will be thrown, and the original transaction will be rolled back. When the application specifies optimistic lock modes, the persistence provider verifies that a particular entity has not changed since it was read from the database even if the entity data was not modified.

Pessimistic locking goes further than optimistic locking. With pessimistic locking, the persistence provider creates a transaction that obtains a long-term lock on the data until the transaction is completed, which prevents other transactions from modifying or deleting the data until the lock has ended. Pessimistic locking is a better strategy than optimistic locking when the underlying data is frequently accessed and modified by many transactions.

Caution – Using pessimistic locks on entities that are not subject to frequent modification may result in decreased application performance.

Using Optimistic Locking

The javax.persistence.Version annotation is used to mark a persistent field or property as a version attribute of an entity. By adding a version attribute, the entity is enabled for optimistic concurrency control. The version attribute is read and updated by the persistence provider when an entity instance is modified during a transaction. The application may read the version attribute, but *must not* modify the value.

Note – Although some persistence providers may support optimistic locking for entities that do not have version attributes, portable applications should always use entities with version attributes when using optimistic locking. If the application attempts to lock an entity without a version attribute, and the persistence provider doesn't support optimistic locking for non-versioned entities, a PersistenceException will be thrown.

The @Version annotation has the following requirements:

- Only a single @Version attribute may be defined per entity.
- The @Version attribute must be in the primary table for an entity mapped to multiple tables.
- The type of the @Version attribute must be one of the following: int, Integer, long, Long, short, Short, or java.sql.Timestamp.

The following code snippet shows how to define a version attribute in an entity with persistent fields:

```
@Version
protected int version;
```

The following code snippet shows how to define a version attribute in an entity with persistent properties:

```
@Version
protected Short getVersion() { ... }
```

Lock Modes

The application may increase the level of locking for an entity by specifying the use of lock modes. Lock modes may be specified to increase the level of optimistic locking or to request the use of pessimistic locks.

The use of optimistic lock modes causes the persistence provider to check the version attributes for entities that were read (but not modified) during a transaction as well as for entities that were updated.

The use of pessimistic lock modes specifies that the persistence provider is to immediately acquire long-term read or write locks for the database data corresponding to entity state.

The lock mode for an entity operation may be set by specifying one of the lock modes defined in the `javax.persistence.LockModeType` enumerated type, listed in Table 17–1.

TABLE 17–1   Lock Modes for Concurrent Entity Access

Lock Mode	Description
OPTIMISTIC	Obtain an optimistic read lock for all entities with version attributes.
OPTIMISTIC_FORCE_INCREMENT	Obtain an optimistic read lock for all entities with version attributes, and increment the version attribute value.
PESSIMISTIC_READ	Immediately obtain a long-term read lock on the data to prevent the data from being modified or deleted. Other transactions may read the data while the lock is maintained, but may not modify or delete the data.
	The persistence provider is permitted to obtain a database write lock when a read lock was requested, but not vice versa.
PESSIMISTIC_WRITE	Immediately obtain a long-term write lock on the data to prevent the data from being read, modified, or deleted.
PESSIMISTIC_FORCE_INCREMENT	Immediately obtain a long-term lock on the data to prevent the data from being modified or deleted, and increment the version attribute of versioned entities.

TABLE 17-1 Lock Modes for Concurrent Entity Access   *(Continued)*

Lock Mode	Description
READ	A synonym for OPTIMISTIC. Use of LockModeType.OPTIMISTIC is to be preferred for new applications.
WRITE	A synonym for OPTIMISTIC_FORCE_INCREMENT. Use of LockModeType.OPTIMISTIC_FORCE_INCREMENT is to be preferred for new applications.
NONE	No additional locking will occur on the data in the database.

Setting the Lock Mode

The lock mode may be specified by one of the following techniques:

- Calling the EntityManager.lock and passing in one of the lock modes:

```
EntityManager em = ...;
Person person = ...;
em.lock(person, LockModeType.OPTIMISTIC);
```

- Calling one of the EntityManager.find methods that takes the lock mode as a parameter:

```
EntityManager em = ...;
String personPK = ...;
Person person = em.find(Person.class, personPK,
        LockModeType.PESSIMISTIC_WRITE);
```

- Calling one of the EntityManager.refresh methods that takes the lock mode as a parameter:

```
EntityManager em = ...;
String personPK = ...;
Person person = em.find(Person.class, personPK);
...
em.refresh(person, LockModeType.OPTIMISTIC_FORCE_INCREMENT);
```

- Calling the Query.setLockMode or TypedQuery.setLockMode method, passing the lock mode as the parameter:

```
Query q = em.createQuery(...);
q.setLockMode(LockModeType.PESSIMISTIC_FORCE_INCREMENT);
```

- Adding a lockMode element to the @NamedQuery annotation:

```
@NamedQuery(name="lockPersonQuery",
  query="SELECT p FROM Person p WHERE p.name LIKE :name",
  lockMode=PESSIMISTIC_READ)
```

Using Pessimistic Locking

Versioned entities as well as entities that do not have version attributes can be locked pessimistically.

To lock entities pessimistically, set the lock mode to PESSIMISTIC_READ, PESSIMISTIC_WRITE, or PESSIMISTIC_FORCE_INCREMENT.

If a pessimistic lock cannot be obtained on the database rows, and the failure to lock the data results in a transaction rollback, a PessimisticLockException is thrown. If a pessimistic lock cannot be obtained, but the locking failure doesn't result in a transaction rollback, a LockTimeoutException is thrown.

Pessimistically locking a version entity with PESSIMISTIC_FORCE_INCREMENT results in the version attribute being incremented even if the entity data is unmodified. When pessimistically locking a versioned entity, the persistence provider will perform the version checks that occur during optimistic locking, and if the version check fails, an OptimisticLockException will be thrown. Attempting to lock a non-versioned entity with PESSIMISTIC_FORCE_INCREMENT is not portable and may result in a PersistenceException if the persistence provider doesn't support optimistic locks for non-versioned entities. Locking a versioned entity with PESSIMISTIC_WRITE results in the version attribute being incremented if the transaction was successfully committed.

Pessimistic Locking Timeouts

The length of time in milliseconds the persistence provider should wait to obtain a lock on the database tables may be specified using the javax.persistence.lock.timeout property. If the time it takes to obtain a lock exceeds the value of this property, a LockTimeoutException will be thrown, but the current transaction will not be marked for rollback. If this property is set to 0, the persistence provider should throw a LockTimeoutException if it cannot immediately obtain a lock.

Note – Portable applications should not rely on the setting of javax.persistence.lock.timeout, as the locking strategy and underlying database may mean that the timeout value cannot be used. The value of javax.persistence.lock.timeout is a hint, not a contract.

This property may be set programmatically by passing it to the EntityManager methods that allow lock modes to be specified, the Query.setLockMode and TypedQuery.setLockMode methods, the @NamedQuery annotation, and as a property to the Persistence.createEntityManagerFactory method. It may also be set as a property in the persistence.xml deployment descriptor.

If `javax.persistence.lock.timeout` is set in multiple places, the value will be determined in the following order:

1. The argument to one of the `EntityManager` or `Query` methods.
2. The setting in the `@NamedQuery` annotation.
3. The argument to the `Persistence.createEntityManagerFactory` method.
4. The value in the `persistence.xml` deployment descriptor.

CHAPTER 18

Using a Second-Level Cache with Java Persistence API Applications

This chapter explains how to modify the second-level cache mode settings to improve the performance of applications that use the Java Persistence API.

The following topics are addressed here:

- "Overview of the Second-Level Cache" on page 303
- "Specifying the Cache Mode Settings to Improve Performance" on page 305

Overview of the Second-Level Cache

A *second-level cache* is a local store of entity data managed by the persistence provider to improve application performance. A second-level cache helps improve performance by avoiding expensive database calls, keeping the entity data local to the application. A second-level cache is typically transparent to the application, as it is managed by the persistence provider and underlies the persistence context of an application. That is, the application reads and commits data through the normal entity manager operations without knowing about the cache.

Note – Persistence providers are not required to support a second-level cache. Portable applications should not rely on support by persistence providers for a second-level cache.

The second-level cache for a persistence unit may be configured to one of several second-level cache modes. The following cache mode settings are defined by the Java Persistence API.

TABLE 18–1 Cache Mode Settings for the Second-Level Cache

Cache Mode Setting	Description
ALL	All entity data is stored in the second-level cache for this persistence unit.
NONE	No data is cached in the persistence unit. The persistence provider must not cache any data.
ENABLE_SELECTIVE	Enable caching for entities that have been explicitly set with the @Cacheable annotation.
DISABLE_SELECTIVE	Enable caching for all entities except those that have been explicitly set with the @Cacheable(false) annotation.
UNSPECIFIED	The caching behavior for the persistence unit is undefined. The persistence provider's default caching behavior will be used.

One consequence of using a second-level cache in an application is that the underlying data may have changed in the database tables, while the value in the cache has not, a circumstance called a *stale read*. Stale reads may be avoided by changing the second-level cache to one of the cache mode settings, controlling which entities may be cached (described in "Controlling Whether Entities May Be Cached" on page 304), or changing the cache's retrieval or store modes (described in "Setting the Cache Retrieval and Store Modes" on page 306). Which strategies best avoid stale reads are application dependent.

Controlling Whether Entities May Be Cached

The javax.persistence.Cacheable annotation is used to specify that an entity class, and any subclasses, may be cached when using the ENABLE_SELECTIVE or DISABLE_SELECTIVE cache modes. Subclasses may override the @Cacheable setting by adding a @Cacheable annotation and changing the value.

To specify that an entity may be cached, add a @Cacheable annotation at the class level:

```
@Cacheable
@Entity
public class Person { ... }
```

By default, the @Cacheable annotation is true. The following example is equivalent:

```
@Cacheable(true)
@Entity
public class Person{ ... }
```

To specify that an entity must not be cached, add a @Cacheable annotation and set it to false:

```
@Cacheable(false)
@Entity
public class OrderStatus { ... }
```

When the ENABLE_SELECTIVE cache mode is set, the persistence provider will cache any entities that have the @Cacheable(true) annotation and any subclasses of that entity that have not been overridden. The persistence provider will not cache entities that have @Cacheable(false) or have no @Cacheable annotation. That is, the ENABLE_SELECTIVE mode will cache only entities that have been explicitly marked for the cache using the @Cacheable annotation.

When the DISABLE_SELECTIVE cache mode is set, the persistence provider will cache any entities that *do not* have the @Cacheable(false) annotation. Entities that do not have @Cacheable annotations, and entities with the @Cacheable(true) annotation will be cached. That is, the DISABLE_SELECTIVE mode will cache all entities that have not been explicitly prevented from being cached.

If the cache mode is set to UNDEFINED, or is left unset, the behavior of entities annotated with @Cacheable is undefined. If the cache mode is set to ALL or NONE, the value of the @Cacheable annotation is ignored by the persistence provider.

Specifying the Cache Mode Settings to Improve Performance

To adjust the cache mode settings for a persistence unit, specify one of the cache modes as the value of the shared-cache-mode element in the persistence.xml deployment descriptor (shown in **bold**):

```
<persistence-unit name="examplePU" transaction-type="JTA">
  <provider>org.eclipse.persistence.jpa.PersistenceProvider</provider>
  <jta-data-source>jdbc/__default</jta-data-source>
  <shared-cache-mode>DISABLE_SELECTIVE</shared-cache-mode>
</persistence-unit>
```

Note – Because support for a second-level cache is not required by the Java Persistence API specification, setting the second-level cache mode in persistence.xml will have no effect when using a persistence provider that does not implement a second-level cache.

Alternatively, the shared cache mode may be specified by setting the
`javax.persistence.sharedCache.mode` property to one of the shared cache mode
settings:

```
EntityManagerFactor emf =
    Persistence.createEntityManagerFactory(
        "myExamplePU", new Properties().add(
            "javax.persistence.sharedCache.mode", "ENABLE_SELECTIVE"));
```

Setting the Cache Retrieval and Store Modes

If the second-level cache has been enabled for a persistence unit by setting the shared
cache mode, the behavior of the second-level cache can be further modified by setting
the `javax.persistence.cache.retrieveMode` and
`javax.persistence.cache.storeMode` properties. These properties may be set at the
persistence context level by passing the property name and value to the
`EntityManager.setProperty` method, or may be set on a per-`EntityManager`
operation (`EntityManager.find` or `EntityManager.refresh`) or per-query level.

Cache Retrieval Mode

The cache retrieval mode, set by the `javax.persistence.retrieveMode` property,
controls how data is read from the cache for calls to the `EntityManager.find` method
and from queries.

The `retrieveMode` property can be set to one of the constants defined by the
`javax.persistence.CacheRetrieveMode` enumerated type, either USE (the default)
or BYPASS. When it is set to USE, data is retrieved from the second-level cache, if
available. If the data is not in the cache, the persistence provider will read it from the
database. When it is set to BYPASS, the second-level cache is bypassed and a call to the
database is made to retrieve the data.

Cache Store Mode

The cache store mode, set by the `javax.persistence.storeMode` property, controls
how data is stored in the cache.

The `storeMode` property can be set to one of the constants defined by the
`javax.persistence.CacheStoreMode` enumerated type, either USE (the default),
BYPASS, or REFRESH. When set to USE the cache data is created or updated when data is
read from or committed to the database. If data is already in the cache, setting the store
mode to USE will not force a refresh when data is read from the database.

When the store mode is set to BYPASS, data read from or committed to the database is
not inserted or updated in the cache. That is, the cache is unchanged.

When the store mode is set to REFRESH, the cache data is created or updated when data is read from or committed to the database, and a refresh is forced on data in the cache upon database reads.

Setting the Cache Retrieval or Store Mode

To set the cache retrieval or store mode for the persistence context, call the EntityManager.setProperty method with the property name and value pair:

```
EntityManager em = ...;
em.setProperty("javax.persistence.cache.storeMode", "BYPASS");
```

To set the cache retrieval or store mode when calling the EntityManger.find or EntityManager.refresh methods, first create a Map<String, Object> instance and add a name/value pair as follows:

```
EntityManager em = ...;
Map<String, Object> props = new HashMap<String, Object>();
props.put("javax.persistence.cache.retrieveMode", "BYPASS");
String personPK = ...;
Person person = em.find(Person.class, personPK, props);
```

Note – The cache retrieve mode is ignored when calling the EntityManager.refresh method, as calls to refresh always result in data being read from the database, not the cache.

To set the retrieval or store mode when using queries, call the Query.setHint or TypedQuery.setHint methods, depending on the type of query:

```
EntityManager em = ...;
CriteriaQuery<Person> cq = ...;
TypedQuery<Person> q = em.createQuery(cq);
q.setHint("javax.persistence.cache.storeMode", "REFRESH");
...
```

Setting the store or retrieve mode in a query or when calling the EntityManager.find or EntityManager.refresh method overrides the setting of the entity manager.

Controlling the Second-Level Cache Programmatically

The javax.persistence.Cache interface defines methods for interacting with the second-level cache programmatically. The Cache interface defines methods to check whether a particular entity has cached data, to remove a particular entity from the cache, to remove all instances (and instances of subclasses) of an entity class from the cache, and to clear the cache of all entity data.

Note – If the second-level cache has been disabled, calls to the Cache interface's methods have no effect, except for contains, which will always return false.

Checking Whether an Entity's Data Is Cached

Call the Cache.contains method to find out whether a given entity is currently in the second-level cache. The contains method returns true if the entity's data is cached, and false if the data is not in the cache.

```
EntityManager em = ...;
Cache cache = em.getEntityManagerFactory().getCache();
String personPK = ...;
if (cache.contains(Person.class, personPK)) {
  // the data is cached
} else {
  // the data is NOT cached
}
```

Removing an Entity from the Cache

Call one of the Cache.evict methods to remove a particular entity or all entities of a given type from the second-level cache. To remove a particular entity from the cache, call the evict method and pass in the entity class and the primary key of the entity:

```
EntityManager em = ...;
Cache cache = em.getEntityManagerFactory().getCache();
String personPK = ...;
cache.evict(Person.class, personPK);
```

To remove all instances of a particular entity class, including subclasses, call the evict method and specify the entity class:

```
EntityManager em = ...;
Cache cache = em.getEntityManagerFactory().getCache();
cache.evict(Person.class);
```

All instances of the Person entity class will be removed from the cache. If the Person entity has a subclass, Student, calls to the above method will remove all instances of Student from the cache as well.

Removing All Data from the Cache

Call the Cache.evictAll method to completely clear the second-level cache:

```
EntityManager em = ...;
Cache cache = em.getEntityManagerFactory().getCache();
cache.evictAll();
```

PART VII

Security

Part VII explores advanced security concepts. This part contains the following chapter:

- Chapter 19, "Java EE Security: Advanced Topics"

Java EE Security: Advanced Topics

This chapter provides advanced information on securing Java EE applications.

The following topics are addressed here:

- "Working with Digital Certificates" on page 311
- "Authentication Mechanisms" on page 316
- "Using Form-Based Login in JavaServer Faces Web Applications" on page 321
- "Using the JDBC Realm for User Authentication" on page 324
- "Securing HTTP Resources" on page 328
- "Securing Application Clients" on page 331
- "Securing Enterprise Information Systems Applications" on page 332
- "Configuring Security Using Deployment Descriptors" on page 336
- "Further Information about Security" on page 337

Working with Digital Certificates

Digital certificates for the GlassFish Server have already been generated and can be found in the directory *domain-dir*/`config/`. These digital certificates are self-signed and are intended for use in a development environment; they are not intended for production purposes. For production purposes, generate your own certificates and have them signed by a certificate authority (CA).

To use the Secure Sockets Layer (SSL), an application or web server must have an associated certificate for each external interface, or IP address, that accepts secure connections. The theory behind this design is that a server should provide some kind of reasonable assurance that its owner is who you think it is, particularly before receiving any sensitive information. It may be useful to think of a certificate as a "digital driver's license" for an Internet address. The certificate states with which company the site is associated, along with some basic contact information about the site owner or administrator.

The digital certificate is cryptographically signed by its owner and is difficult for anyone else to forge. For sites involved in e-commerce or in any other business transaction in which authentication of identity is important, a certificate can be purchased from a well-known CA such as VeriSign or Thawte. If your server certificate is self-signed, you must install it in the GlassFish Server keystore file (keystore.jks). If your client certificate is self-signed, you should install it in the GlassFish Server truststore file (cacerts.jks).

Sometimes, authentication is not really a concern. For example, an administrator might simply want to ensure that data being transmitted and received by the server is private and cannot be snooped by anyone eavesdropping on the connection. In such cases, you can save the time and expense involved in obtaining a CA certificate and simply use a self-signed certificate.

SSL uses *public-key cryptography*, which is based on key pairs. *Key pairs* contain one public key and one private key. Data encrypted with one key can be decrypted only with the other key of the pair. This property is fundamental to establishing trust and privacy in transactions. For example, using SSL, the server computes a value and encrypts it by using its private key. The encrypted value is called a *digital signature*. The client decrypts the encrypted value by using the server's public key and compares the value to its own computed value. If the two values match, the client can trust that the signature is authentic, because only the private key could have been used to produce such a signature.

Digital certificates are used with HTTPS to authenticate web clients. The HTTPS service of most web servers will not run unless a digital certificate has been installed. Use the procedure outlined in the next section to set up a digital certificate that can be used by your application or web server to enable SSL.

One tool that can be used to set up a digital certificate is keytool, a key and certificate management utility that ships with the JDK. This tool enables users to administer their own public/private key pairs and associated certificates for use in self-authentication, whereby the user authenticates himself or herself to other users or services, or data integrity and authentication services, using digital signatures. The tool also allows users to cache the public keys, in the form of certificates, of their communicating peers.

For a better understanding of keytool and public-key cryptography, see "Further Information about Security" on page 337 for a link to the keytool documentation.

Creating a Server Certificate

A server certificate has already been created for the GlassFish Server and can be found in the *domain-dir*/config/ directory. The server certificate is in keystore.jks. The cacerts.jks file contains all the trusted certificates, including client certificates.

If necessary, you can use keytool to generate certificates. The keytool utility stores the keys and certificates in a file termed a *keystore*, a repository of certificates used for identifying a client or a server. Typically, a keystore is a file that contains one client's or one server's identity. The keystore protects private keys by using a password.

If you don't specify a directory when specifying the keystore file name, the keystores are created in the directory from which the keytool command is run. This can be the directory where the application resides, or it can be a directory common to many applications.

The general steps for creating a server certificate are as follows.

1. Create the keystore.

2. Export the certificate from the keystore.

3. Sign the certificate.

4. Import the certificate into a *truststore*: a repository of certificates from parties with which you expect to communicate or from Certificate Authorities that you trust to identify parties. The truststore is used by the client to verify the certificate that is sent by the server. A truststore typically contains more than one certificate.

The next section provides specific information on using the keytool utility to perform these steps.

▼ To Use keytool to Create a Server Certificate

Run keytool to generate a new key pair in the default development keystore file, keystore.jks. This example uses the alias server-alias to generate a new public/private key pair and wrap the public key into a self-signed certificate inside keystore.jks. The key pair is generated by using an algorithm of type RSA, with a default password of changeit. For more information and other examples of creating and managing keystore files, read the keytool documentation.

Note – RSA is public-key encryption technology developed by RSA Data Security, Inc.

From the directory in which you want to create the key pair, run keytool as shown in the following steps.

1   Generate the server certificate.

Type the keytool command all on one line:

```
java-home/bin/keytool -genkey -alias server-alias -keyalg RSA -keypass changeit
-storepass changeit -keystore keystore.jks
```

When you press Enter, keytool prompts you to enter the server name, organizational unit, organization, locality, state, and country code.

You must type the server name in response to keytool's first prompt, in which it asks for first and last names. For testing purposes, this can be localhost.

When you run the example applications, the host (server name) specified in the keystore must match the host identified in the javaee.server.name property specified in the *tut-install*/examples/bp-project/build.properties file (by default, this is localhost).

2 **Export the generated server certificate in keystore.jks into the file server.cer.**

Type the keytool command all on one line:

java-home/bin/keytool -export -alias server-alias -storepass changeit
-file server.cer -keystore keystore.jks

3 **If you want to have the certificate signed by a CA, read the example in the keytool documentation.**

4 **To add the server certificate to the truststore file, cacerts.jks, run keytool from the directory where you created the keystore and server certificate.**

Use the following parameters:

java-home/bin/keytool -import -v -trustcacerts -alias server-alias
-file server.cer -keystore cacerts.jks -keypass changeit -storepass changeit

Information on the certificate, such as that shown next, will appear:

```
Owner: CN=localhost, OU=My Company, O=Software, L=Santa Clara, ST=CA, C=US
Issuer: CN=localhost, OU=My Company, O=Software, L=Santa Clara, ST=CA, C=US
Serial number: 3e932169
Valid from: Mon Nov 26 18:15:47 EST 2012 until: Sun Feb 24 18:15:47 EST 2013
Certificate fingerprints:
         MD5:  52:9F:49:68:ED:78:6F:39:87:F3:98:B3:6A:6B:0F:90
         SHA1: EE:2E:2A:A6:9E:03:9A:3A:1C:17:4A:28:5E:97:20:78:3F:
         SHA256: 80:05:EC:7E:50:50:5D:AA:A3:53:F1:11:9B:19:EB:0D:20:67:C1:12:
AF:42:EC:CD:66:8C:BD:99:AD:D9:76:95
         Signature algorithm name: SHA256withRSA
         Version: 3
         ...
Trust this certificate? [no]:
```

5 **Type yes, then press the Enter or Return key.**

The following information appears:

```
Certificate was added to keystore
[Storing cacerts.jks]
```

Adding Users to the Certificate Realm

In the certificate realm, user identity is set up in the GlassFish Server security context and populated with user data obtained from cryptographically verified client certificates. For step-by-step instructions for creating this type of certificate, see "Working with Digital Certificates" on page 311.

Using a Different Server Certificate with the GlassFish Server

Follow the steps in "Creating a Server Certificate" on page 312 to create your own server certificate, have it signed by a CA, and import the certificate into keystore.jks.

Make sure that when you create the certificate, you follow these rules:

- When you create the server certificate, keytool prompts you to enter your first and last name. In response to this prompt, you must enter the name of your server. For testing purposes, this can be localhost.

- The server/host specified in the keystore must match the host identified in the javaee.server.name property specified in the *tut-install*/examples/bp-project/build.properties file for running the example applications.

- Your key/certificate password in keystore.jks should match the password of your keystore, keystore.jks. This is a bug. If there is a mismatch, the Java SDK cannot read the certificate and you get a "tampered" message.

- If you want to replace the existing keystore.jks, you must either change your keystore's password to the default password (changeit) or change the default password to your keystore's password.

▼ To Specify a Different Server Certificate

To specify that the GlassFish Server should use the new keystore for authentication and authorization decisions, you must set the JVM options for the GlassFish Server so that they recognize the new keystore. To use a different keystore from the one provided for development purposes, follow these steps.

1 Start the GlassFish Server if you haven't already done so. Information on starting the GlassFish Server can be found in "Starting and Stopping the GlassFish Server" on page 41.

2 Open the GlassFish Server Administration Console in a web browser at http://localhost:4848.

3 Expand Configurations, then expand server-config, then click JVM Settings.

4 Select the JVM Options tab.

5   Change the following JVM options so that they point to the location and name of the new keystore. The current settings are shown below:

```
-Djavax.net.ssl.keyStore=${com.sun.aas.instanceRoot}/config/keystore.jks
-Djavax.net.ssl.trustStore=${com.sun.aas.instanceRoot}/config/cacerts.jks
```

6   If you've changed the keystore password from its default value, you need to add the password option as well:

```
-Djavax.net.ssl.keyStorePassword=your-new-password
```

7   Click Save, then restart GlassFish Server.

Authentication Mechanisms

This section discusses the client authentication and mutual authentication mechanisms.

Client Authentication

With *client authentication*, the web server authenticates the client by using the client's public key certificate. Client authentication is a more secure method of authentication than either basic or form-based authentication. It uses HTTP over SSL (HTTPS), in which the server authenticates the client using the client's public key certificate. SSL technology provides data encryption, server authentication, message integrity, and optional client authentication for a TCP/IP connection. You can think of a public key certificate as the digital equivalent of a passport. The certificate is issued by a trusted organization, a certificate authority (CA), and provides identification for the bearer.

Before using client authentication, make sure the client has a valid public key certificate. For more information on creating and using public key certificates, read "Working with Digital Certificates" on page 311.

The following example shows how to declare client authentication in your deployment descriptor:

```
<login-config>
    <auth-method>CLIENT-CERT</auth-method>
</login-config>
```

Mutual Authentication

With *mutual authentication*, the server and the client authenticate each other. Mutual authentication is of two types:

- Certificate-based (see Figure 19–1)
- User name/password-based (see Figure 19–2)

When using certificate-based mutual authentication, the following actions occur.

1. A client requests access to a protected resource.

2. The web server presents its certificate to the client.

3. The client verifies the server's certificate.

4. If successful, the client sends its certificate to the server.

5. The server verifies the client's credentials.

6. If successful, the server grants access to the protected resource requested by the client.

Figure 19–1 shows what occurs during certificate-based mutual authentication.

FIGURE 19-1   Certificate-Based Mutual Authentication

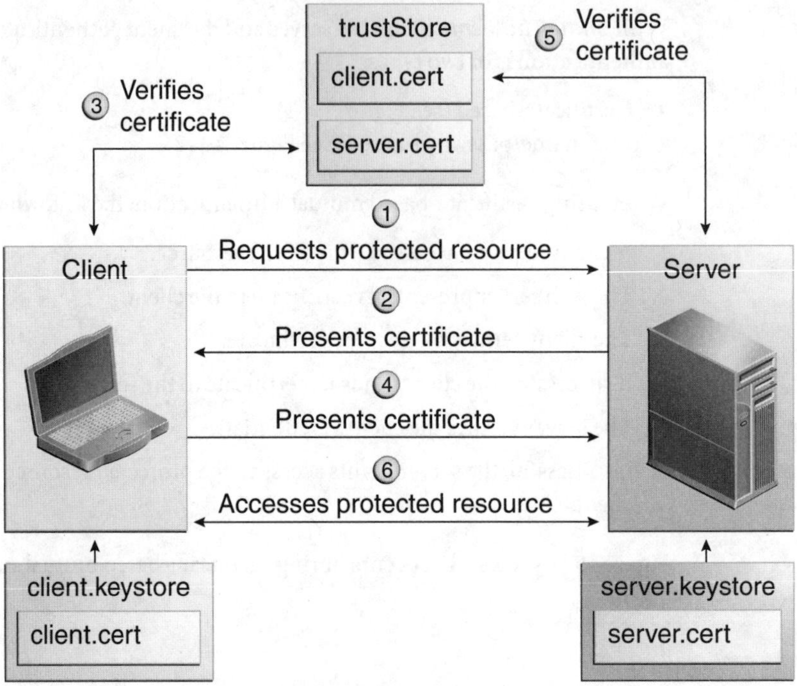

In user name/password-based mutual authentication, the following actions occur.

1. A client requests access to a protected resource.

2. The web server presents its certificate to the client.

3. The client verifies the server's certificate.

4. If successful, the client sends its user name and password to the server.

5. The server verifies the client's credentials.

6. If the verification is successful, the server grants access to the protected resource requested by the client.

Figure 19–2 shows what occurs during user name/password-based mutual authentication.

FIGURE 19–2   User Name/Password-Based Mutual Authentication

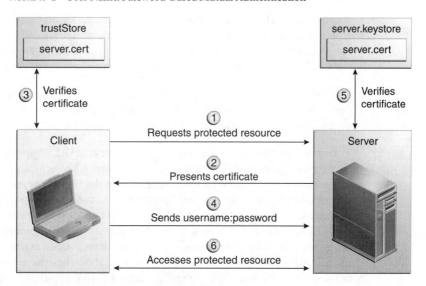

Enabling Mutual Authentication over SSL

This section discusses setting up client-side authentication. Enabling both server-side and client-side authentication is called mutual, or two-way, authentication. In client authentication, clients are required to submit certificates issued by a certificate authority that you choose to accept.

There are at least two ways to enable mutual authentication over SSL:

- The preferred method is to set the method of authentication in the web.xml application deployment descriptor to CLIENT-CERT. This enforces mutual authentication by modifying the deployment descriptor of the given application. In this way, client authentication is enabled only for a specific resource controlled by the security constraint, and the check is performed only when the application requires client authentication.

- A less commonly used method is to set the clientAuth property in the certificate realm to true if you want the SSL stack to require a valid certificate chain from the client before accepting a connection. A false value (which is the default) will not require a certificate chain unless the client requests a resource protected by a security constraint that uses CLIENT-CERT authentication. When you enable client authentication by setting the clientAuth property to true, client authentication will be required for all the requests going through the specified SSL port. If you turn clientAuth on, it is on all of the time, which can severely degrade performance.

When client authentication is enabled in both of these ways, client authentication will be performed twice.

Creating a Client Certificate for Mutual Authentication

If you have a certificate signed by a trusted Certificate Authority (CA) such as Verisign, and the GlassFish Server cacerts.jks file already contains a certificate verified by that CA, you do not need to complete this step. You need to install your certificate in the GlassFish Server certificate file only when your certificate is self-signed.

From the directory where you want to create the client certificate, run keytool as outlined here. When you press Enter, keytool prompts you to enter the server name, organizational unit, organization, locality, state, and country code.

You must enter the server name in response to keytool's first prompt, in which it asks for first and last names. For testing purposes, this can be localhost. The host specified in the keystore must match the host identified in the javee.server.host variable specified in your *tut-install*/examples/bp-project/build.properties file. If this example is to verify mutual authentication and you receive a runtime error stating that the HTTPS host name is wrong, re-create the client certificate, being sure to use the same host name you will use when running the example. For example, if your machine name is duke, then enter duke as the certificate CN or when prompted for first and last names. When accessing the application, enter a URL that points to the same location (for example, https://duke:8181/mutualauth/hello). This is necessary because during SSL handshake, the server verifies the client certificate by comparing the certificate name to the host name from which it originates.

▼ To Create a Client Certificate and Keystore

To create a keystore named client_keystore.jks that contains a client certificate named client.cer, follow these steps.

1 Create a backup copy of the server truststore file. To do this,

   a. Change to the directory containing the server's keystore and truststore files, *domain-dir*\config.

   b. Copy cacerts.jks to cacerts.backup.jks.

   c. Copy keystore.jks to keystore.backup.jks.

   Do not put client certificates in the cacerts.jks file. Any certificate you add to the cacerts file effectively can be a trusted root for any and all certificate chains. After you have completed development, delete the development version of the cacerts file and replace it with the original copy.

2 Generate the client certificate. Enter the following command from the directory where you want to generate the client certificate:

```
java-home\bin\keytool -genkey -alias client-alias -keyalg RSA
-keypass changeit -storepass changeit -keystore client_keystore.jks
```

3 Export the generated client certificate into the file `client.cer`:

```
java-home\bin\keytool -export -alias client-alias -storepass changeit
-file client.cer -keystore client_keystore.jks
```

4 Add the certificate to the truststore file *domain-dir*/`config/cacerts.jks`. Run `keytool` from the directory where you created the keystore and client certificate. Use the following parameters:

```
java-home\bin\keytool -import -v -trustcacerts -alias client-alias
-file client.cer -keystore domain-dir/config/cacerts.jks
-keypass changeit -storepass changeit
```

The keytool utility returns a message like this one:

```
Owner: CN=localhost, OU=My Company, O=Software, L=Santa Clara, ST=CA, C=US
Issuer: CN=localhost, OU=My Company, O=Software, L=Santa Clara, ST=CA, C=US
Serial number: 3e39e66a
Valid from: Tue Nov 27 12:22:47 EST 2012 until: Mon Feb 25 12:22:47 EST 2013
Certificate fingerprints:
    MD5: 5A:B0:4C:88:4E:F8:EF:E9:E5:8B:53:BD:D0:AA:8E:5A
    SHA1:90:00:36:5B:E0:A7:A2:BD:67:DB:EA:37:B9:61:3E:26:B3:89:46:32
    Signature algorithm name: SHA1withRSA
    Version: 3
Trust this certificate? [no]: yes
Certificate was added to keystore
[Storing cacerts.jks]
```

5 Restart GlassFish Server.

Using Form-Based Login in JavaServer Faces Web Applications

This section describes strategies for implementing form-based login in JavaServer Faces applications.

Using `j_security_check` in JavaServer Faces Forms

The most common way of authenticating a user in web applications is through a login form. As described in "Form-Based Authentication" in *The Java EE 6 Tutorial: Basic Concepts*, Java EE security defines the `j_security_check` action for login forms. This allows the web container to authenticate users from many different web application resources. Facelets forms, using the `h:form`, `h:inputText`, and `h:inputSecret` tags, however, generate the action and input IDs automatically, which means developers are unable to specify `j_security_check` as the form action, nor can they set the user name and password input field IDs to `j_username` and `j_password`, respectively.

Using standard HTML form tags allows developers to specify the correct action and input IDs for the form.

```
<form action="j_security_check" method="POST">
  <input type="text" name="j_username" />
  <input type="secret" name="j_password" />
...
</form>
```

This form, however, doesn't have access to the features of a JavaServer Faces application, such as automatic localization of strings and the use of templating to define the look and feel of the pages. A standard HTML form, in combination with Facelets and HTML tags, allows developers to use localized strings for the input field labels while still ensuring the form uses standard Java EE security:

```
<form action="j_security_check" method="POST">
    <h:outputLabel for="j_username">#{bundle['login.username']}:</h:outputLabel>
    <h:inputText id="j_username" size="20" />

    <h:outputLabel for="j_password">#{bundle['login.password']}:</h:outputLabel>
    <h:inputSecret id="j_password" size="20"/>

    <input type="submit" value="#{bundle['login.submit']}" />
</form>
```

Using a Managed Bean for Authentication in JavaServer Faces Applications

A managed bean can authenticate users of a JavaServer Faces application, which allows regular Facelets form tags to be used instead of a mix of standard HTML and Facelets tags. In this case, the managed bean defines login and logout methods, and Facelets forms call these methods in the action attribute. The managed bean's methods call the javax.servlet.http.HttpServletRequest.login and HttpServletRequest.logout methods to manage user authentication.

In the following managed bean, a stateless session bean uses the user credentials passed to the login method to authenticate the user and resets the caller identity of the request when the logout method is called.

```
@Stateless
@Named
public class LoginBean {
  private String username;
  private String password;

  public String getUsername() {
    return this.username;
  }

  public void setUserName(String username) {
    this.username = username;
  }
```

```
      public String getPassword() {
        return this.password;
      }

      public void setPassword() {
        this.password = password;
      }

...

      public String login () {
        FacesContext context = FacesContext.getCurrentInstance();
        HttpServletRequest request = (HttpServletRequest)
            context.getExternalContext().getRequest();
        try {
          request.login(this.username, this.password);
        } catch (ServletException e) {
          ...
          context.addMessage(null, new FacesMessage("Login failed."));
          return "error";
        }
        return "admin/index";
      }

      public void logout() {
        FacesContext context = FacesContext.getCurrentInstance();
        HttpServletRequest request = (HttpServletRequest)
            context.getExternalContext().getRequest();
        try {
          request.logout();
        } catch (ServletException e) {
          ...
          context.addMessage(null, new FacesMessage("Logout failed."));
        }
      }
  }
}
```

The Facelets form then calls these methods for user login and logout.

```
<h:form>
    <h:outputLabel for="usernameInput">
        #{bundle['login.username']}:
    </h:outputLabel>
    <h:inputText id="usernameInput" value="#{loginBean.username}"
                 required="true" />
    <br />
    <h:outputLabel for="passwordInput">
        #{bundle['login.password']}:
    </h:outputLabel>
    <h:inputSecret id="passwordInput" value="#{loginBean.password}"
                   required="true" />
    <br />
    <h:commandButton value="${bundle['login.submit']}"
                     action="#{loginBean.login}" />
</h:form>
```

Using the JDBC Realm for User Authentication

An authentication realm, sometimes called a *security policy domain* or *security domain*, is a scope over which an application server defines and enforces a common security policy. A realm contains a collection of users, who may or may not be assigned to a group. GlassFish Server comes preconfigured with the file, certificate, and administration realms. An administrator can also set up LDAP, JDBC, digest, or custom realms.

An application can specify in its deployment descriptor which realm to use. If the application does not specify a realm, GlassFish Server uses its default realm, the file realm. If an application specifies that a JDBC realm is to be used for user authentication, GlassFish Server will retrieve user credentials from a database. The application server uses the database information and the enabled JDBC realm option in the configuration file.

A database provides an easy way to add, edit, or delete users at runtime and enables users to create their own accounts without any administrative assistance. Using a database also has an additional benefit, providing a place to securely store any extra user information. A realm can be thought of as a database of user names and passwords that identify valid users of a web application or set of web applications with an enumeration of the list of roles associated with each valid user. Access to specific web application resources is granted to all users in a particular role, instead of enumerating a list of associated users. A user name can have any number of roles associated with it.

Two of the tutorial case studies, Chapter 26, "Duke's Tutoring Case Study Example," and Chapter 27, "Duke's Forest Case Study Example," use the JDBC realm for user authentication. Where appropriate, reference will be made to one or both of these examples.

▼ To Configure a JDBC Authentication Realm

GlassFish Server enables administrators to specify a user's credentials (user name and password) in the JDBC realm instead of in the connection pool. This prevents other applications from browsing the database tables for user credentials. By default, storing passwords as clear text is not supported in the JDBC realm. Under normal circumstances, passwords should not be stored as clear text.

1 Create the database tables in which user credentials for the realm will be stored.

How you create the database tables depends on the database you are using. Duke's Forest uses an Ant task, `create-tables`, in the `build.xml` file for the Entities project.

The task executes an SQL script, `create.sql`, that creates the `FOREST.PERSON`, `FOREST.GROUPS`, and `FOREST.PERSON_GROUPS` database tables, as shown below:

```sql
CREATE TABLE "FOREST"."PERSON"
(
  ID int NOT NULL PRIMARY KEY GENERATED ALWAYS AS IDENTITY
      (START WITH 1, INCREMENT BY 1),
  FIRSTNAME varchar(50) NOT NULL,
  LASTNAME varchar(100) NOT NULL,
  EMAIL varchar(45) NOT NULL UNIQUE,
  ADDRESS varchar(45) NOT NULL,
  CITY varchar(45) NOT NULL,
  PASSWORD varchar(100),
  DTYPE varchar(31)
)
;
CREATE UNIQUE INDEX SQL_PERSON_EMAIL_INDEX ON "FOREST"."PERSON"(EMAIL)
;
CREATE UNIQUE INDEX SQL_PERSON_ID_INDEX ON "FOREST"."PERSON"(ID)
;
CREATE TABLE "FOREST"."GROUPS"
(
   ID int NOT NULL PRIMARY KEY GENERATED ALWAYS AS IDENTITY
       (START WITH 1, INCREMENT BY 1),
   NAME varchar(50) NOT NULL,
   DESCRIPTION varchar(300)
)
;
CREATE TABLE "FOREST"."PERSON_GROUPS"
(
  GROUPS_ID int NOT NULL,
  EMAIL varchar(45) NOT NULL
)
;
ALTER TABLE "FOREST"."PERSON_GROUPS"
ADD CONSTRAINT FK_PERSON_GROUPS_PERSON
FOREIGN KEY (EMAIL)
REFERENCES "FOREST"."PERSON"(EMAIL)
;
ALTER TABLE "FOREST"."PERSON_GROUPS"
ADD CONSTRAINT FK_PERSON_GROUPS_GROUPS
FOREIGN KEY (GROUPS_ID)
REFERENCES "FOREST"."GROUPS"(ID)
;
CREATE INDEX SQL_PERSONGROUPS_EMAIL_INDEX ON "FOREST"."PERSON_GROUPS"(EMAIL)
;
CREATE INDEX SQL_PERSONGROUPS_ID_INDEX ON "FOREST"."PERSON_GROUPS"(GROUPS_ID)
;
```

The Duke's Tutoring case study uses a singleton bean, `ConfigBean`, to create its database tables, instead of using SQL commands.

2   Add user credentials to the database tables you created.

How you add user credentials to the database tables depends on the database that you are using. Duke's Forest uses an Ant task. The create-tables Ant task for Duke's Forest adds the user credentials to the tables created in the previous step:

```
INSERT INTO "FOREST"."PERSON" (FIRSTNAME,LASTNAME,EMAIL,ADDRESS,CITY,
PASSWORD,DTYPE) VALUES ('Robert','Exampler','robert@example.com',
'Example street','San Francisco','81dc9bdb52d04dc20036dbd8313ed055',
'Customer');
INSERT INTO "FOREST"."PERSON" (FIRSTNAME,LASTNAME,EMAIL,ADDRESS,CITY,
PASSWORD,DTYPE) VALUES ('Admin','Admin','admin@example.com','Example street',
'Belmont','81dc9bdb52d04dc20036dbd8313ed055','Administrator');
INSERT INTO "FOREST"."PERSON" (FIRSTNAME,LASTNAME,EMAIL,ADDRESS,CITY,
PASSWORD,DTYPE) VALUES ('Jack','Frost','jack@example.com','Example Blvd',
'San Francisco','81dc9bdb52d04dc20036dbd8313ed055','Customer');
INSERT INTO "FOREST"."PERSON" (FIRSTNAME,LASTNAME,EMAIL,ADDRESS,CITY,
PASSWORD,DTYPE) VALUES ('Payment','User','paymentUser@dukesforest.com',
'-','-','58175e1df62779046a3a4e2483575937','Customer');

INSERT INTO "FOREST"."GROUPS" (NAME, DESCRIPTION)
VALUES ('USERS', 'Users of the store');
INSERT INTO "FOREST"."GROUPS" (NAME, DESCRIPTION)
VALUES ('ADMINS', 'Administrators of the store');

INSERT INTO "FOREST"."PERSON_GROUPS" (GROUPS_ID,EMAIL)
VALUES (1,'robert@example.com');
INSERT INTO "FOREST"."PERSON_GROUPS" (GROUPS_ID,EMAIL)
VALUES (2,'admin@example.com');
INSERT INTO "FOREST"."PERSON_GROUPS" (GROUPS_ID,EMAIL)
VALUES (1,'jack@example.com');
INSERT INTO "FOREST"."PERSON_GROUPS" (GROUPS_ID,EMAIL)
VALUES (1,'paymentUser@dukesforest.com');
```

The Duke's Tutoring case study uses a singleton bean, ConfigBean, to populate its database tables, instead of using SQL commands.

3   Create a JDBC connection pool for the database.

Duke's Forest uses an Ant task, create-forest-pool, to create the derby_net_forest_forestPool JDBC connection pool for the database:

```
<target name="create-forest-pool"
    description="create JDBC connection pool">
    <antcall target="create-jdbc-connection-pool">
        <param name="pool.name" value="derby_net_forest_forestPool" />
    </antcall>
</target>
```

You can also use the Administration Console or the command line to create a connection pool.

4   Create a JDBC resource for the database.

Duke's Forest uses an Ant task, create-forest-resource, to create the jdbc/forest JDBC resource for the database:

```
<target name="create-forest-resource" depends="create-forest-pool"
    description="create JDBC resource">
```

```
        <antcall target="create-jdbc-resource">
            <param name="pool.name" value="derby_net_forest_forestPool" />
            <param name="jdbc.resource.name" value="jdbc/forest" />
        </antcall>
</target>
```

You can also use the Administration Console or the command line to create a JDBC resource.

5   Create a realm.

Duke's Forest uses an Ant task, `create-forest-realm`, to create `jdbcRealm`, the JDBC realm used for user authentication:

```
<target name="create-forest-realm" depends="create-forest-resource"
    description="create JDBC realm">
    <antcall target="create-jdbc-realm">
        <param name="jdbc.resource.name" value="jdbc/forest" />
        <param name="jdbc.realm.name" value="jdbcRealm" />
        <param name="user.table.name" value="forest.PERSON" />
        <param name="user.name.column" value="email" />
        <param name="password.column" value="password" />
        <param name="group.table" value="forest.GROUPS" />
        <param name="group.name.column" value="name" />
        <param name="assign.groups" value="USERS,ADMINS" />
        <param name="digest.algorithm" value="MD5" />
    </antcall>
</target>
```

This task associates the resource with the realm, defines the tables and columns for users and groups used for authentication, and defines the digest algorithm that will be used for storing passwords in the database.

You can also use the Administration Console or the command line to create a realm.

6   Modify the deployment descriptor for your application to specify the JDBC realm:

- For an enterprise application in an EAR file, modify the `glassfish-application.xml` file.

- For a web application in a WAR file, modify the `web.xml` file.

- For an enterprise bean in an EJB JAR file, modify the `glassfish-ejb-jar.xml` file.

For example, for the Duke's Forest application, the `web.xml` file specifies the `jdbcRealm` realm:

```
<login-config>
    <auth-method>FORM</auth-method>
    <realm-name>jdbcRealm</realm-name>
    <form-login-config>
        <form-login-page>/login.xhtml</form-login-page>
        <form-error-page>/login.xhtml</form-error-page>
    </form-login-config>
</login-config>
<security-constraint>
    <web-resource-collection>
```

```
        <web-resource-name>Secure Pages</web-resource-name>
        <description/>
        <url-pattern>/admin/*</url-pattern>
    </web-resource-collection>
    <auth-constraint>
        <role-name>ADMINS</role-name>
    </auth-constraint>
</security-constraint>
```

Form-based login is specified for all web pages under /admin. Access to those pages will be allowed only to users in the ADMINS role.

7 Assign security roles to users or groups of users in the realm.

To assign a security role to a group or to a user, add a security-role-mapping element to the application server-specific deployment descriptor, in this case glassfish-web.xml:

```
<security-role-mapping>
    <role-name>USERS</role-name>
    <group-name>USERS</group-name>
</security-role-mapping>
<security-role-mapping>
    <role-name>ADMINS</role-name>
    <group-name>ADMINS</group-name>
</security-role-mapping>
```

Since GlassFish Server users are assigned to groups during the user creation process, this is more efficient than mapping security roles to individual users.

Securing HTTP Resources

When a request URI is matched by multiple constrained URL patterns, the constraints that apply to the request are those that are associated with the best matching URL pattern. The servlet matching rules defined in Chapter 12, "Mapping Requests To Servlets," in the Java Servlet 3.0 Specification, are used to determine the best matching URL pattern to the request URI. No protection requirements apply to a request URI that is not matched by a constrained URL pattern. The HTTP method of the request plays no role in selecting the best matching URL pattern for a request.

When HTTP methods are listed within a constraint definition, the protections defined by the constraint are applied to the listed methods only.

When HTTP methods are not listed within a constraint definition, the protections defined by the constraint apply to the complete set of HTTP methods, including HTTP extension methods.

When constraints with different protection requirements apply to the same combination of URL patterns and HTTP methods, the rules for combining the protection requirements are as defined in Section 13.8.1, "Combining Constraints," in the Java Servlet 3.0 Specification.

Follow these guidelines to properly secure a web application:

- Do not list HTTP methods within constraint definitions. This is the simplest way to ensure that you are not leaving HTTP methods unprotected. For example:

```
<!-- SECURITY CONSTRAINT #1 -->
<security-constraint>
    <display-name>Do not enumerate Http Methods</display-name>
    <web-resource-collection>
        <url-pattern>/company/*</url-pattern>
    </web-resource-collection>
    <auth-constraint>
        <role-name>sales</role-name>
    </auth-constraint>
</security-constraint>
```

If you list methods in a constraint, all non-listed methods of the effectively infinite set of possible HTTP methods, including extension methods, will be *unprotected*. The following example shows a constraint that lists the GET method and thus defines no protection on any of the other possible HTTP methods. Do not use such a constraint unless you are certain that this is the protection scheme you intend to define.

```
<!-- SECURITY CONSTRAINT #2 -->
<security-constraint>
    <display-name>
        Protect GET only, leave all other methods unprotected
    </display-name>
    <web-resource-collection>
        <url-pattern>/company/*</url-pattern>
        <http-method>GET</http-method>
    </web-resource-collection>
    <auth-constraint>
        <role-name>sales</role-name>
    </auth-constraint>
</security-constraint>
```

- If you need to apply specific types of protection to specific HTTP methods, make sure you define constraints to cover every method that you want to permit, with or without constraint, at the corresponding URL patterns. If there are any methods that you do not want to permit, you must also create a constraint that denies access to those methods at the same patterns; for an example, see security constraint #5 in the next bullet.

For example, to permit GET and POST, where POST requires authentication and GET is permitted without constraint, you could define the following constraints:

```
<!-- SECURITY CONSTRAINT #3 -->
<security-constraint>
    <display-name>Allow unprotected GET</display-name>
    <web-resource-collection>
        <url-pattern>/company/*</url-pattern>
        <http-method>GET</http-method>
    </web-resource-collection>
</security-constraint>
```

```
<!-- SECURITY CONSTRAINT #4 -->
<security-constraint>
    <display-name>Require authentication for POST</display-name>
    <web-resource-collection>
        <url-pattern>/company/*</url-pattern>
        <http-method>POST</http-method>
    </web-resource-collection>
    <auth-constraint>
        <role-name>sales</role-name>
    </auth-constraint>
</security-constraint>
```

- The simplest way to ensure that you deny all HTTP methods except those that you want to be permitted is to use http-method-omission elements to omit those HTTP methods from the security constraint, and also to define an auth-constraint that names no roles. The security constraint will apply to all methods except those that were named in the omissions, and the constraint will apply only to the resources matched by the patterns in the constraint.

  For example, the following constraint excludes access to all methods except GET and POST at the resources matched by the pattern /company/*:

```
<!-- SECURITY CONSTRAINT #5 -->
<security-constraint>
    <display-name>Deny all HTTP methods except GET and POST</display-name>
    <web-resource-collection>
        <url-pattern>/company/*</url-pattern>
        <http-method-omission>GET</http-method-omission>
        <http-method-omission>POST</http-method-omission>
    </web-resource-collection>
    <auth-constraint/>
</security-constraint>
```

  If you want to extend these exclusions to the unconstrained parts of your application, also include the URL pattern / (forward slash):

```
<!-- SECURITY CONSTRAINT #6 -->
<security-constraint>
    <display-name>Deny all HTTP methods except GET and POST</display-name>
    <web-resource-collection>
        <url-pattern>/company/*</url-pattern>
        <url-pattern>/</url-pattern>
        <http-method-omission>GET</http-method-omission>
        <http-method-omission>POST</http-method-omission>
    </web-resource-collection>
    <auth-constraint/>
</security-constraint>
```

- If, for your web application, you do not want any resource to be accessible unless you explicitly define a constraint that permits access to it, you can define an auth-constraint that names no roles and associate it with the URL pattern /. The URL pattern / is the weakest matching pattern. Do not list any HTTP methods in this constraint.

```
<!-- SECURITY CONSTRAINT #7 -->
<security-constraint>
    <display-name>
```

```
        Switch from Constraint to Permission model
        (where everything is denied by default)
    </display-name>
    <web-resource-collection>
        <url-pattern>/</url-pattern>
    </web-resource-collection>
    <auth-constraint/>
</security-constraint>
```

Securing Application Clients

The Java EE authentication requirements for application clients are the same as for other Java EE components, and the same authentication techniques can be used as for other Java EE application components. No authentication is necessary when accessing unprotected web resources.

When accessing protected web resources, the usual varieties of authentication can be used: HTTP basic authentication, HTTP login-form authentication, or SSL client authentication. "Specifying an Authentication Mechanism in the Deployment Descriptor" in *The Java EE 6 Tutorial: Basic Concepts* describes how to specify HTTP basic authentication and HTTP login-form authentication. "Client Authentication" on page 316 describes how to specify SSL client authentication.

Authentication is required when accessing protected enterprise beans. The authentication mechanisms for enterprise beans are discussed in "Securing Enterprise Beans" in *The Java EE 6 Tutorial: Basic Concepts*.

An application client makes use of an authentication service provided by the application client container for authenticating its users. The container's service can be integrated with the native platform's authentication system so that a single sign-on capability is used. The container can authenticate the user either when the application is started or when a protected resource is accessed.

An application client can provide a class, called a *login module*, to gather authentication data. If so, the javax.security.auth.callback.CallbackHandler interface must be implemented, and the class name must be specified in its deployment descriptor. The application's callback handler must fully support Callback objects specified in the javax.security.auth.callback package.

Using Login Modules

An application client can use the Java Authentication and Authorization Service (JAAS) to create login modules for authentication. A JAAS-based application implements the javax.security.auth.callback.CallbackHandler interface so that it can interact with users to enter specific authentication data, such as user names or passwords, or to display error and warning messages.

Applications implement the `CallbackHandler` interface and pass it to the login context, which forwards it directly to the underlying login modules. A login module uses the callback handler both to gather input, such as a password or smart card PIN, from users and to supply information, such as status information, to users. Because the application specifies the callback handler, an underlying login module can remain independent of the various ways applications interact with users.

For example, the implementation of a callback handler for a GUI application might display a window to solicit user input, or the implementation of a callback handler for a command-line tool might simply prompt the user for input directly from the command line.

The login module passes an array of appropriate callbacks to the callback handler's `handle` method, such as a `NameCallback` for the user name and a `PasswordCallback` for the password; the callback handler performs the requested user interaction and sets appropriate values in the callbacks. For example, to process a `NameCallback`, the `CallbackHandler` might prompt for a name, retrieve the value from the user, and call the `setName` method of the `NameCallback` to store the name.

For more information on using JAAS for authentication in login modules, refer to the documentation listed in "Further Information about Security" on page 337.

Using Programmatic Login

Programmatic login enables the client code to supply user credentials. If you are using an EJB client, you can use the `com.sun.appserv.security.ProgrammaticLogin` class with its convenient `login` and `logout` methods. Programmatic login is specific to a server.

Securing Enterprise Information Systems Applications

In Enterprise Information Systems (EIS) applications, components request a connection to an EIS resource. As part of this connection, the EIS can require a sign-on for the requester to access the resource. The application component provider has two choices for the design of the EIS sign-on:

- **Container-managed sign-on**: The application component lets the container take the responsibility of configuring and managing the EIS sign-on. The container determines the user name and password for establishing a connection to an EIS instance. For more information, see "Container-Managed Sign-On" on page 333.

- **Component-managed sign-on**: The application component code manages EIS sign-on by including code that performs the sign-on process to an EIS. For more information, see "Component-Managed Sign-On" on page 333.

You can also configure security for resource adapters. See "Configuring Resource Adapter Security" on page 334.

Container-Managed Sign-On

In container-managed sign-on, an application component does not have to pass any sign-on security information to the getConnection() method. The security information is supplied by the container, as shown in the following example (the method call is highlighted in **bold**):

```
// Business method in an application component
Context initctx = new InitialContext();
// Perform JNDI lookup to obtain a connection factory
javax.resource.cci.ConnectionFactory cxf =
    (javax.resource.cci.ConnectionFactory)initctx.lookup(
    "java:comp/env/eis/MainframeCxFactory");
// Invoke factory to obtain a connection. The security
// information is not passed in the getConnection method
javax.resource.cci.Connection cx = cxf.getConnection();
...
```

Component-Managed Sign-On

In component-managed sign-on, an application component is responsible for passing the needed sign-on security information for the resource to the getConnection method. For example, security information might be a user name and password, as shown here (the method call is highlighted in **bold**):

```
// Method in an application component
Context initctx = new InitialContext();

// Perform JNDI lookup to obtain a connection factory
javax.resource.cci.ConnectionFactory cxf =
    (javax.resource.cci.ConnectionFactory)initctx.lookup(
    "java:comp/env/eis/MainframeCxFactory");

// Get a new ConnectionSpec
com.myeis.ConnectionSpecImpl properties = //..

// Invoke factory to obtain a connection
properties.setUserName("...");
properties.setPassword("...");
javax.resource.cci.Connection cx =
    cxf.getConnection(properties);
...
```

Configuring Resource Adapter Security

A resource adapter is a system-level software component that typically implements network connectivity to an external resource manager. A resource adapter can extend the functionality of the Java EE platform either by implementing one of the Java EE standard service APIs, such as a JDBC driver, or by defining and implementing a resource adapter for a connector to an external application system. Resource adapters can also provide services that are entirely local, perhaps interacting with native resources. Resource adapters interface with the Java EE platform through Java EE service provider interfaces (Java EE SPI). A resource adapter that uses Java EE SPIs to attach to the Java EE platform will be able to work with all Java EE products.

To configure the security settings for a resource adapter, you need to edit the resource adapter descriptor file, `ra.xml`. Here is an example of the part of an `ra.xml` file that configures security properties for a resource adapter:

```
<authentication-mechanism>
    <authentication-mechanism-type>
        BasicPassword
    </authentication-mechanism-type>
    <credential-interface>
        javax.resource.spi.security.PasswordCredential
    </credential-interface>
</authentication-mechanism>
<reauthentication-support>false</reauthentication-support>
```

You can find out more about the options for configuring resource adapter security by reviewing *as-install*/`lib/dtds/connector_1_0.dtd`. You can configure the following elements in the resource adapter deployment descriptor file:

- **Authentication mechanisms**: Use the `authentication-mechanism` element to specify an authentication mechanism supported by the resource adapter. This support is for the resource adapter, not for the underlying EIS instance.

   There are two supported mechanism types:

   - `BasicPassword`, which supports the following interface:

      `javax.resource.spi.security.PasswordCredential`
   - `Kerbv5`, which supports the following interface:

      `javax.resource.spi.security.GenericCredential`

   The GlassFish Server does not currently support this mechanism type.

- **Reauthentication support**: Use the `reauthentication-support` element to specify whether the resource adapter implementation supports reauthentication of existing `Managed-Connection` instances. Options are `true` or `false`.

- **Security permissions**: Use the `security-permission` element to specify a security permission that is required by the resource adapter code. Support for security permissions is optional and is not supported in the current release of the GlassFish

Server. You can, however, manually update the `server.policy` file to add the relevant permissions for the resource adapter.

The security permissions listed in the deployment descriptor are different from those required by the default permission set as specified in the connector specification.

For more information on the implementation of the security permission specification, see the security policy file documentation listed in "Further Information about Security" on page 337.

In addition to specifying resource adapter security in the `ra.xml` file, you can create a security map for a connector connection pool to map an application principal or a user group to a back-end EIS principal. The security map is usually used if one or more EIS back-end principals are used to execute operations (on the EIS) initiated by various principals or user groups in the application.

▼ To Map an Application Principal to EIS Principals

When using the GlassFish Server, you can use security maps to map the caller identity of the application (principal or user group) to a suitable EIS principal in container-managed transaction-based scenarios. When an application principal initiates a request to an EIS, the GlassFish Server first checks for an exact principal by using the security map defined for the connector connection pool to determine the mapped back-end EIS principal. If there is no exact match, the GlassFish Server uses the wildcard character specification, if any, to determine the mapped back-end EIS principal. Security maps are used when an application user needs to execute an EIS operation that requires execution as a specific identity in the EIS.

To work with security maps, use the Administration Console. From the Administration Console, follow these steps to get to the security maps page.

1 In the navigation tree, expand the Resources node.

2 Expand the Connectors node.

3 Select the Connector Connection Pools node.

4 On the Connector Connection Pools page, click the name of the connection pool for which you want to create a security map.

5 Click the Security Maps tab.

6 Click New to create a new security map for the connection pool.

7   Type a name by which you will refer to the security map, as well as the other required
    information.

Click the Help button for more information on the individual options.

Configuring Security Using Deployment Descriptors

The recommended way to configure security in the Java EE 6 platform is with
annotations. If you wish to override the security settings at deployment time, you can
use security elements in the web.xml deployment descriptor to do so. This section
describes how to use the deployment descriptor to specify basic authentication and to
override default principal-to-role mapping.

Specifying Security for Basic Authentication in the Deployment Descriptor

The elements of the deployment descriptor that add basic authentication to an
example tell the server or browser to perform the following tasks:

- Send a standard login dialog to collect user name and password data
- Verify that the user is authorized to access the application
- If authorized, display the servlet to the user

The following sample code shows the security elements for a deployment descriptor
that could be used in the example of basic authentication found in the
tut-install/examples/security/hello2_basicauth/ directory:

```
<security-constraint>
    <display-name>SecurityConstraint</display-name>
    <web-resource-collection>
        <web-resource-name>WRCollection</web-resource-name>
        <url-pattern>/greeting</url-pattern>
    </web-resource-collection>
    <auth-constraint>
        <role-name>TutorialUser</role-name>
    </auth-constraint>
    <user-data-constraint>
        <transport-guarantee>CONFIDENTIAL</transport-guarantee>
    </user-data-constraint>
</security-constraint>
<login-config>
    <auth-method>BASIC</auth-method>
    <realm-name>file</realm-name>
</login-config>
    <security-role>
        <role-name>TutorialUser</role-name>
    </security-role>
```

This deployment descriptor specifies that the request URI /greeting can be accessed only by users who have entered their user names and passwords and have been authorized to access this URL because they have been verified to be in the role TutorialUser. The user name and password data will be sent over a protected transport in order to keep it from being read in transit.

Specifying Non-Default Principal-to-Role Mapping in the Deployment Descriptor

To map a role name permitted by the application or module to principals (users) and groups defined on the server, use the security-role-mapping element in the runtime deployment descriptor file (glassfish-application.xml, glassfish-web.xml, or glassfish-ejb-jar.xml). The entry needs to declare a mapping between a security role used in the application and one or more groups or principals defined for the applicable realm of the GlassFish Server. An example for the glassfish-web.xml file is shown below:

```
<glassfish-web-app>
    <security-role-mapping>
        <role-name>DIRECTOR</role-name>
        <principal-name>schwartz</principal-name>
    </security-role-mapping>
    <security-role-mapping>
        <role-name>DEPT-ADMIN</role-name>
        <group-name>dept-admins</group-name>
    </security-role-mapping>
</glassfish-web-app>
```

The role name can be mapped to either a specific principal (user), a group, or both. The principal or group names referenced must be valid principals or groups in the current default realm of the GlassFish Server. The role-name in this example must exactly match the role-name in the security-role element of the corresponding web.xml file or the role name defined in the @DeclareRoles and/or @RolesAllowed annotations.

Further Information about Security

For more information about security, see:

- Documentation on the keytool command:

  http://docs.oracle.com/
  javase/6/docs/technotes/tools/solaris/keytool.html

- *Java Authentication and Authorization Service (JAAS) Reference Guide*

  http://docs.oracle.com/
  javase/6/docs/technotes/guides/security/jaas/JAASRefGuide.html

- *Java Authentication and Authorization Service (JAAS): LoginModule Developer's Guide*

  ```
  http://docs.oracle.com/
  javase/6/docs/technotes/guides/security/jaas/JAASLMDevGuide.html
  ```

- Documentation on security policy file syntax:

  ```
  http://docs.oracle.com/
  javase/6/docs/technotes/guides/security/PolicyFiles.html#FileSyntax
  ```

Java EE Supporting Technologies

Part VIII explores advanced technologies that support the Java EE platform. This part contains the following chapters:

Java Message Service Concepts

This chapter provides an introduction to the Java Message Service (JMS) API, a Java API that allows applications to create, send, receive, and read messages using reliable, asynchronous, loosely coupled communication. It covers the following topics:

- "Overview of the JMS API" on page 341
- "Basic JMS API Concepts" on page 345
- "The JMS API Programming Model" on page 348
- "Creating Robust JMS Applications" on page 359
- "Using the JMS API in Java EE Applications" on page 368
- "Further Information about JMS" on page 376

Overview of the JMS API

This overview defines the concept of messaging, describes the JMS API and when it can be used, and explains how the JMS API works within the Java EE platform.

What Is Messaging?

Messaging is a method of communication between software components or applications. A messaging system is a peer-to-peer facility: A messaging client can send messages to, and receive messages from, any other client. Each client connects to a messaging agent that provides facilities for creating, sending, receiving, and reading messages.

Messaging enables distributed communication that is *loosely coupled*. A component sends a message to a destination, and the recipient can retrieve the message from the destination. However, the sender and the receiver do not have to be available at the same time in order to communicate. In fact, the sender does not need to know anything about the receiver; nor does the receiver need to know anything about the sender. The sender and the receiver need to know only which message format and which destination to use. In this respect, messaging differs from tightly coupled technologies, such as Remote Method Invocation (RMI), which require an application to know a remote application's methods.

Messaging also differs from electronic mail (email), which is a method of communication between people or between software applications and people. Messaging is used for communication between software applications or software components.

What Is the JMS API?

The Java Message Service is a Java API that allows applications to create, send, receive, and read messages. Designed by Sun and several partner companies, the JMS API defines a common set of interfaces and associated semantics that allow programs written in the Java programming language to communicate with other messaging implementations.

The JMS API minimizes the set of concepts a programmer must learn in order to use messaging products but provides enough features to support sophisticated messaging applications. It also strives to maximize the portability of JMS applications across JMS providers in the same messaging domain.

The JMS API enables communication that is not only loosely coupled but also:

- **Asynchronous**: A JMS provider can deliver messages to a client as they arrive; a client does not have to request messages in order to receive them.

- **Reliable**: The JMS API can ensure that a message is delivered once and only once. Lower levels of reliability are available for applications that can afford to miss messages or to receive duplicate messages.

The current version of the JMS specification is Version 1.1. You can download a copy of the specification from the JMS web site: `http://www.oracle.com/technetwork/java/index-jsp-142945.html`.

When Can You Use the JMS API?

An enterprise application provider is likely to choose a messaging API over a tightly coupled API, such as a remote procedure call (RPC), under the following circumstances.

- The provider wants the components not to depend on information about other components' interfaces, so components can be easily replaced.
- The provider wants the application to run whether or not all components are up and running simultaneously.
- The application business model allows a component to send information to another and to continue to operate without receiving an immediate response.

For example, components of an enterprise application for an automobile manufacturer can use the JMS API in situations like these:

- The inventory component can send a message to the factory component when the inventory level for a product goes below a certain level so the factory can make more cars.
- The factory component can send a message to the parts components so the factory can assemble the parts it needs.
- The parts components in turn can send messages to their own inventory and order components to update their inventories and to order new parts from suppliers.
- Both the factory and the parts components can send messages to the accounting component to update budget numbers.
- The business can publish updated catalog items to its sales force.

Using messaging for these tasks allows the various components to interact with one another efficiently, without tying up network or other resources. Figure 20–1 illustrates how this simple example might work.

FIGURE 20–1 Messaging in an Enterprise Application

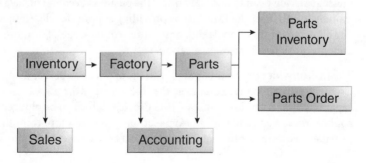

Manufacturing is only one example of how an enterprise can use the JMS API. Retail applications, financial services applications, health services applications, and many others can make use of messaging.

How Does the JMS API Work with the Java EE Platform?

When the JMS API was introduced in 1998, its most important purpose was to allow Java applications to access existing messaging-oriented middleware (MOM) systems, such as MQSeries from IBM. Since that time, many vendors have adopted and implemented the JMS API, so a JMS product can now provide a complete messaging capability for an enterprise.

Beginning with the 1.3 release of the Java EE platform, the JMS API has been an integral part of the platform, and application developers have been able to use messaging with Java EE components.

The JMS API in the Java EE platform has the following features.

- Application clients, Enterprise JavaBeans (EJB) components, and web components can send or synchronously receive a JMS message. Application clients can in addition receive JMS messages asynchronously. (Applets, however, are not required to support the JMS API.)

- Message-driven beans, which are a kind of enterprise bean, enable the asynchronous consumption of messages. A JMS provider can optionally implement concurrent processing of messages by message-driven beans.

- Message send and receive operations can participate in distributed transactions, which allow JMS operations and database accesses to take place within a single transaction.

The JMS API enhances the Java EE platform by simplifying enterprise development, allowing loosely coupled, reliable, asynchronous interactions among Java EE components and legacy systems capable of messaging. A developer can easily add new behavior to a Java EE application that has existing business events by adding a new message-driven bean to operate on specific business events. The Java EE platform, moreover, enhances the JMS API by providing support for distributed transactions and allowing for the concurrent consumption of messages. For more information, see the Enterprise JavaBeans specification, v3.1.

The JMS provider can be integrated with the application server using the Java EE Connector architecture. You access the JMS provider through a resource adapter. This capability allows vendors to create JMS providers that can be plugged in to multiple application servers, and it allows application servers to support multiple JMS providers. For more information, see the Java EE Connector architecture specification, v1.6.

Basic JMS API Concepts

This section introduces the most basic JMS API concepts, the ones you must know to get started writing simple application clients that use the JMS API.

The next section introduces the JMS API programming model. Later sections cover more advanced concepts, including the ones you need in order to write applications that use message-driven beans.

JMS API Architecture

A JMS application is composed of the following parts.

- A *JMS provider* is a messaging system that implements the JMS interfaces and provides administrative and control features. An implementation of the Java EE platform includes a JMS provider.

- *JMS clients* are the programs or components, written in the Java programming language, that produce and consume messages. Any Java EE application component can act as a JMS client.

- *Messages* are the objects that communicate information between JMS clients.

- *Administered objects* are preconfigured JMS objects created by an administrator for the use of clients. The two kinds of JMS administered objects are destinations and connection factories, described in "JMS Administered Objects" on page 349.

Figure 20–2 illustrates the way these parts interact. Administrative tools allow you to bind destinations and connection factories into a JNDI namespace. A JMS client can then use resource injection to access the administered objects in the namespace and then establish a logical connection to the same objects through the JMS provider.

FIGURE 20–2 JMS API Architecture

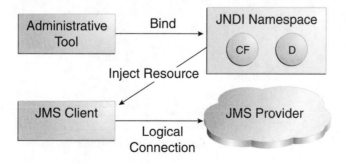

Messaging Domains

Before the JMS API existed, most messaging products supported either the point-to-point or the publish/subscribe approach to messaging. The JMS specification provides a separate domain for each approach and defines compliance for each domain. A stand-alone JMS provider can implement one or both domains. A Java EE provider must implement both domains.

In fact, most implementations of the JMS API support both the point-to-point and the publish/subscribe domains, and some JMS clients combine the use of both domains in a single application. In this way, the JMS API has extended the power and flexibility of messaging products.

The JMS specification goes one step further: It provides common interfaces that enable you to use the JMS API in a way that is not specific to either domain. The following subsections describe the two messaging domains and the use of the common interfaces.

Point-to-Point Messaging Domain

A *point-to-point* (PTP) product or application is built on the concept of message *queues*, senders, and receivers. Each message is addressed to a specific queue, and receiving clients extract messages from the queues established to hold their messages. Queues retain all messages sent to them until the messages are consumed or expire.

PTP messaging, illustrated in Figure 20–3, has the following characteristics:

- Each message has only one consumer.
- A sender and a receiver of a message have no timing dependencies. The receiver can fetch the message whether or not it was running when the client sent the message.
- The receiver acknowledges the successful processing of a message.

FIGURE 20–3   Point-to-Point Messaging

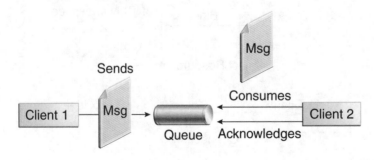

Use PTP messaging when every message you send must be processed successfully by one consumer.

Publish/Subscribe Messaging Domain

In a *publish/subscribe* (pub/sub) product or application, clients address messages to a *topic*, which functions somewhat like a bulletin board. Publishers and subscribers are generally anonymous and can dynamically publish or subscribe to the content hierarchy. The system takes care of distributing the messages arriving from a topic's multiple publishers to its multiple subscribers. Topics retain messages only as long as it takes to distribute them to current subscribers.

Pub/sub messaging has the following characteristics.

- Each message can have multiple consumers.
- Publishers and subscribers have a timing dependency. A client that subscribes to a topic can consume only messages published after the client has created a subscription, and the subscriber must continue to be active in order for it to consume messages.

The JMS API relaxes this timing dependency to some extent by allowing subscribers to create *durable subscriptions*, which receive messages sent while the subscribers are not active. Durable subscriptions provide the flexibility and reliability of queues but still allow clients to send messages to many recipients. For more information about durable subscriptions, see "Creating Durable Subscriptions" on page 364.

Use pub/sub messaging when each message can be processed by any number of consumers (or none). Figure 20–4 illustrates pub/sub messaging.

FIGURE 20–4   Publish/Subscribe Messaging

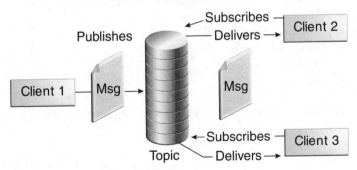

Programming with the Common Interfaces

Version 1.1 of the JMS API allows you to use the same code to send and receive messages under either the PTP or the pub/sub domain. The destinations you use remain domain-specific, and the behavior of the application will depend in part on whether you are using a queue or a topic. However, the code itself can be common to both domains, making your applications flexible and reusable. This tutorial describes and illustrates these common interfaces.

Message Consumption

Messaging products are inherently asynchronous: There is no fundamental timing dependency between the production and the consumption of a message. However, the JMS specification uses this term in a more precise sense. Messages can be consumed in either of two ways:

- **Synchronously**: A subscriber or a receiver explicitly fetches the message from the destination by calling the `receive` method. The `receive` method can block until a message arrives or can time out if a message does not arrive within a specified time limit.

- **Asynchronously**: A client can register a *message listener* with a consumer. A message listener is similar to an event listener. Whenever a message arrives at the destination, the JMS provider delivers the message by calling the listener's `onMessage` method, which acts on the contents of the message.

The JMS API Programming Model

The basic building blocks of a JMS application are:

- Administered objects: connection factories and destinations
- Connections
- Sessions
- Message producers
- Message consumers
- Messages

Figure 20–5 shows how all these objects fit together in a JMS client application.

FIGURE 20–5   The JMS API Programming Model

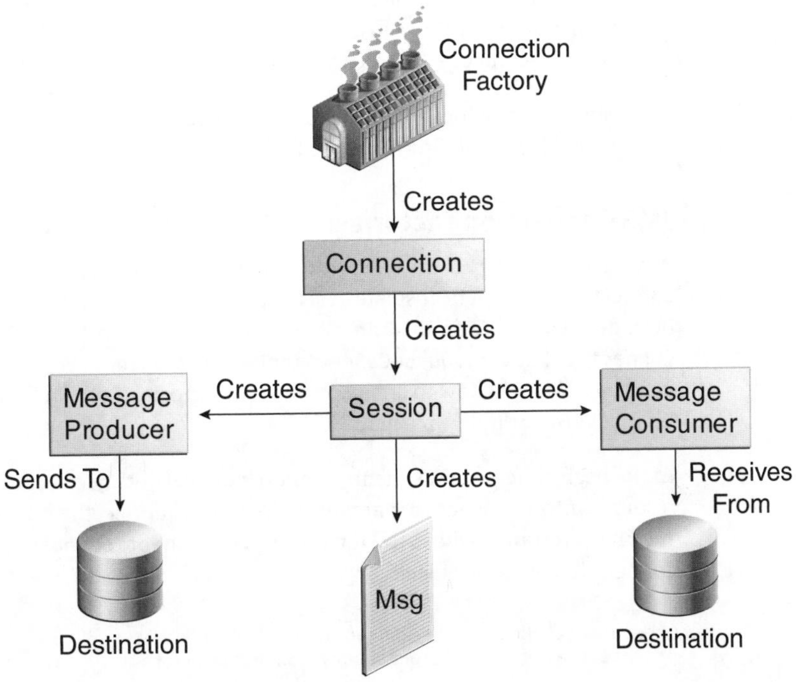

This section describes all these objects briefly and provides sample commands and code snippets that show how to create and use the objects. The last subsection briefly describes JMS API exception handling.

Examples that show how to combine all these objects in applications appear in later sections. For more detail, see the JMS API documentation, part of the Java EE API documentation.

JMS Administered Objects

Two parts of a JMS application, destinations and connection factories, are best maintained administratively rather than programmatically. The technology underlying these objects is likely to be very different from one implementation of the JMS API to another. Therefore, the management of these objects belongs with other administrative tasks that vary from provider to provider.

JMS clients access these objects through interfaces that are portable, so a client application can run with little or no change on more than one implementation of the JMS API. Ordinarily, an administrator configures administered objects in a JNDI namespace, and JMS clients then access them by using resource injection.

With GlassFish Server, you can use the asadmin create-jms-resource command or the Administration Console to create JMS administered objects in the form of connector resources. You can also specify the resources in a file named glassfish-resources.xml that you can bundle with an application.

NetBeans IDE provides a wizard that allows you to create JMS resources for GlassFish Server. See "To Create JMS Resources Using NetBeans IDE" on page 381 for details.

JMS Connection Factories

A *connection factory* is the object a client uses to create a connection to a provider. A connection factory encapsulates a set of connection configuration parameters that has been defined by an administrator. Each connection factory is an instance of the ConnectionFactory, QueueConnectionFactory, or TopicConnectionFactory interface. To learn how to create connection factories, see "To Create JMS Resources Using NetBeans IDE" on page 381.

At the beginning of a JMS client program, you usually inject a connection factory resource into a ConnectionFactory object. For example, the following code fragment specifies a resource whose JNDI name is jms/ConnectionFactory and assigns it to a ConnectionFactory object:

```
@Resource(lookup = "jms/ConnectionFactory")
private static ConnectionFactory connectionFactory;
```

In a Java EE application, JMS administered objects are normally placed in the jms naming subcontext.

JMS Destinations

A *destination* is the object a client uses to specify the target of messages it produces and the source of messages it consumes. In the PTP messaging domain, destinations are called queues. In the pub/sub messaging domain, destinations are called topics. A JMS application can use multiple queues or topics (or both). To learn how to create destination resources, see "To Create JMS Resources Using NetBeans IDE" on page 381.

To create a destination using the GlassFish Server, you create a JMS destination resource that specifies a JNDI name for the destination.

In the GlassFish Server implementation of JMS, each destination resource refers to a physical destination. You can create a physical destination explicitly, but if you do not, the Application Server creates it when it is needed and deletes it when you delete the destination resource.

In addition to injecting a connection factory resource into a client program, you usually inject a destination resource. Unlike connection factories, destinations are specific to one domain or the other. To create an application that allows you to use the same code for both topics and queues, you assign the destination to a `Destination` object.

The following code specifies two resources, a queue and a topic. The resource names are mapped to destination resources created in the JNDI namespace.

```
@Resource(lookup = "jms/Queue")
private static Queue queue;

@Resource(lookup = "jms/Topic")
private static Topic topic;
```

With the common interfaces, you can mix or match connection factories and destinations. That is, in addition to using the `ConnectionFactory` interface, you can inject a `QueueConnectionFactory` resource and use it with a `Topic`, and you can inject a `TopicConnectionFactory` resource and use it with a `Queue`. The behavior of the application will depend on the kind of destination you use and not on the kind of connection factory you use.

JMS Connections

A *connection* encapsulates a virtual connection with a JMS provider. For example, a connection could represent an open TCP/IP socket between a client and a provider service daemon. You use a connection to create one or more sessions.

Note – In the Java EE platform, the ability to create multiple sessions from a single connection is limited to application clients. In web and enterprise bean components, a connection can create no more than one session.

Connections implement the `Connection` interface. When you have a `ConnectionFactory` object, you can use it to create a `Connection`:

```
Connection connection = connectionFactory.createConnection();
```

Before an application completes, you must close any connections you have created. Failure to close a connection can cause resources not to be released by the JMS provider. Closing a connection also closes its sessions and their message producers and message consumers.

```
connection.close();
```

Before your application can consume messages, you must call the connection's `start` method; for details, see "JMS Message Consumers" on page 353. If you want to stop message delivery temporarily without closing the connection, you call the `stop` method.

JMS Sessions

A *session* is a single-threaded context for producing and consuming messages. You use sessions to create the following:

- Message producers
- Message consumers
- Messages
- Queue browsers
- Temporary queues and topics (see "Creating Temporary Destinations" on page 363)

Sessions serialize the execution of message listeners; for details, see "JMS Message Listeners" on page 354.

A session provides a transactional context with which to group a set of sends and receives into an atomic unit of work. For details, see "Using JMS API Local Transactions" on page 366.

Sessions implement the Session interface. After you create a Connection object, you use it to create a Session:

```
Session session = connection.createSession(false,
    Session.AUTO_ACKNOWLEDGE);
```

The first argument means the session is not transacted; the second means the session automatically acknowledges messages when they have been received successfully. (For more information, see "Controlling Message Acknowledgment" on page 360.)

To create a transacted session, use the following code:

```
Session session = connection.createSession(true, 0);
```

Here, the first argument means the session is transacted; the second indicates that message acknowledgment is not specified for transacted sessions. For more information on transactions, see "Using JMS API Local Transactions" on page 366. For information about the way JMS transactions work in Java EE applications, see "Using the JMS API in Java EE Applications" on page 368.

JMS Message Producers

A *message producer* is an object that is created by a session and used for sending messages to a destination. It implements the MessageProducer interface.

You use a Session to create a MessageProducer for a destination. The following examples show that you can create a producer for a Destination object, a Queue object, or a Topic object.

```
MessageProducer producer = session.createProducer(dest);
MessageProducer producer = session.createProducer(queue);
MessageProducer producer = session.createProducer(topic);
```

You can create an unidentified producer by specifying `null` as the argument to `createProducer`. With an unidentified producer, you do not specify a destination until you send a message.

After you have created a message producer, you can use it to send messages by using the send method:

```
producer.send(message);
```

You must first create the messages; see "JMS Messages" on page 355.

If you have created an unidentified producer, use an overloaded send method that specifies the destination as the first parameter. For example:

```
MessageProducer anon_prod = session.createProducer(null);
anon_prod.send(dest, message);
```

JMS Message Consumers

A *message consumer* is an object that is created by a session and used for receiving messages sent to a destination. It implements the `MessageConsumer` interface.

A message consumer allows a JMS client to register interest in a destination with a JMS provider. The JMS provider manages the delivery of messages from a destination to the registered consumers of the destination.

For example, you could use a `Session` to create a `MessageConsumer` for a `Destination` object, a `Queue` object, or a `Topic` object:

```
MessageConsumer consumer = session.createConsumer(dest);
MessageConsumer consumer = session.createConsumer(queue);
MessageConsumer consumer = session.createConsumer(topic);
```

You use the `Session.createDurableSubscriber` method to create a durable topic subscriber. This method is valid only if you are using a topic. For details, see "Creating Durable Subscriptions" on page 364.

After you have created a message consumer it becomes active, and you can use it to receive messages. You can use the `close` method for a `MessageConsumer` to make the message consumer inactive. Message delivery does not begin until you start the connection you created by calling its `start` method. (Remember always to call the `start` method; forgetting to start the connection is one of the most common JMS programming errors.)

You use the receive method to consume a message synchronously. You can use this method at any time after you call the start method:

```
connection.start();
Message m = consumer.receive();
connection.start();
Message m = consumer.receive(1000); // time out after a second
```

To consume a message asynchronously, you use a message listener, as described in the next section.

JMS Message Listeners

A message listener is an object that acts as an asynchronous event handler for messages. This object implements the MessageListener interface, which contains one method, onMessage. In the onMessage method, you define the actions to be taken when a message arrives.

You register the message listener with a specific MessageConsumer by using the setMessageListener method. For example, if you define a class named Listener that implements the MessageListener interface, you can register the message listener as follows:

```
Listener myListener = new Listener();
consumer.setMessageListener(myListener);
```

Note – In the Java EE platform, a MessageListener can be used only in an application client, not in a web component or enterprise bean.

After you register the message listener, you call the start method on the Connection to begin message delivery. (If you call start before you register the message listener, you are likely to miss messages.)

When message delivery begins, the JMS provider automatically calls the message listener's onMessage method whenever a message is delivered. The onMessage method takes one argument of type Message, which your implementation of the method can cast to any of the other message types (see "Message Bodies" on page 357).

A message listener is not specific to a particular destination type. The same listener can obtain messages from either a queue or a topic, depending on the type of destination for which the message consumer was created. A message listener does, however, usually expect a specific message type and format.

Your onMessage method should handle all exceptions. It must not throw checked exceptions, and throwing a RuntimeException is considered a programming error.

The session used to create the message consumer serializes the execution of all message listeners registered with the session. At any time, only one of the session's message listeners is running.

In the Java EE platform, a message-driven bean is a special kind of message listener. For details, see "Using Message-Driven Beans to Receive Messages Asynchronously" on page 370.

JMS Message Selectors

If your messaging application needs to filter the messages it receives, you can use a JMS API message selector, which allows a message consumer to specify the messages that interest it. Message selectors assign the work of filtering messages to the JMS provider rather than to the application. For an example of an application that uses a message selector, see "An Application That Uses the JMS API with a Session Bean" on page 416.

A message selector is a `String` that contains an expression. The syntax of the expression is based on a subset of the SQL92 conditional expression syntax. The message selector in the example selects any message that has a `NewsType` property that is set to the value `'Sports'` or `'Opinion'`:

```
NewsType = 'Sports' OR NewsType = 'Opinion'
```

The `createConsumer` and `createDurableSubscriber` methods allow you to specify a message selector as an argument when you create a message consumer.

The message consumer then receives only messages whose headers and properties match the selector. (See "Message Headers" on page 356, and "Message Properties" on page 356.) A message selector cannot select messages on the basis of the content of the message body.

JMS Messages

The ultimate purpose of a JMS application is to produce and consume messages that can then be used by other software applications. JMS messages have a basic format that is simple but highly flexible, allowing you to create messages that match formats used by non-JMS applications on heterogeneous platforms.

A JMS message can have three parts: a header, properties, and a body. Only the header is required. The following sections describe these parts.

For complete documentation of message headers, properties, and bodies, see the documentation of the `Message` interface in the API documentation.

Message Headers

A JMS message header contains a number of predefined fields that contain values used by both clients and providers to identify and route messages. Table 20–1 lists the JMS message header fields and indicates how their values are set. For example, every message has a unique identifier, which is represented in the header field JMSMessageID. The value of another header field, JMSDestination, represents the queue or the topic to which the message is sent. Other fields include a timestamp and a priority level.

Each header field has associated setter and getter methods, which are documented in the description of the Message interface. Some header fields are intended to be set by a client, but many are set automatically by the send or the publish method, which overrides any client-set values.

TABLE 20–1   How JMS Message Header Field Values Are Set

Header Field	Set By
JMSDestination	send or publish method
JMSDeliveryMode	send or publish method
JMSExpiration	send or publish method
JMSPriority	send or publish method
JMSMessageID	send or publish method
JMSTimestamp	send or publish method
JMSCorrelationID	Client
JMSReplyTo	Client
JMSType	Client
JMSRedelivered	JMS provider

Message Properties

You can create and set properties for messages if you need values in addition to those provided by the header fields. You can use properties to provide compatibility with other messaging systems, or you can use them to create message selectors (see "JMS Message Selectors" on page 355). For an example of setting a property to be used as a message selector, see "An Application That Uses the JMS API with a Session Bean" on page 416.

The JMS API provides some predefined property names that a provider can support. The use of these predefined properties or of user-defined properties is optional.

Message Bodies

The JMS API defines five message body formats, also called message types, which allow you to send and receive data in many different forms and which provide compatibility with existing messaging formats. Table 20–2 describes these message types.

TABLE 20–2   JMS Message Types

Message Type	Body Contains
TextMessage	A java.lang.String object (for example, the contents of an XML file).
MapMessage	A set of name-value pairs, with names as String objects and values as primitive types in the Java programming language. The entries can be accessed sequentially by enumerator or randomly by name. The order of the entries is undefined.
BytesMessage	A stream of uninterpreted bytes. This message type is for literally encoding a body to match an existing message format.
StreamMessage	A stream of primitive values in the Java programming language, filled and read sequentially.
ObjectMessage	A Serializable object in the Java programming language.
Message	Nothing. Composed of header fields and properties only. This message type is useful when a message body is not required.

The JMS API provides methods for creating messages of each type and for filling in their contents. For example, to create and send a TextMessage, you might use the following statements:

```
TextMessage message = session.createTextMessage();
message.setText(msg_text);      // msg_text is a String
producer.send(message);
```

At the consuming end, a message arrives as a generic Message object and must be cast to the appropriate message type. You can use one or more getter methods to extract the message contents. The following code fragment uses the getText method:

```
Message m = consumer.receive();
if (m instanceof TextMessage) {
    TextMessage message = (TextMessage) m;
    System.out.println("Reading message: " + message.getText());
} else {
    // Handle error
}
```

JMS Queue Browsers

Messages sent to a queue remain in the queue until the message consumer for that queue consumes them. The JMS API provides a QueueBrowser object that allows you to browse the messages in the queue and display the header values for each message. To create a QueueBrowser object, use the Session.createBrowser method. For example:

```
QueueBrowser browser = session.createBrowser(queue);
```

See "A Simple Example of Browsing Messages in a Queue" on page 394 for an example of using a QueueBrowser object.

The createBrowser method allows you to specify a message selector as a second argument when you create a QueueBrowser. For information on message selectors, see "JMS Message Selectors" on page 355.

The JMS API provides no mechanism for browsing a topic. Messages usually disappear from a topic as soon as they appear: If there are no message consumers to consume them, the JMS provider removes them. Although durable subscriptions allow messages to remain on a topic while the message consumer is not active, no facility exists for examining them.

JMS Exception Handling

The root class for exceptions thrown by JMS API methods is JMSException. Catching JMSException provides a generic way of handling all exceptions related to the JMS API.

The JMSException class includes the following subclasses, described in the API documentation:

- IllegalStateException
- InvalidClientIDException
- InvalidDestinationException
- InvalidSelectorException
- JMSSecurityException
- MessageEOFException
- MessageFormatException
- MessageNotReadableException
- MessageNotWriteableException
- ResourceAllocationException
- TransactionInProgressException
- TransactionRolledBackException

All the examples in the tutorial catch and handle JMSException when it is appropriate to do so.

Creating Robust JMS Applications

This section explains how to use features of the JMS API to achieve the level of reliability and performance your application requires. Many people choose to implement JMS applications because they cannot tolerate dropped or duplicate messages and because they require that every message be received once and only once. The JMS API provides this functionality.

The most reliable way to produce a message is to send a PERSISTENT message within a transaction. JMS messages are PERSISTENT by default. A *transaction* is a unit of work into which you can group a series of operations, such as message sends and receives, so that the operations either all succeed or all fail. For details, see "Specifying Message Persistence" on page 361 and "Using JMS API Local Transactions" on page 366.

The most reliable way to consume a message is to do so within a transaction, either from a queue or from a durable subscription to a topic. For details, see "Creating Temporary Destinations" on page 363, "Creating Durable Subscriptions" on page 364, and "Using JMS API Local Transactions" on page 366.

For other applications, a lower level of reliability can reduce overhead and improve performance. You can send messages with varying priority levels (see "Setting Message Priority Levels" on page 362) and you can set them to expire after a certain length of time (see "Allowing Messages to Expire" on page 362).

The JMS API provides several ways to achieve various kinds and degrees of reliability. This section divides them into two categories, basic and advanced.

The following sections describe these features as they apply to JMS clients. Some of the features work differently in Java EE applications; in these cases, the differences are noted here and are explained in detail in "Using the JMS API in Java EE Applications" on page 368.

Using Basic Reliability Mechanisms

The basic mechanisms for achieving or affecting reliable message delivery are as follows:

- **Controlling message acknowledgment**: You can specify various levels of control over message acknowledgment.

- **Specifying message persistence**: You can specify that messages are persistent, meaning they must not be lost in the event of a provider failure.

- **Setting message priority levels**: You can set various priority levels for messages, which can affect the order in which the messages are delivered.

- **Allowing messages to expire**: You can specify an expiration time for messages so they will not be delivered if they are obsolete.

- **Creating temporary destinations**: You can create temporary destinations that last only for the duration of the connection in which they are created.

Controlling Message Acknowledgment

Until a JMS message has been acknowledged, it is not considered to be successfully consumed. The successful consumption of a message ordinarily takes place in three stages.

1. The client receives the message.

2. The client processes the message.

3. The message is acknowledged. Acknowledgment is initiated either by the JMS provider or by the client, depending on the session acknowledgment mode.

In transacted sessions (see "Using JMS API Local Transactions" on page 366), acknowledgment happens automatically when a transaction is committed. If a transaction is rolled back, all consumed messages are redelivered.

In nontransacted sessions, when and how a message is acknowledged depend on the value specified as the second argument of the `createSession` method. The three possible argument values are as follows:

- `Session.AUTO_ACKNOWLEDGE`: The session automatically acknowledges a client's receipt of a message either when the client has successfully returned from a call to `receive` or when the `MessageListener` it has called to process the message returns successfully.

  A synchronous receive in an `AUTO_ACKNOWLEDGE` session is the one exception to the rule that message consumption is a three-stage process as described earlier. In this case, the receipt and acknowledgment take place in one step, followed by the processing of the message.

- `Session.CLIENT_ACKNOWLEDGE`: A client acknowledges a message by calling the message's `acknowledge` method. In this mode, acknowledgment takes place on the session level: Acknowledging a consumed message automatically acknowledges the receipt of *all* messages that have been consumed by its session. For example, if a message consumer consumes ten messages and then acknowledges the fifth message delivered, all ten messages are acknowledged.

Note – In the Java EE platform, a `CLIENT_ACKNOWLEDGE` session can be used only in an application client, not in a web component or enterprise bean.

- `Session.DUPS_OK_ACKNOWLEDGE`: This option instructs the session to lazily acknowledge the delivery of messages. This is likely to result in the delivery of some duplicate messages if the JMS provider fails, so it should be used only by consumers that can tolerate duplicate messages. (If the JMS provider redelivers a message, it must set the value of the `JMSRedelivered` message header to `true`.) This option can reduce session overhead by minimizing the work the session does to prevent duplicates.

If messages have been received from a queue but not acknowledged when a session terminates, the JMS provider retains them and redelivers them when a consumer next accesses the queue. The provider also retains unacknowledged messages for a terminated session that has a durable `TopicSubscriber`. (See "Creating Durable Subscriptions" on page 364.) Unacknowledged messages for a nondurable `TopicSubscriber` are dropped when the session is closed.

If you use a queue or a durable subscription, you can use the `Session.recover` method to stop a nontransacted session and restart it with its first unacknowledged message. In effect, the session's series of delivered messages is reset to the point after its last acknowledged message. The messages it now delivers may be different from those that were originally delivered, if messages have expired or if higher-priority messages have arrived. For a nondurable `TopicSubscriber`, the provider may drop unacknowledged messages when its session is recovered.

The sample program in "A Message Acknowledgment Example" on page 406 demonstrates two ways to ensure that a message will not be acknowledged until processing of the message is complete.

Specifying Message Persistence

The JMS API supports two delivery modes specifying whether messages are lost if the JMS provider fails. These delivery modes are fields of the `DeliveryMode` interface.

- The `PERSISTENT` delivery mode, the default, instructs the JMS provider to take extra care to ensure that a message is not lost in transit in case of a JMS provider failure. A message sent with this delivery mode is logged to stable storage when it is sent.

- The `NON_PERSISTENT` delivery mode does not require the JMS provider to store the message or otherwise guarantee that it is not lost if the provider fails.

You can specify the delivery mode in either of two ways.

- You can use the `setDeliveryMode` method of the `MessageProducer` interface to set the delivery mode for all messages sent by that producer. For example, the following call sets the delivery mode to `NON_PERSISTENT` for a producer:

```
producer.setDeliveryMode(DeliveryMode.NON_PERSISTENT);
```

- You can use the long form of the send or the publish method to set the delivery mode for a specific message. The second argument sets the delivery mode. For example, the following send call sets the delivery mode for message to NON_PERSISTENT:

```
producer.send(message, DeliveryMode.NON_PERSISTENT, 3, 10000);
```

The third and fourth arguments set the priority level and expiration time, which are described in the next two subsections.

If you do not specify a delivery mode, the default is PERSISTENT. Using the NON_PERSISTENT delivery mode may improve performance and reduce storage overhead, but you should use it only if your application can afford to miss messages.

Setting Message Priority Levels

You can use message priority levels to instruct the JMS provider to deliver urgent messages first. You can set the priority level in either of two ways.

- You can use the setPriority method of the MessageProducer interface to set the priority level for all messages sent by that producer. For example, the following call sets a priority level of 7 for a producer:

```
producer.setPriority(7);
```

- You can use the long form of the send or the publish method to set the priority level for a specific message. The third argument sets the priority level. For example, the following send call sets the priority level for message to 3:

```
producer.send(message, DeliveryMode.NON_PERSISTENT, 3, 10000);
```

The ten levels of priority range from 0 (lowest) to 9 (highest). If you do not specify a priority level, the default level is 4. A JMS provider tries to deliver higher-priority messages before lower-priority ones but does not have to deliver messages in exact order of priority.

Allowing Messages to Expire

By default, a message never expires. If a message will become obsolete after a certain period, however, you may want to set an expiration time. You can do this in either of two ways.

- You can use the setTimeToLive method of the MessageProducer interface to set a default expiration time for all messages sent by that producer. For example, the following call sets a time to live of one minute for a producer:

```
producer.setTimeToLive(60000);
```

- You can use the long form of the send or the publish method to set an expiration time for a specific message. The fourth argument sets the expiration time in milliseconds. For example, the following send call sets a time to live of 10 seconds:

```
producer.send(message, DeliveryMode.NON_PERSISTENT, 3, 10000);
```

If the specified `timeToLive` value is 0, the message never expires.

When the message is sent, the specified `timeToLive` is added to the current time to give the expiration time. Any message not delivered before the specified expiration time is destroyed. The destruction of obsolete messages conserves storage and computing resources.

Creating Temporary Destinations

Normally, you create JMS destinations (queues and topics) administratively rather than programmatically. Your JMS provider includes a tool to create and remove destinations, and it is common for destinations to be long-lasting.

The JMS API also enables you to create destinations (`TemporaryQueue` and `TemporaryTopic` objects) that last only for the duration of the connection in which they are created. You create these destinations dynamically using the `Session.createTemporaryQueue` and the `Session.createTemporaryTopic` methods.

The only message consumers that can consume from a temporary destination are those created by the same connection that created the destination. Any message producer can send to the temporary destination. If you close the connection to which a temporary destination belongs, the destination is closed and its contents are lost.

You can use temporary destinations to implement a simple request/reply mechanism. If you create a temporary destination and specify it as the value of the `JMSReplyTo` message header field when you send a message, then the consumer of the message can use the value of the `JMSReplyTo` field as the destination to which it sends a reply. The consumer can also reference the original request by setting the `JMSCorrelationID` header field of the reply message to the value of the `JMSMessageID` header field of the request. For example, an `onMessage` method can create a session so that it can send a reply to the message it receives. It can use code such as the following:

```
producer = session.createProducer(msg.getJMSReplyTo());
replyMsg = session.createTextMessage("Consumer " +
    "processed message: " + msg.getText());
replyMsg.setJMSCorrelationID(msg.getJMSMessageID());
producer.send(replyMsg);
```

For more examples, see Chapter 21, "Java Message Service Examples."

Using Advanced Reliability Mechanisms

The more advanced mechanisms for achieving reliable message delivery are the following:

- **Creating durable subscriptions**: You can create durable topic subscriptions, which receive messages published while the subscriber is not active. Durable subscriptions offer the reliability of queues to the publish/subscribe message domain.

- **Using local transactions**: You can use local transactions, which allow you to group a series of sends and receives into an atomic unit of work. Transactions are rolled back if they fail at any time.

Creating Durable Subscriptions

To ensure that a pub/sub application receives all published messages, use PERSISTENT delivery mode for the publishers and durable subscriptions for the subscribers.

The Session.createConsumer method creates a nondurable subscriber if a topic is specified as the destination. A nondurable subscriber can receive only messages that are published while it is active.

At the cost of higher overhead, you can use the Session.createDurableSubscriber method to create a durable subscriber. A durable subscription can have only one active subscriber at a time.

A durable subscriber registers a durable subscription by specifying a unique identity that is retained by the JMS provider. Subsequent subscriber objects that have the same identity resume the subscription in the state in which it was left by the preceding subscriber. If a durable subscription has no active subscriber, the JMS provider retains the subscription's messages until they are received by the subscription or until they expire.

You establish the unique identity of a durable subscriber by setting the following:

- A client ID for the connection
- A topic and a subscription name for the subscriber

You set the client ID administratively for a client-specific connection factory using either the command line or the Administration Console.

After using this connection factory to create the connection and the session, you call the createDurableSubscriber method with two arguments: the topic and a string that specifies the name of the subscription:

```
String subName = "MySub";
MessageConsumer topicSubscriber =
    session.createDurableSubscriber(myTopic, subName);
```

The subscriber becomes active after you start the Connection or TopicConnection. Later, you might close the subscriber:

```
topicSubscriber.close();
```

The JMS provider stores the messages sent or published to the topic, as it would store messages sent to a queue. If the program or another application calls createDurableSubscriber using the same connection factory and its client ID, the same topic, and the same subscription name, then the subscription is reactivated and the JMS provider delivers any messages that were published while the subscriber was inactive.

To delete a durable subscription, first close the subscriber, then use the unsubscribe method with the subscription name as the argument:

```
topicSubscriber.close();
session.unsubscribe("MySub");
```

The unsubscribe method deletes the state the provider maintains for the subscriber.

Figure 20–6 and Figure 20–7 show the difference between a nondurable and a durable subscriber. With an ordinary, nondurable subscriber, the subscriber and the subscription begin and end at the same point and are, in effect, identical. When a subscriber is closed, the subscription also ends. Here, create stands for a call to Session.createConsumer with a Topic argument, and close stands for a call to MessageConsumer.close. Any messages published to the topic between the time of the first close and the time of the second create are not consumed by the subscriber. In Figure 20–6, the subscriber consumes messages M1, M2, M5, and M6, but messages M3 and M4 are lost.

FIGURE 20–6 Nondurable Subscribers and Subscriptions

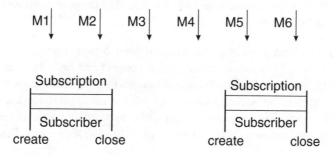

With a durable subscriber, the subscriber can be closed and re-created, but the subscription continues to exist and to hold messages until the application calls the unsubscribe method. In Figure 20–7, create stands for a call to Session.createDurableSubscriber, close stands for a call to

MessageConsumer.close, and unsubscribe stands for a call to
Session.unsubscribe. Messages published while the subscriber is closed are received
when the subscriber is created again, so even though messages M2, M4, and M5 arrive
while the subscriber is closed, they are not lost.

FIGURE 20-7   A Durable Subscriber and Subscription

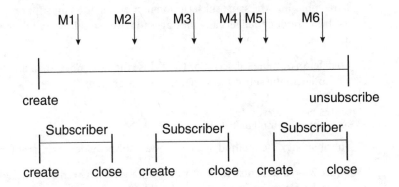

See "A Message Acknowledgment Example" on page 406, "A Durable Subscription
Example" on page 409, and "An Application That Uses the JMS API with a Session
Bean" on page 416 for examples of Java EE applications that use durable subscriptions.

Using JMS API Local Transactions

You can group a series of operations into an atomic unit of work called a *transaction*. If
any one of the operations fails, the transaction can be rolled back, and the operations
can be attempted again from the beginning. If all the operations succeed, the
transaction can be committed.

In a JMS client, you can use local transactions to group message sends and receives.
The JMS API Session interface provides commit and rollback methods you can use
in a JMS client. A transaction commit means that all produced messages are sent and
all consumed messages are acknowledged. A transaction rollback means that all
produced messages are destroyed and all consumed messages are recovered and
redelivered unless they have expired (see "Allowing Messages to Expire" on page 362).

A transacted session is always involved in a transaction. As soon as the commit or the
rollback method is called, one transaction ends and another transaction begins.
Closing a transacted session rolls back its transaction in progress, including any
pending sends and receives.

In an Enterprise JavaBeans component, you cannot use the `Session.commit` and `Session.rollback` methods. Instead, you use distributed transactions, described in "Using the JMS API in Java EE Applications" on page 368.

You can combine several sends and receives in a single JMS API local transaction. If you do so, you need to be careful about the order of the operations. You will have no problems if the transaction consists of all sends or all receives, or if the receives all come before the sends. However, if you try to use a request/reply mechanism, in which you send a message and then try to receive a reply to that message in the same transaction, the program will hang, because the send cannot take place until the transaction is committed. The following code fragment illustrates the problem:

```
// Don't do this!
outMsg.setJMSReplyTo(replyQueue);
producer.send(outQueue, outMsg);
consumer = session.createConsumer(replyQueue);
inMsg = consumer.receive(); session.commit();
```

Because a message sent during a transaction is not actually sent until the transaction is committed, the transaction cannot contain any receives that depend on that message's having been sent.

In addition, the production and the consumption of a message cannot both be part of the same transaction. The reason is that the transactions take place between the clients and the JMS provider, which intervenes between the production and the consumption of the message. Figure 20–8 illustrates this interaction.

FIGURE 20–8 Using JMS API Local Transactions

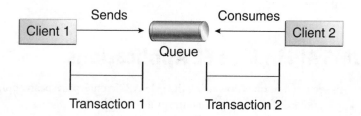

The sending of one or more messages to one or more destinations by Client 1 can form a single transaction, because it forms a single set of interactions with the JMS provider using a single session. Similarly, the receiving of one or more messages from one or more destinations by Client 2 also forms a single transaction using a single session. But because the two clients have no direct interaction and are using two different sessions, no transactions can take place between them.

Another way of putting this is that the act of producing and/or consuming messages in a session can be transactional, but the act of producing and consuming a specific message across different sessions cannot be transactional.

This is the fundamental difference between messaging and synchronized processing. Instead of tightly coupling the sending and receiving of data, message producers and consumers use an alternative approach to reliability, built on a JMS provider's ability to supply a once-and-only-once message delivery guarantee.

When you create a session, you specify whether it is transacted. The first argument to the createSession method is a boolean value. A value of true means the session is transacted; a value of false means it is not transacted. The second argument to this method is the acknowledgment mode, which is relevant only to nontransacted sessions (see "Controlling Message Acknowledgment" on page 360). If the session is transacted, the second argument is ignored, so it is a good idea to specify 0 to make the meaning of your code clear. For example:

```
session = connection.createSession(true, 0);
```

The commit and the rollback methods for local transactions are associated with the session. You can combine queue and topic operations in a single transaction if you use the same session to perform the operations. For example, you can use the same session to receive a message from a queue and send a message to a topic in the same transaction.

You can pass a client program's session to a message listener's constructor function and use it to create a message producer. In this way, you can use the same session for receives and sends in asynchronous message consumers.

"A Local Transaction Example" on page 411 provides an example of using JMS API local transactions.

Using the JMS API in Java EE Applications

This section describes how using the JMS API in enterprise bean applications or web applications differs from using it in application clients.

A general rule in the Java EE platform specification applies to all Java EE components that use the JMS API within EJB or web containers: Application components in the web and EJB containers must not attempt to create more than one active (not closed) Session object per connection.

This rule does not apply to application clients. The application client container supports the creation of multiple sessions for each connection.

Using @Resource Annotations in Enterprise Bean or Web Components

When you use the @Resource annotation in an application client component, you normally declare the JMS resource static:

```
@Resource(lookup = "jms/ConnectionFactory")
private static ConnectionFactory connectionFactory;

@Resource(lookup = "jms/Queue")
private static Queue queue;
```

However, when you use this annotation in a session bean, a message-driven bean, or a web component, do *not* declare the resource static:

```
@Resource(lookup = "jms/ConnectionFactory")
private ConnectionFactory connectionFactory;

@Resource(lookup = "jms/Topic")
private Topic topic;
```

If you declare the resource static in these components, runtime errors will result.

Using Session Beans to Produce and to Synchronously Receive Messages

An application that produces messages or synchronously receives them can use a session bean to perform these operations. The example in "An Application That Uses the JMS API with a Session Bean" on page 416 uses a stateless session bean to publish messages to a topic.

Because a blocking synchronous receive ties up server resources, it is not a good programming practice to use such a receive call in an enterprise bean. Instead, use a timed synchronous receive, or use a message-driven bean to receive messages asynchronously. For details about blocking and timed synchronous receives, see "Writing the Clients for the Synchronous Receive Example" on page 378.

Using the JMS API in an enterprise bean is in many ways similar to using it in an application client. The main differences are the areas of resource management and transactions.

Managing JMS Resources in Session Beans

The JMS API resources are a JMS API connection and a JMS API session. In general, it is important to release JMS resources when they are no longer being used. Here are some useful practices to follow:

- If you wish to maintain a JMS API resource only for the life span of a business method, it is a good idea to close the resource in a `finally` block within the method.

- If you would like to maintain a JMS API resource for the life span of an enterprise bean instance, it is a good idea to use a `@PostConstruct` callback method to create the resource and to use a `@PreDestroy` callback method to close the resource. If you use a stateful session bean and you wish to maintain the JMS API resource in a cached state, you must close the resource in a `@PrePassivate` callback method and set its value to `null`, and you must create it again in a `@PostActivate` callback method.

Managing Transactions in Session Beans

Instead of using local transactions, you use container-managed transactions for bean methods that perform sends or receives, allowing the EJB container to handle transaction demarcation. Because container-managed transactions are the default, you do not have to use an annotation to specify them.

You can use bean-managed transactions and the `javax.transaction.UserTransaction` interface's transaction demarcation methods, but you should do so only if your application has special requirements and you are an expert in using transactions. Usually, container-managed transactions produce the most efficient and correct behavior. This tutorial does not provide any examples of bean-managed transactions.

Using Message-Driven Beans to Receive Messages Asynchronously

The sections "What Is a Message-Driven Bean?" in *The Java EE 6 Tutorial: Basic Concepts* and "How Does the JMS API Work with the Java EE Platform?" on page 344 describe how the Java EE platform supports a special kind of enterprise bean, the message-driven bean, which allows Java EE applications to process JMS messages asynchronously. Session beans allow you to send messages and to receive them synchronously but not asynchronously.

A message-driven bean is a message listener that can reliably consume messages from a queue or a durable subscription. The messages can be sent by any Java EE component (from an application client, another enterprise bean, or a web component) or from an application or a system that does not use Java EE technology.

Like a message listener in an application client, a message-driven bean contains an onMessage method that is called automatically when a message arrives. Like a message listener, a message-driven bean class can implement helper methods invoked by the onMessage method to aid in message processing.

A message-driven bean, however, differs from an application client's message listener in the following ways:

- Certain setup tasks are performed by the EJB container.
- The bean class uses the @MessageDriven annotation to specify properties for the bean or the connection factory, such as a destination type, a durable subscription, a message selector, or an acknowledgment mode. The examples in Chapter 21, "Java Message Service Examples," show how the JMS resource adapter works in the GlassFish Server.

The EJB container automatically performs several setup tasks that a stand-alone client must perform:

- Creating a message consumer to receive the messages. Instead of creating a message consumer in your source code, you associate the message-driven bean with a destination and a connection factory at deployment time. If you want to specify a durable subscription or use a message selector, you do this at deployment time also.
- Registering the message listener. You must not call setMessageListener.
- Specifying a message acknowledgment mode. The default mode, AUTO_ACKNOWLEDGE, is used unless it is overridden by a property setting.

If JMS is integrated with the application server using a resource adapter, the JMS resource adapter handles these tasks for the EJB container.

Your message-driven bean class must implement the javax.jms.MessageListener interface and the onMessage method.

It may implement a @PostConstruct callback method to create a connection, and a @PreDestroy callback method to close the connection. Typically, it implements these methods if it produces messages or performs synchronous receives from another destination.

The bean class commonly injects a MessageDrivenContext resource, which provides some additional methods you can use for transaction management.

The main difference between a message-driven bean and a session bean is that a message-driven bean has no local or remote interface. Instead, it has only a bean class.

A message-driven bean is similar in some ways to a stateless session bean: Its instances are relatively short-lived and retain no state for a specific client. The instance variables of the message-driven bean instance can contain some state across the handling of client messages: for example, a JMS API connection, an open database connection, or an object reference to an enterprise bean object.

Like a stateless session bean, a message-driven bean can have many interchangeable instances running at the same time. The container can pool these instances to allow streams of messages to be processed concurrently. The container attempts to deliver messages in chronological order when that would not impair the concurrency of message processing, but no guarantees are made as to the exact order in which messages are delivered to the instances of the message-driven bean class. Because concurrency can affect the order in which messages are delivered, you should write your applications to handle messages that arrive out of sequence.

For example, your application could manage conversations by using application-level sequence numbers. An application-level conversation control mechanism with a persistent conversation state could cache later messages until earlier messages have been processed.

Another way to ensure order is to have each message or message group in a conversation require a confirmation message that the sender blocks on receipt of. This forces the responsibility for order back onto the sender and more tightly couples senders to the progress of message-driven beans.

To create a new instance of a message-driven bean, the container does the following:

- Instantiates the bean
- Performs any required resource injection
- Calls the @PostConstruct callback method, if it exists

To remove an instance of a message-driven bean, the container calls the @PreDestroy callback method.

Figure 20–9 shows the lifecycle of a message-driven bean.

FIGURE 20–9   Lifecycle of a Message-Driven Bean

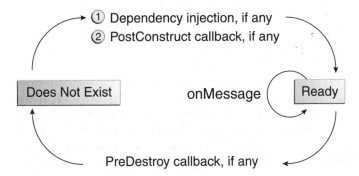

Managing Distributed Transactions

JMS client applications use JMS API local transactions (described in "Using JMS API Local Transactions" on page 366), which allow the grouping of sends and receives within a specific JMS session. Java EE applications commonly use distributed transactions to ensure the integrity of accesses to external resources. For example, distributed transactions allow multiple applications to perform atomic updates on the same database, and they allow a single application to perform atomic updates on multiple databases.

In a Java EE application that uses the JMS API, you can use transactions to combine message sends or receives with database updates and other resource manager operations. You can access resources from multiple application components within a single transaction. For example, a servlet can start a transaction, access multiple databases, invoke an enterprise bean that sends a JMS message, invoke another enterprise bean that modifies an EIS system using the Connector architecture, and finally commit the transaction. Your application cannot, however, both send a JMS message and receive a reply to it within the same transaction; the restriction described in "Using JMS API Local Transactions" on page 366 still applies.

Distributed transactions within the EJB container can be either of two kinds:

- **Container-managed transactions**: The EJB container controls the integrity of your transactions without your having to call commit or rollback. Container-managed transactions are recommended for Java EE applications that use the JMS API. You can specify appropriate transaction attributes for your enterprise bean methods.

  Use the Required transaction attribute (the default) to ensure that a method is always part of a transaction. If a transaction is in progress when the method is called, the method will be part of that transaction; if not, a new transaction will be started before the method is called and will be committed when the method returns.

- **Bean-managed transactions**: You can use these in conjunction with the javax.transaction.UserTransaction interface, which provides its own commit and rollback methods you can use to delimit transaction boundaries. Bean-managed transactions are recommended only for those who are experienced in programming transactions.

You can use either container-managed transactions or bean-managed transactions with message-driven beans. To ensure that all messages are received and handled within the context of a transaction, use container-managed transactions and use the Required transaction attribute (the default) for the onMessage method. This means that if there is no transaction in progress, a new transaction will be started before the method is called and will be committed when the method returns.

When you use container-managed transactions, you can call the following MessageDrivenContext methods:

- setRollbackOnly: Use this method for error handling. If an exception occurs, setRollbackOnly marks the current transaction so that the only possible outcome of the transaction is a rollback.

- getRollbackOnly: Use this method to test whether the current transaction has been marked for rollback.

If you use bean-managed transactions, the delivery of a message to the onMessage method takes place outside the distributed transaction context. The transaction begins when you call the UserTransaction.begin method within the onMessage method, and it ends when you call UserTransaction.commit or UserTransaction.rollback. Any call to the Connection.createSession method must take place within the transaction. If you call UserTransaction.rollback, the message is not redelivered, whereas calling setRollbackOnly for container-managed transactions does cause a message to be redelivered.

Neither the JMS API specification nor the Enterprise JavaBeans specification (available from http://jcp.org/en/jsr/detail?id=318) specifies how to handle calls to JMS API methods outside transaction boundaries. The Enterprise JavaBeans specification does state that the EJB container is responsible for acknowledging a message that is successfully processed by the onMessage method of a message-driven bean that uses bean-managed transactions. Using bean-managed transactions allows you to process the message by using more than one transaction or to have some parts of the message processing take place outside a transaction context. In most cases, however, container-managed transactions provide greater reliability and are therefore preferable.

When you create a session in an enterprise bean, the container ignores the arguments you specify, because it manages all transactional properties for enterprise beans. It is still a good idea to specify arguments of `true` and `0` to the `createSession` method to make this situation clear:

```
session = connection.createSession(true, 0);
```

When you use container-managed transactions, you normally use the `Required` transaction attribute (the default) for your enterprise bean's business methods.

You do not specify a message acknowledgment mode when you create a message-driven bean that uses container-managed transactions. The container acknowledges the message automatically when it commits the transaction.

If a message-driven bean uses bean-managed transactions, the message receipt cannot be part of the bean-managed transaction, so the container acknowledges the message outside the transaction.

If the `onMessage` method throws a `RuntimeException`, the container does not acknowledge processing the message. In that case, the JMS provider will redeliver the unacknowledged message in the future.

Using the JMS API with Application Clients and Web Components

An application client in a Java EE application can use the JMS API in much the same way that a stand-alone client program does. It can produce messages, and it can consume messages by using either synchronous receives or message listeners. See Chapter 11, "A Message-Driven Bean Example," for an example of an application client that produces messages. For an example of using an application client to produce and to consume messages, see "An Application Example That Deploys a Message-Driven Bean on Two Servers" on page 436.

The Java EE platform specification does not impose strict constraints on how web components should use the JMS API. In the GlassFish Server, a web component can send messages and consume them synchronously but cannot consume them asynchronously.

Because a blocking synchronous receive ties up server resources, it is not a good programming practice to use such a `receive` call in a web component. Instead, use a timed synchronous receive. For details about blocking and timed synchronous receives, see "Writing the Clients for the Synchronous Receive Example" on page 378.

Further Information about JMS

For more information about JMS, see:

- Java Message Service web site:

  `http://www.oracle.com/technetwork/java/index-jsp-142945.html`

- Java Message Service specification, version 1.1, available from:

  `http://www.oracle.com/technetwork/java/docs-136352.html`

CHAPTER 21

Java Message Service Examples

This chapter provides examples that show how to use the JMS API in various kinds of Java EE applications. It covers the following topics:

- "Writing Simple JMS Applications" on page 378
- "Writing Robust JMS Applications" on page 406
- "An Application That Uses the JMS API with a Session Bean" on page 416
- "An Application That Uses the JMS API with an Entity" on page 421
- "An Application Example That Consumes Messages from a Remote Server" on page 429
- "An Application Example That Deploys a Message-Driven Bean on Two Servers" on page 436

The examples are in the *tut-install*/examples/jms/ directory.

The steps to build and run each example are as follows:

1. Use NetBeans IDE or Ant to compile and package the example.
2. Use NetBeans IDE or Ant to deploy the example and create resources for it.
3. Use NetBeans IDE, the appclient command, or Ant to run the client.

Each example has a build.xml file that refers to files in the *tut-install*/examples/bp-project/ directory.

Each example has a setup/glassfish-resources.xml file that is used to create resources for the example.

See Chapter 11, "A Message-Driven Bean Example," for a simpler example of a Java EE application that uses the JMS API.

Writing Simple JMS Applications

This section shows how to create, package, and run simple JMS clients that are packaged as application clients and deployed to a Java EE server. The clients demonstrate the basic tasks a JMS application must perform:

- Creating a connection and a session
- Creating message producers and consumers
- Sending and receiving messages

In a Java EE application, some of these tasks are performed, in whole or in part, by the container. If you learn about these tasks, you will have a good basis for understanding how a JMS application works on the Java EE platform.

Each example uses two clients: one that sends messages and one that receives them. You can run the clients in NetBeans IDE or in two terminal windows.

When you write a JMS client to run in an enterprise bean application, you use many of the same methods in much the same sequence as for an application client. However, there are some significant differences. "Using the JMS API in Java EE Applications" on page 368 describes these differences, and this chapter provides examples that illustrate them.

The examples for this section are in the *tut-install*/examples/jms/simple/ directory, under the following four subdirectories:

```
producer
synchconsumer
asynchconsumer
messagebrowser
```

A Simple Example of Synchronous Message Receives

This section describes the sending and receiving clients in an example that uses the receive method to consume messages synchronously. This section then explains how to compile, package, and run the clients using the GlassFish Server.

The following subsections describe the steps in creating and running the example.

Writing the Clients for the Synchronous Receive Example

The sending client, producer/src/java/Producer.java, performs the following steps:

1. Injects resources for a connection factory, queue, and topic:

    ```
    @Resource(lookup = "jms/ConnectionFactory")
    private static ConnectionFactory connectionFactory;
    ```

```
@Resource(lookup = "jms/Queue")private static Queue queue;
@Resource(lookup = "jms/Topic")private static Topic topic;
```

2. Retrieves and verifies command-line arguments that specify the destination type and the number of arguments:

```
final int NUM_MSGS;
String destType = args[0];
System.out.println("Destination type is " + destType);
if ( ! ( destType.equals("queue") || destType.equals("topic") ) ) {
    System.err.println("Argument must be \"queue\" or " + "\"topic\"");
    System.exit(1);
}
if (args.length == 2){
    NUM_MSGS = (new Integer(args[1])).intValue();
}
else {
    NUM_MSGS = 1;
}
```

3. Assigns either the queue or the topic to a destination object, based on the specified destination type:

```
Destination dest = null;
try {
    if (destType.equals("queue")) {
        dest = (Destination) queue;
    } else {
        dest = (Destination) topic;
    }
}
catch (Exception e) {
    System.err.println("Error setting destination: " + e.toString());
    e.printStackTrace();
    System.exit(1);
}
```

4. Creates a Connection and a Session:

```
Connection connection = connectionFactory.createConnection();
Session session = connection.createSession(
            false,
            Session.AUTO_ACKNOWLEDGE);
```

5. Creates a MessageProducer and a TextMessage:

```
MessageProducer producer = session.createProducer(dest);
TextMessage message = session.createTextMessage();
```

6. Sends one or more messages to the destination:

```
for (int i = 0; i < NUM_MSGS; i++) {
    message.setText("This is message " + (i + 1) + " from producer");
    System.out.println("Sending message: " + message.getText());
    producer.send(message);
}
```

7. Sends an empty control message to indicate the end of the message stream:

```
producer.send(session.createMessage());
```

Sending an empty message of no specified type is a convenient way to indicate to the consumer that the final message has arrived.

8. Closes the connection in a `finally` block, automatically closing the session and MessageProducer:

```
} finally {
    if (connection != null) {
        try { connection.close(); }
        catch (JMSException e) { }
    }
}
```

The receiving client, `synchconsumer/src/java/SynchConsumer.java`, performs the following steps:

1. Injects resources for a connection factory, queue, and topic.

2. Assigns either the queue or the topic to a destination object, based on the specified destination type.

3. Creates a `Connection` and a `Session`.

4. Creates a `MessageConsumer`:

```
consumer = session.createConsumer(dest);
```

5. Starts the connection, causing message delivery to begin:

```
connection.start();
```

6. Receives the messages sent to the destination until the end-of-message-stream control message is received:

```
while (true) {
    Message m = consumer.receive(1);
    if (m != null) {
        if (m instanceof TextMessage) {
            message = (TextMessage) m;
            System.out.println("Reading message: " + message.getText());
        } else {
            break;
        }
    }
}
```

Because the control message is not a `TextMessage`, the receiving client terminates the `while` loop and stops receiving messages after the control message arrives.

7. Closes the connection in a `finally` block, automatically closing the session and MessageConsumer.

The `receive` method can be used in several ways to perform a synchronous receive. If you specify no arguments or an argument of `0`, the method blocks indefinitely until a message arrives:

```
Message m = consumer.receive();
Message m = consumer.receive(0);
```

For a simple client, this may not matter. But if you do not want your application to consume system resources unnecessarily, use a timed synchronous receive. Do one of the following:

- Call the receive method with a timeout argument greater than 0:

```
Message m = consumer.receive(1); // 1 millisecond
```

- Call the receiveNoWait method, which receives a message only if one is available:

```
Message m = consumer.receiveNoWait();
```

The SynchConsumer client uses an indefinite while loop to receive messages, calling receive with a timeout argument. Calling receiveNoWait would have the same effect.

Starting the JMS Provider

When you use the GlassFish Server, your JMS provider is the GlassFish Server. Start the server as described in "Starting and Stopping the GlassFish Server" on page 41.

JMS Administered Objects for the Synchronous Receive Example

This example uses the following JMS administered objects:

- A connection factory
- Two destination resources: a topic and a queue

NetBeans IDE and the Ant tasks for the JMS examples create needed JMS resources when you deploy the applications, using a file named setup/glassfish-resources.xml. This file is most easily created using NetBeans IDE, although you can create it by hand.

You can also use the asadmin create-jms-resource command to create resources, the asadmin list-jms-resources command to display their names, and the asadmin delete-jms-resource command to remove them.

▼ To Create JMS Resources Using NetBeans IDE

Follow these steps to create a JMS resource in GlassFish Server using NetBeans IDE. Repeat these steps for each resource you need.

The example applications in this chapter already have the resources, so you will need to follow these steps only when you create your own applications.

1 **Right-click the project for which you want to create resources and choose New, then choose Other.**

The New File wizard opens.

2 **Under Categories, select GlassFish.**

3   **Under File Types, select JMS Resource.**

The General Attributes - JMS Resource page opens.

4   **In the JNDI Name field, type the name of the resource.**

By convention, JMS resource names begin with `jms/`.

5   **Select the radio button for the resource type.**

Normally, this is either `javax.jms.Queue`, `javax.jms.Topic`, or `javax.jms.ConnectionFactory`.

6   **Click Next.**

The JMS Properties page opens.

7   **For a queue or topic, type a name for a physical queue in the Value field for the Name property.**

You can type any value for this required field.

Connection factories have no required properties. In a few situations, discussed in later sections, you may need to specify a property.

8   **Click Finish.**

A file named `glassfish-resources.xml` is created in your project, in a directory named `setup`. In the project pane, you can find it under the Server Resources node. If this file exists, resources are created automatically by NetBeans IDE when you deploy the project.

▼ To Delete JMS Resources Using NetBeans IDE

1   **In the Services pane, expand the Servers node, then expand the GlassFish Server 3+ node.**

2   **Expand the Resources node, then expand the Connector Resources node.**

3   **Expand the Admin Object Resources node.**

4   **Right-click any destination you want to remove and select Unregister.**

5   **Expand the Connector Connection Pools node.**

6 **Right-click any connection factory you want to remove and select Unregister.**

Every connection factory has both a connector connection pool and an associated connector resource. When you remove the connector connection pool, the resource is removed automatically. You can verify the removal by expanding the Connector Resources node.

Running the Clients for the Synchronous Receive Example

To run these examples using the GlassFish Server, package each one in an application client JAR file. The application client JAR file requires a manifest file, located in the src/conf directory for each example, along with the .class file.

The build.xml file for each example contains Ant targets that compile, package, and deploy the example. The targets place the .class file for the example in the build/jar directory. Then the targets use the jar command to package the class file and the manifest file in an application client JAR file.

Because the examples use the common interfaces, you can run them using either a queue or a topic.

▼ To Build and Package the Clients for the Synchronous Receive Example Using NetBeans IDE

1 **From the File menu, choose Open Project.**

2 **In the Open Project dialog, navigate to:**

tut-install/examples/jms/simple/

3 **Select the producer folder.**

4 **Select the Open as Main Project check box.**

5 **Click Open Project.**

6 **In the Projects tab, right-click the project and select Build.**

7 **From the File menu, choose Open Project again.**

8 **Select the synchconsumer folder.**

9 **Select the Open as Main Project check box.**

10 **Click Open Project.**

11 **In the Projects tab, right-click the project and select Build.**

▼ **To Deploy and Run the Clients for the Synchronous Receive Example Using NetBeans IDE**

1 Deploy and run the `Producer` example:

   a. Right-click the `producer` project and select Properties.

   b. Select Run from the Categories tree.

   c. In the Arguments field, type the following:

```
queue 3
```

   d. Click OK.

   e. Right-click the project and select Run.

   The output of the program looks like this (along with some additional output):

```
Destination type is queue
Sending message: This is message 1 from producer
Sending message: This is message 2 from producer
Sending message: This is message 3 from producer
```

   The messages are now in the queue, waiting to be received.

Note – When you run an application client, the command often takes a long time to complete.

---

2 Now deploy and run the `SynchConsumer` example:

   a. Right-click the `synchconsumer` project and select Properties.

   b. Select Run from the Categories tree.

   c. In the Arguments field, type the following:

```
queue
```

   d. Click OK.

   e. Right-click the project and select Run.

   The output of the program looks like this (along with some additional output):

```
Destination type is queue
Reading message: This is message 1 from producer
Reading message: This is message 2 from producer
Reading message: This is message 3 from producer
```

3 Now try running the programs in the opposite order. Right-click the `synchconsumer` project and select Run.

The Output pane displays the destination type and then appears to hang, waiting for messages.

4 Right-click the `producer` project and select Run.

When the messages have been sent, the SynchConsumer client receives them and exits. The Output pane shows the output of both programs, in two different tabs.

5 Now run the `Producer` example using a topic instead of a queue.

a. Right-click the `producer` project and select Properties.

b. Select Run from the Categories tree.

c. In the Arguments field, type the following:

```
topic 3
```

d. Click OK.

e. Right-click the project and select Run.

The output looks like this (along with some additional output):

```
Destination type is topic
Sending message: This is message 1 from producer
Sending message: This is message 2 from producer
Sending message: This is message 3 from producer
```

6 Now run the `SynchConsumer` example using the topic.

a. Right-click the `synchconsumer` project and select Properties.

b. Select Run from the Categories tree.

c. In the Arguments field, type the following:

```
topic
```

d. Click OK.

e. Right-click the project and select Run.

The result, however, is different. Because you are using a topic, messages that were sent before you started the consumer cannot be received. (See "Publish/Subscribe Messaging Domain" on page 347 for details.) Instead of receiving the messages, the program appears to hang.

7   Run the `Producer` example again. Right-click the `producer` project and select Run.

Now the `SynchConsumer` example receives the messages:

```
Destination type is topic
Reading message: This is message 1 from producer
Reading message: This is message 2 from producer
Reading message: This is message 3 from producer
```

▼ To Build and Package the Clients for the Synchronous Receive Example Using Ant

1   In a terminal window, go to the `producer` directory:

```
cd producer
```

2   Type the following command:

```
ant
```

3   In a terminal window, go to the `synchconsumer` directory:

```
cd ../synchconsumer
```

4   Type the following command:

```
ant
```

The targets place the application client JAR file in the `dist` directory for each example.

▼ To Deploy and Run the Clients for the Synchronous Receive Example Using Ant and the `appclient` Command

You can run the clients using the `appclient` command. The `build.xml` file for each project includes a target that creates resources, deploys the client, and then retrieves the client stubs that the `appclient` command uses. Each of the clients takes one or more command-line arguments: a destination type and, for `Producer`, a number of messages.

To build, deploy, and run the `Producer` and `SynchConsumer` examples using Ant and the `appclient` command, follow these steps.

To run the clients, you need two terminal windows.

1   In a terminal window, go to the `producer` directory:

```
cd ../producer
```

2   Create any needed resources, deploy the client JAR file to the GlassFish Server, then retrieve the client stubs:

```
ant getclient
```

Ignore the message that states that the application is deployed at a URL.

3   Run the `Producer` program, sending three messages to the queue:

```
appclient -client client-jar/producerClient.jar queue 3
```

The output of the program looks like this (along with some additional output):

```
Destination type is queue
Sending message: This is message 1 from producer
Sending message: This is message 2 from producer
Sending message: This is message 3 from producer
```

The messages are now in the queue, waiting to be received.

Note – When you run an application client, the command often takes a long time to complete.

---

4   In the same window, go to the `synchconsumer` directory:

```
cd ../synchconsumer
```

5   Deploy the client JAR file to the GlassFish Server, then retrieve the client stubs:

```
ant getclient
```

Ignore the message that states that the application is deployed at a URL.

6   Run the `SynchConsumer` client, specifying the queue:

```
appclient -client client-jar/synchconsumerClient.jar queue
```

The output of the client looks like this (along with some additional output):

```
Destination type is queue
Reading message: This is message 1 from producer
Reading message: This is message 2 from producer
Reading message: This is message 3 from producer
```

7   Now try running the clients in the opposite order. Run the `SynchConsumer` client:

```
appclient -client client-jar/synchconsumerClient.jar queue
```

The client displays the destination type and then appears to hang, waiting for messages.

8   In a different terminal window, run the `Producer` client.

```
cd tut-install/examples/jms/simple/producer
appclient -client client-jar/producerClient.jar queue 3
```

When the messages have been sent, the `SynchConsumer` client receives them and exits.

9   Now run the `Producer` client using a topic instead of a queue:

```
appclient -client client-jar/producerClient.jar topic 3
```

The output of the client looks like this (along with some additional output):

```
Destination type is topic
Sending message: This is message 1 from producer
Sending message: This is message 2 from producer
Sending message: This is message 3 from producer
```

10   Now run the SynchConsumer client using the topic:

`appclient -client client-jar/synchconsumerClient.jar topic`

The result, however, is different. Because you are using a topic, messages that were sent before you started the consumer cannot be received. (See "Publish/Subscribe Messaging Domain" on page 347 for details.) Instead of receiving the messages, the client appears to hang.

11   Run the Producer client again.

Now the SynchConsumer client receives the messages (along with some additional output):

```
Destination type is topic
Reading message: This is message 1 from producer
Reading message: This is message 2 from producer
Reading message: This is message 3 from producer
```

A Simple Example of Asynchronous Message Consumption

This section describes the receiving clients in an example that uses a message listener to consume messages asynchronously. This section then explains how to compile and run the clients using the GlassFish Server.

Writing the Clients for the Asynchronous Receive Example

The sending client is producer/src/java/Producer.java, the same client used in the example in "A Simple Example of Synchronous Message Receives" on page 378.

An asynchronous consumer normally runs indefinitely. This one runs until the user types the character q or Q to stop the client.

The receiving client, asynchconsumer/src/java/AsynchConsumer.java, performs the following steps:

1. Injects resources for a connection factory, queue, and topic.

2. Assigns either the queue or the topic to a destination object, based on the specified destination type.

3. Creates a Connection and a Session.

4. Creates a MessageConsumer.

5. Creates an instance of the `TextListener` class and registers it as the message listener for the `MessageConsumer`:

```
listener = new TextListener();consumer.setMessageListener(listener);
```

6. Starts the connection, causing message delivery to begin.

7. Listens for the messages published to the destination, stopping when the user types the character q or Q:

```
System.out.println("To end program, type Q or q, " + "then <return>");
inputStreamReader = new InputStreamReader(System.in);
while (!((answer == 'q') || (answer == 'Q'))) {
    try {
        answer = (char) inputStreamReader.read();
    } catch (IOException e) {
        System.out.println("I/O exception: " + e.toString());
    }
}
```

8. Closes the connection, which automatically closes the session and `MessageConsumer`.

The message listener, `asynchconsumer/src/java/TextListener.java`, follows these steps:

1. When a message arrives, the `onMessage` method is called automatically.

2. The `onMessage` method converts the incoming message to a `TextMessage` and displays its content. If the message is not a text message, it reports this fact:

```
public void onMessage(Message message) {
    TextMessage msg = null;
    try {
        if (message instanceof TextMessage) {
            msg = (TextMessage) message;
            System.out.println("Reading message: " + msg.getText());
        } else {
            System.out.println("Message is not a " + "TextMessage");
        }
    } catch (JMSException e) {
        System.out.println("JMSException in onMessage(): " + e.toString());
    } catch (Throwable t) {
        System.out.println("Exception in onMessage():" + t.getMessage());
    }
}
```

For this example, you will use the connection factory and destinations you created for "A Simple Example of Synchronous Message Receives" on page 378.

▼ To Build and Package the `AsynchConsumer` Client Using NetBeans IDE

1   From the File menu, choose Open Project.

2   In the Open Project dialog, navigate to:
    tut-install/examples/jms/simple/

3   Select the `asynchconsumer` folder.

4   Select the Open as Main Project check box.

5   Click Open Project.

6   In the Projects tab, right-click the project and select Build.

▼ To Deploy and Run the Clients for the Asynchronous Receive Example Using NetBeans IDE

1   Run the `AsynchConsumer` example:

   a. Right-click the `asynchconsumer` project and select Properties.

   b. Select Run from the Categories tree.

   c. In the Arguments field, type the following:
    `topic`

   d. Click OK.

   e. Right-click the project and select Run.
    The client displays the following lines and appears to hang:
```
Destination type is topic
To end program, type Q or q, then <return>
```

2   Now run the `Producer` example:

   a. Right-click the `producer` project and select Properties.

   b. Select Run from the Categories tree.

   c. In the Arguments field, type the following:
    `topic 3`

d. **Click OK.**

e. **Right-click the project and select Run.**

The output of the client looks like this:

```
Destination type is topic
Sending message: This is message 1 from producer
Sending message: This is message 2 from producer
Sending message: This is message 3 from producer
```

In the other tab, the AsynchConsumer client displays the following:

```
Destination type is topic
To end program, type Q or q, then <return>
Reading message: This is message 1 from producer
Reading message: This is message 2 from producer
Reading message: This is message 3 from producer
Message is not a TextMessage
```

The last line appears because the client has received the non-text control message sent by the Producer client.

3 **Type Q or q in the Output window and press Return to stop the client.**

4 **Now run the Producer client using a queue.**

In this case, as with the synchronous example, you can run the Producer client first, because there is no timing dependency between the sender and the receiver.

a. **Right-click the producer project and select Properties.**

b. **Select Run from the Categories tree.**

c. **In the Arguments field, type the following:**

queue 3

d. **Click OK.**

e. **Right-click the project and select Run.**

The output of the client looks like this:

```
Destination type is queue
Sending message: This is message 1 from producer
Sending message: This is message 2 from producer
Sending message: This is message 3 from producer
```

5 **Run the AsynchConsumer client.**

a. **Right-click the asynchconsumer project and select Properties.**

b. **Select Run from the Categories tree.**

c. In the Arguments field, type the following:

```
queue
```

d. Click OK.

e. Right-click the project and select Run.

The output of the client looks like this:

```
Destination type is queue
To end program, type Q or q, then <return>
Reading message: This is message 1 from producer
Reading message: This is message 2 from producer
Reading message: This is message 3 from producer
Message is not a TextMessage
```

6 Type Q or q in the Output window and press Return to stop the client.

▼ To Build and Package the AsynchConsumer Client Using Ant

1 In a terminal window, go to the asynchconsumer directory:

```
cd ../asynchconsumer
```

2 Type the following command:

```
ant
```

The targets package both the main class and the message listener class in the JAR file and place the file in the dist directory for the example.

▼ To Deploy and Run the Clients for the Asynchronous Receive Example Using Ant and the appclient Command

1 Deploy the client JAR file to the GlassFish Server, then retrieve the client stubs:

```
ant getclient
```

Ignore the message that states that the application is deployed at a URL.

2 Run the AsynchConsumer client, specifying the topic destination type.

```
appclient -client client-jar/asynchconsumerClient.jar topic
```

The client displays the following lines (along with some additional output) and appears to hang:

```
Destination type is topic
To end program, type Q or q, then <return>
```

3 **In the terminal window where you ran the** `Producer` **client previously, run the client again, sending three messages.**

```
appclient -client client-jar/producerClient.jar topic 3
```

The output of the client looks like this (along with some additional output):

```
Destination type is topic
Sending message: This is message 1 from producer
Sending message: This is message 2 from producer
Sending message: This is message 3 from producer
```

In the other window, the `AsynchConsumer` client displays the following (along with some additional output):

```
Destination type is topic
To end program, type Q or q, then <return>
Reading message: This is message 1 from producer
Reading message: This is message 2 from producer
Reading message: This is message 3 from producer
Message is not a TextMessage
```

The last line appears because the client has received the non-text control message sent by the `Producer` client.

4 **Type** Q **or** q **and press Return to stop the client.**

5 **Now run the clients using a queue.**

In this case, as with the synchronous example, you can run the `Producer` client first, because there is no timing dependency between the sender and receiver:

```
appclient -client client-jar/producerClient.jar queue 3
```

The output of the client looks like this:

```
Destination type is queue
Sending message: This is message 1 from producer
Sending message: This is message 2 from producer
Sending message: This is message 3 from producer
```

6 **Run the** `AsynchConsumer` **client:**

```
appclient -client client-jar/asynchconsumerClient.jar queue
```

The output of the client looks like this (along with some additional output):

```
Destination type is queue
To end program, type Q or q, then <return>
Reading message: This is message 1 from producer
Reading message: This is message 2 from producer
Reading message: This is message 3 from producer
Message is not a TextMessage
```

7 **Type** Q **or** q **to stop the client.**

A Simple Example of Browsing Messages in a Queue

This section describes an example that creates a QueueBrowser object to examine messages on a queue, as described in "JMS Queue Browsers" on page 358. This section then explains how to compile, package, and run the example using the GlassFish Server.

Writing the Client for the QueueBrowser Example

To create a QueueBrowser for a queue, you call the Session.createBrowser method with the queue as the argument. You obtain the messages in the queue as an Enumeration object. You can then iterate through the Enumeration object and display the contents of each message.

The messagebrowser/src/java/MessageBrowser.java client performs the following steps:

1. Injects resources for a connection factory and a queue.

2. Creates a Connection and a Session.

3. Creates a QueueBrowser:

   ```
   QueueBrowser browser = session.createBrowser(queue);
   ```

4. Retrieves the Enumeration that contains the messages:

   ```
   Enumeration msgs = browser.getEnumeration();
   ```

5. Verifies that the Enumeration contains messages, then displays the contents of the messages:

   ```
   if ( !msgs.hasMoreElements() ) {
       System.out.println("No messages in queue");
   } else {
       while (msgs.hasMoreElements()) {
           Message tempMsg = (Message)msgs.nextElement();
           System.out.println("Message: " + tempMsg);
       }
   }
   ```

6. Closes the connection, which automatically closes the session and the QueueBrowser.

The format in which the message contents appear is implementation-specific. In the GlassFish Server, the message format looks something like this:

```
Message contents:
Text: This is message 3 from producer
Class: com.sun.messaging.jmq.jmsclient.TextMessageImpl
getJMSMessageID(): ID:14-128.149.71.199(f9:86:a2:d5:46:9b)-40814-1255980521747
getJMSTimestamp(): 1129061034355
getJMSCorrelationID(): null
JMSReplyTo: null
JMSDestination: PhysicalQueue
```

```
getJMSDeliveryMode(): PERSISTENT
getJMSRedelivered(): false
getJMSType(): null
getJMSExpiration(): 0
getJMSPriority(): 4
Properties: null
```

For this example, you will use the connection factory and queue you created for "A Simple Example of Synchronous Message Receives" on page 378.

▼ To Run the `MessageBrowser` Client Using NetBeans IDE

To build, package, deploy, and run the `MessageBrowser` example using NetBeans IDE, follow these steps.

You also need the `Producer` example to send the message to the queue, and one of the consumer clients to consume the messages after you inspect them. If you did not do so already, package these examples.

1   From the File menu, choose Open Project.

2   In the Open Project dialog, navigate to:
    tut-install/examples/jms/simple/

3   Select the `messagebrowser` folder.

4   Select the Open as Main Project check box.

5   Click Open Project.

6   In the Projects tab, right-click the project and select Build.

7   Run the `Producer` client, sending one message to the queue:

    a. Right-click the `producer` project and select Properties.

    b. Select Run from the Categories tree.

    c. In the Arguments field, type the following:
        queue

    d. Click OK.

    e. Right-click the project and select Run.

        The output of the client looks like this:
        ```
        Destination type is queue
        Sending message: This is message 1 from producer
        ```

8 Run the `MessageBrowser` client. Right-click the `messagebrowser` project and select Run.

The output of the client looks something like this:

```
Message:
Text: This is message 1 from producer
Class: com.sun.messaging.jmq.jmsclient.TextMessageImpl
getJMSMessageID(): ID:12-128.149.71.199(8c:34:4a:1a:1b:b8)-40883-1255980521747
getJMSTimestamp(): 1129062957611
getJMSCorrelationID(): null
JMSReplyTo: null
JMSDestination: PhysicalQueue
getJMSDeliveryMode(): PERSISTENT
getJMSRedelivered(): false
getJMSType(): null
getJMSExpiration(): 0
getJMSPriority(): 4
Properties: null
Message:
Class: com.sun.messaging.jmq.jmsclient.MessageImpl
getJMSMessageID(): ID:13-128.149.71.199(8c:34:4a:1a:1b:b8)-40883-1255980521747
getJMSTimestamp(): 1129062957616
getJMSCorrelationID(): null
JMSReplyTo: null
JMSDestination: PhysicalQueue
getJMSDeliveryMode(): PERSISTENT
getJMSRedelivered(): false
getJMSType(): null
getJMSExpiration(): 0
getJMSPriority(): 4
Properties: null
```

The first message is the TextMessage, and the second is the non-text control message.

9 Run the `SynchConsumer` client to consume the messages.

a. Right-click the `synchconsumer` project and select Properties.

b. Select Run from the Categories tree.

c. In the Arguments field, type the following:

`queue`

d. Click OK.

e. Right-click the project and select Run.

The output of the client looks like this:

```
Destination type is queue
Reading message: This is message 1 from producer
```

▼ To Run the `MessageBrowser` Client Using Ant and the `appclient` Command

To build, package, deploy, and run the `MessageBrowser` example using Ant, follow these steps.

You also need the `Producer` example to send the message to the queue, and one of the consumer clients to consume the messages after you inspect them. If you did not do so already, package these examples.

To run the clients, you need two terminal windows.

1 In a terminal window, go to the `messagebrowser` directory.

```
cd ../messagebrowser
```

2 Type the following command:

```
ant
```

The targets place the application client JAR file in the `dist` directory for the example.

3 In another terminal window, go to the `producer` directory.

4 Run the `Producer` client, sending one message to the queue:

```
appclient -client client-jar/producerClient.jar queue
```

The output of the client looks like this (along with some additional output):

```
Destination type is queue
Sending message: This is message 1 from producer
```

5 Go to the `messagebrowser` directory.

6 Deploy the client JAR file to the GlassFish Server, then retrieve the client stubs:

```
ant getclient
```

Ignore the message that states that the application is deployed at a URL.

7 Because this example takes no command-line arguments, you can run the `MessageBrowser` client using the following command:

```
ant run
```

Alternatively, you can type the following command:

```
appclient -client client-jar/messagebrowserClient.jar
```

The output of the client looks something like this (along with some additional output):

```
Message:
Text: This is message 1 from producer
```

```
Class: com.sun.messaging.jmq.jmsclient.TextMessageImpl
getJMSMessageID(): ID:12-128.149.71.199(8c:34:4a:1a:1b:b8)-40883-1255980521747
getJMSTimestamp(): 1255980521747
getJMSCorrelationID(): null
JMSReplyTo: null
JMSDestination: PhysicalQueue
getJMSDeliveryMode(): PERSISTENT
getJMSRedelivered(): false
getJMSType(): null
getJMSExpiration(): 0
getJMSPriority(): 4
Properties: null
Message:
Class: com.sun.messaging.jmq.jmsclient.MessageImpl
getJMSMessageID(): ID:13-128.149.71.199(8c:34:4a:1a:1b:b8)-40883-1255980521767
getJMSTimestamp(): 1255980521767
getJMSCorrelationID(): null
JMSReplyTo: null
JMSDestination: PhysicalQueue
getJMSDeliveryMode(): PERSISTENT
getJMSRedelivered(): false
getJMSType(): null
getJMSExpiration(): 0
getJMSPriority(): 4
Properties: null
```

The first message is the TextMessage, and the second is the non-text control message.

8   Go to the synchconsumer directory.

9   Run the SynchConsumer client to consume the messages:

`appclient -client client-jar/synchconsumerClient.jar queue`

The output of the client looks like this (along with some additional output):

```
Destination type is queue
Reading message: This is message 1 from producer
```

Running JMS Clients on Multiple Systems

JMS clients that use the GlassFish Server can exchange messages with each other when they are running on different systems in a network. The systems must be visible to each other by name (the UNIX host name or the Microsoft Windows computer name) and must both be running the GlassFish Server.

Note – Any mechanism for exchanging messages between systems is specific to the Java EE server implementation. This tutorial describes how to use the GlassFish Server for this purpose.

Suppose you want to run the Producer client on one system, earth, and the SynchConsumer client on another system, jupiter. Before you can do so, you need to perform these tasks:

1. Create two new connection factories

2. Change the name of the default JMS host on one system

3. Edit the source code for the two examples

4. Recompile and repackage the examples

Note – A limitation in the JMS provider in the GlassFish Server may cause a runtime failure to create a connection to systems that use the Dynamic Host Configuration Protocol (DHCP) to obtain an IP address. You can, however, create a connection *from* a system that uses DHCP *to* a system that does not use DHCP. In the examples in this tutorial, earth can be a system that uses DHCP, and jupiter can be a system that does not use DHCP.

When you run the clients, they will work as shown in Figure 21–1. The client run on earth needs the queue on earth only so the resource injection will succeed. The connection, session, and message producer are all created on jupiter using the connection factory that points to jupiter. The messages sent from earth will be received on jupiter.

FIGURE 21–1 Sending Messages from One System to Another

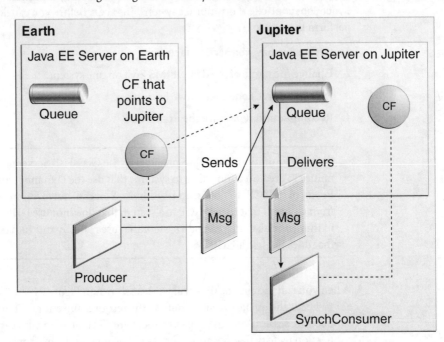

For examples showing how to deploy more complex applications on two different systems, see "An Application Example That Consumes Messages from a Remote Server" on page 429 and "An Application Example That Deploys a Message-Driven Bean on Two Servers" on page 436.

▼ To Create Administered Objects for Multiple Systems

To run these clients, you must do the following:

- Create a new connection factory on both earth and jupiter
- Create a destination resource on both earth and jupiter

You do not have to install the tutorial examples on both systems, but you must be able to access the file system where it is installed. You may find it more convenient to install the tutorial examples on both systems if the two use different operating systems (for example, Windows and UNIX). Otherwise you will have to edit the *tut-install*/examples/bp-project/build.properties file and change the location of the javaee.home property each time you build or run a client on a different system.

1 **Start the GlassFish Server on earth.**

2 **Start the GlassFish Server on jupiter.**

3   To create a new connection factory on jupiter, follow these steps:

  a. From a command shell on jupiter, go to the
      tut-install/**examples/jms/simple/producer/** directory.

  b. Type the following command:

      ```
      ant create-local-factory
      ```

      The create-local-factory target, defined in the build.xml file for the Producer example, creates a connection factory named jms/JupiterConnectionFactory.

4   To create a new connection factory on earth that points to the connection factory on jupiter, follow these steps:

  a. From a command shell on earth, go to the
      tut-install/**examples/jms/simple/producer/** directory.

  b. Type the following command:

      ```
      ant create-remote-factory -Dsys=remote-system-name
      ```

      Replace *remote-system-name* with the actual name of the remote system.

      The create-remote-factory target, defined in the build.xml file for the Producer example, also creates a connection factory named jms/JupiterConnectionFactory. In addition, it sets the AddressList property for this factory to the name of the remote system.

Additional resources will be created when you deploy the application, if they have not been created before.

The reason the glassfish-resources.xml file does not specify jms/JupiterConnectionFactory is that on earth the connection factory requires the AddressList property setting, whereas on jupiter it does not. You can examine the targets in the build.xml file for details.

Changing the Default Host Name

By default, the default host name for the JMS service on the GlassFish Server is localhost. To access the JMS service from another system, however, you must change the host name. You can change it either to the actual host name or to 0.0.0.0.

You can change the default host name using either the Administration Console or the asadmin command.

▼ To Change the Default Host Name Using the Administration Console

1   On jupiter, start the Administration Console by opening a browser at http://localhost:4848/.

2   In the navigation tree, expand the Configurations node, then expand the server-config node.

3   Under the server-config node, expand the Java Message Service node.

4   Under the Java Message Service node, expand the JMS Hosts node.

5   Under the JMS Hosts node, select default_JMS_host.
    The Edit JMS Host page opens.

6   In the Host field, type the name of the system, or type 0.0.0.0.

7   Click Save.

8   Restart the GlassFish Server.

▼ To Change the Default Host Name Using the asadmin Command

1   Specify a command like one of the following:

```
asadmin set server-config.jms-service.jms-host.default_JMS_host.host="0.0.0.0"
```

```
asadmin set server-config.jms-service.jms-host.default_JMS_host.host="hostname"
```

2   Restart the GlassFish Server.

▼ To Run the Clients Using NetBeans IDE

These steps assume you have the tutorial installed on both of the systems you are using and that you are able to access the file system of jupiter from earth or vice versa. You will edit the source files to specify the new connection factory. Then you will rebuild and run the clients.

1   To edit the source files, follow these steps:

    a. On earth, open the following file in NetBeans IDE:

        tut-install/examples/jms/simple/producer/src/java/Producer.java

b. Find the following line:

```
@Resource(lookup = "jms/ConnectionFactory")
```

c. Change the line to the following:

```
@Resource(lookup = "jms/JupiterConnectionFactory")
```

d. Save the file.

e. On jupiter, open the following file in NetBeans IDE:

tut-install/examples/jms/simple/synchconsumer/src/java/SynchConsumer.java

f. Repeat Step b and Step c, then save the file.

2 To recompile and repackage the Producer example on earth, right-click the producer project and select Clean and Build.

3 To recompile and repackage the SynchConsumer example on jupiter, right-click the synchconsumer project and select Clean and Build.

4 On earth, deploy and run Producer. Follow these steps:

a. Right-click the producer project and select Properties.

b. Select Run from the Categories tree.

c. In the Arguments field, type the following:

```
queue 3
```

d. Click OK.

e. Right-click the project and select Run.

The output looks like this (along with some additional output):

```
Destination type is topic
Sending message: This is message 1 from producer
Sending message: This is message 2 from producer
Sending message: This is message 3 from producer
```

5 On jupiter, run SynchConsumer. Follow these steps:

a. Right-click the synchconsumer project and select Properties.

b. Select Run from the Categories tree.

c. In the Arguments field, type the following:

```
queue
```

d. Click OK.

e. Right-click the project and select Run.

The output of the program looks like this (along with some additional output):

```
Destination type is queue
Reading message: This is message 1 from producer
Reading message: This is message 2 from producer
Reading message: This is message 3 from producer
```

▼ To Run the Clients Using Ant and the appclient Command

These steps assume you have the tutorial installed on both of the systems you are using and that you are able to access the file system of jupiter from earth or vice versa. You will edit the source files to specify the new connection factory. Then you will rebuild and run the clients.

1 To edit the source files, follow these steps:

a. On earth, open the following file in a text editor:

tut-install/examples/jms/simple/producer/src/java/Producer.java

b. Find the following line:

```
@Resource(lookup = "jms/ConnectionFactory")
```

c. Change the line to the following:

```
@Resource(lookup = "jms/JupiterConnectionFactory")
```

d. Save and close the file.

e. On jupiter, open the following file in a text editor:

tut-install/examples/jms/simple/synchconsumer/src/java/SynchConsumer.java

f. Repeat Step b and Step c, then save and close the file.

2 To recompile and repackage the Producer example on earth, type the following:

```
ant
```

3 To recompile and repackage the SynchConsumer example on jupiter, go to the synchconsumer directory and type the following:

```
ant
```

4 On earth, deploy and run `Producer`. Follow these steps:

a. On earth, from the `producer` directory, create any needed resources, deploy the client JAR file to the GlassFish Server, then retrieve the client stubs:

```
ant getclient
```

Ignore the message that states that the application is deployed at a URL.

b. To run the client, type the following:

```
appclient -client client-jar/producerClient.jar queue 3
```

The output looks like this (along with some additional output):

```
Destination type is topic
Sending message: This is message 1 from producer
Sending message: This is message 2 from producer
Sending message: This is message 3 from producer
```

5 On jupiter, run `SynchConsumer`. Follow these steps:

a. From the `synchconsumer` directory, create any needed resources, deploy the client JAR file to the GlassFish Server, then retrieve the client stubs:

```
ant getclient
```

Ignore the message that states that the application is deployed at a URL.

b. To run the client, type the following:

```
appclient -client client-jar/synchconsumerClient.jar queue
```

The output of the program looks like this (along with some additional output):

```
Destination type is queue
Reading message: This is message 1 from producer
Reading message: This is message 2 from producer
Reading message: This is message 3 from producer
```

Undeploying and Cleaning the Simple JMS Examples

After you finish running the examples, you can undeploy them and remove the build artifacts.

You can also use the `asadmin delete-jms-resource` command to delete the destinations and connection factories you created. However, it is recommended that you keep them, because they will be used in most of the examples later in this chapter. After you have created them, they will be available whenever you restart the GlassFish Server.

Writing Robust JMS Applications

The following examples show how to use some of the more advanced features of the JMS API.

A Message Acknowledgment Example

The AckEquivExample.java client shows how both of the following scenarios ensure that a message will not be acknowledged until processing of it is complete:

- Using an asynchronous message consumer (a message listener) in an AUTO_ACKNOWLEDGE session
- Using a synchronous receiver in a CLIENT_ACKNOWLEDGE session

---

Note – In the Java EE platform, message listeners and CLIENT_ACKNOWLEDGE sessions can be used only in application clients, as in this example.

With a message listener, the automatic acknowledgment happens when the onMessage method returns (that is, after message processing has finished). With a synchronous receiver, the client acknowledges the message after processing is complete. If you use AUTO_ACKNOWLEDGE with a synchronous receive, the acknowledgment happens immediately after the receive call; if any subsequent processing steps fail, the message cannot be redelivered.

The example is in the following directory:

tut-install/examples/jms/advanced/ackequivexample/src/java/

The example contains an AsynchSubscriber class with a TextListener class, a MultiplePublisher class, a SynchReceiver class, a SynchSender class, a main method, and a method that runs the other classes' threads.

The example uses the following objects:

- jms/ConnectionFactory, jms/Queue, and jms/Topic: resources that you created for "A Simple Example of Synchronous Message Receives" on page 378.
- jms/ControlQueue: an additional queue
- jms/DurableConnectionFactory: a connection factory with a client ID (see "Creating Durable Subscriptions" on page 364 for more information)

The new queue and connection factory are created at deployment time.

You can use either NetBeans IDE or Ant to build, package, deploy, and run ackequivexample.

▼ To Run `ackequivexample` Using NetBeans IDE

1   To build and package the client, follow these steps.

    a. From the File menu, choose Open Project.

    b. In the Open Project dialog, navigate to:

        tut-install/examples/jms/advanced/

    c. Select the `ackequivexample` folder.

    d. Select the Open as Main Project check box.

    e. Click Open Project.

    f. In the Projects tab, right-click the project and select Build.

2   To run the client, right-click the `ackequivexample` project and select Run.

The client output looks something like this (along with some additional output):

```
Queue name is jms/ControlQueue
Queue name is jms/Queue
Topic name is jms/Topic
Connection factory name is jms/DurableConnectionFactory
  SENDER: Created client-acknowledge session
  SENDER: Sending message: Here is a client-acknowledge message
  RECEIVER: Created client-acknowledge session
  RECEIVER: Processing message: Here is a client-acknowledge message
  RECEIVER: Now I'll acknowledge the message
SUBSCRIBER: Created auto-acknowledge session
SUBSCRIBER: Sending synchronize message to control queue
PUBLISHER: Created auto-acknowledge session
PUBLISHER: Receiving synchronize messages from control queue; count = 1
PUBLISHER: Received synchronize message;  expect 0 more
PUBLISHER: Publishing message: Here is an auto-acknowledge message 1
PUBLISHER: Publishing message: Here is an auto-acknowledge message 2
SUBSCRIBER: Processing message: Here is an auto-acknowledge message 1
PUBLISHER: Publishing message: Here is an auto-acknowledge message 3
SUBSCRIBER: Processing message: Here is an auto-acknowledge message 2
SUBSCRIBER: Processing message: Here is an auto-acknowledge message 3
```

3   After you run the client, you can delete the destination resource `jms/ControlQueue` by using the following command:

`asadmin delete-jms-resource jms/ControlQueue`

You will need the other resources for other examples.

▼ To Run `ackequivexample` Using Ant

1 In a terminal window, go to the following directory:

tut-install/examples/jms/advanced/ackequivexample/

2 To compile and package the client, type the following command:

`ant`

3 To create needed resources, deploy the client JAR file to the GlassFish Server, then retrieve the client stubs, type the following command:

`ant getclient`

Ignore the message that states that the application is deployed at a URL.

4 Because this example takes no command-line arguments, you can run the client using the following command:

`ant run`

Alternatively, you can type the following command:

`appclient -client client-jar/ackequivexampleClient.jar`

The client output looks something like this (along with some additional output):

```
Queue name is jms/ControlQueue
Queue name is jms/Queue
Topic name is jms/Topic
Connection factory name is jms/DurableConnectionFactory
  SENDER: Created client-acknowledge session
  SENDER: Sending message: Here is a client-acknowledge message
  RECEIVER: Created client-acknowledge session
  RECEIVER: Processing message: Here is a client-acknowledge message
  RECEIVER: Now I'll acknowledge the message
SUBSCRIBER: Created auto-acknowledge session
SUBSCRIBER: Sending synchronize message to control queue
PUBLISHER: Created auto-acknowledge session
PUBLISHER: Receiving synchronize messages from control queue; count = 1
PUBLISHER: Received synchronize message;  expect 0 more
PUBLISHER: Publishing message: Here is an auto-acknowledge message 1
PUBLISHER: Publishing message: Here is an auto-acknowledge message 2
SUBSCRIBER: Processing message: Here is an auto-acknowledge message 1
PUBLISHER: Publishing message: Here is an auto-acknowledge message 3
SUBSCRIBER: Processing message: Here is an auto-acknowledge message 2
SUBSCRIBER: Processing message: Here is an auto-acknowledge message 3
```

5 After you run the client, you can delete the destination resource `jms/ControlQueue` by using the following command:

`asadmin delete-jms-resource jms/ControlQueue`

You will need the other resources for other examples.

A Durable Subscription Example

DurableSubscriberExample.java shows how durable subscriptions work. It demonstrates that a durable subscription is active even when the subscriber is not active. The example contains a DurableSubscriber class, a MultiplePublisher class, a main method, and a method that instantiates the classes and calls their methods in sequence.

The example is in the
tut-install/examples/jms/advanced/durablesubscriberexample/src/java/
directory.

The example begins in the same way as any publish/subscribe client: The subscriber starts, the publisher publishes some messages, and the subscriber receives them. At this point, the subscriber closes itself. The publisher then publishes some messages while the subscriber is not active. The subscriber then restarts and receives those messages.

You can use either NetBeans IDE or Ant to build, package, deploy, and run durablesubscriberexample.

▼ To Run durablesubscriberexample Using NetBeans IDE

1   To compile and package the client, follow these steps:

a.   From the File menu, choose Open Project.

b.   In the Open Project dialog, navigate to:
     tut-install/examples/jms/advanced/

c.   Select the durablesubscriberexample folder.

d.   Select the Open as Main Project check box.

e.   Click Open Project.

f.   In the Projects tab, right-click the project and select Build.

2   To run the client, right-click the durablesubscriberexample project and select Run.

The output looks something like this (along with some additional output):

```
Connection factory without client ID is jms/ConnectionFactory
Connection factory with client ID is jms/DurableConnectionFactory
Topic name is jms/Topic
Starting subscriber
PUBLISHER: Publishing message: Here is a message 1
```

```
SUBSCRIBER: Reading message: Here is a message 1
PUBLISHER: Publishing message: Here is a message 2
SUBSCRIBER: Reading message: Here is a message 2
PUBLISHER: Publishing message: Here is a message 3
SUBSCRIBER: Reading message: Here is a message 3
Closing subscriber
PUBLISHER: Publishing message: Here is a message 4
PUBLISHER: Publishing message: Here is a message 5
PUBLISHER: Publishing message: Here is a message 6
Starting subscriber
SUBSCRIBER: Reading message: Here is a message 4
SUBSCRIBER: Reading message: Here is a message 5
SUBSCRIBER: Reading message: Here is a message 6
Closing subscriber
Unsubscribing from durable subscription
```

3   After you run the client, you can delete the connection factory
     `jms/DurableConnectionFactory` by using the following command:

     `asadmin delete-jms-resource jms/DurableConnectionFactory`

▼ To Run durablesubscriberexample Using Ant

1   In a terminal window, go to the following directory:

     tut-install/examples/jms/advanced/durablesubscriberexample/

2   To compile and package the client, type the following command:

     `ant`

3   To create any needed resources, deploy the client JAR file to the GlassFish Server, then
     retrieve the client stubs, type the following command:

     `ant getclient`

     Ignore the message that states that the application is deployed at a URL.

4   Because this example takes no command-line arguments, you can run the client using
     the following command:

     `ant run`

     Alternatively, you can type the following command:

     `appclient -client client-jar/durablesubscriberexampleClient.jar`

5   After you run the client, you can delete the connection factory
     `jms/DurableConnectionFactory` by using the following command:

     `asadmin delete-jms-resource jms/DurableConnectionFactory`

A Local Transaction Example

`TransactedExample.java` demonstrates the use of transactions in a JMS client application. The example is in the *tut-install*/examples/jms/advanced/transactedexample/src/java/ directory.

This example shows how to use a queue and a topic in a single transaction as well as how to pass a session to a message listener's constructor function. The example represents a highly simplified e-commerce application in which the following actions occur.

1. A retailer sends a `MapMessage` to the vendor order queue, ordering a quantity of computers, and waits for the vendor's reply:

```
producer = session.createProducer(vendorOrderQueue);
outMessage = session.createMapMessage();
outMessage.setString("Item", "Computer(s)");
outMessage.setInt("Quantity", quantity);
outMessage.setJMSReplyTo(retailerConfirmQueue);
producer.send(outMessage);
System.out.println("Retailer: ordered " + quantity + " computer(s)");
orderConfirmReceiver = session.createConsumer(retailerConfirmQueue);
connection.start();
```

2. The vendor receives the retailer's order message and sends an order message to the supplier order topic in one transaction. This JMS transaction uses a single session, so you can combine a receive from a queue with a send to a topic. Here is the code that uses the same session to create a consumer for a queue and a producer for a topic:

```
vendorOrderReceiver = session.createConsumer(vendorOrderQueue);
supplierOrderProducer = session.createProducer(supplierOrderTopic);
```

The following code receives the incoming message, sends an outgoing message, and commits the session. The message processing has been removed to keep the sequence simple:

```
inMessage = vendorOrderReceiver.receive();
// Process the incoming message and format the outgoing
// message
...
supplierOrderProducer.send(orderMessage);
...
session.commit();
```

For simplicity, there are only two suppliers, one for CPUs and one for hard drives.

3. Each supplier receives the order from the order topic, checks its inventory, and then sends the items ordered to the queue named in the order message's `JMSReplyTo` field. If it does not have enough of the item in stock, the supplier sends what it has. The synchronous receive from the topic and the send to the queue take place in one JMS transaction.

```
receiver = session.createConsumer(orderTopic);
...
inMessage = receiver.receive();
if (inMessage instanceof MapMessage) {
    orderMessage = (MapMessage) inMessage;
}
// Process message
MessageProducer producer =
    session.createProducer((Queue) orderMessage.getJMSReplyTo());
outMessage = session.createMapMessage();
// Add content to message
producer.send(outMessage);
// Display message contentssession.commit();
```

4. The vendor receives the suppliers' replies from its confirmation queue and updates the state of the order. Messages are processed by an asynchronous message listener; this step shows the use of JMS transactions with a message listener.

```
MapMessage component = (MapMessage) message;
...
orderNumber = component.getInt("VendorOrderNumber");
Order order = Order.getOrder(orderNumber).processSubOrder(component);
session.commit();
```

5. When all outstanding replies are processed for a given order, the vendor message listener sends a message notifying the retailer whether it can fulfill the order.

```
Queue replyQueue = (Queue) order.order.getJMSReplyTo();
MessageProducer producer = session.createProducer(replyQueue);
MapMessage retailerConfirmMessage = session.createMapMessage();
// Format the message
producer.send(retailerConfirmMessage);
session.commit();
```

6. The retailer receives the message from the vendor:

```
inMessage = (MapMessage) orderConfirmReceiver.receive();
```

Figure 21–2 illustrates these steps.

FIGURE 21–2 Transactions: JMS Client Example

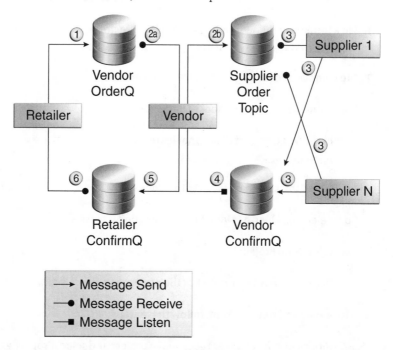

The example contains five classes: GenericSupplier, Order, Retailer, Vendor, and VendorMessageListener. The example also contains a main method and a method that runs the threads of the Retailer, Vendor, and two supplier classes.

All the messages use the MapMessage message type. Synchronous receives are used for all message reception except when the vendor processes the replies of the suppliers. These replies are processed asynchronously and demonstrate how to use transactions within a message listener.

At random intervals, the Vendor class throws an exception to simulate a database problem and cause a rollback.

All classes except Retailer use transacted sessions.

The example uses three queues named jms/AQueue, jms/BQueue, and jms/CQueue, and one topic named jms/OTopic.

You can use either NetBeans IDE or Ant to build, package, deploy, and run transactedexample.

▼ To Run `transactedexample` Using NetBeans IDE

1   In a terminal window, go to the following directory:

tut-install/examples/jms/advanced/transactedexample/

2   To compile and package the client, follow these steps:

a.   From the File menu, choose Open Project.

b.   In the Open Project dialog, navigate to:

tut-install/examples/jms/advanced/

c.   Select the `transactedexample` folder.

d.   Select the Open as Main Project check box.

e.   Click Open Project.

f.   In the Projects tab, right-click the project and select Build.

3   To deploy and run the client, follow these steps:

a.   Right-click the `transactedexample` project and select Properties.

b.   Select Run from the Categories tree.

c.   In the Arguments field, type a number that specifies the number of computers to order:

3

d.   Click OK.

e.   Right-click the project and select Run.

The output looks something like this (along with some additional output):

```
Quantity to be ordered is 3
Retailer: ordered 3 computer(s)
Vendor: Retailer ordered 3 Computer(s)
Vendor: ordered 3 CPU(s) and hard drive(s)
CPU Supplier: Vendor ordered 3 CPU(s)
CPU Supplier: sent 3 CPU(s)
  CPU Supplier: committed transaction
  Vendor: committed transaction 1
Hard Drive Supplier: Vendor ordered 3 Hard Drive(s)
Hard Drive Supplier: sent 1 Hard Drive(s)
Vendor: Completed processing for order 1
  Hard Drive Supplier: committed transaction
```

```
Vendor: unable to send 3 computer(s)
  Vendor: committed transaction 2
Retailer: Order not filled
Retailer: placing another order
Retailer: ordered 6 computer(s)
Vendor: JMSException occurred: javax.jms.JMSException:
Simulated database concurrent access exception
javax.jms.JMSException: Simulated database concurrent access exception
        at TransactedExample$Vendor.run(Unknown Source)
  Vendor: rolled back transaction 1
Vendor: Retailer ordered 6 Computer(s)
Vendor: ordered 6 CPU(s) and hard drive(s)
CPU Supplier: Vendor ordered 6 CPU(s)
Hard Drive Supplier: Vendor ordered 6 Hard Drive(s)
CPU Supplier: sent 6 CPU(s)
  CPU Supplier: committed transaction
Hard Drive Supplier: sent 6 Hard Drive(s)
  Hard Drive Supplier: committed transaction
  Vendor: committed transaction 1
Vendor: Completed processing for order 2
Vendor: sent 6 computer(s)
Retailer: Order filled
  Vendor: committed transaction 2
```

4 After you run the client, you can delete the destination resources in NetBeans IDE or by using the following commands:

```
asadmin delete-jms-resource jms/AQueue
asadmin delete-jms-resource jms/BQueue
asadmin delete-jms-resource jms/CQueue
asadmin delete-jms-resource jms/OTopic
```

▼ To Run transactedexample Using Ant and the appclient Command

1 In a terminal window, go to the following directory:

tut-install/examples/jms/advanced/transactedexample/

2 To build and package the client, type the following command:

ant

3 Create needed resources, deploy the client JAR file to the GlassFish Server, then retrieve the client stubs:

ant getclient

Ignore the message that states that the application is deployed at a URL.

4 Use a command like the following to run the client.

The argument specifies the number of computers to order.

appclient -client client-jar/transactedexampleClient.jar 3

The output looks something like this (along with some additional output):

```
Quantity to be ordered is 3
Retailer: ordered 3 computer(s)
Vendor: Retailer ordered 3 Computer(s)
Vendor: ordered 3 CPU(s) and hard drive(s)
CPU Supplier: Vendor ordered 3 CPU(s)
CPU Supplier: sent 3 CPU(s)
  CPU Supplier: committed transaction
  Vendor: committed transaction 1
Hard Drive Supplier: Vendor ordered 3 Hard Drive(s)
Hard Drive Supplier: sent 1 Hard Drive(s)
Vendor: Completed processing for order 1
  Hard Drive Supplier: committed transaction
Vendor: unable to send 3 computer(s)
  Vendor: committed transaction 2
Retailer: Order not filled
Retailer: placing another order
Retailer: ordered 6 computer(s)
Vendor: JMSException occurred: javax.jms.JMSException:
Simulated database concurrent access exception
javax.jms.JMSException: Simulated database concurrent access exception
        at TransactedExample$Vendor.run(Unknown Source)
  Vendor: rolled back transaction 1
Vendor: Retailer ordered 6 Computer(s)
Vendor: ordered 6 CPU(s) and hard drive(s)
CPU Supplier: Vendor ordered 6 CPU(s)
Hard Drive Supplier: Vendor ordered 6 Hard Drive(s)
CPU Supplier: sent 6 CPU(s)
  CPU Supplier: committed transaction
Hard Drive Supplier: sent 6 Hard Drive(s)
  Hard Drive Supplier: committed transaction
  Vendor: committed transaction 1
Vendor: Completed processing for order 2
Vendor: sent 6 computer(s)
Retailer: Order filled
  Vendor: committed transaction 2
```

5   After you run the client, you can delete the destination resources by using the following commands:

```
asadmin delete-jms-resource jms/AQueue
asadmin delete-jms-resource jms/BQueue
asadmin delete-jms-resource jms/CQueue
asadmin delete-jms-resource jms/OTopic
```

An Application That Uses the JMS API with a Session Bean

This section explains how to write, compile, package, deploy, and run an application that uses the JMS API in conjunction with a session bean. The application contains the following components:

- An application client that invokes a session bean
- A session bean that publishes several messages to a topic

- A message-driven bean that receives and processes the messages using a durable topic subscriber and a message selector

You will find the source files for this section in the *tut-install*/examples/jms/clientsessionmdb/ directory. Path names in this section are relative to this directory.

Writing the Application Components for the clientsessionmdb Example

This application demonstrates how to send messages from an enterprise bean (in this case, a session bean) rather than from an application client, as in the example in Chapter 11, "A Message-Driven Bean Example." Figure 21–3 illustrates the structure of this application.

FIGURE 21–3 An Enterprise Bean Application: Client to Session Bean to Message-Driven Bean

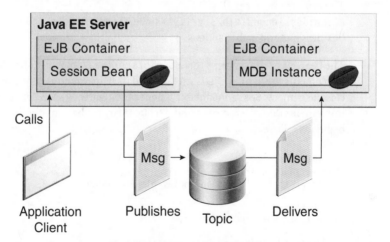

The Publisher enterprise bean in this example is the enterprise-application equivalent of a wire-service news feed that categorizes news events into six news categories. The message-driven bean could represent a newsroom, where the sports desk, for example, would set up a subscription for all news events pertaining to sports.

The application client in the example injects the Publisher enterprise bean's remote home interface and then calls the bean's business method. The enterprise bean creates 18 text messages. For each message, it sets a String property randomly to one of six values representing the news categories and then publishes the message to a topic. The message-driven bean uses a message selector for the property to limit which of the published messages it receives.

Coding the Application Client: `MyAppClient.java`

The application client,
`clientsessionmdb-app-client/src/java/MyAppClient.java`, performs no JMS
API operations and so is simpler than the client in Chapter 11, "A Message-Driven
Bean Example." The client uses dependency injection to obtain the Publisher
enterprise bean's business interface:

```
@EJB(name="PublisherRemote")
static private PublisherRemote publisher;
```

The client then calls the bean's business method twice.

Coding the Publisher Session Bean

The Publisher bean is a stateless session bean that has one business method. The
Publisher bean uses a remote interface rather than a local interface because it is
accessed from the application client.

The remote interface,
`clientsessionmdb-ejb/src/java/sb/PublisherRemote.java`, declares a single
business method, `publishNews`.

The bean class, `clientsessionmdb-ejb/src/java/sb/PublisherBean.java`,
implements the `publishNews` method and its helper method `chooseType`. The bean
class also injects `SessionContext`, `ConnectionFactory`, and `Topic` resources and
implements `@PostConstruct` and `@PreDestroy` callback methods. The bean class
begins as follows:

```
@Stateless
@Remote({PublisherRemote.class})
public class PublisherBean implements PublisherRemote {

    @Resource
    private SessionContext sc;

    @Resource(lookup = "jms/ConnectionFactory")
    private ConnectionFactory connectionFactory;

    @Resource(lookup = "jms/Topic")
    private Topic topic;
    ...
```

The `@PostConstruct` callback method of the bean class, `makeConnection`, creates the
`Connection` used by the bean. The business method `publishNews` creates a `Session`
and a `MessageProducer` and publishes the messages.

The `@PreDestroy` callback method, `endConnection`, deallocates the resources that
were allocated by the `@PostConstruct` callback method. In this case, the method closes
the `Connection`.

Coding the Message-Driven Bean: `MessageBean.java`

The message-driven bean class,
`clientsessionmdb-ejb/src/java/mdb/MessageBean.java`, is almost identical to the
one in Chapter 11, "A Message-Driven Bean Example." However, the `@MessageDriven`
annotation is different, because instead of a queue, the bean is using a topic with a
durable subscription, and it is also using a message selector. Therefore, the annotation
sets the activation config properties `messageSelector`, `subscriptionDurability`,
`clientId`, and `subscriptionName`, as follows:

```
@MessageDriven(mappedName = "jms/Topic", activationConfig =  {
    @ActivationConfigProperty(propertyName = "messageSelector",
            propertyValue = "NewsType = 'Sports' OR NewsType = 'Opinion'")
    , @ActivationConfigProperty(propertyName = "subscriptionDurability",
            propertyValue = "Durable")
    , @ActivationConfigProperty(propertyName = "clientId",
            propertyValue = "MyID")
    , @ActivationConfigProperty(propertyName = "subscriptionName",
            propertyValue = "MySub")
})
```

Note – For a message-driven bean, the destination is specified with the `mappedName`
element instead of the `lookup` element.

The JMS resource adapter uses these properties to create a connection factory for the
message-driven bean that allows the bean to use a durable subscriber.

Creating Resources for the `clientsessionmdb` Example

This example uses the topic named `jms/Topic` and the connection factory
`jms/ConnectionFactory`, which are also used in previous examples. If you deleted the
connection factory or topic, they will be recreated when you deploy the example.

Running the `clientsessionmdb` Example

You can use either NetBeans IDE or Ant to build, package, deploy, and run the
`clientsessionmdb` example.

▼ To Run the `clientsessionmdb` Example Using NetBeans IDE

1   To compile and package the project, follow these steps:

   a. From the File menu, choose Open Project.

   b. In the Open Project dialog, navigate to:

      tut-install/examples/jms/

   c. Select the `clientsessionmdb` folder.

   d. Select the Open as Main Project check box and the Open Required Projects check box.

   e. Click Open Project.

   f. In the Projects tab, right-click the `clientsessionmdb` project and select Build.

     This task creates the following:

      ■ An application client JAR file that contains the client class file and the session bean's remote interface, along with a manifest file that specifies the main class and places the EJB JAR file in its classpath

      ■ An EJB JAR file that contains both the session bean and the message-driven bean

      ■ An application EAR file that contains the two JAR files

2   Right-click the project and select Run.

This command creates any needed resources, deploys the project, returns a JAR file named `clientsessionmdbClient.jar`, and then executes it.

The output of the application client in the Output pane looks like this (preceded by application client container output):

```
To view the bean output,
 check <install_dir>/domains/domain1/logs/server.log.
```

The output from the enterprise beans appears in the server log (*domain-dir*/`logs/server.log`), wrapped in logging information. The Publisher session bean sends two sets of 18 messages numbered 0 through 17. Because of the message selector, the message-driven bean receives only the messages whose `NewsType` property is `Sports` or `Opinion`.

▼ To Run the `clientsessionmdb` Example Using Ant

1 **Go to the following directory:**

tut-install/examples/jms/clientsessionmdb/

2 **To compile the source files and package the application, use the following command:**

`ant`

The ant command creates the following:

- An application client JAR file that contains the client class file and the session bean's remote interface, along with a manifest file that specifies the main class and places the EJB JAR file in its classpath
- An EJB JAR file that contains both the session bean and the message-driven bean
- An application EAR file that contains the two JAR files

The `clientsessionmdb.ear` file is created in the `dist` directory.

3 **To create any needed resources, deploy the application, and run the client, use the following command:**

`ant run`

Ignore the message that states that the application is deployed at a URL.

The client displays these lines (preceded by application client container output):

```
To view the bean output,
 check <install_dir>/domains/domain1/logs/server.log.
```

The output from the enterprise beans appears in the server log file, wrapped in logging information. The Publisher session bean sends two sets of 18 messages numbered 0 through 17. Because of the message selector, the message-driven bean receives only the messages whose NewsType property is Sports or Opinion.

An Application That Uses the JMS API with an Entity

This section explains how to write, compile, package, deploy, and run an application that uses the JMS API with an entity. The application uses the following components:

- An application client that both sends and receives messages
- Two message-driven beans
- An entity class

You will find the source files for this section in the *tut-install*/examples/jms/clientmdbentity/ directory. Path names in this section are relative to this directory.

Overview of the `clientmdbentity` Example Application

This application simulates, in a simplified way, the work flow of a company's human resources (HR) department when it processes a new hire. This application also demonstrates how to use the Java EE platform to accomplish a task that many JMS applications need to perform.

A JMS client must often wait for several messages from various sources. It then uses the information in all these messages to assemble a message that it then sends to another destination. The common term for this process is *joining messages*. Such a task must be transactional, with all the receives and the send as a single transaction. If not all the messages are received successfully, the transaction can be rolled back. For an application client example that illustrates this task, see "A Local Transaction Example" on page 411.

A message-driven bean can process only one message at a time in a transaction. To provide the ability to join messages, an application can have the message-driven bean store the interim information in an entity. The entity can then determine whether all the information has been received; when it has, the entity can report this back to one of the message-driven beans, which then creates and sends the message to the other destination. After it has completed its task, the entity can be removed.

The basic steps of the application are as follows.

1. The HR department's application client generates an employee ID for each new hire and then publishes a message (M1) containing the new hire's name, employee ID, and position. The client then creates a temporary queue, `ReplyQueue`, with a message listener that waits for a reply to the message. (See "Creating Temporary Destinations" on page 363 for more information.)

2. Two message-driven beans process each message: One bean, `OfficeMDB`, assigns the new hire's office number, and the other bean, `EquipmentMDB`, assigns the new hire's equipment. The first bean to process the message creates and persists an entity named `SetupOffice`, then calls a business method of the entity to store the information it has generated. The second bean locates the existing entity and calls another business method to add its information.

3. When both the office and the equipment have been assigned, the entity business method returns a value of `true` to the message-driven bean that called the method. The message-driven bean then sends to the reply queue a message (M2) describing the assignments. Then it removes the entity. The application client's message listener retrieves the information.

Figure 21–4 illustrates the structure of this application. Of course, an actual HR application would have more components; other beans could set up payroll and benefits records, schedule orientation, and so on.

Figure 21–4 assumes that `OfficeMDB` is the first message-driven bean to consume the message from the client. `OfficeMDB` then creates and persists the `SetupOffice` entity and stores the office information. `EquipmentMDB` then finds the entity, stores the equipment information, and learns that the entity has completed its work. `EquipmentMDB` then sends the message to the reply queue and removes the entity.

FIGURE 21–4   An Enterprise Bean Application: Client to Message-Driven Beans to Entity

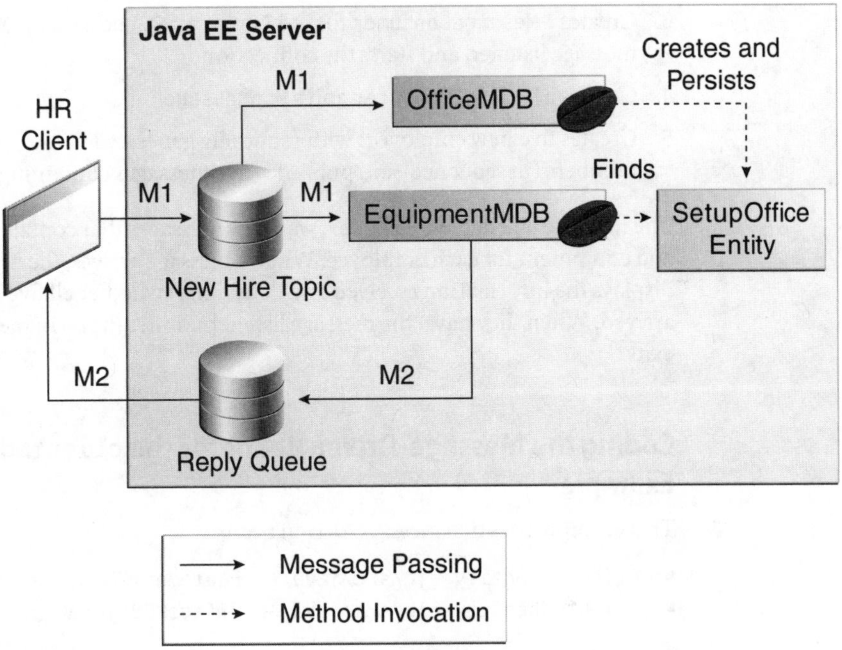

Writing the Application Components for the clientmdbentity Example

Writing the components of the application involves coding the application client, the message-driven beans, and the entity class.

Coding the Application Client: `HumanResourceClient.java`

The application client,
`clientmdbentity-app-client/src/java/HumanResourceClient.java`, performs
the following steps:

1. Injects `ConnectionFactory` and `Topic` resources

2. Creates a `TemporaryQueue` to receive notification of processing that occurs, based
   on new-hire events it has published

3. Creates a `MessageConsumer` for the `TemporaryQueue`, sets the `MessageConsumer`'s
   message listener, and starts the connection

4. Creates a `MessageProducer` and a `MapMessage`

5. Creates five new employees with randomly generated names, positions, and ID
   numbers (in sequence) and publishes five messages containing this information

The message listener, `HRListener`, waits for messages that contain the assigned office
and equipment for each employee. When a message arrives, the message listener
displays the information received and determines whether all five messages have
arrived. When they have, the message listener notifies the `main` method, which then
exits.

Coding the Message-Driven Beans for the `clientmdbentity` Example

This example uses two message-driven beans:

- `clientmdbentity-ejb/src/java/eb/EquipmentMDB.java`
- `clientmdbentity-ejb/src/java/eb/OfficeMDB.java`

The beans take the following steps:

1. They inject `MessageDrivenContext` and `ConnectionFactory` resources.

2. The `onMessage` method retrieves the information in the message. The
   `EquipmentMDB`'s `onMessage` method chooses equipment, based on the new hire's
   position; the `OfficeMDB`'s `onMessage` method randomly generates an office
   number.

3. After a slight delay to simulate real world processing hitches, the `onMessage`
   method calls a helper method, `compose`.

4. The `compose` method takes the following steps:

   a. It either creates and persists the `SetupOffice` entity or finds it by primary key.

   b. It uses the entity to store the equipment or the office information in the
      database, calling either the `doEquipmentList` or the `doOfficeNumber` business
      method.

c. If the business method returns true, meaning that all of the information has been stored, it creates a connection and a session, retrieves the reply destination information from the message, creates a MessageProducer, and sends a reply message that contains the information stored in the entity.

d. It removes the entity.

Coding the Entity Class for the clientmdbentity Example

The SetupOffice class, clientmdbentity-ejb/src/java/eb/SetupOffice.java, is an entity class. The entity and the message-driven beans are packaged together in an EJB JAR file. The entity class is declared as follows:

```
@Entity
public class SetupOffice implements Serializable {
```

The class contains a no-argument constructor and a constructor that takes two arguments, the employee ID and name. It also contains getter and setter methods for the employee ID, name, office number, and equipment list. The getter method for the employee ID has the @Id annotation to indicate that this field is the primary key:

```
@Id
public String getEmployeeId() {
    return id;
}
```

The class also implements the two business methods, doEquipmentList and doOfficeNumber, and their helper method, checkIfSetupComplete.

The message-driven beans call the business methods and the getter methods.

The persistence.xml file for the entity specifies the most basic settings:

```
<?xml version="1.0" encoding="UTF-8"?>
<persistence version="2.0"
             xmlns="http://java.sun.com/xml/ns/persistence"
             xmlns:xsi="http://www.w3.org/2001/XMLSchema-instance"
             xsi:schemaLocation="http://java.sun.com/xml/ns/persistence
                http://java.sun.com/xml/ns/persistence/persistence_2_0.xsd">
  <persistence-unit name="clientmdbentity-ejbPU" transaction-type="JTA">
    <provider>org.eclipse.persistence.jpa.PersistenceProvider</provider>
    <jta-data-source>jdbc/__default</jta-data-source>
    <class>eb.SetupOffice</class>
    <properties>
      <property name="eclipselink.ddl-generation"
                value="drop-and-create-tables"/>
    </properties>
  </persistence-unit>
</persistence>
```

Creating Resources for the `clientmdbentity` Example

This example uses the connection factory `jms/ConnectionFactory` and the topic `jms/Topic`, both of which you used in "An Application That Uses the JMS API with a Session Bean" on page 416. It also uses the JDBC resource named `jdbc/__default`, which is enabled by default when you start the GlassFish Server.

If you deleted the connection factory or topic, they will be created when you deploy the example.

Running the `clientmdbentity` Example

You can use either NetBeans IDE or Ant to build, package, deploy, and run the `clientmdbentity` example.

▼ To Run the `clientmdbentity` Example Using NetBeans IDE

1 From the File menu, choose Open Project.

2 In the Open Project dialog, navigate to:

   tut-install/examples/jms/

3 Select the `clientmdbentity` folder.

4 Select the Open as Main Project check box and the Open Required Projects check box.

5 Click Open Project.

6 In the Projects tab, right-click the `clientmdbentity` project and select Build.

This task creates the following:

- An application client JAR file that contains the client class and listener class files, along with a manifest file that specifies the main class

- An EJB JAR file that contains the message-driven beans and the entity class, along with the `persistence.xml` file

- An application EAR file that contains the two JAR files along with an `application.xml` file

7 If the Java DB database is not already running, follow these steps:

   a. Click the Services tab.

   b. Expand the Databases node.

c. Right-click the Java DB node and select Start Server.

8   In the Projects tab, right-click the project and select Run.

This command creates any needed resources, deploys the project, returns a client JAR file named clientmdbentityClient.jar, and then executes it.

The output of the application client in the Output pane looks something like this:

```
PUBLISHER: Setting hire ID to 50, name Bill Tudor, position Programmer
PUBLISHER: Setting hire ID to 51, name Carol Jones, position Senior Programmer
PUBLISHER: Setting hire ID to 52, name Mark Wilson, position Manager
PUBLISHER: Setting hire ID to 53, name Polly Wren, position Senior Programmer
PUBLISHER: Setting hire ID to 54, name Joe Lawrence, position Director
Waiting for 5 message(s)
New hire event processed:
  Employee ID: 52
  Name: Mark Wilson
  Equipment: PDA
  Office number: 294
Waiting for 4 message(s)
New hire event processed:
  Employee ID: 53
  Name: Polly Wren
  Equipment: Laptop
  Office number: 186
Waiting for 3 message(s)
New hire event processed:
  Employee ID: 54
  Name: Joe Lawrence
  Equipment: Java Phone
  Office number: 135
Waiting for 2 message(s)
New hire event processed:
  Employee ID: 50
  Name: Bill Tudor
  Equipment: Desktop System
  Office number: 200
Waiting for 1 message(s)
New hire event processed:
  Employee ID: 51
  Name: Carol Jones
  Equipment: Laptop
  Office number: 262
```

The output from the message-driven beans and the entity class appears in the server log, wrapped in logging information.

For each employee, the application first creates the entity and then finds it. You may see runtime errors in the server log, and transaction rollbacks may occur. The errors occur if both of the message-driven beans discover at the same time that the entity does not yet exist, so they both try to create it. The first attempt succeeds, but the second fails because the bean already exists. After the rollback, the second message-driven bean tries again and succeeds in finding the entity. Container-managed transactions allow the application to run correctly, in spite of these errors, with no special programming.

▼ **To Run the `clientmdbentity` Example Using Ant**

1 **Go to the following directory:**

   tut-install/examples/jms/clientmdbentity/

2 **To compile the source files and package the application, use the following command:**

   ant

   The ant command creates the following:

   - An application client JAR file that contains the client class and listener class files, along with a manifest file that specifies the main class

   - An EJB JAR file that contains the message-driven beans and the entity class, along with the `persistence.xml` file

   - An application EAR file that contains the two JAR files along with an `application.xml` file

3 **To create any needed resources, deploy the application, and run the client, use the following command:**

   ant run

   This command starts the database server if it is not already running, then deploys and runs the application.

   Ignore the message that states that the application is deployed at a URL.

   The output in the terminal window looks something like this (preceded by application client container output):

```
running application client container.
PUBLISHER: Setting hire ID to 50, name Bill Tudor, position Programmer
PUBLISHER: Setting hire ID to 51, name Carol Jones, position Senior Programmer
PUBLISHER: Setting hire ID to 52, name Mark Wilson, position Manager
PUBLISHER: Setting hire ID to 53, name Polly Wren, position Senior Programmer
PUBLISHER: Setting hire ID to 54, name Joe Lawrence, position Director
Waiting for 5 message(s)
New hire event processed:
  Employee ID: 52
  Name: Mark Wilson
  Equipment: PDA
  Office number: 294
Waiting for 4 message(s)
New hire event processed:
  Employee ID: 53
  Name: Polly Wren
  Equipment: Laptop
  Office number: 186
Waiting for 3 message(s)
New hire event processed:
  Employee ID: 54
  Name: Joe Lawrence
```

```
    Equipment: Java Phone
    Office number: 135
Waiting for 2 message(s)
New hire event processed:
    Employee ID: 50
    Name: Bill Tudor
    Equipment: Desktop System
    Office number: 200
Waiting for 1 message(s)
New hire event processed:
    Employee ID: 51
    Name: Carol Jones
    Equipment: Laptop
    Office number: 262
```

The output from the message-driven beans and the entity class appears in the server log, wrapped in logging information.

For each employee, the application first creates the entity and then finds it. You may see runtime errors in the server log, and transaction rollbacks may occur. The errors occur if both of the message-driven beans discover at the same time that the entity does not yet exist, so they both try to create it. The first attempt succeeds, but the second fails because the bean already exists. After the rollback, the second message-driven bean tries again and succeeds in finding the entity. Container-managed transactions allow the application to run correctly, in spite of these errors, with no special programming.

An Application Example That Consumes Messages from a Remote Server

This section and the following section explain how to write, compile, package, deploy, and run a pair of Java EE modules that run on two Java EE servers and that use the JMS API to interchange messages with each other. It is a common practice to deploy different components of an enterprise application on different systems within a company, and these examples illustrate on a small scale how to do this for an application that uses the JMS API.

The two examples work in slightly different ways. In the first example, the deployment information for a message-driven bean specifies the remote server from which it will *consume* messages. In the next example, described in "An Application Example That Deploys a Message-Driven Bean on Two Servers" on page 436, the same message-driven bean is deployed on two different servers, so it is the client module that specifies the servers (one local, one remote) to which it is *sending* messages.

This first example divides the example in Chapter 11, "A Message-Driven Bean Example," into two modules: one containing the application client, and the other containing the message-driven bean.

You will find the source files for this section in the *tut-install*/examples/jms/consumeremote/ directory. Path names in this section are relative to this directory.

Overview of the `consumeremote` Example Modules

This example is very similar to the one in Chapter 11, "A Message-Driven Bean Example," except for the fact that it is packaged as two separate modules:

- One module contains the application client, which runs on the remote system and sends three messages to a queue.
- The other module contains the message-driven bean, which is deployed on the local server and consumes the messages from the queue on the remote server.

The basic steps of the modules are as follows:

1. The administrator starts two Java EE servers, one on each system.
2. On the local server, the administrator deploys the message-driven bean module, which specifies the remote server where the client is deployed.
3. On the remote server, the administrator places the client JAR file.
4. The client module sends three messages to a queue.
5. The message-driven bean consumes the messages.

Figure 21–5 illustrates the structure of this application. You can see that it is almost identical to Figure 11–1 except that there are two Java EE servers. The queue used is the one on the remote server; the queue must also exist on the local server for resource injection to succeed.

FIGURE 21–5 A Java EE Application That Consumes Messages from a Remote Server

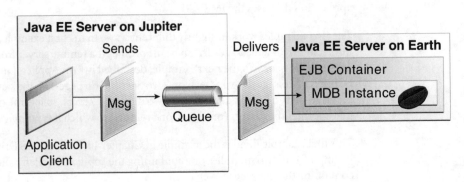

Writing the Module Components for the consumeremote Example

Writing the components of the modules involves

- Coding the application client
- Coding the message-driven bean

The application client, jupiterclient/src/java/SimpleClient.java, is almost identical to the one in "The simplemessage Application Client" on page 228.

Similarly, the message-driven bean, earthmdb/src/java/MessageBean.java, is almost identical to the one in "The Message-Driven Bean Class" on page 229. The only significant difference is that the activation config properties include one property that specifies the name of the remote system. You need to edit the source file to specify the name of your system.

Creating Resources for the consumeremote Example

The application client can use any connection factory that exists on the remote server; in this example, it uses jms/ConnectionFactory. Both components use the queue named jms/Queue, which you created for "A Simple Example of Synchronous Message Receives" on page 378. The message-driven bean does not need a previously created connection factory; the resource adapter creates one for it.

Any missing resources will be created when you deploy the example.

Using Two Application Servers for the consumeremote Example

As in "Running JMS Clients on Multiple Systems" on page 398, the two servers are referred to as earth and jupiter.

The GlassFish Server must be running on both systems.

Before you can run the example, you must change the default name of the JMS host on jupiter, as described in "To Change the Default Host Name Using the Administration Console" on page 402. If you have already performed this task, you do not have to repeat it.

Which system you use to package and deploy the modules and which system you use to run the client depend on your network configuration (specifically, which file system you can access remotely). These instructions assume you can access the file system of jupiter from earth but cannot access the file system of earth from jupiter. (You can use the same systems for jupiter and earth that you used in "Running JMS Clients on Multiple Systems" on page 398.)

You can package both modules on earth and deploy the message-driven bean there. The only action you perform on jupiter is running the client module.

Running the consumeremote Example

You can use either NetBeans IDE or Ant to build, package, deploy, and run the consumeremote example.

▼ To Run the consumeremote Example Using NetBeans IDE

To edit the message-driven bean source file and then package, deploy, and run the modules using NetBeans IDE, follow these steps.

1 From the File menu, choose Open Project.

2 In the Open Project dialog, navigate to:

tut-install/examples/jms/consumeremote/

3 Select the earthmdb folder.

4 Select the Open as Main Project check box.

5 Click Open Project.

6 Edit the MessageBean.java file as follows:

a. In the Projects tab, expand the earthmdb, Source Packages, and mdb nodes, then double-click MessageBean.java.

b. Find the following line within the @MessageDriven annotation:

```
@ActivationConfigProperty(propertyName = "addressList",
        propertyValue = "remotesystem"),
```

c. Replace remotesystem with the name of your remote system.

7 Right-click the earthmdb project and select Build.

This command creates a JAR file that contains the bean class file.

8 From the File menu, choose Open Project.

9   Select the `jupiterclient` folder.

10 Select the Open as Main Project check box.

11 Click Open Project.

12 In the Projects tab, right-click the `jupiterclient` project and select Build.

This command creates a JAR file that contains the client class file and a manifest file.

13 Right-click the `earthmdb` project and select Deploy.

14 To copy the `jupiterclient` module to the remote system, follow these steps:

a. Change to the directory `jupiterclient/dist`:

```
cd tut-install/examples/jms/consumeremote/jupiterclient/dist
```

b. Type a command like the following:

```
cp jupiterclient.jar F:/
```

That is, copy the client JAR file to a location on the remote file system. You can use the file system graphical user interface on your system instead of the command line.

15 To run the application client, follow these steps:

a. If you did not previously create the queue and connection factory on the remote system (`jupiter`), go to the `tut-install`/**examples/jms/consumeremote/jupiterclient/** directory on the remote system and type the following command:

```
ant add-resources
```

b. Go to the directory on the remote system (`jupiter`) where you copied the client JAR file.

c. To deploy the client module and retrieve the client stubs, use the following command:

```
asadmin deploy --retrieve . jupiterclient.jar
```

This command deploys the client JAR file and retrieves the client stubs in a file named `jupiterclientClient.jar`

d. To run the client, use the following command:

```
appclient -client jupiterclientClient.jar
```

On jupiter, the output of the appclient command looks like this (preceded by application client container output):

```
Sending message: This is message 1 from jupiterclient
Sending message: This is message 2 from jupiterclient
Sending message: This is message 3 from jupiterclient
```

On earth, the output in the server log looks something like this (preceded by logging information):

```
MESSAGE BEAN: Message received: This is message 1 from jupiterclient
MESSAGE BEAN: Message received: This is message 2 from jupiterclient
MESSAGE BEAN: Message received: This is message 3 from jupiterclient
```

e. **To undeploy the client after you finish running it, use the following command:**

```
asadmin undeploy jupiterclient
```

▼ To Run the consumeremote Example Using Ant

To edit the message-driven bean source file and then package, deploy, and run the modules using Ant, follow these steps.

1 Open the following file in an editor:

tut-install/examples/jms/consumeremote/earthmdb/src/java/mdb/MessageBean.java

2 Find the following line within the @MessageDriven annotation:

```
@ActivationConfigProperty(propertyName = "addressList",
        propertyValue = "remotesystem"),
```

3 Replace remotesystem with the name of your remote system, then save and close the file.

4 Go to the following directory:

tut-install/examples/jms/consumeremote/earthmdb/

5 Type the following command:

```
ant
```

This command creates a JAR file that contains the bean class file.

6 Type the following command:

```
ant deploy
```

7 Go to the jupiterclient directory:

```
cd ../jupiterclient
```

8 Type the following command:

```
ant
```

This command creates a JAR file that contains the client class file and a manifest file.

9 To copy the `jupiterclient` module to the remote system, follow these steps:

a. Change to the directory `jupiterclient/dist`:

```
cd ../jupiterclient/dist
```

b. Type a command like the following:

```
cp jupiterclient.jar F:/
```

That is, copy the client JAR file to a location on the remote file system.

10 To run the application client, follow these steps:

a. If you did not previously create the queue and connection factory on the remote system (`jupiter`), go to the *tut-install*/**examples/jms/consumeremote/jupiterclient/** directory on the remote system and type the following command:

```
ant add-resources
```

b. Go to the directory on the remote system (`jupiter`) where you copied the client JAR file.

c. To deploy the client module and retrieve the client stubs, use the following command:

```
asadmin deploy --retrieve . jupiterclient.jar
```

This command deploys the client JAR file and retrieves the client stubs in a file named `jupiterclientClient.jar`

d. To run the client, use the following command:

```
appclient -client jupiterclientClient.jar
```

On `jupiter`, the output of the `appclient` command looks like this (preceded by application client container output):

```
Sending message: This is message 1 from jupiterclient
Sending message: This is message 2 from jupiterclient
Sending message: This is message 3 from jupiterclient
```

On `earth`, the output in the server log looks something like this (preceded by logging information):

```
MESSAGE BEAN: Message received: This is message 1 from jupiterclient
MESSAGE BEAN: Message received: This is message 2 from jupiterclient
```

```
MESSAGE BEAN: Message received: This is message 3 from jupiterclient
```

e. **To undeploy the client after you finish running it, use the following command:**

```
asadmin undeploy jupiterclient
```

An Application Example That Deploys a Message-Driven Bean on Two Servers

This section, like the preceding one, explains how to write, compile, package, deploy, and run a pair of Java EE modules that use the JMS API and run on two Java EE servers. These modules are slightly more complex than the ones in the first example.

The modules use the following components:

- An application client that is deployed on the local server. It uses two connection factories, an ordinary one and one configured to communicate with the remote server, to create two publishers and two subscribers and to publish and consume messages.

- A message-driven bean that is deployed twice: once on the local server, and once on the remote one. It processes the messages and sends replies.

In this section, the term *local server* means the server on which both the application client and the message-driven bean are deployed (earth in the preceding example). The term *remote server* means the server on which only the message-driven bean is deployed (jupiter in the preceding example).

You will find the source files for this section in the *tut-install*/examples/jms/sendremote/ directory. Path names in this section are relative to this directory.

Overview of the sendremote Example Modules

This pair of modules is somewhat similar to the modules in "An Application Example That Consumes Messages from a Remote Server" on page 429 in that the only components are a client and a message-driven bean. However, the modules here use these components in more complex ways. One module consists of the application client. The other module contains only the message-driven bean and is deployed twice, once on each server.

The basic steps of the modules are as follows.

1. You start two Java EE servers, one on each system.

2. On the local server (earth), you create two connection factories: one local and one that communicates with the remote server (jupiter). On the remote server, you create a connection factory that has the same name as the one that communicates with the remote server.

3. The application client looks up the two connection factories (the local one and the one that communicates with the remote server) to create two connections, sessions, publishers, and subscribers. The subscribers use a message listener.

4. Each publisher publishes five messages.

5. Each of the local and the remote message-driven beans receives five messages and sends replies.

6. The client's message listener consumes the replies.

Figure 21–6 illustrates the structure of this application. M1 represents the first message sent using the local connection factory, and RM1 represents the first reply message sent by the local MDB. M2 represents the first message sent using the remote connection factory, and RM2 represents the first reply message sent by the remote MDB.

FIGURE 21–6   A Java EE Application That Sends Messages to Two Servers

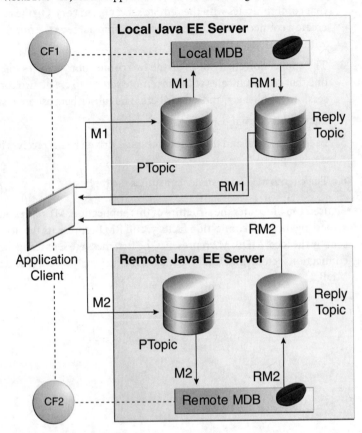

Writing the Module Components for the sendremote Example

Writing the components of the modules involves coding the application client and the message-driven bean.

Coding the Application Client: MultiAppServerClient.java

The application client class, `multiclient/src/java/MultiAppServerClient.java`, does the following.

1. It injects resources for two connection factories and a topic.

2. For each connection factory, it creates a connection, a publisher session, a publisher, a subscriber session, a subscriber, and a temporary topic for replies.

3. Each subscriber sets its message listener, `ReplyListener`, and starts the connection.

4. Each publisher publishes five messages and creates a list of the messages the listener should expect.

5. When each reply arrives, the message listener displays its contents and removes it from the list of expected messages.

6. When all the messages have arrived, the client exits.

Coding the Message-Driven Bean: `ReplyMsgBean.java`

The message-driven bean class, `replybean/src/ReplyMsgBean.java`, does the following:

1. Uses the `@MessageDriven` annotation:

    ```
    @MessageDriven(mappedName = "jms/Topic")
    ```

2. Injects resources for the `MessageDrivenContext` and for a connection factory. It does not need a destination resource because it uses the value of the incoming message's `JMSReplyTo` header as the destination.

3. Uses a `@PostConstruct` callback method to create the connection, and a `@PreDestroy` callback method to close the connection.

The `onMessage` method of the message-driven bean class does the following:

1. Casts the incoming message to a `TextMessage` and displays the text
2. Creates a connection, a session, and a publisher for the reply message
3. Publishes the message to the reply topic
4. Closes the connection

On both servers, the bean will consume messages from the topic `jms/Topic`.

Creating Resources for the `sendremote` Example

This example uses the connection factory named `jms/ConnectionFactory` and the topic named `jms/Topic`. These objects must exist on both the local and the remote servers.

This example uses an additional connection factory, `jms/JupiterConnectionFactory`, which communicates with the remote system; you created it in "To Create Administered Objects for Multiple Systems" on page 400. This connection factory must exist on the local server.

The `build.xml` file for the `multiclient` module contains targets you can use to create these resources if you deleted them previously.

To create the resource needed only on the local system, use the following command:

```
ant create-remote-factory -Dsys=remote-system-name
```

The other resources will be created when you deploy the application.

▼ To Enable Deployment on the Remote System

GlassFish Server by default does not allow deployment from a remote system. You must create a password for the administrator, then execute an `asadmin` command on the remote system to enable deployment of the message-driven bean on that system.

1 On `jupiter`, start the Administration Console by opening a browser at `http://localhost:4848/`.

2 In the navigation tree, expand the Configurations node, then expand the server-config node.

3 Expand the Security node.

4 Expand the Realms node.

5 Select the admin-realm node.

6 On the Edit Realm page, click Manage Users.

7 In the File Users table, click admin in the User ID column.

8 On the Edit File Realm Users page, type a password (for example, jmsadmin) in the New Password and Confirm New Password fields, then click Save.

9 From a command prompt on the remote system (`jupiter`), run the following command:

```
asadmin enable-secure-admin
```

10 Stop and restart the server on `jupiter`.

▼ To Use Two Application Servers for the `sendremote` Example

If you are using NetBeans IDE, you need to add the remote server in order to deploy the message-driven bean there. To do so, follow these steps.

1 In NetBeans IDE, click the Services tab.

2   Right-click the Servers node and select Add Server. In the Add Server Instance dialog, follow these steps:

    a.   Select GlassFish Server 3+ from the Server list.

    b.   In the Name field, specify a name slightly different from that of the local server, such as GlassFish Server 3+ (2).

    c.   Click Next.

    d.   For the Server Location, browse to the location of the GlassFish Server on the remote system. This location must be visible from the local system.

    e.   Click Next.

    f.   Select the Register Remote Domain radio button.

    g.   In the Host Name field, type the name of the remote system.

    h.   Click Finish.

    i.   In the dialog that appears, enter the user name (admin) and the password you created.

Next Steps   Before you can run the example, you must change the default name of the JMS host on jupiter, as described in "To Change the Default Host Name Using the Administration Console" on page 402. If you have already performed this task, you do not have to repeat it.

Running the sendremote Example

You can use either NetBeans IDE or Ant to build, package, deploy, and run the sendremote example.

▼ To Run the sendremote Example Using NetBeans IDE

1   To build the replybean module, follow these steps:

    a.   From the File menu, choose Open Project.

    b.   In the Open Project dialog, navigate to:

       tut-install/examples/jms/sendremote/

   c. **Select the** `replybean` **folder.**

   d. **Select the Open as Main Project check box.**

   e. **Click Open Project.**

   f. **In the Projects tab, right-click the** `replybean` **project and select Build.**

     This command creates a JAR file that contains the bean class file.

2   **To build the** `multiclient` **module, follow these steps:**

   a. **From the File menu, choose Open Project.**

   b. **Select the** `multiclient` **folder.**

   c. **Select the Open as Main Project check box.**

   d. **Click Open Project.**

   e. **In the Projects tab, right-click the** `multiclient` **project and select Build.**

     This command creates a JAR file that contains the client class file and a manifest file.

3   **To create any needed resources and deploy the** `multiclient` **module on the local server, follow these steps:**

   a. **Right-click the** `multiclient` **project and select Properties.**

   b. **Select Run from the Categories tree.**

   c. **From the Server list, select GlassFish Server 3+ (the local server).**

   d. **Click OK.**

   e. **Right-click the** `multiclient` **project and select Deploy.**

     You can use the Services tab to verify that `multiclient` is deployed as an App Client Module on the local server.

4   **To deploy the** `replybean` **module on the local and remote servers, follow these steps:**

   a. **Right-click the** `replybean` **project and select Properties.**

   b. **Select Run from the Categories tree.**

c. From the Server list, select GlassFish Server 3+ (the local server).

d. Click OK.

e. Right-click the `replybean` project and select Deploy.

f. Right-click the `replybean` project again and select Properties.

g. Select Run from the Categories tree.

h. From the Server list, select GlassFish Server 3+ (2) (the remote server).

i. Click OK.

j. Right-click the `replybean` project and select Deploy.

You can use the Services tab to verify that `replybean` is deployed as an EJB Module on both servers.

5 **To run the application client, right-click the `multiclient` project and select Run.**

This command returns a JAR file named `multiclientClient.jar` and then executes it.

On the local system, the output of the `appclient` command looks something like this:

```
running application client container.
...
Sent message: text: id=1 to local app server
Sent message: text: id=2 to remote app server
ReplyListener: Received message: id=1, text=ReplyMsgBean processed message:
text: id=1 to local app server
Sent message: text: id=3 to local app server
ReplyListener: Received message: id=3, text=ReplyMsgBean processed message:
text: id=3 to local app server
ReplyListener: Received message: id=2, text=ReplyMsgBean processed message:
text: id=2 to remote app server
Sent message: text: id=4 to remote app server
ReplyListener: Received message: id=4, text=ReplyMsgBean processed message:
text: id=4 to remote app server
Sent message: text: id=5 to local app server
ReplyListener: Received message: id=5, text=ReplyMsgBean processed message:
text: id=5 to local app server
Sent message: text: id=6 to remote app server
ReplyListener: Received message: id=6, text=ReplyMsgBean processed message:
text: id=6 to remote app server
Sent message: text: id=7 to local app server
ReplyListener: Received message: id=7, text=ReplyMsgBean processed message:
text: id=7 to local app server
Sent message: text: id=8 to remote app server
ReplyListener: Received message: id=8, text=ReplyMsgBean processed message:
text: id=8 to remote app server
Sent message: text: id=9 to local app server
ReplyListener: Received message: id=9, text=ReplyMsgBean processed message:
```

```
text: id=9 to local app server
Sent message: text: id=10 to remote app server
ReplyListener: Received message: id=10, text=ReplyMsgBean processed message:
text: id=10 to remote app server
Waiting for 0 message(s) from local app server
Waiting for 0 message(s) from remote app server
Finished
Closing connection 1
Closing connection 2
```

On the local system, where the message-driven bean receives the odd-numbered messages, the output in the server log looks like this (wrapped in logging information):

```
ReplyMsgBean: Received message: text: id=1 to local app server
ReplyMsgBean: Received message: text: id=3 to local app server
ReplyMsgBean: Received message: text: id=5 to local app server
ReplyMsgBean: Received message: text: id=7 to local app server
ReplyMsgBean: Received message: text: id=9 to local app server
```

On the remote system, where the bean receives the even-numbered messages, the output in the server log looks like this (wrapped in logging information):

```
ReplyMsgBean: Received message: text: id=2 to remote app server
ReplyMsgBean: Received message: text: id=4 to remote app server
ReplyMsgBean: Received message: text: id=6 to remote app server
ReplyMsgBean: Received message: text: id=8 to remote app server
ReplyMsgBean: Received message: text: id=10 to remote app server
```

▼ To Run the sendremote Example Using Ant

1 To package the modules, follow these steps:

a. Go to the following directory:

tut-install/examples/jms/sendremote/multiclient/

b. Type the following command:

`ant`

This command creates a JAR file that contains the client class file and a manifest file.

c. Change to the directory replybean:

`cd ../replybean`

d. Type the following command:

`ant`

This command creates a JAR file that contains the bean class file.

2 To deploy the `replybean` module on the local and remote servers, follow these steps:

   a. Verify that you are still in the directory `replybean`.

   b. Type the following command:

```
ant deploy
```

Ignore the message that states that the application is deployed at a URL.

   c. Type the following command:

```
ant deploy-remote -Dsys=remote-system-name
```

Replace *remote-system-name* with the actual name of the remote system.

3 To deploy the client, follow these steps:

   a. Change to the directory `multiclient`:

```
cd ../multiclient
```

   b. Type the following command:

```
ant getclient
```

4 To run the client, type the following command:

```
ant run
```

On the local system, the output looks something like this:

```
running application client container.
...
Sent message: text: id=1 to local app server
Sent message: text: id=2 to remote app server
ReplyListener: Received message: id=1, text=ReplyMsgBean processed message:
text: id=1 to local app server
Sent message: text: id=3 to local app server
ReplyListener: Received message: id=3, text=ReplyMsgBean processed message:
text: id=3 to local app server
ReplyListener: Received message: id=2, text=ReplyMsgBean processed message:
text: id=2 to remote app server
Sent message: text: id=4 to remote app server
ReplyListener: Received message: id=4, text=ReplyMsgBean processed message:
text: id=4 to remote app server
Sent message: text: id=5 to local app server
ReplyListener: Received message: id=5, text=ReplyMsgBean processed message:
text: id=5 to local app server
Sent message: text: id=6 to remote app server
ReplyListener: Received message: id=6, text=ReplyMsgBean processed message:
text: id=6 to remote app server
Sent message: text: id=7 to local app server
ReplyListener: Received message: id=7, text=ReplyMsgBean processed message:
text: id=7 to local app server
Sent message: text: id=8 to remote app server
ReplyListener: Received message: id=8, text=ReplyMsgBean processed message:
```

```
text: id=8 to remote app server
Sent message: text: id=9 to local app server
ReplyListener: Received message: id=9, text=ReplyMsgBean processed message:
text: id=9 to local app server
Sent message: text: id=10 to remote app server
ReplyListener: Received message: id=10, text=ReplyMsgBean processed message:
text: id=10 to remote app server
Waiting for 0 message(s) from local app server
Waiting for 0 message(s) from remote app server
Finished
Closing connection 1
Closing connection 2
```

On the local system, where the message-driven bean receives the odd-numbered messages, the output in the server log looks like this (wrapped in logging information):

```
ReplyMsgBean: Received message: text: id=1 to local app server
ReplyMsgBean: Received message: text: id=3 to local app server
ReplyMsgBean: Received message: text: id=5 to local app server
ReplyMsgBean: Received message: text: id=7 to local app server
ReplyMsgBean: Received message: text: id=9 to local app server
```

On the remote system, where the bean receives the even-numbered messages, the output in the server log looks like this (wrapped in logging information):

```
ReplyMsgBean: Received message: text: id=2 to remote app server
ReplyMsgBean: Received message: text: id=4 to remote app server
ReplyMsgBean: Received message: text: id=6 to remote app server
ReplyMsgBean: Received message: text: id=8 to remote app server
ReplyMsgBean: Received message: text: id=10 to remote app server
```

▼ To Disable Deployment on the Remote System

After running this example, you will probably want to return the GlassFish Server on jupiter to its previous state of not requiring a user name and password for administration.

1 **From a command prompt on the remote system (jupiter), enter the following command:**

   `asadmin disable-secure-admin`

   You will need to type the administration user name and password.

2 **Stop and restart the GlassFish Server on jupiter.**

3 **Start the Administration Console by opening a browser at http://localhost:4848/.**

   You will need to log in.

4 **In the navigation tree, expand the Configurations node, then expand the server-config node.**

5   Expand the Security node.

6   Expand the Realms node.

7   Select the admin-realm node.

8   On the Edit Realm page, click Manage Users.

9   In the File Users table, click admin in the User ID column.

10 On the Edit File Realm Users page, click Save.

11 In the dialog that asks you to confirm that you are setting an empty password for the specified user, click OK.

    The next time you start the Administration Console or issue an `asadmin` command, you will not need to provide login credentials.

CHAPTER 22

Bean Validation: Advanced Topics

This chapter describes how to create custom constraints, custom validator messages, and constraint groups using the Java API for JavaBeans Validation (Bean Validation).

The following topics are addressed here:

Creating Custom Constraints

Bean Validation defines annotations, interfaces, and classes to allow developers to create custom constraints.

Using the Built-In Constraints to Make a New Constraint

Bean Validation includes several built-in constraints that can be combined to create new, reusable constraints. This can simplify constraint definition by allowing developers to define a custom constraint made up of several built-in constraints that may then be applied to component attributes with a single annotation.

```
@Pattern.List({
  @Pattern(regexp = "[a-z0-9!#$%&'*+/=?^_'{|}~-]+(?:\\."
    +"[a-z0-9!#$%&'*+/=?^_'{|}~-]+)*"
    +"@(?:[a-z0-9](?:[a-z0-9-]*[a-z0-9])?\\.)+[a-z0-9](?:[a-z0-9-]*[a-z0-9])?")
})
@Constraint(validatedBy = {})
@Documented
@Target({ElementType.METHOD,
    ElementType.FIELD,
```

```
        ElementType.ANNOTATION_TYPE,
        ElementType.CONSTRUCTOR,
        ElementType.PARAMETER})
@Retention(RetentionPolicy.RUNTIME)
public @interface Email {

    String message() default "{invalid.email}";

    Class<?>[] groups() default {};

    Class<? extends Payload>[] payload() default {};

    @Target({ElementType.METHOD,
        ElementType.FIELD,
        ElementType.ANNOTATION_TYPE,
        ElementType.CONSTRUCTOR,
        ElementType.PARAMETER})
    @Retention(RetentionPolicy.RUNTIME)
    @Documented
    @interface List {
        Email[] value();
    }
}
```

This custom constraint can then be applied to an attribute.

```
...
@Email
protected String email;
...
```

Customizing Validator Messages

Bean Validation includes a resource bundle of default messages for the built-in constraints. These messages can be customized, and localized for non-English speaking locales.

The `ValidationMessages` Resource Bundle

The `Validationmessages` resource bundle and the locale variants of this resource bundle contain strings that override the default validation messages. The `ValidationMessages` resource bundle is typically a properties file, `ValidationMessages.properties`, in the default package of an application.

Localizing Validation Messages

Locale variants of `ValidationMessages.properties` are added by appending an underscore and the locale prefix to the base name of the file. For example, the Spanish locale variant resource bundle would be `ValidationMessages_es.properties`.

Grouping Constraints

Constraints may be added to one or more groups. Constraint groups are used to create subsets of constraints so only certain constraints will be validated for a particular object. By default, all constraints are included in the `Default` constraint group.

Constraint groups are represented by interfaces.

```
public interface Employee {}

public interface Contractor {}
```

Constraint groups can inherit from other groups.

```
public interface Manager extends Employee {}
```

When a constraint is added to an element, the constraint declares the groups to which that constraint belongs by specifying the class name of the group interface name in the `groups` element of the constraint.

```
@NotNull(groups=Employee.class)
Phone workPhone;
```

Multiple groups can be declared by surrounding the groups with angle brackets ({ and }) and separating the groups' class names with commas.

```
@NotNull(groups={ Employee.class, Contractor.class })
Phone workPhone;
```

If a group inherits from another group, validating that group results in validating all constraints declared as part of the supergroup. For example, validating the `Manager` group results in the `workPhone` field being validated, because `Employee` is a superinterface of `Manager`.

Customizing Group Validation Order

By default, constraint groups are validated in no particular order. There are cases where some groups should be validated before others. For example, in a particular class, basic data should be validated before more advanced data.

To set the validation order for a group, add a `javax.validation.GroupSequence` annotation to the interface definition, listing the order in which the validation should occur.

```
@GroupSequence({Default.class, ExpensiveValidationGroup.class})
public interface FullValidationGroup {}
```

When validating FullValidationGroup, first the Default group is validated. If all the data passes validation, then the ExpensiveValidationGroup group is validated. If a constraint is part of both the Default and the ExpensiveValidationGroup groups, the constraint is validated as part of the Default group, and will not be validated on the subsequent ExpensiveValidationGroup pass.

CHAPTER 23

Using Java EE Interceptors

This chapter discusses how to create interceptor classes and methods that interpose on method invocations or lifecycle events on a target class.

The following topics are addressed here:

- "Overview of Interceptors" on page 453
- "Using Interceptors" on page 455
- "The interceptor Example Application" on page 460

Overview of Interceptors

Interceptors are used in conjunction with Java EE managed classes to allow developers to invoke interceptor methods on an associated *target class*, in conjunction with method invocations or lifecycle events. Common uses of interceptors are logging, auditing, and profiling.

The Interceptors 1.1 specification is part of the final release of JSR 318, Enterprise JavaBeans 3.1, available from `http://jcp.org/en/jsr/detail?id=318`.

An interceptor can be defined within a target class as an *interceptor method*, or in an associated class called an *interceptor class*. Interceptor classes contain methods that are invoked in conjunction with the methods or lifecycle events of the target class.

Interceptor classes and methods are defined using metadata annotations, or in the deployment descriptor of the application containing the interceptors and target classes.

Note – Applications that use the deployment descriptor to define interceptors are not portable across Java EE servers.

Interceptor methods within the target class or in an interceptor class are annotated with one of the metadata annotations defined in Table 23–1.

TABLE 23–1 Interceptor Metadata Annotations

Interceptor Metadata Annotation	Description
`javax.interceptor.AroundInvoke`	Designates the method as an interceptor method.
`javax.interceptor.AroundTimeout`	Designates the method as a timeout interceptor, for interposing on timeout methods for enterprise bean timers.
`javax.annotation.PostConstruct`	Designates the method as an interceptor method for post-construct lifecycle events.
`javax.annotation.PreDestroy`	Designates the method as an interceptor method for pre-destroy lifecycle events.

Interceptor Classes

Interceptor classes may be designated with the optional `javax.interceptor.Interceptor` annotation, but interceptor classes aren't required to be so annotated. An interceptor class *must* have a public, no-argument constructor.

The target class can have any number of interceptor classes associated with it. The order in which the interceptor classes are invoked is determined by the order in which the interceptor classes are defined in the `javax.interceptor.Interceptors` annotation. However, this order can be overridden in the deployment descriptor.

Interceptor classes may be targets of dependency injection. Dependency injection occurs when the interceptor class instance is created, using the naming context of the associated target class, and before any @PostConstruct callbacks are invoked.

Interceptor Lifecycle

Interceptor classes have the same lifecycle as their associated target class. When a target class instance is created, an interceptor class instance is also created for each declared interceptor class in the target class. That is, if the target class declares multiple interceptor classes, an instance of each class is created when the target class instance is created. The target class instance and all interceptor class instances are fully instantiated before any @PostConstruct callbacks are invoked, and any @PreDestroy callbacks are invoked before the target class and interceptor class instances are destroyed.

Interceptors and CDI

Contexts and Dependency Injection for the Java EE Platform (CDI) builds on the basic functionality of Java EE interceptors. For information on CDI interceptors, including a discussion of interceptor binding types, see "Using Interceptors in CDI Applications" on page 260.

Using Interceptors

An interceptor is defined using one of the interceptor metadata annotations listed in Table 23–1 within the target class, or in a separate interceptor class. The following code declares an @AroundTimeout interceptor method within a target class.

```
@Stateless
public class TimerBean {
...
    @Schedule(minute="*/1", hour="*")
    public void automaticTimerMethod() { ... }

    @AroundTimeout
    public void timeoutInterceptorMethod(InvocationContext ctx) { ... }
...
}
```

If interceptor classes are used, use the javax.interceptor.Interceptors annotation to declare one or more interceptors at the class or method level of the target class. The following code declares interceptors at the class level.

```
@Stateless
@Interceptors({PrimaryInterceptor.class, SecondaryInterceptor.class})
public class OrderBean { ... }
```

The following code declares a method-level interceptor class.

```
@Stateless
public class OrderBean {
...
    @Interceptors(OrderInterceptor.class)
    public void placeOrder(Order order) { ... }
...
}
```

Intercepting Method Invocations

The `@AroundInvoke` annotation is used to designate interceptor methods for managed object methods. Only one around-invoke interceptor method per class is allowed. Around-invoke interceptor methods have the following form:

```
@AroundInvoke
visibility Object method-name(InvocationContext) throws Exception { ... }
```

For example:

```
@AroundInvoke
public void interceptOrder(InvocationContext ctx) { ... }
```

Around-invoke interceptor methods can have public, private, protected, or package-level access, and must not be declared static or final.

An around-invoke interceptor can call any component or resource callable by the target method on which it interposes, have the same security and transaction context as the target method, and run in the same Java virtual machine call-stack as the target method.

Around-invoke interceptors can throw any exception allowed by the throws clause of the target method. They may catch and suppress exceptions, and then recover by calling the `InvocationContext.proceed` method.

Using Multiple Method Interceptors

Use the `@Interceptors` annotation to declare multiple interceptors for a target method or class.

```
@Interceptors({PrimaryInterceptor.class, SecondaryInterceptor.class,
        LastInterceptor.class})
public void updateInfo(String info) { ... }
```

The order of the interceptors in the `@Interceptors` annotation is the order in which the interceptors are invoked.

Multiple interceptors may also be defined in the deployment descriptor. The order of the interceptors in the deployment descriptor is the order in which the interceptors will be invoked.

```
...
<interceptor-binding>
    <target-name>myapp.OrderBean</target-name>
    <interceptor-class>myapp.PrimaryInterceptor.class</interceptor-class>
    <interceptor-class>myapp.SecondaryInterceptor.class</interceptor-class>
    <interceptor-class>myapp.LastInterceptor.class</interceptor-class>
    <method-name>updateInfo</method-name>
</interceptor-binding>
...
```

To explicitly pass control to the next interceptor in the chain, call the `InvocationContext.proceed` method.

Data can be shared across interceptors:

- The same `InvocationContext` instance is passed as an input parameter to each interceptor method in the interceptor chain for a particular target method. The `InvocationContext` instance's `contextData` property is used to pass data across interceptor methods. The `contextData` property is a `java.util.Map<String, Object>` object. Data stored in `contextData` is accessible to interceptor methods further down the interceptor chain.

- The data stored in `contextData` is not sharable across separate target class method invocations. That is, a different `InvocationContext` object is created for each invocation of the method in the target class.

Accessing Target Method Parameters From an Interceptor Class

The `InvocationContext` instance passed to each around-invoke method may be used to access and modify the parameters of the target method. The `parameters` property of `InvocationContext` is an array of `Object` instances that corresponds to the parameter order of the target method. For example, for the following target method, the `parameters` property, in the `InvocationContext` instance passed to the around-invoke interceptor method in `PrimaryInterceptor`, is an `Object` array containing two `String` objects (`firstName` and `lastName`) and a `Date` object (`date`):

```
@Interceptors(PrimaryInterceptor.class)
public void updateInfo(String firstName, String lastName, Date date) { ... }
```

The parameters can be accessed and modified using the `InvocationContext.getParameters` and `InvocationContext.setParameters` methods, respectively.

Intercepting Lifecycle Callback Events

Interceptors for lifecycle callback events (post-create and pre-destroy) may be defined in the target class or in interceptor classes. The `@PostCreate` annotation is used to designate a method as a post-create lifecycle event interceptor. The `@PreDestroy` annotation is used to designate a method as a pre-destroy lifecycle event interceptor.

Lifecycle event interceptors defined within the target class have the following form:

```
void method-name() { ... }
```

For example:

```
@PostCreate
void initialize() { ... }
```

Lifecycle event interceptors defined in an interceptor class have the following form:

```
void <method-name>(InvocationContext) { ... }
```

For example:

```
@PreDestroy
void cleanup(InvocationContext ctx) { ... }
```

Lifecycle interceptor methods can have public, private, protected, or package-level access, and must not be declared static or final.

Lifecycle interceptor methods are called in an unspecified security and transaction context. That is, portable Java EE applications should not assume the lifecycle event interceptor method has access to a security or transaction context. Only one interceptor method for each lifecycle event (post-create and pre-destroy) is allowed per class.

Using Multiple Lifecycle Callback Interceptors

Multiple lifecycle interceptors may be defined for a target class by specifying the interceptor classes in the @Interceptors annotation:

```
@Interceptors({PrimaryInterceptor.class, SecondaryInterceptor.class,
        LastInterceptor.class})
@Stateless
public class OrderBean { ... }
```

The order in which the interceptor classes are listed in the @Interceptors annotation defines the order in which the interceptors are invoked.

Data stored in the contextData property of InvocationContext is not sharable across different lifecycle events.

Intercepting Timeout Events

Interceptors for EJB timer service timeout methods may be defined using the @AroundTimeout annotation on methods in the target class or in an interceptor class. Only one @AroundTimeout method per class is allowed.

Timeout interceptors have the following form:

```
Object <method-name>(InvocationContext) throws Exception { ... }
```

For example:

```
@AroundTimeout
protected void timeoutInterceptorMethod(InvocationContext ctx) { ... }
```

Timeout interceptor methods can have public, private, protected, or package-level access, and must not be declared static or final.

Timeout interceptors can call any component or resource callable by the target timeout method, and are invoked in the same transaction and security context as the target method.

Timeout interceptors may access the timer object associated with the target timeout method through the InvocationContext instance's getTimer method.

Using Multiple Timeout Interceptors

Multiple timeout interceptors may be defined for a given target class by specifying the interceptor classes containing @AroundTimeout interceptor methods in an @Interceptors annotation at the class level.

If a target class specifies timeout interceptors in an interceptor class, and also has a @AroundTimeout interceptor method within the target class itself, the timeout interceptors in the interceptor classes are called first, followed by the timeout interceptors defined in the target class. For example, in the following example, assume that both the PrimaryInterceptor and SecondaryInterceptor classes have timeout interceptor methods.

```
@Interceptors({PrimaryInterceptor.class, SecondaryInterceptor.class})
@Stateful
public class OrderBean {
...
    @AroundTimeout
    private void last(InvocationContext ctx) { ... }
...
}
```

The timeout interceptor in PrimaryInterceptor will be called first, followed by the timeout interceptor in SecondaryInterceptor, and finally the last method defined in the target class.

The `interceptor` **Example Application**

The `interceptor` example demonstrates how to use an interceptor class, containing an `@AroundInvoke` interceptor method, with a stateless session bean.

The `HelloBean` stateless session bean is a simple enterprise bean with two business methods, `getName` and `setName`, to retrieve and modify a string. The `setName` business method has an `@Interceptors` annotation that specifies an interceptor class, `HelloInterceptor`, for that method.

```
@Interceptors(HelloInterceptor.class)
public void setName(String name) {
    this.name = name;
}
```

The `HelloInterceptor` class defines an `@AroundInvoke` interceptor method, `modifyGreeting`, that converts the string passed to `HelloBean.setName` to lowercase.

```
@AroundInvoke
public Object modifyGreeting(InvocationContext ctx) throws Exception {
    Object[] parameters = ctx.getParameters();
    String param = (String) parameters[0];
    param = param.toLowerCase();
    parameters[0] = param;
    ctx.setParameters(parameters);
    try {
        return ctx.proceed();
    } catch (Exception e) {
        logger.warning("Error calling ctx.proceed in modifyGreeting()");
        return null;
    }
}
```

The parameters to `HelloBean.setName` are retrieved and stored in an `Object` array by calling the `InvocationContext.getParameters` method. Because `setName` has only one parameter, it is the first and only element in the array. The string is set to lowercase and stored in the `parameters` array, then passed to `InvocationContext.setParameters`. To return control to the session bean, `InvocationContext.proceed` is called.

The user interface of `interceptor` is a JavaServer Faces web application that consists of two Facelets views: `index.xhtml`, which contains a form for entering the name, and `response.xhtml`, which displays the final name.

Running the `interceptor` **Example**

You can use either NetBeans IDE or Ant to build, package, deploy, and run the `interceptor` example.

▼ To Run the interceptor Example Using NetBeans IDE

1 From the File menu, choose Open Project.

2 In the Open Project dialog, navigate to *tut-install*/**examples/ejb/**.

3 Select the interceptor folder and click Open Project.

4 In the Projects tab, right-click the interceptor project and select Run.

   This will compile, deploy, and run the interceptor example, opening a web browser page to http://localhost:8080/interceptor/.

5 Type a name into the form and select Submit.

   The name will be converted to lowercase by the method interceptor defined in the HelloInterceptor class.

▼ To Run the interceptor Example Using Ant

1 Go to the following directory:

   tut-install/examples/ejb/interceptor/

2 To compile the source files and package the application, use the following command:

   ant

   This command calls the default target, which builds and packages the application into a WAR file, interceptor.war, located in the dist directory.

3 To deploy and run the application using Ant, use the following command:

   ant run

   This command deploys and runs the interceptor example, opening a web browser page to http://localhost:8080/interceptor/.

4 Type a name into the form and select Submit.

   The name will be converted to lowercase by the method interceptor defined in the HelloInterceptor class.

CHAPTER 24

The Resource Adapter Example

The `mailconnector` example shows how you can use a resource adapter, a message-driven bean (MDB), and JavaServer Faces technology to create an application that can send email messages and browse for messages. This example uses a sample implementation of the JavaMail API called `mock-javamail`. The resource adapter is deployed separately, while the MDB and the web application are packaged in an EAR file.

The following topics are addressed here:

The Resource Adapter

The `mailconnector` resource adapter enables the MDB to receive email messages that are delivered to a specific mailbox folder on a mail server. It also provides connection factory objects clients can use to obtain connection objects that allow them to synchronously query email servers for new messages in a specific mailbox folder.

In this example, the MDB activates the resource adapter, but it does not receive email messages. Instead, this example allows users to synchronously query an email server for new messages.

The components of the resource adapter are as follows:

- `mailconnector.ra`: Base class of the `mailconnector` resource adapter

- `mailconnector.ra/inbound`: Classes that implement the inbound resource adapter, which supports delivery of JavaMail messages to MDBs

- `mailconnector.ra/outbound`: Classes that implement the outbound resource adapter, which supports synchronous queries to email servers
- `mailconnector.api`: Interfaces that are implemented by MDBs associated with this resource adapter and by the `Connection` and `ConnectionFactoryinterfaces` provided by the outbound resource adapter
- `mailconnector.share`: JavaBeans class that implements the `ConnectionSpec` interface, allowing properties to be passed to the outbound resource adapter

When the resource adapter is deployed, it uses the Work Management facilities available to resource adapters to start a thread that monitors mailbox folders for new messages. The polling thread of the resource adapter monitors the mailbox folders every 30 seconds for new messages.

The Message-Driven Bean

The `mailconnector` message-driven bean, `JavaMailMessageBean`, activates the resource adapter. When an MDB is deployed, the application server passes the MDB's activation config properties (commented out in this case) to the `mailconnector` resource adapter, which forwards it to the polling thread. When the MDB is undeployed, the application server notifies the resource adapter, which notifies the polling thread to stop monitoring the mail folder associated with the MDB being undeployed.

The MDB is packaged in an EJB JAR file.

The Web Application

The web application in the `mailconnector` example contains an HTML page (`index.html`), Facelets pages, and managed beans that let you log in, send email messages to a mailbox folder, and query for new messages in a mail folder using the connection interfaces provided by the `mailconnector` resource adapter.

The application protects the Facelets pages by using form-based authentication, specified through a security constraint in the `web.xml` file.

The web application is packaged in a WAR file.

Running the `mailconnector` Example

You can use either NetBeans IDE or Ant to build, package, deploy, and run the `mailconnector` example.

▼ Before You Deploy the `mailconnector` Example

Before you deploy the `mailconnector` application, perform the following steps.

1 Download `mock-javamail-1.9.jar` from
  `http://download.java.net/maven/2/org/jvnet/mock-javamail/mock-javamail/1.9/`.

2 Copy this JAR file to the directory *as-install*/`lib`.

3 Restart GlassFish Server.

4 Open the GlassFish Server Administration Console in a web browser at
  `http://localhost:4848`.

5 In the Administration Console, expand the Configurations node, then expand the
  `server-config` node.

6 Select the Security node.

7 Select the Default Principal to Role Mapping Enabled check box.

8 Click Save.

▼ To Build, Package, and Deploy the `mailconnector` Example Using NetBeans IDE

1 From the File menu, choose Open Project.

2 In the Open Project dialog, navigate to:
  tut-install/`examples/connectors/mailconnector/`

3 Select the `mailconnector-ra` folder and click Open Project.

4 In the Projects tab, right-click the `mailconnector-ra` project and select Build.
  This command builds the resource adapter. It also places identical files named
  `mailconnector.rar` and `mailconnector.jar` in the `mailconnector` directory.

5   In the Projects tab, right-click the `mailconnector-ra` project and select Deploy.

6   From the File menu, choose Open Project.

7   In the Open Project dialog, navigate to:

     tut-install/examples/connectors/mailconnector/

8   Select the `mailconnector-ear` folder.

9   Select the Open Required Projects check box and click Open Project.

10   In the Projects tab, right-click the `mailconnector-ear` project and select Build.

11   In a terminal window, navigate to:

     tut-install/examples/connectors/mailconnector/mailconnector-ear/

12   Enter the following command to create the resources and users:

     `ant setup`

13   In NetBeans IDE, in the Projects tab, right-click the `mailconnector-ear` project and select Deploy.

▼ To Build, Package, and Deploy the `mailconnector` Example Using Ant

1   In a terminal window, go to:

     tut-install/examples/connectors/mailconnector/mailconnector-ear/

2   Enter the following command:

     `ant all`

     This command builds and deploys the `mailconnector-ra` RAR file, sets up users and resources, then builds and deploys the `mailconnector-ear` EAR file. It also places identical files named `mailconnector.rar` and `mailconnector.jar` in the `mailconnector` directory.

▼ To Run the `mailconnector` Example

1   In a web browser, navigate to the following URL:

     `http://localhost:8080/mailconnector-war/`

2 **Log in with a user name of either user1, user2, user3, or user4. The password is the same as the user name.**

You can send messages and browse for the messages you sent. The messages you sent are available 30 seconds after you sent them.

For example, you can log in as user1 and send a message to user4, then log in as user4 and query for messages. In the form for browsing messages, verify that the fields are correct, then click Browse.

View the server log to follow the flow of the application. Most classes and methods specify logging information that makes the sequence of events easy to follow.

3 **Before you undeploy the application, in a terminal window, navigate to** *tut-install*/**examples/connectors/mailconnector/mailconnector-ear/ and enter the following command to remove the resources and users:**

`ant takedown`

You cannot undeploy the resource adapter until you run this command.

Next Steps When you clean the application, you can also remove the mailconnector.rar and mailconnector.jar files from the mailconnector directory.

Remove the mock-javamail-1.9.jar file from the *as-install*/lib directory if you might run any other applications that use the JavaMail API (for example, "The async Example Application" on page 244).

PART IX

Case Studies

Part IX presents case studies that use a variety of Java EE technologies. This part contains the following chapters:

CHAPTER 25

Duke's Bookstore Case Study Example

The Duke's Bookstore example is a simple e-commerce application that illustrates some of the more advanced features of JavaServer Faces technology in combination with Contexts and Dependency Injection for the Java EE Platform (CDI), enterprise beans, and the Java Persistence API. Users can select books from an image map, view the bookstore catalog, and purchase books. No security is used in this application.

The following topics are addressed here:

- "Design and Architecture of Duke's Bookstore" on page 471
- "The Duke's Bookstore Interface" on page 472
- "Running the Duke's Bookstore Case Study Application" on page 477

Design and Architecture of Duke's Bookstore

Duke's Bookstore is a simple web application that uses many features of JavaServer Faces technology, in addition to other Java EE 6 features:

- JavaServer Faces technology, as well as Contexts and Dependency Injection for the Java EE Platform (CDI):

    - A set of Facelets pages, along with a template, provides the user interface to the application.

    - CDI managed beans are associated with each of the Facelets pages.

    - A custom image map component on the front page allows you to select a book to enter the store. Each area of the map is represented by a JavaServer Faces managed bean. Text hyperlinks are also provided for accessibility.

    - Action listeners are registered on the image map and the text hyperlinks. These listeners retrieve the ID value for the selected book and store it in the session map so it can be retrieved by the managed bean for the next page.

    - The h:dataTable tag is used to render the book catalog and shopping cart contents dynamically.

- A custom converter is registered on the credit card field on the checkout page, bookcashier.xhtml, which also uses an f:validateRegEx tag to ensure that the input is correctly formatted.
- A value-change listener is registered on the name field on bookcashier.xhtml. This listener saves the name in a parameter so the following page, bookreceipt.xhtml, can access it.

- Enterprise beans: Local, no-interface-view stateless session bean and singleton bean
- A Java Persistence API entity

The packages of the Duke's Bookstore application, located in the *tut-install*/examples/case-studies/dukes-bookstore/src/java/dukesbookstore/ directory, are as follows:

- components: Includes the custom UI component classes, MapComponent and AreaComponent
- converters: Includes the custom converter class, CreditCardConverter
- ejb: Includes two enterprise beans:
  - A singleton bean, ConfigBean, that initializes the data in the database
  - A stateless session bean, BookRequestBean, that contains the business logic to manage the entity
- entity: Includes the Book entity class
- exceptions: Includes three exception classes
- listeners: Includes the event handler and event listener classes
- model: Includes a model JavaBeans class
- renderers: Includes the custom renderers for the custom UI component classes
- web.managedbeans: Includes the managed beans for the Facelets pages
- web.messages: Includes the resource bundle files for localized messages

The Duke's Bookstore Interface

This section provides additional detail regarding the components of the Duke's Bookstore example and how they interact.

The Book Java Persistence API Entity

The Book entity, located in the dukesbookstore.entity package, encapsulates the book data stored by Duke's Bookstore.

The Book entity defines attributes used in the example:

- A book ID
- The author's first name
- The author's surname
- The title
- The price
- Whether the book is on sale
- The publication year
- A description of the book
- The number of copies in the inventory

The Book entity also defines a simple named query, findBooks.

Enterprise Beans Used in Duke's Bookstore

Two enterprise beans located in the dukesbookstore.ejb package provide the business logic for Duke's Bookstore.

BookRequestBean is a stateless session bean that contains the business methods for the application. The methods create, retrieve, and purchase books, and update the inventory for a book. To retrieve the books, the getBooks method calls the findBooks named query defined in the Book entity.

ConfigBean is a singleton session bean used to create the books in the catalog when the application is initially deployed. It calls the createBook method defined in BookRequestBean.

Facelets Pages and Managed Beans Used in Duke's Bookstore

The Duke's Bookstore application uses Facelets and its templating features to display the user interface. The Facelets pages interact with a set of CDI managed beans that provide the underlying properties and methods for the user interface. The front page also interacts with the custom components used by the application.

The application uses the following Facelets pages, which are located in the *tut-install*/examples/case-studies/dukes-bookstore/web/ directory:

bookstoreTemplate.xhtml   The template file, which specifies a header used on every page as well as the style sheet used by all the pages. The template also retrieves the language set in the web browser.

Uses the LocaleBean managed bean.

`index.xhtml`	Landing page, which lays out the custom map and area components using managed beans configured in the `faces-config.xml` file, and allows the user to select a book and advance to the `bookstore.xhtml` page.
`bookstore.xhtml`	Page that allows the user to obtain details on the selected book or the featured book, to add either book to the shopping cart, and to advance to the `bookcatalog.xhtml` page.
	Uses the `BookstoreBean` managed bean.
`bookdetails.xhtml`	Page that shows details on a book selected from `bookstore.xhtml` or other pages and allows the user to add the book to the cart and/or advance to the `bookcatalog.xhtml`.
	Uses the `BookDetailsBean` managed bean.
`bookcatalog.xhtml`	Page that displays the books in the catalog and allows the user to add books to the shopping cart, view the details for any book, view the shopping cart, empty the shopping cart, or purchase the books in the shopping cart.
	Uses the `CatalogBean` and `ShoppingCart` managed beans.
`bookshowcart.xhtml`	Page that displays the contents of the shopping cart and allows the user to remove items, view the details for an item, empty the shopping cart, purchase the books in the shopping cart, or return to the catalog.
	Uses the `ShowCartBean` and `ShoppingCart` managed beans.
`bookcashier.xhtml`	Page that allows the user to purchase books, specify a shipping option, subscribe to newsletters, or join the Duke Fan Club with a purchase over a certain amount.
	Uses the `CashierBean` and `ShoppingCart` managed beans.

bookreceipt.xhtml   Page that confirms the user's purchase and allows the
                           user to return to the catalog page to continue
                           shopping.

                           Uses the `CashierBean` managed bean.

In addition to the managed beans used by the Facelets template and pages, the
application uses the following managed beans:

AbstractBean   Contains utility methods called by other managed beans.

ShoppingCartItem   Contains methods called by `ShoppingCart`, `CatalogBean`, and
                           `ShowCartBean`.

Custom Components and Other Custom Objects Used in Duke's Bookstore

The map and area custom components for Duke's Bookstore, along with associated
renderer, listener, and model classes, are defined in the following packages in the
tut-install/examples/case-studies/dukes-bookstore/src/java/dukesbookstore/
directory:

components   Contains the `MapComponent` and `AreaComponent` classes. See
                           "Creating Custom Component Classes" on page 106.

listeners   Contains the `AreaSelectedEvent` class, along with other listener
                           classes. See "Handling Events for Custom Components" on page 119.

model   Contains the `ImageArea` class. See "Configuring Model Data" on
                           page 103.

renderers   Contains the `MapRenderer` and `AreaRenderer` classes. See
                           "Delegating Rendering to a Renderer" on page 114.

The *tut-install*/examples/case-studies/dukes-bookstore/src/java/
dukesbookstore/ directory also contains a custom converter and other custom
listeners not specifically tied to the custom components:

converters   Contains the `CreditCardConverter` class. See "Creating and Using a
                           Custom Converter" on page 123.

listeners   Contains the `LinkBookChangeListener`, `MapBookChangeListener`,
                           and `NameChanged` classes. See "Implementing an Event Listener" on
                           page 117.

Properties Files Used in Duke's Bookstore

The strings used in the Duke's Bookstore application are encapsulated into resource bundles to allow the display of localized strings in multiple locales. The properties files, located in the *tut-install*/examples/case-studies/dukes-bookstore/src/java/ dukesbookstore/web/messages/ directory, consist of a default file containing English strings and three additional files for other locales. The files are as follows:

Messages.properties   Default file, containing English strings

Messages_de.properties   File containing German strings

Messages_es.properties   File containing Spanish strings

Messages_fr.properties   File containing French strings

The language setting in the user's web browser determines which locale is used. The html tag in bookstoreTemplate.xhtml retrieves the language setting from the language property of LocaleBean:

```
<html lang="#{localeBean.language}"
...
```

For more information about resource bundles, see Chapter 9, "Internationalizing and Localizing Web Applications."

The resource bundle is configured as follows in the faces-config.xml file:

```
<application>
    <resource-bundle>
        <base-name>dukesbookstore.web.messages.Messages</base-name>
        <var>bundle</var>
    </resource-bundle>
    <locale-config>
        <default-locale>en</default-locale>
        <supported-locale>de</supported-locale>
        <supported-locale>fr</supported-locale>
        <supported-locale>es</supported-locale>
    </locale-config>
</application>
```

This configuration means that in the Facelets pages, messages are retrieved using the prefix bundle with the key found in the Messages_*locale*.properties file, as in the following example from the index.xhtml page:

```
<h:outputText style="font-weight:bold"
              value="#{bundle.ChooseBook}" />
```

In Messages.properties, the key string is defined as follows:

```
ChooseBook=Choose a Book from our Catalog
```

Deployment Descriptors Used in Duke's Bookstore

The following deployment descriptors are used in Duke's Bookstore:

src/conf/persistence.xml	The Java Persistence API configuration file
web/WEB-INF/beans.xml	An empty deployment descriptor file used to enable the CDI runtime
web/WEB-INF/bookstore.taglib.xml	The tag library descriptor file for the custom components
web/WEB-INF/faces-config.xml	The JavaServer Faces configuration file, which configures the managed beans for the map component as well as the resource bundles for the application
web/WEB-INF/glassfish-web.xml	The GlassFish-specific configuration file
web/WEB-INF/web.xml	The web application configuration file

Running the Duke's Bookstore Case Study Application

You can use either NetBeans IDE or Ant to build, package, deploy, and run the Duke's Bookstore application.

▼ To Build and Deploy Duke's Bookstore Using NetBeans IDE

Before You Begin You must have already configured GlassFish Server as a Java EE server in NetBeans IDE, as described in "To Add GlassFish Server as a Server in NetBeans IDE" on page 40.

1 From the File menu, choose Open Project.

2 In the Open Project dialog, navigate to:

   tut-install/examples/case-studies/

3 Select the Open as Main Project check box.

4 Click Open Project.

5 Right-click dukes-bookstore in the project pane and select Deploy.

   This will build, package, and deploy Duke's Bookstore to the GlassFish Server, starting the Java DB database and GlassFish Server if they have not already been started.

▼ To Build and Deploy Duke's Bookstore Using Ant

Before You Begin Make sure the GlassFish Server is started as described in "Starting and Stopping the GlassFish Server" on page 41 and the Java DB server is started as described in "Starting and Stopping the Java DB Server" on page 43.

1 In a terminal window, go to:

   tut-install/examples/case-studies/dukes-bookstore/

2 Type the following command:

   ant all

   This command builds, packages, and deploys Duke's Bookstore to the GlassFish Server.

▼ To Run Duke's Bookstore

1 In a web browser, type the following URL:

   http://localhost:8080/dukesbookstore/

2 On the Duke's Bookstore main page, click a book in the graphic, or click one of the links at the bottom of the page.

3 Use the pages in the application to view and purchase books.

CHAPTER 26

Duke's Tutoring Case Study Example

The Duke's Tutoring example application is a tracking system for a tutoring center for students. Students or their guardians can check in and out. The tutoring center can track attendance and status updates and can store contact information for guardians and students.

The following topics are addressed here:

- "Design and Architecture of Duke's Tutoring" on page 479
- "Main Interface" on page 481
- "Administration Interface" on page 486
- "Running the Duke's Tutoring Case Study Application" on page 487

Design and Architecture of Duke's Tutoring

Duke's Tutoring is a web application that incorporates several Java EE technologies. It exposes both a main interface (for students, guardians, and tutoring center staff) and an administration interface (for staff to maintain the system). The business logic for both interfaces is provided by enterprise beans. The enterprise beans use the Java Persistence API to create and store the application's data in the database. Figure 26–1 illustrates the architecture of the application.

FIGURE 26-1   Architecture of the Duke's Tutoring Example Application

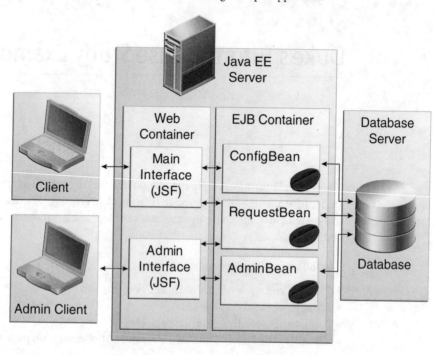

The Duke's Tutoring application is organized into two main projects, the dukes-tutoring-common library, and the dukes-tutoring-war web application. The dukes-tutoring-common library project contains the entity classes and helper classes used by the dukes-tutoring-war web application, and dukes-tutoring-common is packaged and deployed with dukes-tutoring-war. The library JAR file is useful for allowing the entity classes and helper classes to be reused by other applications, such as a JavaFX client application.

Duke's Tutoring uses the following Java EE 6 platform features:

- Java Persistence API entities

  - Java API for JavaBeans Validation (Bean Validation) annotations on the entities for verifying data

  - A custom Bean Validation annotation, @Email, for validating email addresses

- Enterprise beans

  - Local, no-interface-view session and singleton beans
  - JAX-RS resources in a session bean
  - Java EE security constraints on the administrative interface business methods
  - All enterprise beans packaged within the WAR

- JavaServer Faces technology, using Facelets for the web front end
  - Templating
  - Composite components
  - A custom formatter, `PhoneNumberFormatter`
  - Security constraints on the administrative interface
  - AJAX-enabled Facelets components
  - Custom converters for the entity classes used in the user-interface components

The Duke's Tutoring application has two main user interfaces, both packaged within a single WAR file:

- The main interface, for students, guardians, and staff
- The administrative interface used by the staff to manage the students and guardians, and to generate attendance reports

Apart from the main and administrative interfaces, there is a JUnit test that demonstrates how to use the embedded EJB container to test the business logic of the session beans.

Main Interface

The main interface allows students and staff to check students in and out, and record when students are outside at the playground.

Java Persistence API Entities Used in the Main Interface

The entities used in the main interface encapsulate data stored and manipulated by Duke's Tutoring, and are located in the `dukestutoring.entity` package in the `dukes-tutoring-common` project.

The `Person` entity defines attributes common to students, guardians, and administrators tracked by the application. These attributes are the person's name and contact information, including phone numbers and email address. The phone number and email address attributes have Bean Validation annotations to ensure that the submitted data is well-formed. The email attribute uses a custom validation class, `dukestutoring.util.Email`. The `Person` entity has three subclasses, `Student`, `Guardian`, and `Administrator`. For additional data common to all people, the `PersonDetails` entity is used to store attributes like pictures and the person's birthday, which aren't included in the `Person` entity for performance reasons.

The `Student` entity stores attributes specific to the students who come to tutoring. This includes information like the student's grade level and school. The `Guardian` entity's attributes are specific to the parents or guardians of a `Student`. Students and guardians have a many-to-many relationship. That is, a student may have a one or more guardians, and a guardian may have one or more students. The Administrator entity is for staff who manage the tutoring center.

The Address entity represents a mailing address, and is associated with Person entities. Addresses and people have a many-to-one relationship. That is, one person may have many addresses.

The TutoringSession entity represents a particular day at the tutoring center. A particular tutoring session tracks which students attended that day, and which students went to the park. Associated with TutoringSession is the StatusEntry entity, which logs when a student's status changes. Students' status changes when they check in to a tutoring session, when they go to the park, and when they check out. The status entry allows the tutoring center staff to track exactly which students attended a tutoring session, when they checked in and out, which students went to the park while they were at the tutoring center, and when they went to and came back from the park.

For information on creating Java Persistence API entities, see Chapter 19, "Introduction to the Java Persistence API," in *The Java EE 6 Tutorial: Basic Concepts*. For information on validating entity data, see "Validating Persistent Fields and Properties" in *The Java EE 6 Tutorial: Basic Concepts* and Chapter 22, "Bean Validation: Advanced Topics."

Enterprise Beans Used in the Main Interface

The enterprise beans used in the main interface provide the business logic for Duke's Tutoring, and are located in the dukestutoring.ejb package in the dukes-tutoring-war project.

ConfigBean is singleton session bean used to create the default students, guardians, and administrator when the application is initially deployed, and to create an automatic EJB timer that creates tutoring session entities every weekday.

RequestBean is a stateless session bean containing the business methods for the main interface. Students or staff can check students in and out and track when they go to and come back from the park. The bean also has business methods for retrieving lists of students. The business methods in RequestBean use strongly-typed Criteria API queries to retrieve data from the database.

For information on creating and using enterprise beans, see Part IV, "Enterprise Beans," in *The Java EE 6 Tutorial: Basic Concepts*. For information on creating strongly-typed Criteria API queries, see Chapter 22, "Using the Criteria API to Create Queries," in *The Java EE 6 Tutorial: Basic Concepts*.

Facelets Files Used in the Main Interface

The Duke's Tutoring application uses Facelets to display the user interface, and makes extensive use of the templating features of Facelets. Facelets is the default display technology for JavaServer Faces, and consists of XHTML files located in the *tut-install*/examples/case-studies/dukes-tutoring/dukes-tutoring-war/web/ directory.

The following Facelets files are used in the main interface:

`template.xhtml`
    Template file for the main interface

`error.xhtml`
    Error file employed if something goes wrong

`index.xhtml`
    Landing page for the main interface

`park.xhtml`
    Page showing who is currently at the park

`current.xhtml`
    Page showing who is currently in today's tutoring session

`statusEntries.xhtml`
    Page showing the detailed status entry log for today's session

`resources/components/allStudentsTable.xhtml`
    A composite component for a table displaying all active students

`resources/components/currentSessionTable.xhtml`
    A composite component for a table displaying all students in today's session

`resources/components/parkTable.xhtml`
    A composite component for a table displaying all students currently at the park

`WEB-INF/includes/navigation.xhtml`
    XHTML fragment for the main interface's navigation bar

`WEB-INF/includes/footer.xhtml`
    XHTML fragment for the main interface's footer

For information on using Facelets, see Chapter 5, "Introduction to Facelets," in *The Java EE 6 Tutorial: Basic Concepts*.

Helper Classes Used in the Main Interface

The following helper classes, found in the dukes-tutoring-common project's dukestutoring.util package, are used in the main interface:

CalendarUtil   A class that provides a method to strip the unnecessary time data from java.util.Calendar instances

Email   A custom Bean Validation annotation class for validating email addresses in the Person entity

StatusType   An enumerated type defining the different statuses that a student can have. Possible values are IN, OUT, and PARK. StatusType is used throughout the application, including in the StatusEntry entity, and throughout the main interface. StatusType also defines a toString method that returns a localized translation of the status based on the locale.

The following helper classes, found in the dukes-tutoring-war project's dukestutoring.web.util package, are used in the JavaServer Faces application:

EntityConverter   A parent class to StudentConverter and GuardianConverter that defines a cache to store the entity classes when converting the entities for use in JavaServer Faces user-interface components. The cache helps increase performance. The cache is stored in the JavaServer Faces context.

StudentConverter   A JavaServer Faces converter for the Student entity class. This class contains methods to convert Student instances to strings and back again, so they can be used in the user-interface components of the application.

GuardianConverter   Similar to StudentConverter, this class is a converter for the Guardian entity class.

Properties Files

The strings used in the main interface are encapsulated into resource bundles to allow the display of localized strings in multiple locales. Each of the properties files has locale-specific files appended with locale codes, containing the translated strings for each locale. For example, Messages_es.properties contains the localized strings for Spanish locales.

The `dukestutoring.util` package in the `dukes-tutoring-common` project has the following resource bundle:

`StatusMessages`   Strings for each of the status types defined in the `StatusType` enumerated type for the default locale. Each supported locale has a property file of the form `StatusMessages_locale prefix.properties` containing the localized strings. For example, the strings for Spanish-speaking locales are located in `StatusMessages_es.properties`.

The `dukes-tutoring-war` project has the following resource bundles:

`ValidationMessages.properties`
Strings for the default locale used by the Bean Validation runtime to display validation messages. This file must be named `ValidationMessages.properties` and located in the default package as required by the Bean Validation specification. Each supported locale has a property file of the form `ValidationMessages_locale prefix.properties` containing the localized strings. For example, the strings for German-speaking locales are located in `ValidationMessages_de.properties`.

`dukestutoring/web/messages/Messages.properties`
Strings for the default locale for the main and administration Facelets interfaces. Each supported locale has a property file of the form `Messages_locale prefix.properties` containing the localized strings. For example, the strings for simplified Chinese-speaking locales are located in `Messages_zh.properties`.

For information on localizing web applications, see "Registering Application Messages" on page 155.

Deployment Descriptors Used in Duke's Tutoring

The following deployment descriptors in the `dukes-tutoring-war` project are used in Duke's Tutoring:

`src/conf/beans.xml`	An empty deployment descriptor file used to enable the CDI runtime
`web/WEB-INF/faces-config.xml`	The JavaServer Faces configuration file
`web/WEB-INF/glassfish-web.xml`	The GlassFish-specific configuration file
`web/WEB-INF/web.xml`	The web application configuration file

The following deployment descriptor in the `dukes-tutoring-common` project is used in Duke's Tutoring:

`src/META-INF/persistence.xml`	The Java Persistence API configuration file

No enterprise bean deployment descriptor is used in Duke's Tutoring. Annotations in the enterprise bean class files are used for the configuration of enterprise beans in this application.

Administration Interface

The administration interface of Duke's Tutoring is used by the tutoring center staff to manage the data employed by the main interface: the students, the students' guardians, and the addresses. The administration interface uses many of the same components as the main interface. Additional components that are only used in the administration interface are described here.

Enterprise Beans Used in the Administration Interface

The following enterprise beans, in the `dukestutoring.ejb` package, are used in the administration interface:

AdminBean   A stateless session bean for all the business logic used in the administration interface. Contains security constraint annotations to allow invocation of the business methods only by authorized users.

Facelets Files Used in the Administration Interface

The following Facelets files are used in the administration interface:

`admin/adminTemplate.xhtml`	Template for the administration interface
`admin/index.xhtml`	Landing page for the administration interface
`admin/login.xhtml`	Login page for the security-constrained administration interface
`admin/loginError.xhtml`	Page displayed if there are errors authenticating the administration user
`admin/address` directory	Pages that allow you to create, edit, and delete `Address` entities

`admin/guardian` directory	Pages that allow you to create, edit, and delete `Guardian` entities
`admin/student` directory	Pages that allow you to create, edit, and delete `Student` entities
`resources/components/formLogin.xhtml`	Composite component for a login form using Java EE security
`WEB-INF/includes/adminNav.xhtml`	XHTML fragment for the administration interface's navigation bar

Running the Duke's Tutoring Case Study Application

This section describes how to build, package, deploy, and run the Duke's Tutoring application.

Setting Up GlassFish Server

Before running the Duke's Tutoring application, set up the security realm used by Duke's Tutoring with users and groups. The user names and passwords set in this security realm are used to log in to the administration interface of Duke's Tutoring.

Duke's Tutoring's security realm maps members of the `Administrator` entity to the `Administrator` role used in the security constraint annotations in `AdminBean`.

▼ To Create the JDBC Realm in GlassFish Server

Create the `tutoringRealm` JDBC security realm in GlassFish Server.

Before You Begin Make sure GlassFish Server is started as described in "Starting and Stopping the GlassFish Server" on page 41, and Java DB is started as described in "Starting and Stopping the Java DB Server" on page 43.

1 In a terminal window, go to:

tut-install/examples/case-studies/dukes-tutoring/dukes-tutoring-war/

2 Enter the following command:

`ant create-tutoring-realm`

This target creates a JDBC realm using the `jdbc/tutoring` JDBC resource, which will be created when `dukes-tutoring-war` has been deployed.

Running Duke's Tutoring

You can use either NetBeans IDE or Ant to build, package, deploy, and run Duke's Tutoring.

▼ To Build and Deploy Duke's Tutoring in NetBeans IDE

Before You Begin   You must have already configured GlassFish Server as a Java EE server in NetBeans IDE, as described in "To Add GlassFish Server as a Server in NetBeans IDE" on page 40.

1   From the File menu, choose Open Project.

2   In the Open Project dialog, navigate to:

tut-install/examples/case-studies/dukes-tutoring/

3   Select the dukes-tutoring-war folder.

4   Select the Open as Main Project check box and the Open Required Projects check box.

The dukes-tutoring-common library project is required by dukes-tutoring-war, and will be opened along with dukes-tutoring-war.

5   Click Open Project.

Note – The first time you open Duke's Tutoring in NetBeans, you will see error glyphs in the project pane. This is expected, as the metamodel files used by the enterprise beans for Criteria API queries have not yet been generated.

---

6   Right-click dukes-tutoring-war in the project pane and select Run.

This will build and package the dukes-tutoring-common and dukes-tutoring-war projects and deploy dukes-tutoring-war to GlassFish Server, starting the Java DB database and GlassFish Server if they have not already been started. The jdbc/tutoring JDBC resource will be created at deploy time. After the application has been successfully deployed, the Duke's Tutoring main interface will open in a web browser if NetBeans IDE has been configured to open web applications in a web browser.

▼ To Build and Deploy Duke's Tutoring Using Ant

Before You Begin   Make sure GlassFish Server is started as described in "Starting and Stopping the GlassFish Server" on page 41, and Java DB server is started as described in "Starting and Stopping the Java DB Server" on page 43.

1   **In a terminal window, go to:**

    tut-install/examples/case-studies/dukes-tutoring/dukes-tutoring-war/

2   **Enter the following command:**

    `ant all`

    This command builds and packages the dukes-tutoring-common and
    dukes-tutoring-war projects, and deploys dukes-tutoring-war to GlassFish Server.

Using Duke's Tutoring

Once Duke's Tutoring is running on GlassFish Server, use the main interface to
experiment with checking students in and out or sending them to the park.

▼ To Use the Main Interface of Duke's Tutoring

1   **In a web browser, open the main interface at the following URL:**

    `http://localhost:8080/dukes-tutoring/`

2   **Use the main interface to check students in and out, and to log when the students go
    to the park.**

▼ To Use the Administration Interface of Duke's Tutoring

Follow these instructions to log in to the administration interface of Duke's Tutoring
and add new students, guardians, and addresses.

1   **In a web browser, open the administration interface at the following URL:**

    `http://localhost:8080/dukes-tutoring/admin/index.xhtml`

    This will redirect you to the login page.

2   **At the login page, enter the user name `admin@example.com` and password `javaee`.**

3   **Use the administration interface to add or modify students, guardians, or addresses.**

Duke's Forest Case Study Example

Duke's Forest is a simple e-commerce application that contains two web applications and illustrates the use of multiple Java EE 6 APIs:

- JavaServer Faces technology, including Ajax
- Contexts and Dependency Injection for the Java EE Platform (CDI)
- Java API for XML Web Services (JAX-WS)
- Java API for RESTful Web Services (JAX-RS)
- Java Persistence API (JPA)
- Java API for JavaBeans Validation (Bean Validation)
- Enterprise JavaBeans (EJB) technology

The application consists of the following projects:

- Duke's Store: A web application that has a product catalog, customer self-registration, and a shopping cart. It also has an administration interface for product, category, and user management. The project name is dukes-store.

- Duke's Shipment: A web application that provides an interface for order shipment management. The project name is dukes-shipment.

- Duke's Payment: A web service application that has a JAX-WS service for order payment. The project name is dukes-payment.

- Duke's Resources: A simple Java archive project that contains all resources used by the web projects. It includes messages, CSS style sheets, images, JavaScript files, and JavaServer Faces composite components. The project name is dukes-resources.

- Entities: A simple Java archive project that contains all JPA entities. This project is shared among other projects that use the entities. The project name is entities.

- Events: A simple Java archive project that contains a POJO class that is used as a CDI event. The project name is events.

The following topics are addressed here:

Design and Architecture of Duke's Forest

Duke's Forest is a complex application consisting of three main projects and three subprojects. Figure 27–1 shows the architecture of the three main projects that you will deploy: Duke's Store, Duke's Shipment, and Duke's Payment. It also shows how Duke's Store makes use of the Events and Entities projects.

FIGURE 27–1   Architecture of the Duke's Forest Example Application

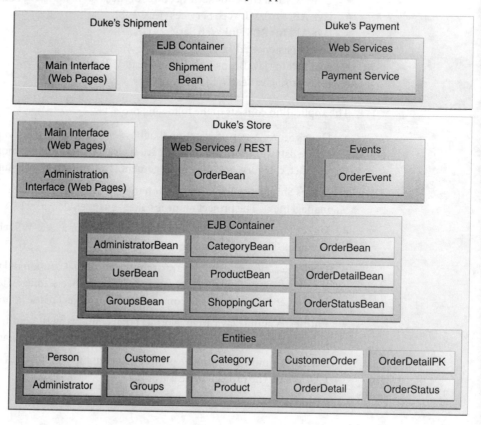

Duke's Forest uses the following Java EE 6 platform features:

- Java Persistence API entities:
  - Bean Validation annotations on the entities for verifying data
  - XML annotations for Java API for XML Binding (JAXB) serialization
- Web services:
  - A JAX-WS web service for payment, with security constraints
  - A JAX-RS web service that is EJB based
- Enterprise beans:
  - Local session beans
  - All enterprise beans packaged within the WAR
- Contexts and Dependency Injection (CDI):
  - CDI annotations for JavaServer Faces components
  - A CDI managed bean used as a shopping cart, with conversation scoping
  - Qualifiers
  - Events and event handlers
- Servlets:
  - A Servlet 3.0 file upload example
  - A servlet for dynamic image presentation
- JavaServer Faces technology, using Facelets for the web front end
  - Templating
  - Composite components
  - Resources packaged in a JAR file so they can be found in the classpath
- Security:
  - Java EE security constraints on the administrative interface business methods (enterprise beans)
  - Security constraints for customers and administrators (web components)

The Duke's Forest application has two main user interfaces, both packaged within the Duke's Store WAR file:

- The main interface, for customers and guests
- The administrative interface used to perform back office operations, such as adding new items to the catalog

The Duke's Shipment application also has a user interface, accessible to administrators.

Figure 27–2 shows how the web applications and the web service interact.

FIGURE 27-2   Interactions between Duke's Forest Components

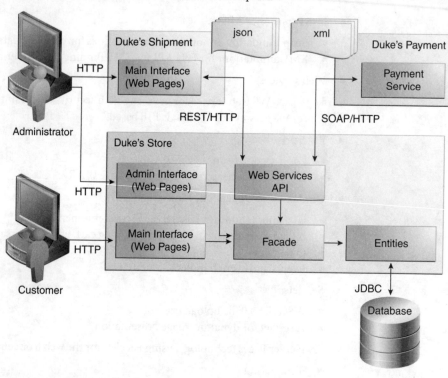

As illustrated in Figure 27–2, the customer interacts with the main interface of Duke's Store, while the administrator interacts with the administration interface. Both interfaces access a façade consisting of managed beans and stateless session beans, which in turn interact with the entities that represent database tables. The façade also interacts with web services APIs that access the Duke's Payment web service. The administrator also interacts with the interface of Duke's Shipment, which can be accessed either directly through Duke's Shipment or from the administration interface of Duke's Store by means of a web service.

The most fundamental building blocks of the application are the Events and Entities projects, which are bundled into Duke's Store and Duke's Shipment along with the Duke's Resources project.

The events Project

Events are one of the core components of Duke's Forest. The events project, included in all three of the main projects, is the most simple project of the application. It has only one class, OrderEvent, but this class is responsible for most of the messages between objects in the application.

The application can send messages based on events to different components and react to them based on the qualification of the event. The application supports the following qualifiers:

- `@LoggedIn`: For authenticated users
- `@New`: When a new order is created by the shopping cart
- `@Paid`: When an order is paid for and ready for shipment

The following code snippet from the `PaymentHandler` class of Duke's Store shows how the `@Paid` event is handled:

```
@Inject @Paid Event<OrderEvent> eventManager;

...
public void onNewOrder(@Observes @New OrderEvent event) {

    if (processPayment(convertForWS(event))) {
        orderBean.setOrderStatus(event.getOrderID(),
                OrderBean.Status.PENDING_PAYMENT.getStatus());
        logger.info("Payment Approved");
        eventManager.fire(event);
    } else {
        orderBean.setOrderStatus(event.getOrderID(),
                OrderBean.Status.CANCELLED_PAYMENT.getStatus())
        logger.info("Payment Denied");
    }
}
...
```

To enable users to add more events to the project easily or update an event class with more fields for a new client, this component is a separate project within the application.

The `entities` Project

The `entities` project is a Java Persistence API (JPA) project used by both Duke's Store and Duke's Shipment. It is generated from the database schema shown in Figure 27–3 and is also used as a base for the entities consumed and produced by the web services through JAXB. Each entity has validation rules based on business requirements, specified using Bean Validation.

FIGURE 27–3 Duke's Forest Database Tables and their Relationships

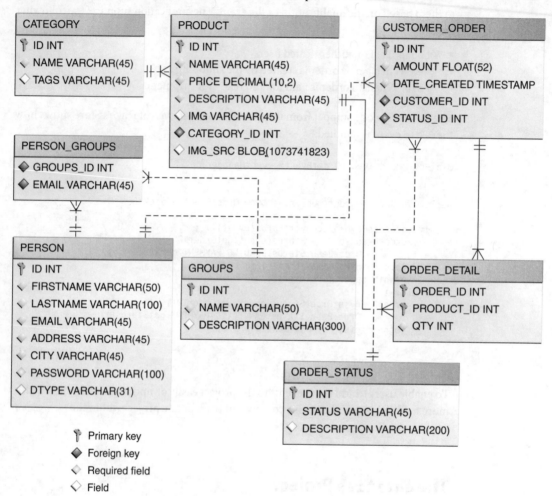

Primary key
Foreign key
Required field
Field

The database schema contains eight tables:

- PERSON, which has a one-to-many relationship with PERSON_GROUPS and CUSTOMER_ORDER

- GROUPS, which has a one-to-many relationship with PERSON_GROUPS

- PERSON_GROUPS, which has a many-to-one relationship with PERSON and GROUPS (it is the join table between those two tables)

- PRODUCT, which has a many-to-one relationship with CATEGORY and a one-to-many relationship with ORDER_DETAIL

- CATEGORY, which has a one-to-many relationship with PRODUCT

- ORDER_DETAIL, which has a many-to-one relationship with PRODUCT and CUSTOMER_ORDER (it is the join table between those two tables)
- CUSTOMER_ORDER, which has a one-to-many relationship with ORDER_DETAIL and a many-to-one relationship with PERSON and ORDER_STATUS
- ORDER_STATUS, which has a one-to-many relationship with CUSTOMER_ORDER

The entity classes that correspond to these tables are as follows:

- Person, which defines attributes common to customers and administrators. These attributes are the person's name and contact information, including street and email addresses. The email address has a Bean Validation annotation to ensure that the submitted data is well-formed. The generated table for Person entities also has a DTYPE field that represents the discriminator column. Its value identifies the subclass (Customer or Administrator) to which the person belongs.
- Customer, a specialization of Person with a specific field for CustomerOrder objects.
- Administrator, a specialization of Person with fields for administration privileges.
- Groups, which represents the group (USERS or ADMINS) to which the user belongs.
- Product, which defines attributes for products. These attributes include name, price, description, associated image, and category.
- Category, which defines attributes for product categories. These attributes include a name and a set of tags.
- CustomerOrder, which defines attributes for orders placed by customers. These attributes include an amount and a date, along with id values for the customer and the order detail.
- OrderDetail, which defines attributes for the order detail. These attributes include a quantity, along with id values for the product and the customer.
- OrderStatus, which defines a status attribute for each order.

The dukes-payment Project

The dukes-payment project is a web project that holds a simple Payment web service. Since this is an example application, it does not obtain any real credit information or even customer status to validate the payment. For now, the only rule imposed by the payment system is to deny all orders above $1,000. This application illustrates a common scenario where a third-party payment service is used to validate credit cards or bank payments.

The project uses HTTP Basic Authentication and JAAS (Java Authentication and Authorization Service) to authenticate a customer to a JAX-WS web service. The implementation itself exposes a simple method, processPayment, which receives an OrderEvent to evaluate and approve or deny the order payment. The method is called from the checkout process of Duke's Store.

The dukes-resources Project

The dukes-resources project contains a number of files used by both Duke's Store and Duke's Shipment, bundled into a JAR file placed in the classpath. The resources are in the src/META-INF/resources directory:

src/META-INF/resources/css	Two style sheets, default.css and jsfcrud.css
src/META-INF/resources/img	Images used by the projects
src/META-INF/resources/js	A JavaScript file, util.js
src/META-INF/resources/util	Composite components used by the projects

The Duke's Store Project

Duke's Store, a web application, is the core application of Duke's Forest. It is responsible for the main store interface for customers as well as the administration interface.

The main interface of Duke's Store allows the user to perform the following tasks:

- Browsing the product catalog
- Signing up as a new customer
- Adding products to the shopping cart
- Checking out
- Viewing order status

The administration interface of Duke's Store allows administrators to perform the following tasks:

- Product maintenance (create, edit, update, delete)
- Category maintenance (create, edit, update, delete)
- Customer maintenance (create, edit, update, delete)
- Group maintenance (create, edit, update, delete)

The project also uses stateless session beans as façades for interactions with the JPA entities described in "The entities Project" on page 495, and CDI managed beans as controllers for interactions with Facelets pages. The project thus follows the MVC (Model-View-Controller) pattern and applies the same pattern to all entities and pages, as in the following example:

- AbstractFacade is an abstract class that receives a Type<T> and implements the common operations (CRUD) for this type, where <T> is a JPA entity.

- ProductBean is a stateless session bean that extends AbstractFacade, applying Product as Type<T>, and injects the PersistenceContext for the Entity Manager. This bean implements any custom methods needed to interact with the Product entity or to call a custom query.

- ProductController is a CDI managed bean that interacts with the necessary enterprise beans and Facelets pages to control the way the data will be displayed.

ProductBean begins as follows:

```
@Stateless
public class ProductBean extends AbstractFacade<Product> {
    private static final Logger logger =
            Logger.getLogger(ProductBean.class.getCanonicalName());

    @PersistenceContext(unitName="forestPU")
    private EntityManager em;

    @Override
    protected EntityManager getEntityManager() {
        return em;
    }
    ...
```

Enterprise Beans Used in Duke's Store

The enterprise beans used in Duke's Store provide the business logic for the application and are located in the com.forest.ejb package. All are stateless session beans.

AbstractFacade is not an enterprise bean but an abstract class that implements common operations for Type<T>, where <T> is a JPA entity.

Most of the other beans extend AbstractFacade, inject the PersistenceContext, and implement any needed custom methods:

- AdministratorBean
- CategoryBean
- GroupsBean
- OrderBean
- OrderDetailBean

- `OrderStatusBean`
- `ProductBean`
- `ShoppingCart`
- `UserBean`

The `ShoppingCart`, although it is in the `ejb` package, is a CDI managed bean with conversation scope, which means that the request information will persist across multiple requests. Also, `ShoppingCart` is responsible for starting the event chain for customer orders, as described in "The `events` Project" on page 494.

Facelets Files Used in the Main Interface of Duke's Store

Like the other case study examples, Duke's Store uses Facelets to display the user interface. The main interface uses a large number of Facelets pages to display different areas. The pages are grouped into directories based on which module they handle.

`template.xhtml`	Template file, used for both main and administration interfaces. It first performs a browser check to verify that the user's browser supports HTML 5, which is required for Duke's Forest. It divides the screen into several areas and specifies the client page for each area.
`topbar.xhtml`	Page for the login area at the top of the screen
`top.xhtml`	Page for the title area
`left.xhtml`	Page for the left sidebar
`index.xhtml`	Page for the main screen content
`login.xhtml`	Login page specified in `web.xml`. The main login interface is provided in `topbar.xhtml`, but this page appears if there is a login error.
`admin` directory	Pages related to the administration interface, described in "Facelets Files Used in the Administration Interface of Duke's Store" on page 501
`customer` directory	Pages related to customers (`Create.xhtml`, `Edit.xhtml`, `List.xhtml`, `Profile.xhtml`, `View.xhtml`)
`order` directory	Pages related to orders (`Create.xhtml`, `List.xhtml`, `MyOrders.xhtml`, `View.xhtml`)
`orderDetail` directory	Popup page allowing users to view details of an order (`View_popup.xhtml`)
`orderStatus` directory	Pages related to order status (`Create.xhtml`, `Edit.xhtml`, `List.xhtml`, `View.xhtml`)

product directory	Pages related to products (`List.xhtml`, `ListCategory.xhtml`, `View.xhtml`)

Facelets Files Used in the Administration Interface of Duke's Store

The Facelets pages for the administration interface of Duke's Store are found in the web/admin directory.

administrator directory	Pages related to administrator management (`Create.xhtml`, `Edit.xhtml`, `List.xhtml`, `View.xhtml`)
category directory	Pages related to product category management (`Create.xhtml`, `Edit.xhtml`, `List.xhtml`, `View.xhtml`)
customer directory	Pages related to customer management (`Create.xhtml`, `Edit.xhtml`, `List.xhtml`, `Profile.xhtml`, `View.xhtml`)
groups folder	Pages related to group management (`Create.xhtml`, `Edit.xhtml`, `List.xhtml`, `View.xhtml`)
order directory	Pages related to order management (`Create.xhtml`, `Edit.xhtml`, `List.xhtml`, `View.xhtml`)
orderDetail directory	Popup page allowing the administrator to view details of an order (`View_popup.xhtml`)
product directory	Pages related to product management (`Confirm.xhtml`, `Create.xhtml`, `Edit.xhtml`, `List.xhtml`, `View.xhtml`)

Managed Beans Used in Duke's Store

Duke's Store uses the following CDI managed beans, which correspond to the enterprise beans. The beans are in the com.forest.web package.

- `AdministratorController`
- `CategoryController`
- `CustomerController`
- `CustomerOrderController`
- `GroupsController`
- `OrderDetailController`
- `OrderStatusController`

- `ProductController`
- `UserController`

Helper Classes Used in Duke's Store

The CDI managed beans in the main interface of Duke's Store use the following helper classes, found in the `com.forest.web.util` package:

`AbstractPaginationHelper`	An abstract class with methods used by the managed beans
`FileUploadServlet, ImageServlet`	Classes used for image processing. `FileUploadServlet` uploads an image and stores its content in the database. `ImageServlet` retrieves the image content from the database and displays it. (JavaServer Faces technology does not provide this functionality, so a servlet is needed.)
`JsfUtil`	Class used for JavaServer Faces operations, such as queuing messages on a `FacesContext` instance
`MD5Util`	Class used by the `CustomerController` managed bean to generate an encrypted password for a user

Qualifiers Used in Duke's Store

Duke's Store defines the following qualifiers in the `com.forest.qualifiers` package:

`@LoggedIn`	Qualifies a user as having logged in.
`@New`	Qualifies an order as new.
`@Paid`	Qualifies an order as paid.

Event Handlers Used in Duke's Store

Duke's Store defines event handlers related to the `OrderEvent` class packaged in "The events Project" on page 494. The event handlers are in the `com.forest.handlers` package:

`IOrderHandler`	The `IOrderHandler` interface defines a method, `onNewOrder`, implemented by the two handler classes.
`PaymentHandler`	The `ShoppingCart` bean fires an `OrderEvent` qualified as `@New`. The `onNewOrder` method of `PaymentHandler` observes these events and, when it intercepts them, processes the payment

using the Duke's Payment web service. After a successful response from the web service, `PaymentHandler` fires the `OrderEvent` again, this time qualified as `@Paid`.

DeliveryHandler   The `onNewOrder` method of `DeliveryHandler` observes `OrderEvent` objects qualified as `@Paid` (orders paid and ready for delivery) and modifies the order status to `PENDING_SHIPMENT`. When an administrator accesses Duke's Shipment, it will call the Order Service, a RESTful web service, and ask for all orders in the database that are ready for delivery.

Properties Files Used in Duke's Store

The strings used in the main and administration interfaces of Duke's Store are encapsulated into resource bundles to allow the display of localized strings in multiple locales. The resource bundles are located in the default package.

`Bundle.properties`	Application messages in English
`Bundle_es.properties`	Application messages in Spanish
`ValidationMessages.properties`	Bean Validation messages in English
`ValidationMessages_es.properties`	Bean Validation messages in Spanish

Deployment Descriptors Used in Duke's Store

Duke's Store uses the following deployment descriptors, located in the `web/WEB-INF` directory:

`beans.xml`	An empty deployment descriptor file used to enable the CDI runtime
`faces-config.xml`	The JavaServer Faces configuration file
`glassfish-web.xml`	The configuration file specific to GlassFish Server
`jaxws-catalog.xml`	A deployment descriptor for a JAX-WS web service client
`web.xml`	The web application configuration file

The Duke's Shipment Project

Duke's Shipment is a web application with a login page, a main Facelets page, and some other objects. This application, which is accessible only to administrators, calls the Order Service (the RESTful web service exposed by Duke's Store) and lists all orders under two status headings: Pending and Shipped. The administrator can either approve or deny a pending order. If approved, the order is shipped, and it appears under the Shipped heading. If denied, the order disappears from the page, and on the customer's Orders list it appears as cancelled.

There is also a gear icon on the Pending list that makes an Ajax call to the Order Service to refresh the list without refreshing the page. The code looks like this:

```
<h:commandLink>
    <h:graphicImage library="img" title="Check for new orders"
                    style="border:0px" name="refresh.png"/>
    <f:ajax execute="refresh" render="out" />
</h:commandLink>
```

Enterprise Bean Used in Duke's Shipment

The enterprise bean used in Duke's Shipment, UserBean, provides the business logic for the application and is located in the com.forest.shipment.session package. It is a stateless session bean.

Like Duke's Store, Duke's Shipment uses the AbstractFacade class. This class is not an enterprise bean but an abstract class that implements common operations for Type<T>, where <T> is a JPA entity.

Facelets Files Used in Duke's Shipment

Duke's Shipment has only one page, so it has many fewer Facelets files than Duke's Store.

template.xhtml	The template file, like the one in Duke's Store, first performs a browser check to verify that the user's browser supports HTML 5, which is required for Duke's Forest. It divides the screen into areas and specifies the client page for each area.
topbar.xhtml	Page for the login area at the top of the screen
top.xhtml	Page for the title area
left.xhtml	Page for the left sidebar (not used in Duke's Shipment)
index.xhtml	Page for the initial main screen content
login.xhtml	Login page specified in web.xml. The main login interface is provided in topbar.xhtml, but this page appears if there is a login error
admin/index.xhtml	Page for the main screen content after authentication

Managed Beans Used in Duke's Shipment

Duke's Shipment uses the following CDI managed beans, in the
`com.forest.shipment` package:

`control.ShippingBean` — Managed bean that acts as a client to the Order Service

`web.UserController` — Managed bean that corresponds to the `UserBean` session bean

Helper Class Used in Duke's Shipment

The Duke's Shipment managed beans use only one helper class, found in the
`com.forest.shipment.web.util` package:

`JsfUtil` — Class used for JavaServer Faces operations, such as queuing messages on a `FacesContext` instance

Qualifier Used in Duke's Shipment

Duke's Shipment defines the following qualifier in the `com.forest.qualifiers` package:

`@LoggedIn` — Qualifies a user as having logged in

Properties Files Used in Duke's Shipment

The Duke's Shipment properties files, located in the default package, are
`Bundle.properties`, containing English strings, and `Bundle_es.properties`,
containing Spanish strings. They are identical to the files in Duke's Store.

Deployment Descriptors Used in Duke's Shipment

Duke's Shipment uses the following deployment descriptors:

`web/WEB-INF/beans.xml` — An empty deployment descriptor file used to enable the CDI runtime

`web/WEB-INF/faces-config.xml` — The JavaServer Faces configuration file

`web/WEB-INF/glassfish-web.xml` — The configuration file specific to GlassFish Server

`web/WEB-INF/web.xml` — The web application configuration file

`src/conf/persistence.xml` — The Java Persistence API configuration file

Building and Deploying the Duke's Forest Case Study Application

You can use NetBeans IDE or Ant to build and deploy Duke's Forest. The prerequisite task requires Ant.

Prerequisite Task

Before you begin this task, you must have already configured GlassFish Server as a Java EE server in NetBeans IDE, as described in "To Add GlassFish Server as a Server in NetBeans IDE" on page 40.

▼ To Create the JDBC Realm and Populate the Database

1 Enable Default Principal to Role Mapping on the GlassFish Server, if you have not done so previously:

    a. From the Administration Console, expand the Configurations node, then expand the server-config node.

    b. Select the Security node.

    c. Select the Default Principal to Role Mapping Enabled check box.

    d. Click Save.

2 In a terminal window, go to:

    tut-install/examples/case-studies/dukes-forest/entities/

3 Execute the create-forest-realm Ant task:

    `ant create-forest-realm`

    This task creates a JDBC connection pool and a JDBC resource as well as the realm.

4 Execute the Ant task:

    `ant`

    This task creates the tables (dropping any existing tables) and builds the JAR file. Ignore any errors if you are running the task for the first time.

▼ To Build and Deploy the Duke's Forest Application Using NetBeans IDE

1 From the File menu, choose Open Project.

2 In the Open Project dialog, navigate to:

   tut-install/examples/case-studies/dukes-forest/

3 Select the dukes-store folder.

4 Select the Open Required Projects check box.

5 Click Open Project.

   The IDE will open the dukes-store, dukes-resources, entities, and events projects.

   The project opens with a message stating that there is a data source problem.

6 Right-click the project and select Resolve Data Source Problem.

7 In the dialog that opens, select jdbc/forest and click Add Connection.

8 Click Finish.

   The connection to the forest database is now established.

   If the project still indicates there is a data source problem but the dialog does not indicate a missing connection, close and reopen the project.

9 Repeat steps 1–5 to open the dukes-shipment project.

10 Repeat steps 1–5 to open the dukes-payment project.

11 Right-click the events project and select Build.

12 Right-click the dukes-resources project and select Build.

13 Right-click the dukes-payment project and select Deploy.

14 Right-click the dukes-store project and select Deploy.

15 Right-click the `dukes-shipment` project and select Deploy.

The `dukes-shipment` project requires the file `jersey-client.jar`, which is located in *as-install*/`lib/modules/`. If you get a Resolve References error when you first try to build `dukes-shipment`, you can resolve the error by locating this file.

▼ To Build and Deploy the Duke's Forest Application Using Ant

1 In a terminal window, go to:

tut-install/`examples/case-studies/dukes-forest/events/`

2 Enter the following command to build the `events.jar` file:

`ant`

3 Go to the `dukes-resources` directory:

`cd ../dukes-resources`

4 Enter the following command to build the `dukes-resources.jar` file:

`ant`

5 Go to the `dukes-payment` directory:

`cd ../dukes-payment`

6 Enter the following command:

`ant all`

7 Go to the `dukes-store` directory:

`cd ../dukes-store`

8 Enter the following command:

`ant all`

9 Go to the `dukes-shipment` directory:

`cd ../dukes-shipment`

10 Enter the following command:

`ant all`

Running the Duke's Forest Application

Running the Duke's Forest application involves several tasks, among them the following:

- Registering as a customer of Duke's Store
- As a customer, purchasing products
- As an administrator, approving shipment of a product
- As an administrator, creating a new product

▼ To Register as a Duke's Store Customer

1   In a web browser, enter the following URL:

`http://localhost:8080/dukes-store`

The Duke's Forest - Store page opens.

2   Click the Sign Up button at the top of the page.

3   Fill in the form fields, then click Save.

All fields are required, and the Password value must be at least 7 characters in length.

▼ To Purchase Products

1   To log in as the user you created, or as one of two users already in the database, enter the user name and password and click Log In.

The preexisting users have the user names `jack@example.com` and `robert@example.com`, and they both have the same password, 1234.

2   Click Products in the left sidebar.

3   On the page that appears, click one of the categories (Plants, Food, Services, or Tools).

4   Choose a product and click Add to Cart.

You can order only one of any one product, but you can order multiple *different* products in multiple categories. The products and a running total appear in the Shopping Cart in the left sidebar.

5   When you have finished choosing products, click Checkout.

A message appears, reporting that your order is being processed.

6   **Click Orders in the left sidebar to verify your order.**

If the total of the order was over $1,000, the status of the order is "Order cancelled," because the Payment web service denies orders over that limit. Otherwise, the status is "Ready to ship."

7   **When you have finished placing orders, click the Logout button at the top of the page.**

▼ To Approve Shipment of a Product

1   **Log in to Duke's Store as an administrator.**

Your user name is `admin@example.com`, and your password is 1234.

The main administration page allows you to view categories, customers, administrators, groups, products, and orders, and to create new objects of all types except orders.

2   **At the bottom of the page, click Approve Shipment.**

This action takes you to Duke's Shipment.

3   **Log in to Duke's Shipment at the top of the page, as `admin@example.com`.**

4   **On the Pending list, click Approve to approve an order and move it to the Shipped area of the page.**

If you click Deny, the order disappears from the page. If you log in to Duke's Store again as the customer, it will appear in the Orders list as "Order Cancelled."

Next Steps   To return to Duke's Store from Duke's Shipment, click Return to Duke's Store.

▼ To Create a New Product

You can create other kinds of objects as well as products. Creating products is more complex than the other creation processes.

1   **Log in to Duke's Store as an administrator.**

2   **On the main administration page, click Create New Product.**

3   **Enter values in the Name, Price, and Description fields.**

4   **Select a category, then click Next.**

5 On the Upload the Product Image page, click Browse to locate an image on your file system using a file chooser.

6 Click Next.

7 On the next page, view the product fields, then click Done.

8 Click Products in the left sidebar, then click the category to verify that the product has been added.

9 Click Administration at the top of the page to return to the main administration page, or click Logout to log out.

Index

X

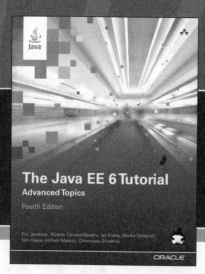

Safari
Books Online

FREE
Online Edition

Your purchase of *Java EE 6 Tutorial: Advanced Topics, Fourth Edition* includes access to a free online edition for 45 days through the **Safari Books Online** subscription service. Nearly every Addison-Wesley Professional book is available online through **Safari Books Online**, along with thousands of books and videos from publishers such as Cisco Press, Exam Cram, IBM Press, O'Reilly Media, Prentice Hall, Que, Sams, and VMware Press.

Safari Books Online is a digital library providing searchable, on-demand access to thousands of technology, digital media, and professional development books and videos from leading publishers. With one monthly or yearly subscription price, you get unlimited access to learning tools and information on topics including mobile app and software development, tips and tricks on using your favorite gadgets, networking, project management, graphic design, and much more.

Activate your FREE Online Edition at
informit.com/safarifree

STEP 1:   Enter the coupon code: SPFFXBI.

STEP 2:   New Safari users, complete the brief registration form.
Safari subscribers, just log in.

If you have difficulty registering on Safari or accessing the online edition,
please e-mail customer-service@safaribooksonline.com